W9-BPS-302

The popular image of the traditional western city has usually been dominated by the cathedral, whose sheer size seemed to create an isolated physical and spiritual focal point.

In this iconoclastic study, the author sets out to reverse some of the romantic myths which have accrued about the medieval cathedral, in particular that the cathedral was a separate entity, self-sufficient, sublime and apart. Here the cathedral is shown to be a dynamic, evolving and unpredictable force in the development of the medieval city. Taking France as the main focus, but including material on England, Germany, Italy, Spain and Bohemia, the author describes the growth of diocesan authority and the consequent experiments in the layout of cathedral plans. Full use is made of recent archaeological research to show how architectural, social, financial and religious considerations combined to form a structure that was above all a practical, functioning concern, a 'city within a city'.

CAMBRIDGE STUDIES IN THE
HISTORY OF ARCHITECTURE

The Cathedral

CAMBRIDGE STUDIES IN THE HISTORY OF ARCHITECTURE

Edited by

ROBIN MIDDLETON
Professor of Art History, Columbia University

JOSEPH RYKWERT
*Paul Philippe Cret Professor of Architecture,
University of Philadelphia*

and DAVID WATKIN
Reader in the History of Architecture, University of Cambridge, and Fellow of Peterhouse

This is a new series of historical studies intended to embrace a wide chronological range, from Antiquity to the twentieth century, and to become a natural counterpart to Cambridge Studies in the History of Art. Volumes in the series are intended primarily for professional historians of architecture and their students, but it is also intended to include a number of volumes for course work or of interest to the general reader.

Titles in the series

Other titles are in preparation

The Cathedral

THE SOCIAL AND ARCHITECTURAL DYNAMICS OF CONSTRUCTION

Alain Erlande-Brandenburg

TRANSLATED BY
Martin Thom

CAMBRIDGE
UNIVERSITY PRESS

Published by the Press Syndicate of the University of Cambridge

The Pitt Building, Trumpington Street, Cambridge CB2 1RP

40 West 20th Street, New York, NY 10011–4211, USA

10 Stamford Road, Oakleigh, Melbourne 3166, Australia

Originally published in French as *La cathédrale*

by Alain Erlande-Brandenburg 1989

and © Librairie Arthème Fayard, 1989

First published in English by Cambridge University Press 1994 as

The cathedral: the social and architectural dynamics of construction

Reprinted 1996

English translation © Cambridge University Press 1994

Printed in Great Britain at the University Press, Cambridge

A catalogue record for this book is available from the British Library

Library of Congress cataloguing in publication data

Erlande-Brandenburg, Alain.

[Cathédrale.   English]

The cathedral: the social and architectural dynamics of construction / Alain Erlande-Brandenburg;

translated by Martin Thom.

p.   cm. – (Cambridge studies in the history of architecture)

Includes bibliographical references and index.

ISBN 0 521 41118 1 (hardback)

1. Cathedrals – France. 2. Architecture, Medieval – France. 3. Architecture and society – France.

4. Cathedrals – England. 5. Architecture, Medieval – England. 6. Architecture and society – England.

I. Title. II. Series.

NA5543.E7413 1994

726′.6′0940902–dc20   93-29216 CIP

ISBN 0 521 41118 1 hardback

For Francis Salet

We shall build so large a cathedral
that those who see it in its finished state will
think that we were mad.

Canon at Sevilla cathedral (1402)

Contents

ix

Illustrations

xiii

xv

Maps and plans produced by the Atelier *Etudes et Cartographie* in Lille.

Preface

I obviously ought to try to justify the bold title which I have chosen. In *The cathedral*, a novel published by Huysmans in 1898, the atmosphere of the cathedral of Chartres is suggested, and an attempt is made to evoke the religious life inside the building. My justification is of a different order, and must lie in the course which led me to the drafting of this book. My historical research is concerned with the long term, and I have tried to transcend piecemeal description and thus to achieve a global perspective. What do I mean by long term? Cathedrals were first introduced, in early Christian times, into towns which had recently been reduced to the status of *castrum*. They were then, as they are now, buildings which believers entered with a feeling of veneration. Cathedrals have always resembled living bodies and, in the centuries since they were first established, have been subjected to ceaseless change. In talking of a global perspective, I would emphasise the fact that the cathedral was originally something far larger than the single monument called by that name today. It consisted of a huge complex of buildings: places of worship, which fell in number with the passage of time, the bishop's palace, the canonial precinct, administrative buildings, and the hôtel-Dieu. Each of these would subsequently expand, in a manner that demands analysis if we are to grasp the full extent of the 'holy town', an entity which was exclusively concerned with God, and which was inhabited by those who prayed day and night for the living and dead of their diocese. The holy town sprang up within the ancient city, first of all, and then within the medieval town, the latter a flourishing place whose prosperity reflected a rapid rate of demographic growth. The image of the holy town owes much to the existence of the cathedral, which dominated it by its sheer mass, and bestowed a meaning upon it.

The emergence of particular buildings, such as the hôtel-Dieu or the canonial precinct, the extension of others, and the construction of the huge Gothic cathedrals, which sometimes measured over one hundred metres in length, cannot be construed in formal terms alone. Indeed, each major transformation was linked to a religious upheaval, for the Middle Ages were no more static than was Antiquity or the modern period. Each epoch established a new order within the holy town.

It has only been possible to address such issues because of the discovery of new sources and the development of a new conception of history. Excavations in urban areas have unearthed fascinating materials whose existence was not even hinted at in written texts. Recent archaeological studies have been concerned with humbler buildings than the cathedral itself, and they have enabled us to appreciate the complexity of the holy town. Current approaches allow us to understand the interaction between the various elements involved, between holy town and town, cathedral and palace, and between canonial precinct and hôtel-Dieu.

Introduction: myth or reality

The *New Illustrated Larousse* defines the cathedral, accurately enough, as the 'episcopal church of the diocese'. We are also told, in somewhat vaguer terms, that a cathedral is a 'large monumental church exemplifying Christian medieval architecture', a key example of which would be Notre-Dame of Paris. So it is that right from the start we have to address the question of what a cathedral essentially is. For the man in the street, with no specialist interest in religious matters, a cathedral is first and foremost a large Catholic building, in the Gothic style. Many buildings declared by tourist notices to be cathedrals are in fact merely parish churches, although this in no way detracts from their essential merit or interest. It is curious to note that this error always concerns Gothic buildings, the implication being, at least as far as France is concerned, that people find it hard to imagine Romanesque or Classical cathedrals. Conversely, one is startled to find that the cathedral of Saint-Denis, the town chosen as the capital of the diocese when the department of Seine-Saint-Denis was created, was still known as a 'basilica', both by the inhabitants and by the authorities, although neither party really knew what this term meant. This designation may have served, however, to reinforce a strictly mythical notion of the Gothic, for the building is not really in the town but in a suburb held to be dangerous because it forms part of the famous red light district.

The myths surrounding the concept of the cathedral date back to the nineteenth century and, more particularly, to the Romantic movement. Through its discovery of Gothic architecture, the generation of 1830, aware both of the power of the Catholic faith and of the strength of the monarchy, was to unleash a movement of such dynamism that even unbelievers would have no choice but to adopt it as their own, while imposing a distinct, lay interpretation.

In addition, each country responded in a different fashion to the image of its own past.

ENGLAND

England was the first country in Europe to be confronted with its own cultural past, and to expound a doctrine, which was indeed to inspire many foreigners. The dissolution of the monasteries, ordered by Henry VIII in 1536 and 1539, led to many of their number being abandoned. Their ruins were a source of passionate interest from an early date. Thus, in the middle of the sixteenth century, John Leland took it upon himself to describe what remained of Malmesbury Abbey, by then a cloth manufactory. Sir William Dugdale followed his example, drafting a *History of Saint-Paul's Cathedral* (London, 1658), in which he sought to preserve for posterity an account of a building which had suffered grave damage at the hands of the Puritans. He therefore explained that the engravings of Wenceslas Hollar disregarded the devastation which had been inflicted upon the building. The London Society of Antiquarians was to put this piecemeal concern on a broader footing, and thus to promote an interest in Gothic architecture. It published a journal, *Archaoelogia* (1770), which contained a number of remarkable monographic studies of the English cathedrals. The high point of this tendency was *Contrasts*, a book published by Pugin in 1836, which drew the attention of the general public, in a somewhat flamboyant fashion, to medieval architecture. For the first time a close link was intimated between religion and architecture, and the superiority of medieval architecture asserted. Also, after the Houses of Parliament had burned down in 1834, he argued strongly in favour of rebuilding the monument in the Gothic style, it being his conviction that, from a moral point of view, this style was to be preferred to all others. The architect, Sir Charles Barry (1796–1860), in spite of his classical tastes, designed a Gothic monument (1836) the decor of which drew its inspiration from the neighbouring chapel of Henry VII but which, as far as the rhythm of the facade fronting the Thames was concerned, was not uninfluenced by a Palladian formalism.

GERMANY

In Germany, the discovery of Gothic architecture, although occurring, as had been the case in England, in the context of Romanticism, assumed a different form. Political factors were involved, for the Napoleonic wars had profoundly shaken this mosaic of countries, leaving them with a thirst for unity. However, Strasburg cathedral had been regarded as a symbol of the German soul at a still earlier date. Endorsing a term (*tedesco*) which Italian humanists of the Renaissance period had applied to twelfth-century architecture, Goethe had drawn the conclusion that Gothic art was an authentically German art (*Von der deutscher Baukunst*, 1773). In his analysis of the facade of Strasburg cathedral which, somewhat fancifully, had been ascribed to Erwin von Steinbach, the poet saw it as the embodiment of an art rooted in nature. Erwin, whose tomb had just been discovered, was to assume a mythical status, rivalling that of Durer as far as invention and national genius were concerned. The writers of the *Stürm und Drang* followed Herder down the trail blazed by Goethe. A veritable resurrection of the Middle Ages occurred, with all the imbalances of an exaggerated nationalism. Nuremberg became one of the capitals of the movement, but the emphasis soon shifted from Strasburg to Köln, which was to serve as a channel for the energy of the German people for almost half a century.

The movement was launched by Joseph Görres who, on 20 November 1814, issued a stirring appeal concerning the cathedral and its eventual completion. The reasons advanced for such a project reflect the mood of the times, and help us to understand the extent of the movement. Köln cathedral immediately became a symbol, of the German people and of their forthcoming liberation from the Napoleonic yoke. The Emperor's wars had not only shattered a fragile equilibrium but also, more importantly, they had given a large proportion of these oppressed peoples a sense of their own identity. Görres' genius lay in having managed to turn Köln, the most remarkable Gothic cathedral in all of the German territories, into a focal point for this new awareness. The cathedral reminded Germans in the most stirring fashion possible of the virtues of the past. Even its unfinished state was significant, for it represented the abandonment of a project which, if revived, would serve to unite the energies of one and all. There was a flood of engravings of the unfinished building, an iconography which served as a constant reproach. Such representations were lent further resonance through the fact that during this same period the 'cathedral' became a pictorial motif, encapsulating in striking fashion the emotional content underlying the word, and the hope which it symbolised. Karl Friedrich Schinkel played an important role here. He had been strongly influenced by the Romantic milieu in which he lived and worked, which saw Gothic architecture as both the quintessential expression of Christianity and as a remarkable affirmation of national art. Schinkel had also read Goethe's study of 1773, and it was in this spirit that he produced a number of his highly evocative paintings. *The Gothic cathedral by the water* (1813), a later copy of which by Wilhelm Alborn may now be seen in the National Gallery, Berlin, was one of the most characteristic of such works, including such features as the link between water and the setting sun and, above all, the bustling human activity unfolding at the foot of the monument and giving the onlooker a clue to its true meaning. The 'city' is dominated by the chevet of the 'cathedral', by means of a massiveness which manages to be both powerful and airy. One quickly comes to realise that the building is in fact a synthesis of several cathedrals built on German territory, namely, Strasburg, Freiburg and Prague. A plan was therefore drawn, but never in fact realised, for a monument commemorating the War of Liberation of 1814–15, a cathedral taking its inspiration from monuments in both Germany (Köln, Freiburg, Strasburg), Italy (Milano) and France (Reims). Finally, the originality of the scheme lay in its centred design, which could not help but call to mind the Temple of the Holy Grail, and in the stylistic choices inspired by its flamboyant architecture.

The failure of this plan, and of many others like it, may serve in part to explain the place won by Köln cathedral in the hearts and minds of the population. Sulpice Boisserée, himself a native of Köln, was to play the crucial role here. He had learned of the importance of his city as regards the painting of the early German masters, and he had accumulated a collection of such works that was exceptional for the period. Having met Friedrich Schlegel in Paris (1803–4), he had managed to persuade him to come to Köln. Schlegel drafted his study on *Les Fondements de l'architecture gothique* (1804–5), which relied very heavily on his analysis of the city's cathedral. In 1814, Georg Moller discovered a medieval drawing featuring the north tower and, in 1815, Boisserée unearthed a second drawing, with a representation of the south tower. Fired by these discoveries, in 1821 Boisserée commissioned an engraving of the completed cathedral, which was widely circulated. In 1815, he had persuaded Goethe to come to the Rhineland, and had drawn his attention to the building. The following year, the great poet launched an appeal for funds to complete Köln cathedral.

The whole of Germany seemed to be involved in the project. First of all, the archbishop's see was re-established there (1821). Secondly, the Prussian state decided to assume responsibility for the completion of the edifice. In 1834, Schinkel was commissioned to draw a plan, which he did forthwith. It was necessary to begin by shoring up the cathedral and it was only through the efforts of Friedrich-Wilhelm IV of Prussia, who had ascended the throne in 1840, that work on the site became both more urgent and more extensive. In 1842, Zwirner, one of Schinkel's pupils, laid the first stone. Work went on until

1880. This drawn-out and delicate venture served to symbolise the fraternity of all Germans, since they were collaborating in the completion of a national monument. German sensibility had in a sense assuaged its thirst for the absolute in the realisation of this dream, the meaning of which transcended the excessively narrow framework of the various *Länder*. It had been profoundly marked by a specific ideology, as had the various expressions of Gothic revivalism in other countries. Some historians have been too ready to regard the project as the loftiest expression of German genius. Nazism was to give a new lease of life to such theories, no matter how contentious they in fact were, and no matter how often their essentially inane nature had been demonstrated.

FRANCE

The rediscovery of Gothic architecture in France was never so ardent and passionate an affair as it had been in Germany, even though the difficulty of addressing so different a reality produced a somewhat febrile state of mind. The myth took longer to assume a definite shape. Its focal point was Notre-Dame of Paris, a building of crucial significance not only in the history of architecture but in politics also. Notre-Dame has never been the object of such outlandish arguments as Köln had occasioned, and it has never served as the symbol of the desire for independence of a people that had suffered oppression for a number of years. National unity had been so long established that it was not at issue. I do not propose to rehearse the emergence of a sensibility responsive to Gothic art, for many excellent studies have been devoted to the question in recent years, and they serve to bring out the complexity of the phenomenon. My aim, rather, will be to discern just what, in relation to the discovery of the Gothic, the meaning of the cathedral was taken to be. By contrast with what took place in England and in Germany, it is only through reference to literature that one may grasp the particular qualities of the cult of the Gothic in France. For it was literature alone that served there to unify, and to draw into a genuine current of opinion, what had been up until then no more than a number of disparate and ill-founded perspectives. For more than a hundred years, Victor Hugo's famous novel, *Notre-Dame de Paris* (1831), was to exert an influence upon the more open-minded, both specialists and amateur enthusiasts. In this novel, one of the most intriguing contributions to French Romanticism, the author depicted a medieval world which readers could readily imagine, and to which later generations remained profoundly attached. Even the cathedral fire seemed to prefigure the

Fig. 1 The spire and roofs of Rouen cathedral ablaze, 15 September 1822.
Lithograph by Périaux, from an original drawing by Langlois.

blaze which, in 1836, set alight the timber frame and the roofing of Chartres
cathedral, and which by the same token seemed to suggest a confusion between
a Hugoesque world and reality. After 1918 the gargoyles on Reims cathedral,
now kept in the Palais du Tau, spat lead. Aside from the imaginative aspects of
the work, which reality was soon to copy, two other elements helped to give the
novel a quality all its own. The first concerns the subject which serves as the
guiding thread of the book, namely, the cathedral itself, conceived as a living,
palpitating being, and not merely as a cold edifice which had been mutilated in
the course of the Revolution and for a long time neglected. The second concerns
the ideas elaborated upon by Hugo, which were in no way contingent but rather
involved themes which had undergone a long process of maturation in his mind
and which, aside from a few points of detail, were never to vary. The majority
of them have been incorporated into public knowledge to such a degree, owing

to the huge success of the novel, that they now seem to be mere commonplaces. Their origin was soon to be forgotten. Emile Mâle, in his thesis on the thirteenth century (1898), acknowledged the debt he owed to Hugo, and Henri Focillon followed suit, in his *Art d'Occident* (Paris, 1938). I do not want to labour arguments that have already been spelled out at length by Jean Mallion, in *Victor Hugo et l'art médiéval* (Paris, 1962), but propose instead to emphasise a number of points which may help the reader to understand just how the myth of the cathedral was consolidated. The doctrine has been considerably reinforced since Hugo's day. Its central tenets include the unity of the arts, the primacy of architecture with respect to the other arts, and the claim that architecture is a form of expression that is by its nature spiritual. Hugo had tried to define the conditions for creation, whether material (climate, geography and materials) or social. It was in this area that his thinking appeared most original, as he drew a sharp contrast between Romanesque art, as Gerville had defined it a short time before, and Gothic art. The distinction was based upon a sociological analysis which, although admittedly somewhat perfunctory, at least had the virtue of being boldly drawn. Hugo claimed that there was a connection between form and social class. Indeed, in his view, authority in the medieval period was vested in two different classes in succession. Romanesque art reflected the rule of a priesthood: 'There is a pervading sense of authority, unity, of what is impenetrable, absolute, of Pope Gregory VII; the priestly caste is everywhere, the people nowhere'. With the coming of the Crusades, the authority of the priesthood was undermined and the people reclaimed its rights: 'The face of Europe had changed and, in like fashion, the face of architecture had changed too; like civilization, it had turned a page...From this point on, the cathedral was invaded by the bourgeoisie, by the commune and by liberty' (*Notre-Dame de Paris*, Book 5, Chapter 2). Architecture was above all a social and a collective art. Architecture died when the ties between art and society were sundered.

Hugo was naturally led to analyse more precisely the role of the creator, and so to introduce the notion of 'collective creation'. Once he had adopted this notion, he tried to render it more systematic: 'The greatest works of architecture are not so much individual as social creations; they are better seen as the giving birth of peoples in labour than as the gushing stream of genius. Such works should be regarded as the deposit left by a nation, as the accumulations of the centuries, as the residue of successive evaporations of human society, briefly, as a kind of geological formation' (3, 1). These peremptory assertions were tempered, however, by Hugo's decision to reintroduce the individual creator in the course of the second stage:

The cathedral itself, a building that in former times was so dogmatic, had now been invaded by the bourgeoisie, by the commune and by liberty, and so eluded the priest and fell into the hands of the artist. The artist built after his own fashion. He bid adieu to mystery, myth and law and in their stead he welcomed phantasy and caprice. Provided that the priest still had his basilica and his altar, he could raise no objection. The four walls now belonged to the artist. The book of architecture no longer belonged to the priesthood, to religion or to Rome, but to the imagination, to poetry and to the people.

(5, 2)

The shift from the first to the second period was effected by means of transitional works, among them the cathedral of Paris:

The colossal work of a man and a people...a prodigious product of all the forces of an epoch in which, upon every single stone, one could see burst forth in a hundred different ways the phantasy of the workman disciplined by the genius of the artist; a form of human creation, in a word, powerful, and fruitful like the divine creation, from which it seemed to have wrested its twofold character of variety and unity.

(5, 2)

If Victor Hugo placed so much emphasis upon the differences between Romanesque art, where the churches were 'sombre, mysterious, low and as if overwhelmed by the weight of the semicircular arch', and Gothic art, with its 'tall, airy churches, rich in stained glass and sculpture...communal and bourgeois as political symbols; free, capricious and unfettered as works of art' (3, 1), he had nonetheless set out to show that the evolution of 'art was achieved without trouble, without effort, and without reaction, as if obeying a tranquil, natural law' (3, 1). The comparison with nature, already operative in the writings of Bernardin de Saint-Pierre and, after him, in those of Chateaubriand, was adopted by Hugo as his own and indeed taken much further. He likened the cathedral to a forest: 'The pillars are thick trunks, at the pinnacle of which the sheafs of fillets interweave like shadow-laden branches' (*En Voyage*, vol. II, 1839, 'Midi de France et Bourgogne', p. 275).

If I have placed such emphasis upon some of the ideas formulated by Victor Hugo, it is because they exerted an immediate and profound influence upon the minds of his contemporaries, who could not help but be impressed by the breadth of his vision. These ideas were not intrinsically original, for a number of them had been formulated by, among others, Sulpice Boisserée, whose writings Hugo had read with care. His contribution, however, was to make such ideas so familiar that a whole generation was in some way marked by them. Didron, in his introduction to his *Manuel d'iconographie chrétienne*...(Paris, 1845), did not conceal his debt to Hugo and, indeed, dedicated the work to him. Many other scholars could be mentioned, and there were a host of literary persons who, after reading the novel, paid their very first visit to the cathedral of Paris, meditated upon Hugo's sublime pages, and succumbed to the strange enchantment worked by such an admirably described monument.

The imposing personality of Victor Hugo should not be allowed to obscure the existence of those others who, during the same period, helped to mould the imaginary conception of the cathedral. Two of their number took the trouble to theorise, and thereby to reduce their analyses to a systematic form. Viollet-le-Duc has been much studied, but Ludovic Vitet (1802 73) has only recently re-emerged from the shadows, even though the role he played, both in practical terms and as a writer, was by no means a negligible one. He served as Inspector of Historical Monuments, an office to which he was appointed by Guizot on 23 October 1830 and which he held up until 1834, when Prosper Mérimée succeeded him. In 1837, the Count of Salvandy founded the Committee of Arts and Monuments, the aim of which was to encourage and coordinate archaeological researches, amongst which the study of cathedrals was to occupy a prominent place. Ludovic Vitet was commissioned to write a monograph on Noyon, while Lassus, an architect, was responsible for drafting a similar work on Chartres.

The publication of Ludovic Vitet's study of Noyon cathedral, in 1845, was of crucial importance, for it was the first monograph to be based upon texts and upon the actual analysis of the monument. It aspired in this respect to rival the work which Sulpice Boisserée had written on Köln, and which had been translated into French in 1823. Vitet's monograph also reflected a new concern with illustration. The volume containing the written text was complemented by an album of plates in which plans, cross-sections, elevations and architectural details had been drawn with the greatest care. Vitet even went so far as to call upon the expertise of one of the great architects of the period, Daniel Ramée (1806–87). If Noyon was given so important a place in the history of Gothic architecture, it was because Vitet believed that a very early date could be ascribed to the monument. He imagined that it had been embarked upon immediately after the fire of 1131, long before work began on Saint-Denis. More important still were the new theories, which played a considerable role at the time, partly because of their clarity of exposition, and partly because the high standing in official milieux enjoyed by their author ensured that his views gained a wide hearing. Vitet had derived some of these theories from Victor Hugo, especially all those arguments which concerned the evolution of architectural forms and sociological explanation. On the other hand, he represented a particular current of thought, which may be characterised as agnostic, if not anti-religious and positivist. Finally, one cannot rule out the possibility that Ramée gave him valuable assistance. This architect, himself born in Germany, was familiar with both the German and the English architectural literature. He later went on to publish a *Manuel de l'histoire de l'architecture chez tous les peuples et particulièrement de l'architecture en France* (1843), in which a number of Vitet's theories were elaborated further.

In many respects, Viollet-le-Duc belonged to this same intellectual current, to which he gave a further, and quite spectacular development. In addition, he had the merit of expounding to a wide audience, both through his various writings and through his actions, the arguments which he professed. Even today, such arguments inform many discussions of medieval architecture, and this is even more apparent in the case of Gothic architecture. I do not propose to rehearse the whole analysis advanced by this famous architect, but what was involved was a system of thought designed to provide a global account of a reality the extraordinary diversity of which had profoundly impressed him. Viollet-le-Duc's ideas were further developed in his *Dictionnaire*, the first volume of which was published in 1854, but earlier formulations were sketched out ten years before in a series of articles published, from 1844 on, in Didron's *Annales archéologiques* ('*De la construction des édifices religieux en France*'). One thus has to accept that it is difficult to identify the authorship of certain arguments propounded at around the same date by Lassus, Verneilh and Vitet, who held very much the same views, and who tended to publish in the *Annales*. The general public, however, was convinced that the theory, as far as medieval rationalism was concerned, had emerged fully fledged from the brain of Viollet-le-Duc.

In order to shed some light on the great debate of the mid-nineteenth century on the cathedral, which preoccupied both scholarly and professional milieux, I want to discuss a few of the central issues. Viollet-le-Duc's position was expounded in 'Cathédrale', an article published in 1854 which in many respects rehearsed the lines of argument advanced by Victor Hugo and Vitet. He too posited a link between urban growth and the building of cathedrals. The populations of the towns had reacted against the monastic and feudal order by constituting themselves as 'communes'. The bishops used such emancipatory movements to their own advantage by building or rebuilding their cathedrals 'with the vigorous participation of the local population'. Using a formula sufficiently striking to persuade the most sceptical of his readers, Viollet-le-Duc went so far as to claim that 'at the end of the twelfth century, the erection of a cathedral was a need, because it constituted a clamorous protest against the feudal order'. Although he was prepared to admit that they were 'religious monuments', he immediately qualified this observation by emphasising that they 'were above all national monuments'. So it was that the French cathedral, built by French society, its labour and its financial contributions, was a 'symbol of French unity', 'the first and the most powerful bid for unity'. It was then a simple matter to conclude, as Viollet-le-Duc showed no hesitation in doing, that it was the wealth of the lay population, eagerly proffered, which had served to raise up 'the first genuinely popular building to be opposed to the feudal castle, which would in the end conquer it'. The historical sequence seemed to accord with such theories for, while the building fever abated around the middle of the thirteenth century, this occurrence could easily be regarded as a consequence of the consolidation of the power of the monarchy. With the crushing of the feudal fortresses, the building of cathedrals ceased to be so urgent and, as a consequence, some of them were left unfinished. It was thanks to the efforts of bishop and canons, who rallied a flagging population, that some of the cathedrals were in fact completed.

Viollet-le-Duc gave a still more coherent formulation of this analysis in his *Histoire d'une cathédrale et d'un hôtel de ville*, which was published in 1854, and which further emphasised the link between the history of the cathedral and the revival of the city. The cathedral was defined as not merely a religious monument but also, and primarily, as the most vibrant expression of municipal existence. Together with the town hall, it allowed one to grasp just what, across history, the rise of the people had been. Indeed, the civil aspect of the cathedral was of greater importance than the religious dimension. In illustration of Viollet-le-Duc's theory, let us consider a concrete example, the alterations to the choir of Laon cathedral. The original plans had featured a rather shallow semicircular chevet, but before long the decision was taken to opt for a long rectangular chevet instead. Viollet-le-Duc interpreted this change in design in terms of the democratic origin of the building, which distinguished it from the cathedrals of Chartres, Amiens or Reims. Laon cathedral was, he claimed, 'the monument of a people that was both resourceful, energetic and full of a virile grandeur' (vol. II, p. 309). The local population had, he argued, helped the bishop to raise the building, by themselves endowing the chevet, 'which was better suited, by its very design, to popular meetings'. Indeed, the bishops had yielded in this matter to the civil authorities, whose might had found expression in the creation of the commune.

22

Fig. 2 Clusy. Plan by Viollet-le-Duc, taken from his *Histoire d'une cathédrale*, 1854.

Jean-Baptiste Lassus, who from 1844 onwards was collaborating with Viollet-le-Duc on the site of Notre-Dame of Paris, belonged to a somewhat different tendency. In his view, social and political restoration should be accompanied by religious restoration. He was therefore opposed to eighteenth-century rationalism, and was an unabashed admirer of the Middle Ages, and of the thirteenth century in particular. He drew inspiration not so much from Chateaubriand as from Joseph de Maistre, whose writings had contained hugely influential meditations upon the Catholic philosophy of history. Lassus shared de Maistre's admiration for the thirteenth century, which he derived in part from his friend Montalambert. He therefore took an opposite view to Viollet-le-Duc, declaring himself to be a Catholic architect, whose efforts would be devoted to the building of religious buildings 'in which art will forever celebrate the glory of God to whom it is consecrated'. In *Histoire et description des moeurs et usages ... en Europe*, a work co-written by Jean-Baptiste Lassus and by Paul Lacroix and published in Paris in 1851, the symbolic signification of the church was emphasised. It was claimed that the church was a 'pure creation of thought', and the plan of the building, which evoked the shape of the cross, was stressed. Lassus died in 1857, and his premature death meant that he was never able to present his arguments in any sort of systematic form. If, however, one analyses the few texts published during his lifetime, it soon becomes apparent that his thought was diametrically opposed to that of Viollet-le-Duc. Indeed, Lassus showed a deeper appreciation of what is, to my mind, one of the most original features of this form of architecture, namely, its affirmation of spatial values. This characteristic of the Gothic is at once wholly at odds with the perceptions of Antiquity and an intimation of modern and contemporary architectural theory and practice.

The theories regarding Gothic architecture advanced during this period were soon to be put into practice, through the rebuilding of the cathedrals. A number of such buildings were in every respect in urgent need of restoration. Their critical condition was due to the general neglect they had suffered during the Revolution, and the less-than-satisfactory state of repairs sustained during the classical period. The cathedrals were also important counters in a religious, political and even local struggle. Public opinion was simply no longer prepared to countenance the failure to preserve such monuments, in a period in which much thought was being given to their nature and history. Finally, the holding of religious services itself demanded that the fabric of the cathedrals be restored. Where so many disparate interests converged, such ventures were bound to prosper, even though large sums of money and protracted building works

Fig. 3 Limoges cathedral at the beginning of the nineteenth century. Lithograph by A. Rouargue, from an original drawing by Chapuy (*Le Moyen Age pittoresque*, 1836).

would be necessary. Some of these restorations took on an exemplary status, because the monuments in question had a particular symbolic value in historical terms. Notre-Dame of Paris was an especially telling instance here, both because of the debates which were staged and because of the choice of architects.

There should be no need to inform the reader that the decision to put the monument to rights was an indirect consequence of the publication of Victor Hugo's novel. Several factors served to make the restoration of Notre-Dame an event of particular significance within the general movement for the refurbishment of medieval monuments: the building had played a particular role in national history, and as a consequence public opinion rallied to the cause. An architectural competition was held, which was won by Lassus and Viollet-le-Duc, their aspiration being to create a site that was animated by the same faith that had prevailed there in the thirteenth century.

The restoration of a monument would often entail returning it to its original state, even if, as Viollet-le-Duc acknowledged in his article 'Restoration' (t. 8, p. 14), such a state had never existed. Sometimes, the attempt was also made to complete unfinished cathedrals. Köln may serve as an example of such a project although, for all its prestige, it had its critics too, Victor Hugo among them (*Le Rhin*). It is a remarkable fact that many schemes to finish cathedrals arose out of local initiatives. This was the case with, for example, Bayonne, Clermont, Moulins, Nantes, Limoges and Toulouse. At Bayonne, in 1847, a generous donor bequeathed an annuity of 40,000 francs, to be used for the rebuilding and decoration of the cathedral. As is well known, the funds that were thus made available allowed those responsible for the building to go much further. In 1858, Emile Boeswillwald, the architect dispatched from Paris to impose some order upon the site, was forced to yield to the wishes of the local population.

If it had proved difficult at Moulins to find sufficient funds to endow the former collegiate church, which, after the administrative reforms of the revolutionary period, had become a cathedral, it was because of the rival claims of the Sacré-Coeur. The problem was finally resolved in 1852, when the prince-president inaugurated an emergency fund. Toulouse was one of the first cities in France to call for the rebuilding of its cathedral. Thus, in 1821, Pascal Virebent suggested that a nave be reconstructed within the extension of the Gothic chevet, and that 'the Raymondine nave' be demolished. Plan after plan was mooted, but financial difficulties prevented any of them from being executed. Finally, in 1844, Léopold Petit's plan was accepted and, with the use of funds raised by a lottery and in spite of the stubborn opposition of the *Société archéologique du Midi*, work was begun. However, the Franco-Prussian war put

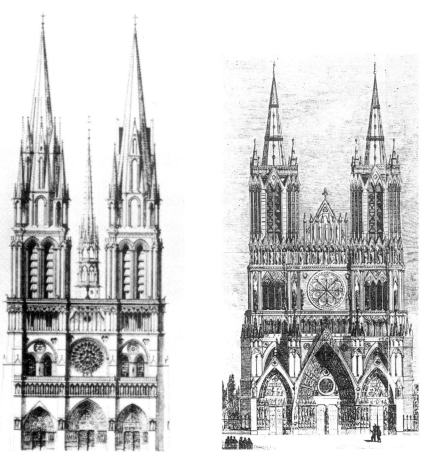

Fig. 4 The facade of Notre-Dame of Paris, surmounted with spires. Plan by Sauvageot.

Fig. 5 Léopold Petit's plan for the western facade of Toulouse cathedral (1864).

a stop to this ambitious but destructive plan. The inspiration behind the planned completion of Limoges cathedral was Monsignor Duquesnoy, who dreamed of linking up the nave to the freestanding bell-tower. He set up a number of committees, whose responsibility it was to raise the necessary sums, solicited subscriptions and subventions and even obtained whatever indulgences were deemed necessary from the Pope. Here too care was taken to recreate the material and spiritual circumstances which had prevailed in the thirteenth century. In April 1875, the sum required had been raised and, on 27 April 1876, the first stone was laid. Local architects had generally encountered

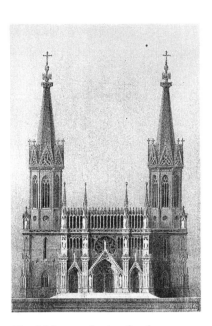

Fig. 6 Marnotte's plan for the western
facade of Besançon (1844).

Fig. 7 Viollet-le-Duc's plan for the
western facade of Lausanne cathedral.

problems on the various sites, and had then been replaced by men of Parisian
origin, such as Boeswillwald in Bayonne, Lassus in Moulins, Viollet-le-Duc in
Toulouse and Bailly in Limoges.

Each and every plan, irrespective of the discussions or polemics to which they
had given rise, took its inspiration from Gothic architecture. The various
drawings for Moulins cathedral show very clearly how difficult it had been to
settle upon a formula – in the end, Lassus' plan had won the competition – but
all of them referred to Gothic architecture of the first half of the thirteenth
century from northern France, and therefore took no account of a chevet
designed at the very end of the fifteenth century. The completion of the western
end of the cathedral posed fewer problems than the building of the nave had
done. In this case too, the architects drew their inspiration from the example of
the great cathedrals of the North, so that the facade, subsequently known as
harmonic, was to have two towers and was to feature three portals. Notre-
Dame of Paris was the usual reference-point, and indeed it actually served to

define what a cathedral was. The sole exception to this rule was Limoges, where those concerned were determined to preserve the bell-tower, one of the most popular sights of the town. Everywhere else a 'harmonic facade' was advocated. In his plan for Toulouse cathedral, Pascal Virebent established the principle which would be retained for all subsequent schemes – such as those of Jean-Pierre Laffont (1825) and Léopold Petit (1864) – regardless of the precise fate of the nave. Only Viollet-le-Duc struck out on his own, his plan being to double the Raymondine nave and to build a single bell-tower on the west side. At Bayonne, Selmersheim was responsible, in the years after 1873, for the completion of the facade, which was to have towers and spires.

One has the sense that everyone, from architects, sponsors, amateur enthusiasts to the general public, entertained a specific conception of the cathedral. Most would seem to have believed that the men of the Middle Ages had dreamed, when the building began, of an 'ideal cathedral', which circumstances had in time either scotched or modified. Viollet-le-Duc gave this mythical image a concrete form in his *Dictionnaire*:

In order to give some impression of what a complete, finished thirteenth-century cathedral was supposed, according to its original conception, to have looked like, we have reproduced a somewhat free representation of a building of the period, executed at Reims. If we set aside those details, which are not of particular concern to us here, the monument designed by Robert of Coucy fits this overall conception, even though the western spires were never finished and the central spires and some transepts were made of wood and lead.

(vol. II, 1859, p. 324)

The image made a profound impression upon contemporaries, if the sheer number of reproductions is anything to go by. I would like to emphasise here that the cathedral was viewed from the outside rather than the inside, a crucial factor where its urban setting was concerned. It was in fact a work of synthesis that was to prove persuasive to many nineteenth-century sensibilities, the breadth of its transept being modelled upon that of Chartres, its lantern-tower being derived from Laon and its western facade being borrowed from Reims.

One might have imagined that the nineteenth century would have been equal to designing a monument that matched up to its own ambitions. The most ambitious plan in France was that proposed for the town of Lille, where it was hoped to build a church of international stature. Lassus submitted a design for Notre-Dame-de-la-Treille in 1855. Admittedly, it was not a cathedral in the strict sense of the term, but the architect set to work as if it were: 'I have

Fig. 8 Viollet-le-Duc's plan for the western facade of Clermont-Ferrand (1864).

Fig. 9 Viollet-le-Duc's 'ideal cathedral', *Dictionnaire d'architecture*, vol. VI.

tried...to create the cathedral of the North'. The outcome of the competition was to prove deeply wounding, for the jury ranked him only third (13 April 1856). The specifications had made it perfectly clear what the sponsors were looking for. The building, they stipulated, 'should remind us of the lovely constructions, at once simple and impressive, of the first half of the thirteenth century'. The dimensions laid down were close to those of the cathedrals of the period, the length being from 100–110 metres. The monument was to have a 'harmonic facade' with spires and three portals with deep arches. The plan featured a nave with three aisles, a transept, a choir, an ambulatory and a number of side chapels, while the elevation showed galleries. In addition, there were chapels of ease, an assembly room, two sacristies, a catechism room, various other rooms and, finally, a cloister. Lassus could not help but be delighted by these specifications, which seemed to match his wildest dreams. His enthusiasm is captured in the surviving drawings, which are indeed of a remarkably high quality. Lassus' plan for this monument gave rise to the most beautiful architectural drawings of the period. The remarkable quality of his contribution should have been evident to the jury on the basis of his views of the interior alone. For the architect had not merely delineated the architectural aspects of the building, but had also taken care to draw the furnishings, including confessionals, stalls, lectern, railings, stoop, high altar, churchwardens' pew, baptismal fonts, chapel altars, organ chest, pulpit and stained glass. Since the specifications had emphasised the importance of chapels of ease, Lassus took care to locate his 'cathedral' in its immediate context. He placed his building in a very close-knit urban fabric, bordered by streets and houses to the north and to the west, preceded in the west by a parvis (51 metres). The chapels of ease were located on the south side, ringing the cloister which gave out directly on to the choir. The bishop's palace was removed to the south-west. This, then, was the milieu in which the place of worship was situated. Lassus showed the same eclecticism as had been perceptible in Viollet-le-Duc's 'ideal cathedral'. The plan featured a double ambulatory and deeply recessed side-chapels (Le Mans), semicircular arms to the transept without aisles (Noyon), and semicircular chapels located on the first bay of the nave. Borrowings were just as visible in the elevation. However, in his report, Lassus emphasised that his plan was not a copy. On the other hand, he took considerable liberties with his programmes for sculpture and stained glass, in part because the specifications in this area remained very vague. He spelled out the reasons for his distancing himself from the Middle Ages, reducing characteristically enough the part played by the New Testament. Indeed, this plan bore witness to a quite sophisticated line of argument, for

Lassus wished to do as the sculptors of the thirteenth century had successfully done, and to incorporate modern procedures into his programme.

THE SPONTANEIST THEORY

The analysis of the conditions governing creation in the medieval period had led to the formulation of a far-reaching doctrine. Here too Victor Hugo had shown the way, by emphasising the ascendancy of architecture and by asserting that the other arts had been subordinated to it. Professional architects found evidence in the documents then in print to support this argument, and were not slow to profess it themselves. The programme may well have been the responsibility of the sponsor, but definition of the overall scheme and of details fell to the master of the fabric fund. The shaping of the fabric was his sole prerogative. Viollet-le-Duc ascribed exemplary importance to this term, 'for by fabric was meant everything which constituted the fixtures and fittings of a building, from foundations to tapestries, candelabras, or even to the smallest furnishings' (*Dictionnaire*, I, p. 107). In Viollet-le-Duc's view, this massive task did not emerge before the Gothic period, which saw the birth of the artist in the modern sense of the term. The artist was therefore of lay origin, and his responsibilities bore a curious resemblance to those of the architects of Viollet-le-Duc's own time. If the cathedral was to have its own coherence, the architect should not only execute drawings for the whole site and for the details of the monument, but should also be responsible for the furnishings and decor. Finally, he should also be involved in the actual running of the site. Both Lassus and Viollet-le-Duc adopted this approach, stipulating in minute detail what the decor should be in the cathedrals of Paris and Moulins and in the church of Notre-Dame-de-la-Treille at Lille. As for the smooth operation of the site, Paris provided a particularly telling example, as scrutiny of the works record shows.

The architects responsible for the restoration of Notre-Dame of Paris concentrated their energies upon the actual organisation of the site, for they wished to recreate the working conditions and spiritual ambience of the Middle Ages. It is in these terms that one should judge their relationship with Geoffroi-Dechaume, the man in overall charge of the team of sculptors, although their task was made the easier by his remarkable personality, his powerful physique and even his place of birth. The works site for the restoration of Notre-Dame of Paris made it possible to imagine what a thirteenth-century site would have looked like.

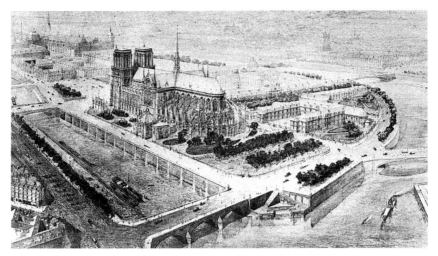

Fig. 10 Viollet-le-Duc's plan for the treatment of the approaches to Notre-Dame of Paris (1859).

This elitist theory of artistic creation nevertheless met with a spectacular failure, since the public, both specialist and amateur, generally favoured the vaguer theory endorsed by Victor Hugo. One should further note that the surviving documentation from the Gothic Middle Ages offered strong grounds for supposing that architectural creation had in fact been both anonymous and spontaneous.

Some texts even served to reinforce this point of view, for example, those concerning Chartres cathedral, one of which, dated 1144, is ascribed to Robert of Torigni: 'In my diocese, there is the most extraordinary sight, for everyone, whether knight, burgess or peasant, hastens to Chartres in order to have the honour of working for Notre-Dame…they rush there in a disordered mass, paying no heed to distinctions of rank; the load is sometimes so heavy that a thousand men are needed for each waggon'. Other documents lent credence to this hypothesis, which was soon regarded as established fact. A number of consequences followed, the most important of them concerning the birth of Gothic art, which is too often reduced to being no more than a matter of the emergence of intersecting ribs in vaults. Up until quite recently, the tendency has been to see the clumsy vaulting of the little churches on the Ile de France as a relatively early development, as if they were the first, hesitant and groping attempts of architects who, becoming surer of themselves after a short while, embarked upon the building of cathedrals. The architecture which had emerged

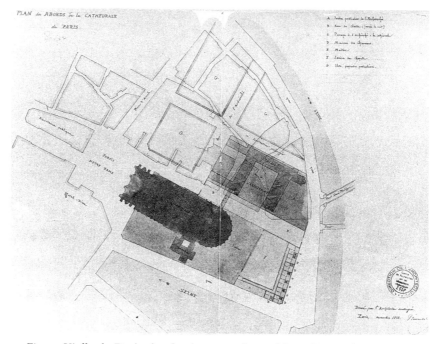

Fig. 11 Viollet-le-Duc's plan for the approaches to Notre-Dame of Paris (1858).

Fig. 12 Project for the treatment of the chevet of Notre-Dame of Paris, by Lassus and Viollet-le-Duc (28 January 1843).

in the countryside of the Ile de France would then have made inroads into the towns and their episcopal churches. It is clear enough what conclusions might be drawn from an argument of this sort. Even Focillon, an independent-minded thinker if ever there was one, claimed that 'the rib was invented by masons', although he went on to add the rider that 'it was as an organ of structure that it was conceived ... it was as an organ of structure that it spread' (*Art d'Occident*, p. 144).

The nineteenth century had had the courage to grapple with the cathedral and, in the process, made a number of errors whose gravity matched the passion brought to the task. Despite the claims that are often advanced, these errors did not have any dramatic consequences overall. We owe a debt to the nineteenth century anyway for having raised the issue once again, and for having handed down this imposing inheritance to us. However, the bestowal of a mythical status upon the cathedral worked to the advantage of the single monument, while the immediate environment was neglected or even condemned. In this respect, the consequences of the rediscovery of the cathedral were catastrophic. Victor Hugo, however, had been quite clear on this point. He had had the exceptional clearsightedness to appreciate that the cathedral of Paris was not isolated, cut off from everyday life and from the town, but in fact participated fully in it, and was irrigated by this teeming mass of human beings and by this proliferation of houses. Fifty years later, the damage had been done, and Notre-Dame stood in splendid isolation on a deserted Ile de la Cité. Baron Haussmann had pursued this work of destruction with particular vigour. Three roads crossed the island running from north to south, along the axis of each of the bridges, the first at the foot of the western face of the cathedral, the second being the Rue de la Cité and the third the Boulevard du Palais. New buildings, which were both cumbersome and out of proportion to the surface area of the island, replaced the countless two-storey residential houses. Among their number one should mention a huge hôtel-Dieu, on the north bank of the river, although it had previously been on the south, a commercial court, and the city barracks, subsequently the Prefecture of police. The episcopal palace, gutted by fire, had already been pulled down, thus freeing the south flank of the cathedral; the canons' residences, to the north, disappeared. The rebuilding of the massive palace to the west would soon weigh down the point of the Cité still more. In front of the facade, the parvis was extended, becoming a huge square 100 metres wide and 200 metres long, which now serves as a parade-ground for the soldiers quartered opposite. As a consequence of these changes, the population of the Ile de la Cité fell from 15,000 inhabitants to around 5,000 by the end of the century.

Notre-Dame of Paris served as a model for many other sites. The example of Amiens is no less striking, even if alterations there were occasioned by strictly external factors. Thus, the damage of two World Wars made it possible to supply a 'parvis' for the western facade, and to free the whole of the northern flank of the building. Every conceivable reason was advanced for isolating the cathedral within the city. At Le Mans, it was thought necessary to clean up the approaches to the cathedral, while at Bourges, it was decided to preserve a vista that had been revealed by accident when a garage was demolished. Equally striking examples of the same general approach were in evidence in Reims, Chartres and Laon, and one could readily extend the list to include Toulouse and Rouen. Indeed, it was everywhere agreed that the monument was self-sufficient, and that it was a building like any other, like a town hall, for example, or a theatre.

Admittedly, there was nothing particularly novel about nineteenth-century thinking in this respect, for eighteenth-century alterations were often done in a similar spirit. Consider, for example, the creation of the square on the southern flank of Metz cathedral. As a result of this, the cathedral is no longer at the heart of the city; indeed, through a failure to grasp its real identity, as a house of God designed to welcome the faithful, it has been deliberately detached. The twentieth century has followed a similar course.

If we are to grasp the real nature of the cathedral, as it was in the medieval period, we must consider it in a long-term perspective, beginning with the introduction of Christianity into Roman Gaul and the establishment of episcopal sees in the ancient cities. We must scrutinise each of the great periods which followed, emphasising whatever was original in its particular contribution. We must break off, however, at the dawn of the Renaissance, because a different reality takes hold then, characterised, among other things, by the emergence of Protestantism, an event of such momentous importance that it led to fratricidal wars, and by the Council of Trent which, after a lengthy period of turbulence, put the Church back on the right path. The breach with the Middle Ages was complete. The new circumstances which then arose, although just as propitious, represented a wholly different reality, and therefore a break with the past.

I

The bishop in the city

✤

Three events were to have a lasting impact upon Roman Gaul, although we have only recently begun to appreciate how important they were. Two of these changes were virtually contemporary with each other, while the third took place later, fitting into an already existing framework. The first two events were not restricted to the geographical boundaries of Gaul, but assumed a highly characteristic form there, and therefore imposed a markedly original pattern on this part of the Empire.

CHRISTIANITY

The first of the three events was the coming of Christianity, brought to Gaul by the Jewish communities of the diaspora, which had settled in the towns. It was only later, through the agency of Saint Martin of Tours, in the sixth century, that the new faith began to impinge upon the rural areas, which had up until then preserved their allegiance to the pagan religions. The etymology of the French word *paysan*, derived from the Latin *paganus*, bears out the point I am making here. Admittedly, anyone wishing to write the history of early Christianity is faced with a number of difficulties, occasioned by the lack of real textual evidence. In recent years, however, archaeological excavations have helped to make good such deficiencies. We now have proof that Christian communities existed at Vienne and Lyon as early as the second century, and that there was another at Autun, in the third century. The unreliable nature of the sources gave rise to many legends which, from the fifth century, grew up around a still unwritten history. Grégoire of Tours, during the seventh century, lent some credence to such legends, among them, the notion that the Gauls had been granted apostolicity. The apostle Peter was supposed to have sent seven bishops to serve as evangelists in Gaul, each of whom was ordained with this purpose in mind: Gatien to Tours, Trophime to Arles, Paul to Narbonne, Saturnin to Toulouse, Denis to Paris, Austremoine to Clermont (then known as Arverne) and Martial to Limoges. This legend, although disputed since the seventeenth century, has remained current until fairly recently. In fact, it is not until the fourth century that we can be sure of treading on firmer ground.

On 28 October 312, the emperor Constantine had a Christian revelation on the Pontus Milvius, outside of Rome, where he was about to do battle with, and in fact crush, his rival Maxencius. In 313, what is generally known as the Edict of Milan was to transform relations between Church and State, with the former being granted precedence rather than being merely tolerated, as had been the case in the past. In the following year, bishops from Africa, Italy, Rome, Britain and Spain met at Arles, at the behest of the city's prelate, Maximus. We know why this assembly was convoked, and it is therefore clear to us why the bishops were vested with such wide-ranging powers. It was necessary to quell the Arian heresy.

In the course of the fourth century, the Church came to be organised in much the same fashion throughout the Empire. Within each *civitas* there arose a Christian community, run by a bishop, who was then known as an *episcopos* or overseer, but who generally preferred the title of pontiff. He was vested with a threefold authority, involving administration, jurisdiction and education, and held sway over a territory whose boundaries were defined by administrative divisions imposed under the Empire. He wielded full sacerdotal powers, and he alone could consecrate other bishops, ordain priests or other clerics. He was responsible for confirmations and, crucially, for baptisms, a function which had important implications for architecture, as we shall see below. One should also bear in mind that, at this period, a bishop was elected by the clergy and the people.

We have very little idea as to the sort of hierarchical organisation which prevailed in the earliest periods of the Church's history. In 398, the Council of Turin confirmed that the metropolitan bishop, resident in the capital city of each province, stood at the head of the hierarchy. A chain of command was thus consolidated, in which the bishop was helped, in his various functions, by priests, deacons, subdeacons and by the whole range of officers over whom he held disciplinary power. At the same time, his own function was more precisely defined. He was to preach against paganism, schism and the ever-recurrent

Fig. 13 Map of ecclesiastical Gaul (after A. Mirot). 1. Metropolis; 2. Bishopric.

heresies, and to provide for the welfare of the local population, making good in this respect the shortcomings of a faltering Roman administration. He had also won the right to visit prisons, and he would, when the occasion arose, ransom prisoners from the barbarians or defend the population from laws which he regarded as unjust.

As well as being responsible for such charitable activities, the bishop was also an administrator. The goods of the church, being divine property, were held to be sacred and inalienable. They were greatly increased by gifts, given by the prelate upon assuming office or at his death, or by generous Christians. With the accession to the episcopate, towards the end of the fifth century, of persons from well-to-do families, the church grew significantly wealthier. The substantial income which accrued was divided by the bishop into several parts, one being allocated to the 'house' (*domus*) of the bishop and his clergy, a second to the construction and maintenance of sacred buildings and a third to charitable institutions.

The bishop also wielded real judicial powers, both over the clergy, which was answerable solely to him, even in the civil sphere, and over the remainder of the population, through arbitration. A law promulgated in 398 in fact required that he be referred to by both groups. Finally, in 408, a subsequent law placed the bishop's rulings on a par with the judgements of the civil courts.

One may gauge the scale of Christianity's triumph in Gaul from the number of bishops attending the various councils. At the Council of Arles, there were sixteen in attendance. In the fourth century, the number rose to twenty-six, while the boundaries of the dioceses were redrawn, with some being fragmented or disappearing off the map, while others were created for purely political reasons (for example, Laon). The changing face of the map bears witness to the remarkably flourishing condition of the Church of Gaul.

THE CITY TURNED IN UPON ITSELF

The bishops exercised their authority in towns which bore little resemblance to the open, ancient cities of the town-planners of the *Pax Romana*. The Roman conquest had had an overwhelming impact upon urbanisation in Gaul. Admittedly, there had been centres of settlement which had, since late prehistoric times, embodied in embryonic form the principle of the town, but it had taken the Roman genius to bring them to fruition. Our own conception of a town should not be confused with that of Antiquity. For us, a town is founded upon the notion of conviviality, and it is therefore meant to serve as a meeting-place for human beings converging from many different places, engaged in quite diverse activities, in a spirit of mutual tolerance and acknowledging the authority of an administration elected by themselves and responsible for rendering this mosaic homogeneous. Antiquity's concept of the town was both simpler and more complex. Its greater simplicity was due to the fact that it judged everything outside of itself to be savage and barbarian, and deemed civilization to be of its essence urban. Its complexity, on the other hand, arose from the fact that its culture, being given a powerful expression through lavish monuments, should be seen in relation to the territory over which the *civitas* wielded power. For the *civitas* included other agglomerations but also, and most importantly, the land cultivated in order to feed the inhabitants of the *urbs*. Gaul was divided into a number of provinces, each of which was governed by a capital. The reforms implemented under Diocletian and during the fourth century were designed to recast the administration of the whole territory, and so to increase the number of provinces, and therefore of governors. The *Notitia Galliarum*, at the end of the fourth century, describes seventeen provinces and their respective capitals. Christian administration experienced no difficulty in adjusting to this strictly hierarchical structure, even going so far as to turn the peculiar features of specific agglomerations to its own account. This was the case with Lyon, for example, where the assembly of the Gallic peoples had met since the first century BC, beside the altar dedicated to Caesar Augustus, which was housed in a sanctuary. In the fourth century, Trèves and Bordeaux were added to the list, and at the beginning of the fifth century Arles replaced the former as capital of Gaul.

The *urbs* could only provide shelter for the living, the dead being cast outside, along approach roads conveying the traveller right up to the sacred boundary of the town, the *pomoerium*, which was sometimes marked by a surrounding wall. The topography of ancient cities was in principle orthogonal in design, but in practice it would be adjusted to suit the terrain. Scholars have therefore concluded that they were planned by 'topographical engineers'. A powerful communications network, less hierarchical than has often being implied, established close links between the constituent elements of the town, leaving, as has been said, areas of land of varying size free of buildings, which could provide sites for public monuments as and when they were needed. Some of these monuments became the symbols of the town, such as the forum, which was both a centre of government and a meeting-place. For this very reason, it is difficult to assess the size of population, since these public monuments were meant to serve the *civitas* as well as the *urbs*. Thus, estimates for Lutetia (Paris) suggest 8,000 inhabitants, although the arenas could accommodate as many as 15,000 spectators. Nevertheless, some agglomerations reached a much higher figure, between 20,000 and 25,000 in the case of Autun, Lyon, Narbonne, Nîmes, Reims and Trèves. Such populations consisted of notables, whose existence is revealed to us through the excavation of their luxurious dwellings, and of those who were less wealthy, workers, artisans and even slaves, slavery being a phenomenon that was intrinsically linked to cities.

In the course of the fourth and fifth centuries, the cities of Gaul underwent a drastic transformation, with their surface area being reduced through the construction of new stone surrounding walls. Pressure from the 'barbarians' along the *limes*, and their incursions from the middle of the third century onwards, put the cities on the defensive. This massive endeavour, which we have known of since Adrien Blanchet's pioneering researches in 1906, has been put into proper proportion since that time, thanks to the work of historians and archaeologists and to the application of a modicum of common sense to the problem.

One should begin by noting that it was an order from Rome that had prompted the decision to restore the defences of the towns of Gaul. A decree promulgated by Honorius in 396, and published subsequently in the *Corpus Juris Civilis*, ordered the senates and the inhabitants of the towns to erect new walls or to rebuild those which already existed, in order to render them more secure (*Ordines et incolas urbium singularum muros vel novos facere debere, vel veteres firmius renovare*). As we have already seen, a number of high defensive walls already existed, and these were simply reinforced. Most such defences, however, were built from the end of the fourth century onwards. It has often been claimed that the building of such walls was highly precipitate, as if the territory lived in fear of imminent catastrophe, but this was not in fact the case. Excavations undertaken in recent years in Paris, together with the analysis of fragments of masonry that have recently come loose, in Bourges, Le Mans, Senlis and Tours, have shown just how carefully such work was done. A number of medieval texts emphasise the difficulties which faced stone-masons when these walls were finally destroyed. So homogeneous was the construction of a number of such walls, as we know from those which are still standing or from extant drawings, that there is good reason to suppose that they were the work of a corps of architects, working to a precise plan as regards both lay-out and construction. Their foundations generally consisted of large blocks of stone, which sometimes reached an impressive number of courses, for example, ten at Sens and thirteen at Périgueux. The blocks had been recovered from ancient monuments of every kind, ranging from funerary stelae, cornices and columns to boundary-posts and capitals. The catastrophic theories advanced in the past to account for the building of these walls, to which I referred above, arose in part from the discovery that such elements were reused for the foundations. A more convincing interpretation of this phenomenon may, however, be advanced. The construction of an enceinte called for the destruction of various buildings that were situated in its path, whether to dig foundation trenches or to ensure circulation of traffic on the inside or the outside, or, most important of all, to create the ramp that was needed to protect the surrounding wall and to enable

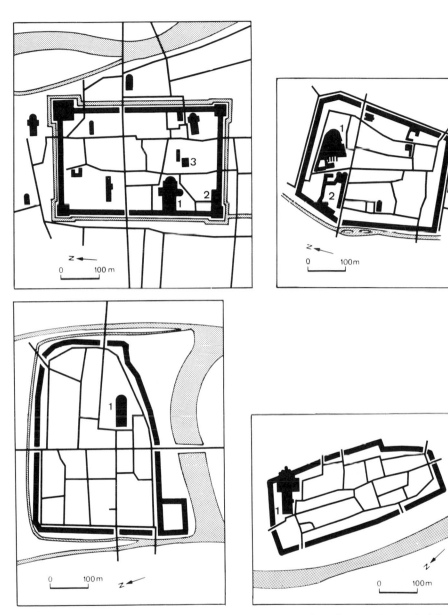

Fig. 14 Plan of ancient Soissons (after A. Blanchet). 1. The cathedral; 2. The episcopal palace; 3. The hôtel-Dieu.

Fig. 16 Plan of ancient Rouen (after A. Blanchet). 1. The cathedral.

Fig. 15 Plan of ancient Beauvais (after A. Blanchet). 1. The cathedral; 2. The episcopal palace.

Fig. 17 Plan of ancient Le Mans (after A. Blanchet). 1. The cathedral.

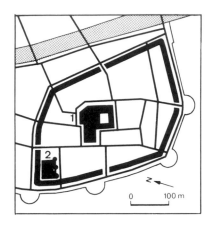

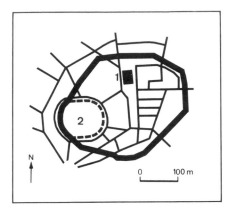

Fig. 18 Plan of ancient Bayonne (after A. Blanchet). 1. The cathedral; 2. The castle.

Fig. 19 Plan of ancient Périgueux (after A. Blanchet). 1. The cathedral; 2. The castle.

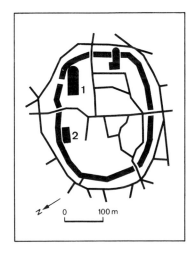

Fig. 20 Plan of ancient Tours (after A. Blanchet). 1. The cathedral.

Fig. 21 Plan of ancient Senlis (after A. Blanchet). 1. The cathedral; 2. The castle.

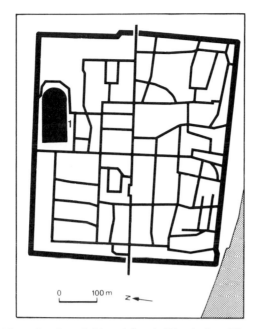

Fig. 22 Plan of ancient Orléans (after A. Blanchet). 1. The cathedral.

the besieged inhabitants to see their assailants. The ramp was sometimes several dozen metres high. One should also add moats to the list, although their existence is by no means proven. The demolition undertaken was substantial, both because it had been necessary to act decisively, and because it made available materials which reduced building costs. It goes without saying that only the finest blocks could be used for such a purpose and, where they were wanting, they were sought for in derelict public monuments, which served as quarries.

The new lay-out led to a considerable reduction in the surface area of those towns which had originally been built on an especially large scale, for example, Autun, Köln, Nîmes and Trèves. The town of Gap was now no more than two hectares in area, while Clermont was three hectares, Bazas four, Senlis seven, Tours between eight and nine and Évreux nine. Other towns were still somewhat larger. Saintes, for example, was sixteen hectares, Rouen and Nantes were eighteen, Sens twenty-five and Bordeaux thirty or so. These dramatic reductions in size lent credence to the catastrophist notion of the fourth and fifth centuries. Up until quite recently, it had been supposed that the urban habitat was entirely concentrated within the surrounding walls, and that the laying waste of the town could be traced back to a fairly early period, but archaeological finds have undermined the more extreme versions of this argument. Thus, in Paris, the discovery of tombs dating from this period but situated outside the Ile de la Cité, which was the only area with proper defences, suggests that there were as many settlements *extra muros*. One can draw the same conclusion from the evidence at Senlis, where the enclosed town corresponded to the medieval *castrum*, with the *urbs* extending well beyond it. In reality, the enceinte was supposed to protect not so much the population as the symbols of the town, the main administrative buildings, among them the palace or the praetorium and the garrisons. This provides a more convincing explanation as to why particular lay-outs, with specific siting of buildings and sizes, were chosen. The architects appointed by the imperial government to build the enceinte had chosen within the *urbs* that part that was most readily protected and defended. When especially dramatic circumstances arose, these redoubts could serve, as in the Middle Ages, as fall-back positions for the population at large.

TEMPORA CHRISTIANA

The religious topography of the towns of Gaul serves to confirm, and even to reinforce the notion that such settlements were permanent, and thereby undermines any idea of discontinuity. The number of attested religious institutions situated *extra muros*, from the earliest times, obviously lends weight to the hypothesis that there were communities within the *urbs* at Paris, and in many other towns, for example, Clermont, Lyon and Vienne. Many other names could even now be added to this list. Within 'the citadel' was to be found, as was only right and proper, the ecclesiastical administration and the bishop.

In addition, archaeologists have disproved the thesis, which was entertained up until very recently, that the cathedral had originally been located *extra muros*, only to be transferred subsequently inside the 'cities'. This thesis was based upon legends which had been fabricated, in the absence of any authenticated documents, at a very early date, or else upon a thoroughly imprecise vocabulary, for example, the term *ecclesia senior*, which conjured up an image of a second cathedral built *intra muros*. Right from the beginning, the cathedral was in fact built inside the walls. At that time it was known by the term *ecclesia*, a word which was wholly unambiguous to contemporaries. It was the church of the bishop, or of the diocese, words which were not employed until later, as we shall see below. The term expresses quite accurately the reality it was supposed to represent, namely, the assembly or community of Christians united around its bishop. The meaning of the term was then extended to embrace the place in which the eucharistic synaxis was celebrated and finally included all places of worship. It was thus replaced in the early Middle Ages by a new word, *cathedra*, which was meant to be more precise, and which originally referred to the symbol of the bishop's power. One can more readily grasp the change in meaning of the term by considering the location in the place of worship of this seat, for it was placed at the end of the apse, from which vantage-point the bishop could both see, and be seen by, the congregation.

The *ecclesia*, and subsequently the cathedral, did not refer to a single reality, but to a whole complex of buildings. The attention of scholars has been drawn to this complex by a more rigorous analysis of ancient texts and plans, and by excavations in urban areas, which have established just how large, complex and diverse early Christian institutions were. All of these discoveries go some way towards explaining the history of towns in Europe.

Tradition has it that beneath the Gothic cathedral lay the Romanesque cathedral and that if by some chance investigations were taken further, a temple from Antiquity would be unearthed and possibly, at a still deeper level, as was believed in the sixteenth century at Chartres, a Druidic grotto. If one makes due allowance for the excessively systematic nature of this schema, it may be judged to be by and large accurate. Excavations carried out inside cathedrals, or in their immediate vicinity, have shown that they contained many venerable memories buried deep within them. If such legends are so tenacious, it is because they rest upon the discoveries of an earlier period. Thus, at Notre-Dame of Paris, in 1711, when work was under way on the building of the archbishops' burial vault within the presbytery, a number of ancient fragments were unearthed, among them the famous 'Pilier des Nautes' ('Boatmen's Pillar'), now the pride of the Musée de Cluny. At Chartres cathedral, up until the eighteenth century, one could see fragments of old walls in the crypt, which gave credence to any number of different hypotheses. In the nineteenth century, chance finds made when heating systems were being installed and, more recently, scientifically rigorous excavations provided ample proof for the view that the *ecclesia* had usually been introduced into a densely populated quarter, generally in close proximity to the city walls. The pegging out of such buildings required the demolition of existing monuments, and we have no grounds for supposing that they were derelict. Sometimes it was even necessary to recast a whole quarter, obliterating *insulae* and roadways and erecting new buildings, and altogether disregarding the original orthogonal plan. Unfortunately, texts are of little use to us in our attempts to grasp what such works were actually like, or to gauge how the townspeople viewed them. However, as we shall see in the case of the Gothic period, there was no shortage of traumatic episodes. This point is borne out by a number of sources, reflecting what was probably a general phenomenon which varied with the terrain, the personality of the bishop, the means that were at his disposal and regarding which, in the absence of written documents, we can only entertain hypotheses. Such events were no doubt so commonplace as to pass all but unnoticed.

We have remarkable evidence from Trèves but, given the exceptional role played by the city in the Later Roman Empire, it cannot be regarded as typical. As capital of *Belgica prima*, capital of the diocese of Gaul, and seat of the prefecture of the praetorium, from the end of the third century it became the residence of the Western Emperors. There was intense economic activity there in the fourth century, with a great number of public buildings and a large population. Evidence for Christian belief appears very early in funereal inscriptions. The scale upon which the *ecclesia* at Trèves was to be built reflects the city's role as capital. The granting of the land for building was probably the work of the imperial administration, under the orders of the Emperor Constantine himself, or rather, under those of his mother, Helena, who owned a very large part of the city. Two *insulae* to the north-east of the centre of the city were thus surrendered; and the roadway running from north to south, which divided the territory into two equal parts – both of which were built upon – ceased to exist. To the north, a recently built palace was demolished in order to make room for the basilica.

At the end of the fourth century, Arles succeeded Trèves as capital of the prefecture of the praetorium of Gaul. Already an important centre for the imperial administration, the mint from Ostia was transferred there in 313. There is mention of a bishop from the middle of the third century. We know from surviving texts that the original cathedral was built in the inside corner of the south-eastern walls, and that Saint Césaire turned it into a nunnery in 514. Under Saint Hilaire, and for reasons that now escape us, the cathedral was moved to one of the most densely populated quarters of the old town, between the forum and the theatre, on the site of a road running from north to south, the most important in the town.

From excavations recently undertaken at Aix, it is possible to date the foundation of Christian buildings there to the fifth century. The bishop responsible, who may perhaps have been Basilius, managed to secure a prestigious site at the very heart of the city, comprising a vast monumental ensemble occupying several small blocks of the ancient grid and situated

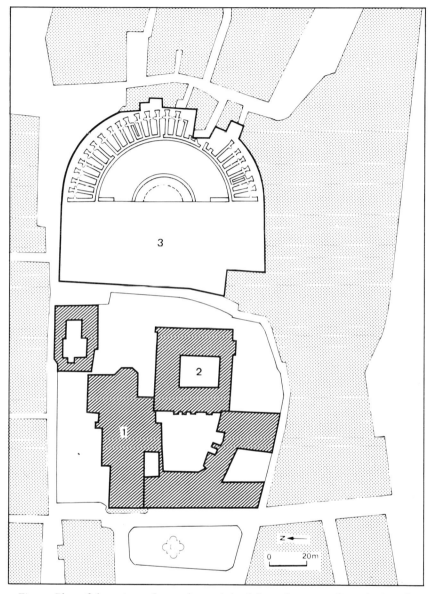

Fig. 23 Plan of the episcopal complex at Arles (after a document from the Musée d'Arles). 1. The cathedral; 2. The cloister; 3. The ancient theatre.

Fig. 24 Plan of the episcopal complex at Genève (after *Topographie religieuse...*). 1.
The north cathedral; 2. The south cathedral; 3. The baptistry; 4. The episcopal
church; 5. The *domus*.

between two roadways, namely, the *cardo maximus* and a secondary *cardo*
discovered beneath the transept of the Gothic cathedral. The site consisted of a
large square, 25 metres wide by 48 metres long, bordered on its east and west
sides by porticos and dominated on its north side by a monument, which may
have been the basilica, perched on a podium. In all probability this was the
forum and its outbuildings, which had been surrendered permanently to the
Christians. The partly destroyed monuments were replaced by the cathedral and
its outlying buildings.

At Genève, equally careful excavations yielded no less spectacular results. The
town, which was raised to the rank of city under the Later Roman Empire, at the
end of the third or the beginning of the fourth century, was immediately
provided with a surrounding wall enclosing the *oppidum*. The site itself was

drastically altered, with the terrain being levelled off, and the buildings being disposed along a north-south axis. The first Christian edifice was built at some point between 350 and the third quarter of the fourth century, in the north-east quadrant, on top of a substantial residence whose buildings surrounded a courtyard. The northern basilica was in part constructed out of the old walls. A probable date for the *domus* built against the eastern wall of the city enclosure would be the end of the fourth or perhaps the beginning of the fifth century. The cathedral complex occupied over a quarter of the available space within the enclosure (5·5 hectares). In order to clear the terrain, several buildings were partly demolished.

A number of other cases prove that the original Christian installation invariably entailed the destruction of important monuments. At Cimiez, for example, the walls of the thermal baths were in part razed, so as to make the building of cathedral and baptistry possible. At Riez, the cathedral was erected on the site of a fine edifice of the Early Empire. In order to establish themselves in the very heart of the city, and to be in the shelter of the walls of the recently established enclosure, the bishops managed to secure well-favoured sites, mostly through gifts from the administration but sometimes through purchases from private individuals. In either case, their presence within the walls was plainly welcome. The consequences were sometimes very serious. An entire quarter might be thrown into disarray, with public monuments destroyed – although there is no reason to suppose that they were derelict – and even major roadways might be eliminated, thus disrupting the flow of traffic across the city. It should also be borne in mind that these early Christian establishments were from the very beginning particularly largescale.

Before tackling this subject, it is worth asking a question which, in the present state of our knowledge, cannot be properly answered, but which touches upon a wide range of issues affecting the future development of cities. On the basis of the plans drawn up by Adrien Blanchet, were the majority of installations situated close to the ancient city walls?

THE 'CATHEDRAL COMPLEX'

The religious complex assumed an increasingly prominent place within the city as, over the centuries, the bishop became responsible for performing a growing number of different roles. Admittedly, the cathedral is generally better known to us than are the other buildings within the complex, which were overhauled at regular intervals, adapted to their new functions, or even demolished when

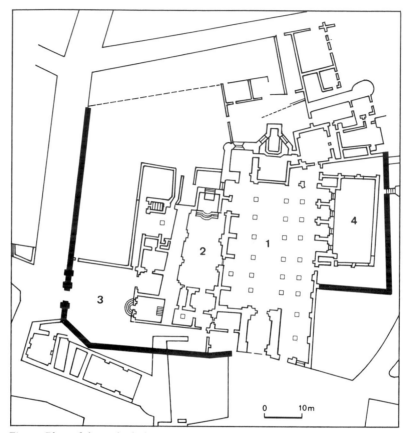

Fig. 25 Plan of the cathedral complex at Grenoble (after a document of 1788). 1.
The south cathedral: Notre-Dame; 2. The north cathedral: Saint-Hugues; 3. The
palace; 4. The cloister.

there was no longer any need for them. It was from the cathedral, the real heart
of the complex, that a number of other buildings, ranged around it, derived their
meaning. Among them, one should note the existence in each town of three
ensembles, namely, the cathedral itself, which consisted of two buildings and the
baptistry, the *domus episcopi* and, lastly, the outbuildings. The organisation of
these buildings varied from city to city, with a greater importance being
accorded one element or another, and with a wide range of overall plans and
internal arrangements. These differences may be readily accounted for, in terms
of what were often severely constraining topographical conditions, which
invariably differed, and for which adjustments had to be made; in terms of
financial resources, about which very little information is available, and which

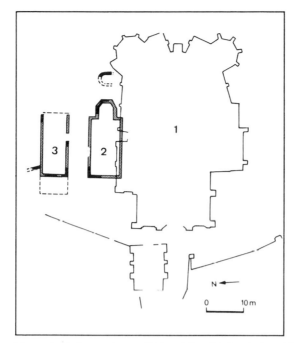

Fig. 26 Plan of the cathedral complex at Viviers (after Y. Esquieu). 1. The cathedral;
2. The north cathedral; 3. Unidentified buildings.

could well have been substantial in some cases (for example, Trèves, Paris, Aix) or, conversely, very restricted; in terms of the architects, regarding whom we have equally little information, but who stamped their personality on what they built; and, finally, in terms of the ambitions of the sponsor, which were necessarily linked to the importance of his diocese.

Two edifices at least were assured of the imperial stamp, which stipulated what the architecture should be, and very probably also dictated the choice of architect. In addition, especially generous funding was made available for their construction. The cathedrals of L'Aquila, in Italy, and of Trèves, belonged to the same group, which may be clearly differentiated from that of the Lateran. The latter is characterised by five aisles, a massively projecting transept and an apse which gives directly on to the transept. This arrangement may also be found in a fair number of buildings commissioned by the Imperial family, for example, at Rome, the churches of San Giovanni, of San Pietro and of San Paolo, at Bethlehem, the church of the Nativity and at Jerusalem the church of the Holy Sepulchre. The lay-out of L'Aquila and Trèves, although likewise developed by

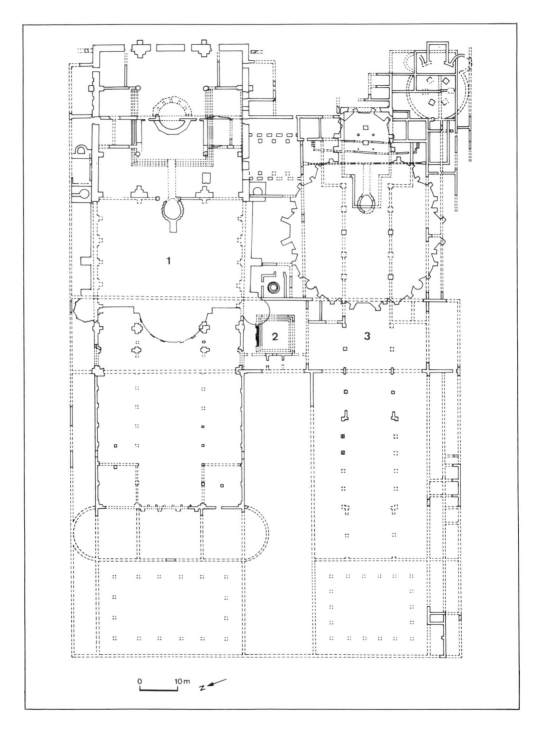

0   10 m

court architects, followed a very different plan, generally known as the 'double cathedral'. Two parallel basilicas, with three naves each, terminated at the east by an apse without a transept, were linked to each other along their transversal axis. The ensemble at Trèves was particularly imposing, being contained within a rectangle 170 metres long by 110 metres wide.

Double cathedrals

Various interpretations of this arrangement have been advanced, none of which is entirely convincing. There is no doubt, however, that it represented a deliberate choice on the part of the emperor, who had dedicated one of the buildings at Constantinople to Saint Eirene (Peace), the other to Saint Sophia (Wisdom). This view is further reinforced by a poem written by Paulinus of Nola, around 403, in honour of a group of edifices which Sulpicius Severus had just built in his *villa*. The twin roofs of the two buildings were compared to the Old and New Testaments, the link between the two being achieved by means of the baptistry, which ran between them and which was surmounted by a tower. The attractive argument has been advanced that each building served a specific function, with one being reserved for the catechumens, the other for baptised Christians, their baptism itself having taken place in the intermediate building. However, in northern Italy, in Milano, Brescia and Vercelli, the two buildings were put to a different use, although this was, admittedly, in the seventh century. The north church, which was almost always dedicated to the Virgin, was the summer church, while the south church, which was named after a martyred saint, was used in winter. The passage from one church to the other took place at Easter and at Advent. We have no evidence that the same procedure applied in Gaul, where such parallel edifices as exist are in the south (for example, Aix and Fréjus). The upheavals suffered by many monuments, from a very early date, render any interpretation of their functions a still more delicate matter. At the end of the fourth century, an atrium measuring 35 by 40 metres was added to the front of the northern basilica of Trèves and, to the east, a huge quadrilateral, the sides of which measured 40 metres, and whose walls were decorated with marble plaques surmounted with mosaics. In the middle there was an aedicule with a centred plan, designed to house a relic, perhaps Christ's tunic, which had been in the town's possession from a fairly early, but unspecifiable, date. It could have been a *memoria*, whose dodecagonal form on

Fig. 27 Plan of the cathedral complex at Trèves (after *Topographie religieuse …*). 1. The north cathedral; 2. The baptistry; 3. The south cathedral.

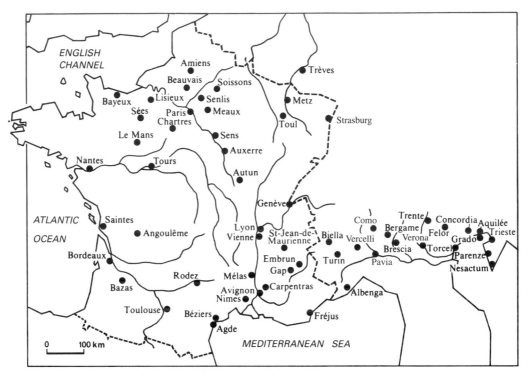

Fig. 28 Map showing the location of cathedral complexes in France and northern
Italy in the Carolingian period (after J. Hubert).

the outside would have called to mind the twelve apostles. This would explain
the appearance, at some point in the eighth century, of the name Saint Pierre for
the basilica. A reference must have been implied to the church of the Holy
Apostles at Constantinople, built by Constantine in order to house the cenotaphs
of the apostles and his own tomb also. This is therefore the earliest recorded
instance of a cathedral being invested with a new meaning through the
development of the cult of relics. We shall shortly come across many other
examples of reliquary cathedrals.

Alongside the imperial design, whose rigorous organisation made it
necessarily something of a rarity, Gaul furnishes an impressive number of double
cathedrals, featuring an equally large number of different lay-outs. The formula
had been quite generally adopted, although we cannot be sure just when, since
the dates at which the different edifices were built are still unknown. A study of
the double cathedrals serves to show just how original Gaul was in architectural
terms, in contrast to the other regions of the Roman Empire. If one consults a

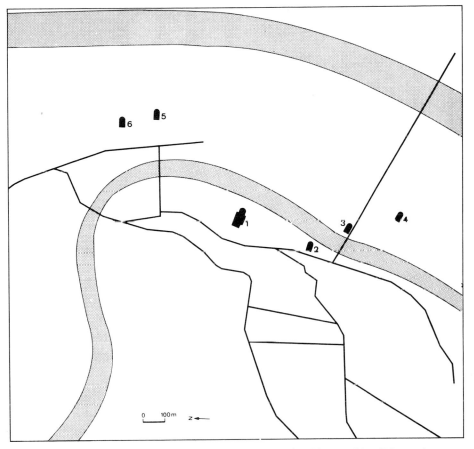

Fig. 29 Lyon in the fourth to seventh centuries (after *Topographie religieuse ...*).
1. The cathedral complex; 2. Saint-Georges; 3. Saint-Michel d'Ainay; 4. Saint-Martin
d'Ainay; 5. Saint-Nizier; 6. Saint-Pierre.

map charting the distribution of such cathedrals, it is quickly apparent that they
are especially densely clustered in the neighbourhood of northern Italy.
However, by contrast with the latter, Gaul had not chosen to follow the
symmetrical plan characteristic of the Imperial cathedrals. One then wonders
whether there had existed an original plan for the ensemble, dating back to the
time of the first Christian establishment in the heart of the city. The second
edifice may have been added later, a fact which would explain its somewhat
dramatic relation to the first.

Recent excavations at Lyon have shed particular light upon this group of
episcopal buildings. Up until the third century, the town consisted of two

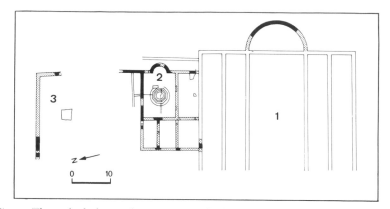

Fig. 30 The cathedral complex at Lyon in the fifth century (after J.-F. Reynaud). 1. Saint-Jean; 2. Saint-Etienne; 3. Sainte-Croix.

settlements, the upper town, which stood on the Fourvière plateau, and the lower town, which was situated at the confluence of the river Saône and the river Rhône. Lyon later consisted of the lower town only, which lay at the foot of the hill, and spread along the banks of the Saône. The cathedral complex, whose situation has remained the same to this day, was inserted into this rapidly expanding quarter.

To the north of, and parallel to the primatical of Saint-Jean stood the baptistry (Saint-Etienne) and the north church (Sainte-Croix), following a pattern already described above. The original plan for the baptistry was particularly simple, being rectangular in shape (12·8 metres by 9·5 metres). The floor was heated, with the piscina, an octagonal tank (3·66 metres in diameter), having been installed at the end of the fourth century, with a system of lead pipes for the delivery and evacuation of the water.

To the north, the church of Sainte-Croix consisted of a substantial hall, measuring 23 metres by 16 metres. To the south stood the *maxima ecclesia*, as Leidrade terms it, but only the gigantic apse, whose diameter was between 13 and 15 metres, has been identified. The archaeological finds assume added importance in the context of a letter which concerns the building of the cathedral by Bishop Patiens. The letter in question was by the hand of Sidonius Apollinaris, one of the greatest writers of the fifth century, Bishop Elect of Clermont, and was dated around 470, and addressed to Hesperius. We know from a number of other surviving examples that it was the custom to draft poems upon such occasions. Sidonius Apollinaris had written his 'in triple trochaic metre', the plan being to have it engraved, alongside other poems by

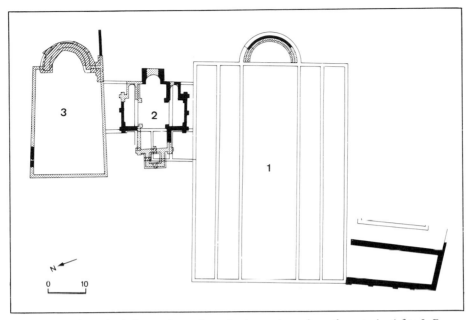

Fig. 31 The cathedral complex at Lyon in the tenth to eleventh centuries (after J.-F. Reynaud); 1. Saint-Jean; 2. Saint-Etienne; 3. Sainte-Croix.

Constantius and Scandinus, on the walls of the apse. It is worth pausing to consider the description of the monument:

The lofty temple sparkles and does not incline to right or left, but with its towering front faces the sunrise of the equinox. Within it the light flashes and the sunshine is so tempted to the gilded ceiling that it travels over the tawny metal, matching its hue. Marble diversified by various shining tints pervades the vaulting, the floor, the windows; framing designs of diverse colour, a verdant grass-green encrustation, brings winding lines of sapphire-hued stones over the leek-green glass. Attached to this edifice is a triple colonnade rising proudly on columns of the marble of Aquitania. A second colonnade on the same plan closes the atrium at the farther end, and a stone forest clothes the middle area with columns standing well apart. On one side is the noisy high road, on the other the echoing Arar; on the first the traveller on foot or on horse and the drivers of creaking carriages turn round; on the other, the company of the bargemen, their backs bent to their work, raise a boatmen's shout to Christ, and the banks echo their alleluia. Sing, traveller, thus; sing, boatman, thus; for towards this place all should make their way, since through it runs the road which leads to salvation.

Sidonius Apollinaris, *Poems and Letters*, translated by W. B. Anderson, London, and Cambridge, Mass., 1936, vol. 1, pp. 464–7 (Loeb editions).

Fig. 32 The cathedral complex at Lyon, as represented on Simon Maupin's plan,
1635 (detail).

The building, oriented in the usual fashion for the period, had its apse facing
the Saône and its west front pointing towards the hill. In front of it there stood
an atrium, whose columns were made of marble from Aquitaine, and it was
flanked by another, whose function is less certain. Sidonius emphasises the
sumptuous nature of the decor, his account of the gold-leaf covering the ceiling
and the mosaic-laden walls serving to remind his readers of the most beautiful
Roman basilicas. He quite rightly draws our attention to the situation of the
cathedral, for it stood at the very heart of the city and therefore played a full part

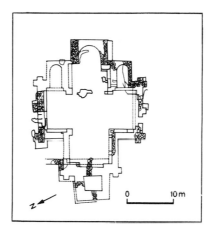

Fig. 33 Plan of Saint-Etienne of Lyon, in the eleventh century (after J.-F. Reynaud).

in its activities. On one side one could hear street-cries, on the other, the sailors' songs, both parties joining forces to pay homage, as if addressing a prayer, in which the whole city participated, to God.

It was not long before the baptistry underwent extensive alteration, ultimately becoming the canons' church, although serving as a place of baptism up until the seventeenth century. The fonts were then transferred to the church of Sainte-Croix with Saint-Etienne being reserved for the baptism of Jews and Muslims.

There was at least one illustrious exception to the 'double cathedral' formula, namely, Paris, which in this regard followed Roman tradition. During this period, the town's destiny was an unusual one, as may be gleaned from the cathedral plan unearthed in the course of the excavations carried out in the mid-nineteenth century and fortunately recommenced in recent years. In front of the Gothic facade, archaeologists have brought to light the foundations of the western part of the original cathedral, which featured five aisles and was thirty-six metres wide. The use of five aisles and the scale of the building remind us of the plan for the Constantinian basilica, and there is no doubt that the cathedral in Paris took its inspiration from that model. Building began at an earlier date than has generally been supposed. Scholars had posited a Merovingian foundation, but the cathedral in fact belongs to the fourth century, if one takes into account the various elements unearthed in the course of the excavations, including marble columns, capitals, likewise of marble, and mosaics. Contrary to what one might have supposed, it consisted of just one edifice, with the small apse uncovered by Viollet-le-Duc around the middle of the last century, when the archbishops' burial vault was being extended, belonging to an oratory with no actual connection to the cathedral. Indeed, the eastern part of the island did not belong to the city in Antiquity. When Clovis was considering which city to choose as the capital of his young kingdom, the presence of such a cathedral, Imperial in inspiration, at Lutetia, clinched the matter.

The baptistry

Baptism, in the Christian religion, is an essential act which enables whoever undergoes it to enter into the 'assembly' and to take part in the miracle of the transubstantiation. The sacrament is seen as an extension of that received by Christ at the hands of St John the Baptist in the waters of the river Jordan. Christ had himself emphasised its importance to his apostles: 'Go, teach all the nations; baptise them in the name of the Father, the Son and the Holy Ghost'. Saint John had rendered more precisely Christ's thoughts in this domain: 'except a man be born of water and *of* the Spirit, he cannot enter into the Kingdom of God' (chapter 3, verse 5). Like Christ who was plunged in the waters of the river Jordan, the catechumen could only be baptised if he had reached adulthood, and only through being immersed in running water. Before receiving his baptism, he had to pass through the various degrees of the Catechumenate. Thus, as an 'auditor', he received the required instruction; as a 'competent', he could take part in the opening part of the Mass; as an 'elect', he received the baptism, either on the eve of Easter or on the eve of Pentecost. This ceremony was solemn in character, because it marked a moment of passage in the life of a human being, who was thereby cleansed of an original stain. The exceptional nature of the monument in which this sacrament was staged may therefore be accounted for in terms of the importance of the institution itself, and of the number of elect called to be baptised. The baptistry had to be clearly separated from the church of the baptised, which the new Christians would then have the right to enter. This accounts for the favoured position of the baptistries in Milano and Trèves, which were compulsory places of passage between the catechumens' church and the church of the Christians. In other cities, they were situated near to the cathedral, very often in front of the west facade, but they were invariably wholly separate from the building itself.

The very first baptistry to be built very probably stood within the Lateran Palace, which Constantine had given to Pope Sylvester. One of the architects attached to the Imperial court had stipulated what architectural programme should be followed for the building, for a particular design was adopted, with various modifications, throughout the Empire. It was based upon a centred plan, so as to surround the piscina dug out of the ground, into which the catechumen would be plunged. The cupola above was pierced with numerous bays, so as to flood the interior volume of the edifice with light, as if in a vision. It was supported by galleries, which themselves rested upon columns opening out on to a ring-shaped corridor.

We are fairly well acquainted with a number of baptistries, either through archaeological excavations or through written documents containing descriptions of them, although it should be borne in mind that they underwent significant alterations from a very early stage, in response to institutional changes. The baptistry in Lyon, which survived up until the time of the Revolution, was the object, prior to its destruction, of plans and engravings and, more recently, of an outstandingly fruitful series of excavations. Its history, together with its architectural development, may therefore be traced, as we have already seen.

A good number of towns in southern France have had the good fortune to keep their baptistries until a fairly recent date, or even until the present day. Study of them allows us to assess how important the diocese was at the time of building, and how many inhabitants there were. The most remarkable example in this respect was the baptistry of Marseille, the existence of which was known from graphic documents but which was in fact rediscovered in 1854. While soundings were being taken for the new cathedral, the Major, its architect, Vaudroyer, came across the foundations of the baptistry. It had been an exceptionally large building, measuring 23 metres by 23 metres, with a frontispiece to the east of it, which had perhaps been a portico. On the outside, the various corners contained niches, as had been the case at Riez, and along the walls were columns supporting the roof over the side aisle. In the centre, the octagonal tank, 4·4 metres in diameter, must have been covered by a cupola. The first mention of a bishop at Marseille dates from 314, when he attended the Council of Arles, and yet the building seems to be no earlier in date than the fifth century. The building must have remained in use up until the twelfth century, when the cathedral was built, whereupon it was turned into a chapel dedicated to Saint Jean-Baptiste, as was a common and well-attested practice. We do not know just what the dimensions of the original cathedral were, but, given the scale of the baptistry, they were undoubtedly large. The Roman Catholic cathedral which replaced it was to be a far more modest affair.

The baptistry of Riez, parts of which still stand and which was built on top of some ancient thermal baths, followed the arrangement adopted at Marseille,

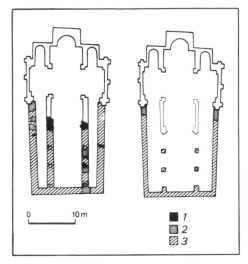

Fig. 34 Plan of Saint-Etienne of Lyon, from the twelfth to the fourteenth centuries (after J.-F. Reynaud). 1. Structures in elevation; 2. Structures at the foundations; 3. Reconstructions.

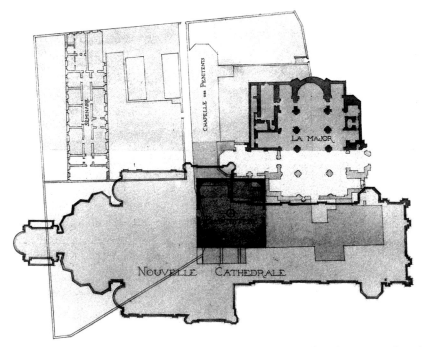

Fig. 35 Plan of the cathedral complex at Marseille, uncovered in the course of work executed in 1854, after P. Roustan.

54

though on a smaller scale (8·25 metres by 9·25 metres). The elevation almost certainly featured vaulted corner recesses with culs-de-four, walls pierced to the north and south with bays, and to the east and west with a door and a rectangular reinforcement. On the inside, eight granite columns supported, by means of galleries, the drum of the dome. The roofing was replaced, as was quite common, during the Norman period, but it very probably reproduced the original design.

The baptistry at Aix, which was square in shape (14 metres by 14 metres), also featured recesses in the corners, although these had not been part of the original plan. The monument underwent a number of alterations, particularly during the eleventh century, but the original design was maintained. The side aisle (2·75 metres), square in shape, left a square area in the centre, which measured 5·5 metres by 5·5 metres, and which contained the octagonal piscina (1·5 metres).

The rectangular but irregular plan of the baptistry at Cimiez may be accounted for in terms of the fact that it had been built on top of ancient thermal baths. Eight columns supported a rotunda, at the centre of which there was a hexagonal piscina (1·6 metres). This monument is so well preserved that it allows us to speculate as to the direction in which people circulated. One entered the building by a narrow door on the eastern side, which gave on to the vestibule, and by a second door, in the south-west corner, which enabled the Christian to enter the cathedral.

The baptistry at Fréjus, which is also in a good state of repair, permits similar observations, although various points of interpretation are still open to dispute. The cathedral complex, located at the very centre of the ancient town, consists today of two linked churches, namely, Saint-Etienne to the north, which was the parish church in the Middle Ages, and Notre-Dame to the south, which was the chapter church during the same period. The baptistry, which was square in plan (11 metres by 11 metres), had been built in front of the church of Notre-Dame, although it was separated from it by a passage leading to the canons' cloister. Originally, therefore, it had stood on its own, and was surrounded by a sort of enclosing wall. One wonders what sort of passage ran between it and the original cathedral.

In fact, all of these baptistries have been modified upon several different occasions, generally at a fairly early date, which makes study of them a particularly delicate matter. We have already noted as much in the case of Aix, Fréjus and Lyon, but Genève offers an equally striking example, its complex history having been clarified in the course of a number of different programmes of excavation. The first baptismal cistern (around 350–70) was undoubtedly

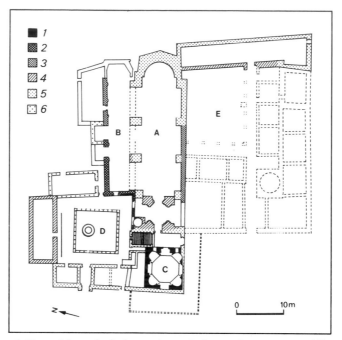

Fig. 36 Plan of the cathedral complex at Fréjus. 1. Ancient; 2. Middle of the eleventh century; 3. Eleventh century. End of the eleventh – beginning of the twelfth century; 4. Twelfth century; 5. Twelfth century; 6. Fourteenth century and more recently. A. Notre-Dame cathedral; B. The church of Saint-Etienne; C. The baptistry; D. The cloister; E. The palace.

located in a chapel of ease of the north church, undergoing alterations shortly afterwards (380–400), with the addition of a second room of exactly equal proportions and with a semi-circular apse. Finally, a new baptistry was built, with a more extended plan, and with an enlarged apse, the cistern being placed in the centre of the building and being surmounted by a stucco ciborium. The water supply was carried along wooden pipes. Lastly, one should note the reduction in size on two separate occasions of the baptismal cistern, as was the case at Poitiers and at Nevers.

In Nevers, the baptistry has been discovered beneath the north ambulatory of the Gothic cathedral. It featured an octagonal plan (16 metres by 12·6 metres), radiating around a rotunda supported by eight marble columns. The side aisle, 1·7 metres wide, gave on to eight apsidal chapels. A second stage involved the raising of the floor and, during a third stage, access to the building was altered. The baptistry's building could not predate the sixth century, which was when the bishopric was established; the first restoration was carried out during the episcopate of Jérôme (775–815), the second in the course of the eleventh century.

At Poitiers, the baptistry suffered such drastic modifications that scholars have been puzzled as to why they were undertaken. The mystery is compounded by its location, some 500 metres away from the cathedral of Saint-Pierre. It was built in the fourth century, in the very heart of residential and artisanal quarters, to a particularly original, rectangular plan, with two halls, the first of which was preceded by three small rooms. The baptismal font was in the last of the three, and was lit by high windows. Excavations have unearthed the brick conduit which supplied the piscina with water, and the brick pipe which drained off water into a cesspool. The building was changed out of all recognition by alterations effected in the Merovingian, Carolingian and Norman periods. In 1096, it is described as an abbey and, in the fourteenth century, as a parish church.

Although profoundly altered subsequently, baptistries would seem to be the most evocative illustrations of early Christianity. If we are to grasp just what this period in the history of western Europe meant, these buildings merit prolonged study. Furthermore, baptistries provide us with quite exceptional evidence of the architectural styles of the period. This was a light architecture, which featured walls that were by no means thick, and which was to a large degree open to the outside, thanks to the use of columns. It was an architecture that was at once airy and, on account of the many bays, flooded with light. The use of a square plan, and of a dome for roofing, represented a breach with the traditions of Antiquity. For several centuries, the architects of the Imperial court continued to furnish a schema, which those of their successors who were responsible for building religious monuments elaborated upon in various respects, although in the main they remained faithful to it up until the great stylistic revolution of the Romanesque period. Because they had lost their function, these monuments remained standing up until a fairly late date, serving as a point of reference for architects until very recently.

THE ADMINISTRATIVE COMPLEX

The domus episcopi

It is a more delicate matter to describe other buildings, so closely linked were they with places of worship that they formed a closely knit ensemble with them, and were conceived as a whole. There was a paucity of documentation for the *ecclesia*, but here there is still less available. One may fairly claim, however, that from the very beginning places of worship and priests' dwellings were closely associated. Indeed, the wish to be in close proximity is a datum which should be borne in mind if what was really at stake is to be understood. The reader will recall the difficulties occasioned by the need to establish a cathedral in an especially dense urban fabric. The townspeople might be prepared to accept the building of places of worship where necessary, but they must have been more hesitant about edifices which could as easily have been erected elsewhere. Even the slightest distance was regarded as unacceptable, for the shepherd was supposed to be in the midst of his flock. The various buildings, the most important of which was the *domus*, therefore tended to be clustered together.

Until it was replaced, very much later, by 'palace', the term *domus* remained in use. It was a word with very strong associations, which were clearly evident to Christians. A very valuable text, the *Life of Saint Césaire* (Bishop of Arles, from 502 to 542–3), probably written before 550, informs us that the *domus* was known as the *domus ecclesiae*, and this indeed was its recognised meaning. It was near to the cathedral of Saint-Etienne, and was on two levels. The ground floor consisted of rooms for clerics in the bishop's service, while the first floor was reserved for the use of the bishop himself, and contained his room. *Domus* and cathedral were so closely linked that one could easily pass from the atrium, to the west of the latter, into the courtyard of the *domus*. The same text throws some light on the communal life of the clerics. They took their meals in common, and we may therefore suppose them to have had a refectory and a kitchen. Hilaire had sought to impose a communal existence upon the clerics around him, such as was followed at Lérins, but Césaire did not aspire to do more than add communal prayers to the daily routine. At Arles, as at Toledo, there was an episcopal school, the purpose of which was to train children for the priesthood. Such schools proliferated in the course of the sixth and seventh centuries.

Archaeological excavations in Genève have supplied us with a wealth of information regarding the various buildings within the *domus* at the end of the fourth, and the beginning of the fifth century. As we have already seen, the cathedral complex at this period took up over a quarter of the area available within the enceinte (5·5 hectares). The *domus* was located between the enceinte wall, against which it leaned, and the cathedral, which lay to the west, from which it was separated by a screen. The regularly oriented buildings included a small chapel, which might have been the bishop's chapel; a huge reception room, which was heated, and which was later enlarged through the addition of an annex to the north; and a number of halls whose precise function is unclear,

Fig. 37 The south gate of the city of Reims:
archbishop's residence in the seventh century.

several of which were heated. Many of them were actually decorated with frescoes or mosaics.

In Genève, the *domus* was rebuilt, but in many other places there was clearly no hesitation in reutilising and redesigning older buildings of this sort. This would seem to have been the case at Aix, if at any rate one accepts that the foundations discovered in 1984–5, in the archbishop's courtyard, formed part of the original *domus*. The long-established nature of the episcopal buildings there would seem to lend credence to such a hypothesis.

The other buildings

Alongside the *domus* there stood a number of other buildings, regarding which we have only the vaguest information, with the surviving texts being highly imprecise. Excavations do not always enable us to specify the function of the

buildings that have been brought to light. One of these problems concerns what I will for the sake of convenience call the hôtel-Dieu, although I am well aware that the word was first used much later, in an institutional framework which is our own. The term has a built-in association with Christianity, but it can refer to a number of different functions, including what we today would call a hospital, a hospice, a hostelry, an orphanage or a place for the care of abandoned children. In Antiquity, the local administration or, to be more precise, the prefect, was responsible for offering assistance to the unfortunate. However, as city government collapsed, the Church, and thus the bishop, inherited such charitable functions, for which it was well suited, through the mission entrusted to it by Christ. From the fourth century, it assumed full responsibility for such tasks, redefining and extending them as society evolved in new directions.

There was no mistaking the recommendations that popes had made in regard to these matters, for they had strongly emphasised the obligation of bishops to bring succour to God's disinherited. Thus, under Pope Simplicius (468–83), Gelasius stipulated that bishops should reserve a quarter of their church's income to *hospitalitas*, a term here interpreted in a very wide sense. Such rulings were reiterated at regular intervals, for example, at the Councils of Orléans (511), Tours (567) and Mâcon (585). In 583, at the Council of Lyon, the care of lepers was added to the list. These exhortations were not only repeated but, in addition, they became prescriptions or even threats. At the Council of Orléans (511), those prelates who failed to fulfil their duties risked being demoted. Especially severe punishments were in fact reserved for those who had embezzled sums of money, the very existence of such penalties being proof that the above prescriptions were not always heeded.

By contrast with the earlier period, new buildings were now placed in a different setting. At Le Mans, admittedly, ancient tradition was followed, and the construction was, according to archaeological evidence, *extra muros*, but usually the decision was taken to build within the enclosure, so as to be near to the cathedral. At Arles, for example, Saint Césaire founded a house for the sick, which was so placed that they could readily visit the cathedral. At Paris, the hôtel-Dieu is supposed to have been founded by Landry in 651, inside the city. This was probably a legend, but one with some basis in fact. We have a number

Fig. 38 Plan of the ancient town of Genève (after *Topographie religieuse...*). 1. The north cathedral; 2. The baptistry; 3. The south cathedral; 4. The episcopal church; 5. The *domus*.

of sources for the following period regarding the presence of hôtels-Dieu *intra muros*, the foundation of which may have dated from an earlier period.

Apart from the above buildings, whose intended function is not in doubt, there were others, unearthed in the course of excavations, which still mystify us: oratories (as at Aix), outbuildings connected to the cathedral, thermal bath complexes, the basic elements of which have been uncovered at Aix, at Cimiez and perhaps at Fréjus.

Into such cities, which were turned in upon themselves, was introduced what even at this early date should be termed a 'holy city', wholly turned towards God and one's fellow man. The 'holy city' took up varying proportions of the enclosed town, but its share was larger than most, at least until recently, have supposed. It was not an expression of the town as such, but of the whole diocese. Indeed, it imposed a rhythm upon everyday life, which was steadily becoming more 'Christian'. In the eyes of the local population, the town was rapidly assuming a markedly religious character, while its administrative role was tending to diminish. The bishop was becoming an important figure, if not the most important. So it was that the invading barbarians encountered a reality which was largely unfamiliar to them, and which they had to reconcile with their own imaginings, and with their perennial concern with conquest. It is only in these terms that one can understand why it was that Clovis chose Paris as the capital of his kingdom.

CLOVIS AND PARIS

In recent years, historians have drastically revised their approach to the period characterised by the fall of the Roman Empire in the West (476), and by the emergence of the barbarian kingdoms. Where nineteenth- and twentieth-century historians had been preoccupied by the notion of a rupture, it is now the permanence and continuity which seem to be the crucial factors, if we are to apprehend the period in all its complexity. The ancient world is now seen in a new configuration, whose origins Henri-Irenée Marrou has identified in the second century, and it is believed to have survived up until the end of the Carolingian period. The Norman incursions now seem to us more dramatic than the barbarian invasions of the third century, for their murderous raids, coming in endless waves, bled the country dry. The rupture with Antiquity occurred in the course of the tenth century. We are better placed today to understand just why the 'barbarians' were in the end fairly well received, more favourably in any case than had been previously supposed. I do not wish to go into this historiographical reappraisal in any detail, but it may be worth putting the case of Clovis into its proper perspective. His victory in 486 over Syagrius, at Soissons, the last bastion of the Roman resistance, was not seen as the destruction of an entire world but merely as the triumph of the stronger party. How then is one to account for the dazzling success of the king of the Franks, the culmination of which was his victory over the Visigoths in 508, at the battle of Vouillé? I have already touched upon this point, but it will bear repeating, for what is at issue affects the whole of the present work. The crucial factor was the conversion of Clovis to Catholicism. The episcopate was resentful of the Arian yoke, for the Visigoth kings showed no hesitation in exiling prelates, or in leaving certain sees vacant. However, the episcopate was the only agency to which the local population might have recourse, once the Roman administration had collapsed, and Visigoths, Burgundians and Alemanni missed no opportunity to harry it. The conversion of the Frankish king to Catholicism must have seemed as miraculous an event as that of Constantine on the Pontus Milvius. Contemporaries showed no hesitation in acclaiming Clovis as the new Constantine. A close tie was immediately forged between the newly converted king and the episcopate. The latter, in the second half of the fifth century, was a perquisite of the upper strata of the population, and it seemed associated with everything that then counted. The episcopate's alignment with the Franks also won the elites over. Relations between Church and State, placed on a secure footing during this period, were permanently marked by this convergence. Thus, from the middle of the sixth century, the Merovingian sovereigns convoked councils and appointed bishops. This fusion was so complete that, from this date, the bishops had German names.

It is within this perspective that Clovis' choice of a capital for his nascent kingdom should be understood. He made his decision after the famous ceremony at Tours in 508, in the course of which he received an embassy sent from Constantinople by the emperor Anastasius. The reasons for his choice appear obscure but, of all those which have been advanced, some of which are by no means insignificant, the clinching factor plainly lay in the fact that at this period Paris was seen as a town in which Catholicism was especially well established. This impression has been reinforced by the discovery, in the nineteenth century, of Christian tombs, and by the presence of numerous Merovingian places of worship. Furthermore, Paris possessed the most remarkable cathedral in the whole of Gaul, exceptional both in design and in scale and, in addition, Imperial in inspiration. Clovis had certainly been impressed by the building, and had grasped its symbolic value. He immediately consolidated the 'Catholic' identity of the town by establishing a royal basilica, each aspect of which was prepared with great care. For his site, Clovis chose a hill, later known as 'Montagne Sainte-Geneviève', which both dominated the city and seemed to offer it protection, and he named the building 'les Saints-Apôtres'. In both respects, he took his inspiration from Constantine, who had built a basilica of the same name, which overlooked his capital and in which were disposed the cenotaphs of the twelve apostles, a thirteenth tomb being prepared for himself. Clovis had likewise decided that his body would lie in the basilica of the Saints-Apôtres. Paris immediately became a sacred town, both because it was the capital of the kingdom, and because it was the place in which the conquering king had avowed his faith. His heirs had judged aright when they had refused to include Paris in the later divisions of the kingdom, for it was indeed the symbol of its unity.

2

The Imperial dream

✦

The Carolingian period saw a complete reorganisation of the Church in Gaul, as a result of the various jolts to which it had been subjected, not only in the religious and political domain but in human terms also. The submission of the episcopate to the Frankish king had a number of disadvantages, such as could legitimately have been anticipated. When the regime went into decline, and was no longer capable of controlling the religious authority, the latter then became a state within the State, whose might had grown as the royal power weakened. This dependence had strained the Church's ties with Rome, so that it had assumed a markedly national character. Since the clerics in Gaul played no part in the great debates on dogma staged during this period, the quality of religious life declined. Terrestrial existence has more attractions than celestial, and the bishops allowed themselves to be seduced by it. This shift was reinforced by the increasing wealth of the Church, due in part to donations from the laity, in part to the expropriation of lands belonging to the Exchequer. Within the towns, the bishops gradually became sole proprietors of much of the land, a tendency which was aggravated throughout the Carolingian period.

DESPOLIATION

In order to consolidate a still vulnerable royal authority, Charles Martel, mayor of the palace, had need of extraordinary financial resources, the Merovingian royal domain having been squandered. He decided upon the 'despoliation' of the property of the Church, the only institution capable of furnishing him with the instruments he needed to implement his policies. He began by placing men

65

loyal to himself in episcopal sees, who would subordinate themselves to his will and support his policies. The monasteries were handled in very much the same fashion. Charles Martel then expropriated the property of the Church. The sums involved were so large that this wholesale expropriation may well have been one of the most massive transactions in history; it had the additional virtue of proving successful. The Church of France was traumatised by this episode, swore that it would never forgive the mayor of the palace and that he would burn in hell. However, it was obliged to accept his body for burial at Saint-Denis, where a cult was soon celebrated.

THE ROLE OF THE EMPEROR

So violent a warning could not help but be heeded. Even though Carloman and Pépin le Bref (Pépin the Short) the sons of Charles Martel, made the Carolingian Church some restitution, it remained an impoverished and morally stricken institution. There was a pressing need both for religious reform and for a reorganisation of the hierarchy, and Charlemagne, the eldest son of Pépin, saw this task as lying within his competence. This point was made quite clearly in the letter which he addressed to Pope Leo III in 796:

Our task [i.e. Charlemagne's] is, with the aid of divine piety, to defend with arms the holy Church of Christ against the attack of pagans and devastation by infidels from without, and to fortify it from within with knowledge of the Catholic faith. Your task, most holy father, is to lift up your hands to God, like Moses, so as to aid our troops; so that through your intercession the Christian people may, with God as its leader and giver of victory, always and everywhere be victorious over enemies of His Holy Name, and so that the name of Our Lord Jesus Christ may be extolled throughout the world.

Likewise, in the *Liber Carolinus*, written in 791, Charlemagne had declared that his role was to 'steer the Church across the breaking waves of the age'. He was prepared to intervene in every domain, ruling on matters of dogma (as earlier Merovingian sovereigns had done), convoking church councils, drafting capitularies, such as the *Admonitio generalis* of 789 and, finally, appointing *missi dominici*.

Historians have regarded the reorganisation of the ecclesiastical hierarchy as being of particular importance. When Rome appointed the Anglo-Saxon Boniface a bishop in 722, but with no responsibility for any diocese in particular, the office was thereby lent fresh lustre. In 731, Pope Gregory III raised him to the dignity of archbishop, permitting him to create new dioceses in the course of his

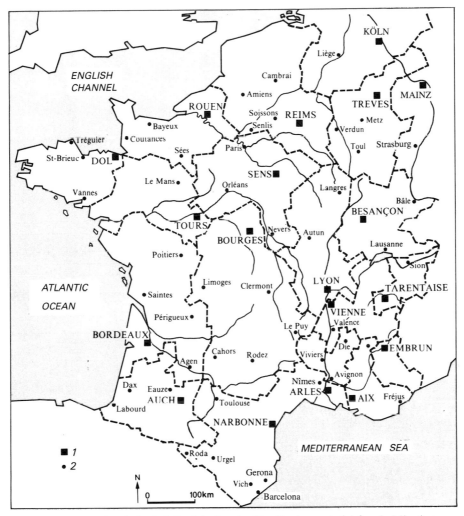

Fig. 39 Map of ecclesiastical Gaul during the Carolingian period (after A. Mirot). 1.
Metropolis; 2. Episcopal see.

missionary work, which he proceeded to do in Hesse-Thuringia and Bavaria.
His fame was such that he prevailed upon Pépin le Bref and Carloman to revive
the tradition of convoking Church councils. He even attempted to re-establish
the old metropolitan sees, bestowing upon the titulars both the title and the
authority of archbishop. He was successful in the case of two or three
ecclesiastical provinces, and won the titulars the right to wear the *pallium*, a
symbol of the delegation of pontifical authority which took the form of a long

band of white wool dotted with crosses, and cut in such a fashion as to pass around the neck and fall fairly low both at the front and the back. Both Charlemagne and Louis le Pieux adopted this policy, thus establishing a college of prelates which, though reduced in size, was capable of presiding over the bishops placed under its authority.

In the Merovingian period, religious authority had taken refuge in the monasteries, which had flourished to such an extent in the seventh century that they posed a real threat to the episcopacy, but could serve as an inspiration also. If these constantly proliferating establishments represented a threat, it was because they attracted honest souls to them, and financial resources also. Some monasteries even asserted their independence from the hierarchy, winning first from the sovereign, then from the pope, a diploma of 'subtraction'. The bishops even felt obliged to accept the election of abbots and abbesses by their own congregations. This success also led to a rise in the number of religious foundations and an increase in the number of monks, largely on account of the intensity of the religious life. This enthusiastic response was occasioned by the communal life, based upon the Rule of Saint Benedetto of Norcia, which was tending to supplant the seemingly over-strict Rule of Saint Columba.

CHRODEGANG'S REFORM

Chrodegang, Bishop of Metz, decided to reform the religious life of the clerics in his entourage. He had received the *pallium*, together with the title of archbishop, from Pope Stephen III and previously had been trained as *nutritus* in the palace of Charles Martel; at that time he was chief clerk to the Frankish chancellery. In other words, his appointment to the see of Metz, the ancient capital of Austrasia, represented a political decision on the part of the Carolingian sovereign. The clerics within the *domus* of Chrodegang had formerly followed the Rule of Saint Augustine, which was based upon two texts, the letter (211) sent in 423 to the women's monastery at Hippo, and the *Regula ad servos Dei*, which was a sixth-century interpretation and adaptation of the same letter. From now on they were to follow the Rule of Saint Benedetto of Norcia. Paul Diacre, in the *Gestes des évêques de Metz* (*c.* 783), commented upon the reasons for Chrodegang's decision, and upon the steps taken to realise it. The clergy was to play no part in the organisation of secular existence, but was supposed to devote itself to worship and to lead a fairly intense communal life, meeting for prayer and sharing both refectories and dormitories. The clerics did not swear an oath of poverty; their possessions reverted to the community, which kept the usufruct. They still had certain pastoral responsibilities, such as preaching. The aim was to fashion a life of prayer for bishop and clerics alike.

In 755, at the Council of Vic, Pépin le Bref tried to impose a reform, formulated in Article XI, such that the clerics would 'live in a monastery under the *Regula* [i.e. the Rule of Saint Benedetto of Norcia] or under the authority of the bishop with the *Institutio canonicorum*'. Charlemagne tried to extend this reform to the entire episcopate of Gaul, although he introduced a number of modifications which were intended to make it more efficient and which took into account the changes effected by Chrodegang's successor at Metz:

We demand that the canons residing with the bishop in the cities live within the close, sleep in the same dormitory, eat in the same refectory, so as to be more readily available in order to celebrate the canonial hours, and that they should be exhorted and instructed for a life of conversion. That they should receive from the bishop, where circumstances permit, food and clothing, so that they should not have to leave the order for reasons of poverty.

In a later version of the *Institutio*, from 816, at Aix-la-Chapelle, these points are made still more emphatically (chapter XVIII):

The life of the canons must be organised very quickly...The close, within which the cleric should live, in obedience to the canonical Rule, should be enclosed by walls on every side, so that no one can enter or leave save by the door; inside there should be a dormitory, a refectory, a storeroom and any such service buildings as the common life of the brothers requires.

However, the 'close' (*claustrum*) was also supposed to contain houses for the sick, the crippled and the elderly monks, This was the first twist given to the ideal of communal life, and such exceptions would soon become routine, as we shall see, for the canons bridled at sleeping in a shared dormitory.

The gradual application of such decisions was to have immediate repercussions for the already existing complex of buildings, which, for the purposes of a communal existence, had now to be extended. As in the past, however, the demands of the religious life required that such buildings still be grouped around the cathedral. It therefore became vital to find some land nearby and, obviously, *intra muros*. Concerned to face up to the readily imaginable difficulties, the legislator took a number of decisions. The capitulary of 819, which placed several means at the bishop's disposal, is particularly explicit in this regard. If the land in question belonged to the Exchequer, the king would present it as a gift. If it already belonged to the cathedral, but was unavailable because leased, it would regain possession of it. If the land belonged to another church or to a freedman, an exchange would entitle the church to recover ownership of it. In this manner legal settlement was made of the questions surrounding the necessary extension of the site.

This organisation of the chapter was soon to give rise to consequences which were unintended and to a large extent unforeseen. It was necessary to provide for the keep of the members of the chapter but, at the Council of Tours (813), the stipulation had merely been that the bishop should assume the responsibility 'insofar as was possible'. Thus, as was noted above, the bishop's want of financial resources could create serious difficulties, not least if the incumbent in question were unduly selfish. Some solution to the problem had to be found, if the success of the reform were not to be jeopardised and if the clerics, fearing for their own livelihood, were to be persuaded to desert the canonial precincts for the monasteries. Steps had in effect been taken towards a division, with the newly built canonial precinct being regarded as the property of the canons. Once embarked upon, this development was seen through to a conclusion: the decision was taken to define the share of the products of the soil which would revert to the community. The Council of Aix (816) ordered the bishop to surrender to it pasture lands and even a part of the alms of the faithful. The idea of a distribution of revenue was gaining ground. Bishops were instructed to divide their income into an episcopal and a canonical income. Responses to this instruction were remarkably diverse, with some complying and others not. Those who complied with the council's ruling did so at widely differing dates, and chose a number of different quota. However, this measure had some advantages for the bishops also, for it enabled them to shed a number of responsibilities which had always proved a hindrance. In the long term, it benefited the canons, for, from the end of the ninth century, they won the right to elect their bishop.

THE RESTRUCTURING OF THE HOLY TOWN

The real importance of the restructuring of the religious quarter, made all the easier by the measures taken by the sovereign, lay in its challenge to an equilibrium established when Christianity was first granted official recognition. The holy town was considerably enlarged in order to respond to its new role. However, it is difficult to gauge the extent of the upheaval, because the documents in question are full of obscure allusions and the plans hard to interpret. A further difficulty concerns the question of chronology, namely, the fact that a movement launched during the Carolingian period continued well beyond it. The dating of the various stages is therefore necessarily approximate, even if the outcome of each is clear.

As chance would have it, most of the strictly architectural information concerns the episcopal town in which the religious reform was realised. Its pioneering role suggests that it served from the start as a reference point for a number of different dioceses. In the eighth century, the cathedral complex in Metz consisted of Saint-Etienne, Saint-Pierre, Notre-Dame and the baptistry, together with the *domus episcopi*. Chrodegang would seem not to have made any substantial alterations to this ancient structure, if one excepts his renovation of the decor, which became far more elaborate. This was the case with the presbyteries of Saint-Etienne and Saint-Pierre-le-Majeur. These buildings were described as standing, from this period onwards, *infra domum*, that is, to the east of the episcopal palace, which itself was located to the west of the nineteenth-century west front. Thanks to the plan published by François and Tabouillot, just before some buildings to the south of the cathedral were demolished in order to make room for a parade-ground, we have a fairly good idea as to the precise location of these buildings. The holy town was then divided into two other complexes, namely, the *domus episcopi* and the chapter precinct (*claustrum*), with the latter being reserved for the use of the canons and their associates. As the Rule stipulated, it consisted of a refectory, a heated hall, a dormitory, some bedrooms, a stove and a kitchen, disposed around a cloister lying to the south of the cathedral, the galleries of which framed a garden. Two other religious buildings also gave out on to this cloister, namely, Saint-Pierre-le-Majeur (to the south-east) and Saint-Paul. This complex of buildings, the organisation of which seems to us to be self-evident, was enclosed within a stone enclosure, with a gate guarded by a porter and his assistant, which only opened at dawn and was closed again at Compline. The canons' routine unfolded in large part within this narrowly circumscribed precinct, according to a rhythm wholly dictated by the communal life, with its prayers and shared meals. The refectory was meticulously planned, with particular places allocated for the reader and for the seven tables, the first being for the bishop, the archdeacon, guests and strangers, the second being for the priests, the third for the deacons, the fourth for the subdeacons, the fifth for minor clerics, the sixth for the abbots and for the prior's guests and the seventh for external clerics. In spite of the many unresolved questions regarding the organisation of the chapter precinct at Metz, it remains a unique testimony for the period.

Elsewhere, it seems certain that the canonial precincts came into being fairly

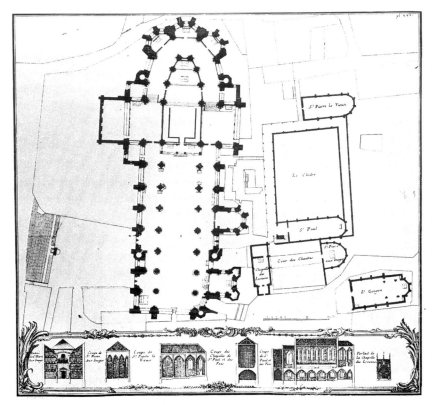

Fig. 40 Plan of the cathedral complex at Metz in the eighteenth century, after
Tabouillot and François.

rapidly. At Châlons, the building of a precinct ran into real difficulties, because
of the especially large dimensions adopted. It seemed as vast as a monastery, with
lodgings, a refectory and a chapter-house. The purchase of additional land led to
an exodus on the part of the lay population, which took refuge *extra muros*,
between the Mau and the Nau, in what was later to become the merchants'
quarter. In 859, Charles le Chauve (Charles the Bald) made a gift of two plots
of land which had belonged to the Exchequer, as he had previously undertaken
to do. Similar gifts of land occurred throughout Gaul. Thus, in 822, the emperor
yielded to the demands of the archbishop of Rouen, who had requested land
belonging to the Exchequer in order to extend the canonial precinct. The title
deed was regarded as so exemplary that it was included in the collection of
Imperial formulae, serving thus as a model. Many other instances of transfers
could be cited. For example, in 817, the church of Tournai obtained a plot of 84

perches, which belonged to the Exchequer, and two others (99 and 32 perches), held in trust from the Exchequer. Louis le Pieux's concessions to Ebbon, Archbishop of Reims, were still more exorbitant, for he authorised the transfer or rerouting of all the public highways encircling the cathedral. Such measures would seem not to have been sufficient since, a few years later, Hincmar, Ebbon's successor, was granted the right to suppress another public highway, once again with a view to enlarging the precinct.

Canonial precincts spread throughout Gaul. At Lyon, Leidrade boasted to Charlemagne of 'having built the clerics' cloister, where all now reside in the same precinct' (verse 813). A precinct is mentioned at Tournai (817). At Le Mans, Aldric, appointed bishop in 832, surrendered, during the reign of Charles le Chauve, a part of his *domus* to the canons. He built them a genuine cloister with galleries, individual houses and even a church dedicated to Saint Etienne. On 20 May 858, Jonas, Bishop of Autun, decided, in order to conform to the practice of other towns, to build a precinct, together with whatever utility rooms the canons required.

It is worth emphasising the care taken by the prelates over such projects. Admittedly, due allowance should be made for exaggeration, and verbal testimonies should therefore be measured against such contemporary structures as are still standing. Chrodegang, at Metz, in order to make his reform as effective as possible, had sought to provide suitable lodgings for his canons. The building work would seem to have been executed with care, and the decoration was lavish. At Le Mans, Aldric insisted that the buildings be to a high standard. At Lyon, Leidrade showed no hesitation in singing his own praises. At Reims, the archbishop took luxury so far as to stipulate bath-houses.

Contemporaries saw these compact constructions – which at Metz included a small garden and at Le Mans galleries, around which were organised the various buildings – in close proximity to the cathedral, the site of communal prayer, as urban monasteries. Indeed, it was in such terms that many canonial precincts, for example, those at Vienne, Le Mans, Reims, Liège, Limoges and Cambrai, were described. The presence of a stone enclosure merely served to lend further weight to the comparison.

THE HÔTEL-DIEU

Not only did these new constructions have the topographic consequences that one might have predicted but, in addition, they required substantial investment. Unfortunately, we have no information on this topic, but we can safely assume that resources were generally insufficient. It was no easy matter to locate the stone that was required, to quarry it and then to transport it. In order to cut the cost of such operations, authorisation was sometimes requested for the recovery of stones from old walls. At Reims, Ebbon asked for permission to demolish a wall, together with a city gate, in order to enlarge the cathedral. Wenilon, Archbishop of Sens, was authorised to take the stones from the walled enclosure of Melun. Such occurrences were especially frequent in the north of the Empire, at Beauvais, for example, at Langres, Frankfurt and Ratisbon.

Bishops and clerics had inherited duties of hospitality for which the prefects had previously been responsible. To this obligation was added the Christian duty of charity. The Carolingian Empire laid particular emphasis upon this point, although responsibility fell upon the clergy. These prescriptions, which were restated in the *Admonitio generalis* (75) of 23 March 789, were addressed to the whole population, and they took as their point of departure the words of Christ: 'I was a stranger and you took me in'. Measures had therefore to be taken to ensure that guests, strangers and the poor had access in various localities to monastery and canonial reception centres. Huge efforts were made in this regard. Thus, in the space of a few years, the Empire was endowed with reception centres serving the needs not only of the poor, the sick and the infirm, but also of pilgrims and travellers. There was no clear distinction, however, between the various categories. Owing to the unstinting efforts of succeeding generations, the roads came to be marked out with establishments offering rest at regular intervals. These hospitable institutions, some of which already existed in the towns, were extended or, where they were not yet in existence, created. It was the episcopate and the canons who were responsible for these innovations, and who therefore deserve the credit for them. Upon several occasions, the central authority took an interest, even going so far as to give precise instructions as to the organisation of such institutions. Such ventures were facilitated by the existence of a college of canons which could, basing its practice upon the procedure in the monasteries, guarantee that pilgrims and the poor were welcomed. The Council of Aix, in 816, laid down the respective obligations of bishop and canons. The prelate was supposed to identify a place, in close proximity to the cathedral, where beggars might take shelter, so that the monks might come and wash the feet of the poor. The monks themselves were supposed to designate one of their own number to guarantee a welcome to those who came. In order to ensure that these institutions survived, it also became crucial to see that regular funding was forthcoming. The legislator took care to share out the responsibility between the bishop and the canons. The bishops were responsible for erecting the buildings, while the canons saw to their maintenance, using harvest tithes and alms for the purpose.

The episcopate would seem to have acquitted itself of this especially onerous responsibility fairly conscientiously. The documents which are extant point to the huge efforts made in this respect, although they assumed different forms from diocese to diocese. Thus, at Le Mans, the abovementioned Bishop Aldric expended considerable effort to found a hôtel-Dieu in the city itself, in close proximity to the cathedral, even though one already existed on the outskirts. The new building was meant to cater for the needs of the poor, the weak, the blind, the lame and other infirm people, to which list should be added the needy. Aldric even went so far as to specify that twelve paupers should be fed and sheltered there. A number of documents listed the church properties serving for the upkeep of the charitable institutions, the domains and the tithes. Aldric took the trouble to leave the poor a bequest, laid down in his will, according to which they would receive the ninth and tenth part of whatever his *villae* contained in the way of wheat, wine, hay and vegetables. Hériman, Bishop of Nevers, founded a hospital in 849, close to the cathedral, which was intended for the use of the poor. The bequest of his own property, together with the lands and tithes of the church, assured the future upkeep of the building. Conversely, in Paris, Bishop Inchade sought, when he was deciding upon the canons' income, to define just what their responsibilities were: the tithes from eight *villae* which had come into their possession were to be used for the maintenance of the hôtel-Dieu. The canons were supposed to attend and, on specified days of the year, to wash the feet of the poor. Hincmar took similar steps at Reims. Thus, having founded a hôtel-Dieu for pilgrims and the poor, he matched the canons' incomes to the resources available to them. At Toul, on the other hand, where there was a hôtel-Dieu for travellers and the poor, Gérard allocated for the purpose the tithes from all the episcopal revenues. He assigned the canons the task of washing the feet of the poor every Saturday after vespers.

I could easily extend this list but, no matter how diverse the examples I have given may seem, in every case the bishop had the final word. If no such institution yet existed, he would found one, in the vicinity of the cathedral, assume responsibility for its upkeep and decide what resources would be allocated for the purpose. The division of responsibilities recommended at the Council of Aix was not always honoured, since an endowment could be arranged from episcopal revenues. There are unfortunately very few accounts extant of the actual construction of these buildings. However, we can reasonably assume that, difficult as it often was to find unencumbered land to build upon, it was easier to resolve the problem than was the case with the much larger canonial precincts. The hôtel-Dieu would seem to have been fairly small, and to have offered accommodation that was by no means luxurious. One important obligation, however, as we know from the Council of Aix, was to build the hôtel-Dieu in the vicinity of the cathedral.

At the beginning of the ninth century, the religious town was thus substantially complete, with the canonial precinct and the charitable institution in place, each closely linked to the other, both in topographic and in institutional terms.

The constitution of a canonial chapter in the episcopal town could easily have led, owing to the perceptible reduction in the size of the bishop's *domus*, to a diminution in his power. If clerics in his entourage had then deserted him, in order to live in communities, some of the buildings which they had previously occupied might then have been left empty. As we shall see, things in fact worked out quite differently. Far from diminishing, the bishop's sphere of responsibility was extended. The prelate assumed responsibility for the town's administration and for supplying it with provisions, as the central government was no longer able to perform these functions, among others. The capitulary of Soissons (744) exhorted the bishops to hold a market in every town, and to ensure that weights and measures were accurate (74); it was also explicitly acknowledged that only they were in a position to address such questions. The bishops, some of whom had already assumed responsibility for such matters, lost no time in shouldering these new obligations. The author of the *Life of Saint Marillus*, Bishop of Angers, praises him for having successfully supplied the inhabitants of the town with wine and cereals at fixed prices, for a full thirty years. A number of markets held until recently in the vicinity of cathedrals in fact date from this period.

It was not long before the running of the town itself was to become their responsibility. The report which Leidrade, Archbishop of Lyon (799–813), gave to Charlemagne is quite explicit on this point. He spelled out the numerous improvements he had made to the town, for its greater glory and in accord with the emperor's own suggestions, ranging from the renovation of the cathedral and of the *domus episcopi* to the building of the canonial precinct. He also mentioned the restoration of numerous churches. Although documents detailing such work are extremely rare, there is good cause to suppose that Leidrade was by no means an isolated example. The Norman invasions added yet another to the bishops' responsibilities, for they were also actively involved in the defence of the kingdom. The attempts made to call a halt to these devastating raids involved massive constructions. Thus, streams and rivers were crossed by bridges, monasteries were ringed by defensive walls and towns renovated their stone defences, which had generally fallen derelict by that time (from around 800). The bishop was responsible for such improvements, although the legislator showed no hesitation in recalling that the 'walls' belonged to the sovereign. Such rebuilding took place at Orléans (865), Reims (883), Langres (885), Troyes (887–8), Tournai (898) and Noyon (898). Generally, it was a question of plugging breaches occasioned by the illegal use of walls as a quarry, of restoring the walls to their proper height and of repairing the external ramp. There was even one instance, without doubt an exceptional occurrence, of the original enclosure being expanded. Thus, at Cambrai, Dudilon took the enclosure surrounding the monastery of Saint-Aubert right up to the *extra muros*. One may readily understand how the bishop's standing was enhanced by these changes and how he appeared in the town to be the sole master, symbolising and synthesising religious and administrative power, in their largest senses. He was the sole authority to whom an anxious population, markedly reduced in size since the Merovingian period, as we shall see below, could have recourse.

THE *DOMUS*

The separation of the *domus* from the canonial precinct was to have important consequences for the latter. The bishop was sometimes ready to surrender it, either wholly or in part, to the canons, and to take up residence elsewhere. This was a development of some significance for, as the example of Aldric at Le Mans shows, the canons immediately found themselves in possession of various buildings. At the end of one of the Canons of the Councils of Meaux and of Paris, it was decreed that the *domus* should be located in the vicinity of the cathedral; the Council of Meaux likewise stipulated that it should be furnished according to the bishop's needs and decorated in a dignified fashion. The majority of such buildings, being inherited from an earlier age, were probably so dilapidated as to be entirely unsuited to a bishop's rank. From this period on, there is also mention in the records of substantial improvements, embellishments and even of rebuilding. At Lyon, Leidrade prided himself upon having restored the old house, which was going to rack and ruin, and even upon having built another, which was twice as large, to receive the emperor. At Auxerre, a fire had caused so much damage to the town that Hérifrid (887–909) had had no option but to rebuild everything. His successors proceeded with the especially largescale works which he had initiated. The *domus*, located in the chevet of the cathedral, consisted of two assembly rooms, one of which was made of timber and, being sheltered from the sun, was used during the summer. The bishop's own apartments looked out on to the other bank of the Yonne, as we shall see below. At Reims, Séulphe (922–5) decorated his own *domus* with pictures, while at Cambrai, Erluin (995–1012) constructed some buildings which are described as 'superb'.

We have, however, almost no information regarding the position of the various buildings of which the *domus* consisted. One suspects that a number of rooms of a particular kind were already considered indispensable, but it is unclear exactly how they were interconnected. However, it seems fair to assume that there was a clear distinction between the public part and the area reserved for the sole use of the prelate. The latter would have contained a room set aside for assemblies, which was often known as the *solarium*, no doubt because it was south-facing. At Lyon, Leidrade had built a room of this nature, in which he gave audiences. The *camera pontificalis* would seem to have been differentiated from the complex as a whole, but there are no grounds for claiming that it was the same as the assembly room. In the shared area, the stables were of some importance, because it was necessary for clerics to travel around the diocese. The garden, which is often mentioned, would have had an orchard and vines, and brought relaxation to the clerics and some variety to the table.

THE EPISCOPAL SCHOOL

The Carolingians also ventured into the field of education, obviously indispensable for the training of clerics. Thus, in one of his earliest capitularies (796), Charlemagne had decreed that ignorant clerics should be defrocked, for 'those who did not know the Law of God could not teach it to others'. He therefore took steps to open a number of schools. He returned to the task in the *Admonitio generalis* of 789 (72), calling for the opening of schools for boys in the monasteries and episcopal palaces. Such exhortations were directed in particular at those bishops who had as yet done nothing in this area. At the Council of Neuching, in 772, it was decided that bishops should found episcopal schools and recruit teachers. The bishops and dukes of Bavaria showed particular initiative in this domain. Arn, Archbishop of Salzburg, in attendance at the Council of 789, called upon each bishop to found an institution of this sort in his diocesan town. However, at the Council of Attigny, in 822, the bishops themselves judged that efforts had up until then proved unsatisfactory. They promised to set up schools next to their cathedrals, and some do in fact date from this period.

The school would be run by a canon, who, according to the *institutio canonicorum*, would be known as *scolasticus*. There was one such institution at Laon, which in the ninth century enjoyed the protection of Bishops Pardule, Hincmar and Didon, and profited from the teaching of masters Bernard and Adalelmo, so that it was in fact one of the centres of pedagogic excellence in the Carolingian period. At Auxerre, the episcopal school soon came to rival that of Saint-Germain. In fact, the standards achieved were still mediocre during the reign of Charlemagne, although they improved under his son, Louis le Pieux, and even more under his grandson, Charles le Chauve. In the early stages, *scriptoria* would seem to have proliferated, without being directly linked to teaching. Laon, however, was an exception, for there *scriptorium*, library and school were in close symbiosis.

Teaching took place at various differing sites, although in no case was a very large space required, for there were not many masters or pupils. In 767, at Lucca, a site near to the portico of the cathedral was used. However, when Foulques, Archbishop of Reims, enlarged his *domus*, he built two schools there, one for future canons, the other for rural clerics.

THE CATHEDRAL COMPLEX

The baptistries

The Carolingian reorganisation also had some impact on monuments, either directly, as was the case with the baptistries, or indirectly, as happened with places of worship.

The baptistry had from the start occupied a prominent position within the Christian church: baptism, involving an initiation ceremony which the building was supposed to render more sublime, was soon to undergo an evolution which was to have immediate repercussions for the building, its role, its meaning and its appearance. Originally, the bishop was the only person with the authority to baptise, and he would administer this sacrament to adults, through immersion in water. From the sixth century, however, the creation of parishes, and their very rapid proliferation, could not help but give the incumbent a larger role. He came not only to celebrate Sunday Mass but also to administer the baptism, for otherwise the christianisation of the rural areas could never have been achieved. The second stage involved changes of an institutional nature. Thus Charlemagne decreed, through the capitulary of 789, that it was no longer necessary to wait until one became an adult, and that baptism should be administered to children

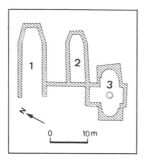

Fig. 41 Plan of the cathedral complex at Thérouanne (seventh–eighth century), after H. Bernard. 1. The north cathedral; 2. The south cathedral; 3. The baptistry (?).

once they were one year old. This decision must have made the baptistry redundant, since the piscina could not be used for children, and dipping replaced total immersion. As was invariably the case, this reform was not implemented immediately. A large number of baptistries remained in use, after having undergone such modifications as were necessary, for example, the covering of the piscina and the installation of a mobile cistern. In other cases, the piscina was reduced in size, for example, at Nevers. There is a far more startling monument at Le Puy, which dates from the Carolingian period, and has a rectangular plan, consisting of two bays and a semi-circular apse hollowed out with deep recesses. At Lyon, Leidrade lost no time in assigning the baptistry of Saint-Etienne to the canons, who used it as their own church.

Places of worship

It soon became necessary to provide the canons with places of worship. We have already seen what shape the complex of buildings assumed at Lyon. In other places, one of the two buildings of the double cathedral may well have been assigned for this purpose at around this period, even if the available testimonies are later (Fréjus). Moreover, new buildings were founded at this time as well. In this respect too, as we have already pointed out, the case of Metz is a representative one, with the churches being built within the precinct of Saint-Pierre-le-Vieux and Saint-Paul. It was in fact the apostle who was the patron saint of the chapter and not, as one might have expected, Saint Etienne. He therefore featured on the chapter seal, and he was also represented in a room located above the refectory, which could well have been the dormitory.

As far as the cathedral was concerned, substantial building was undertaken, involving both repairs, decoration, expansion, equipping and renovation. The majority of monuments would seem to have been in a fairly parlous condition, either because they were old or because they had not been properly maintained.

Here too the initiative was taken by the central government, which was simply not prepared to accept that the House of God was not in a fitting condition. Individual bishops were responsible for the restoration of the churches.

Chrodegang had concerned himself not only with the canonial precinct, but also with the internal lay-out of Saint-Etienne. He took particular care, as may readily be understood, with the sanctuary. The high altar was renovated and crowned with a ciborium. He rearranged the choir in a manner which, though no doubt highly systematic, is none too easy to reconstruct. Choir screens made their appearance, their purpose being to differentiate between the various parts of the building. It is hard for us to imagine how these Carolingian sanctuaries were organised. However, the *Gesta Aldrici* provides sufficient information as regards Saint-Sauveur of Le Mans for it to be feasible to attempt a drawing of the lay-out of the sanctuary in 835. Everywhere else, we have to be satisfied with very vague information. At Lyon, Leidrade partly rebuilt the building, including the apse, his main concern being with the decoration. At Nevers, Jérôme (795–815) set out to renovate the cathedral, which he endowed with relics of Saint Cyr, and to improve the baptistry, which was raised up and decorated with mosaics. Comparable work was undertaken in many other buildings, for example at Narbonne.

A number of cathedrals were both renovated and then subjected to even more striking changes. Thus, at Auxerre, Héribald (849) began by renovating the cathedral, which was in an especially poor state of repair. He therefore rebuilt the walls and ceilings, decorated the building with frescoes and closed off the bays with stained glass. His successor, Abbon (857–60), persevered with the work, building a tower on the west side, which remained unfinished at his death. On the first floor, a gallery directly overlooked the nave, with an altar dedicated to the Holy Cross. Guy (933–41) made a number of significant alterations to the new tower, adding a portico decorated with frescoes, while on the east side, he enlarged the choir.

Since most of the available information derives from written sources, it is not always very clear, because even the last vestiges of the buildings described have generally disappeared. Contemporary accounts give very little sense of the sheer inventiveness of the work executed in this period, an aspect which only archaeological excavations are able to bring home to us. This is true of Köln, seemingly one of the best-known of the Carolingian cathedrals, where texts and documents together give us a coherent picture of the main stages in its history. The various upheavals suffered by the monument are of particular importance in this regard. The work undertaken by Hiltibolde (787–818) around 800, who,

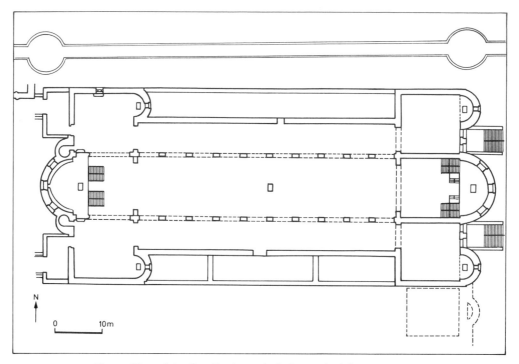

Fig. 42 Plan of the Carolingian cathedral at Köln (after W. Weyres).

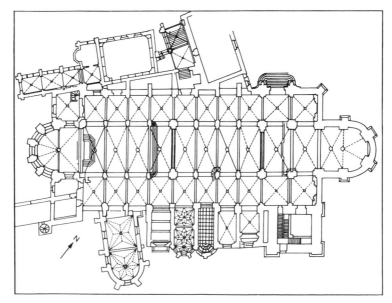

Fig. 43 Plan of Besançon cathedral (after Tournier).

it should be borne in mind, had formerly been arch-chaplain at Aix, was finished when the building was consecrated by Willibert, in 870. The western part of the cathedral, which had been wholly transformed, acquired an apse surrounded by two semi-circular foundations, reminiscent of the lay-out sketched out on the *Plan of Saint-Gall* (816–17?), a chevet of the Roman type consisting of a rather shallow apse ringed by two stairway turrets, overlooking the *augmenta*. It formed a portico on the ground floor and a gallery on the first floor. On the east side, there was a large western transept with a chapel oriented on each of its arms. The eastern chevet, on the other hand, retained its original lay-out. The building was thus on a huge scale, 94·5 metres long, 24·6 metres wide at the nave, and 38·6 metres wide at the transept. At the same time, the whole of the holy town had been reorganised; the canonial precinct at the west and the *domus* occupied a significant part of the town along the northern wall of the ancient enceinte.

Besançon features a similar lay-out, attributable to another great figure of the period, Bernouin (797–830), who was in fact related to the emperor. The emperor of Constantinople, Constantine VI, had lavished gifts upon him, in order to ensure that the venture was successfully completed. The cathedral also featured an apse on its western flank but, by contrast with Köln, it served as a place of worship.

The shifting of churches westwards did not affect only cathedrals, for example, Auxerre, Angoulême, Nevers, Reims, Trèves and Verdun, for a similar transformation occurred in the case of certain monastic churches, one of the most famous of which was Saint-Michel of Cuxa, known to us through archaeological excavations. This tendency testifies to the importance of the liturgical reforms imposed by the Carolingian sovereigns. Gaul had so far refused to adopt the usages of Rome wholesale, an attitude which had caused some important aspects of religious life to be neglected. To remedy this shortcoming, Pépin imposed the Roman practice, which was characterised, among other things, by the fact that the great churches founded by Constantine faced west (S. Salvatore-in-Laterano, Saint Peter's): ceremonies there took the western position of the altar into account. In some cases, adoption of the Roman liturgy therefore required that the altar be shifted to the west.

However, such alterations were not universally adopted. A number of other buildings featured complex constructions on their western flank, which are none too easy to analyse, and which have variously, and somewhat vaguely, been called *Westwerk*, in Germany, and *massif occidental*, in France. The remarkable diversity of such constructions serves merely to show that the authorities could do little more than offer encouragement in this domain. The bishop maintained

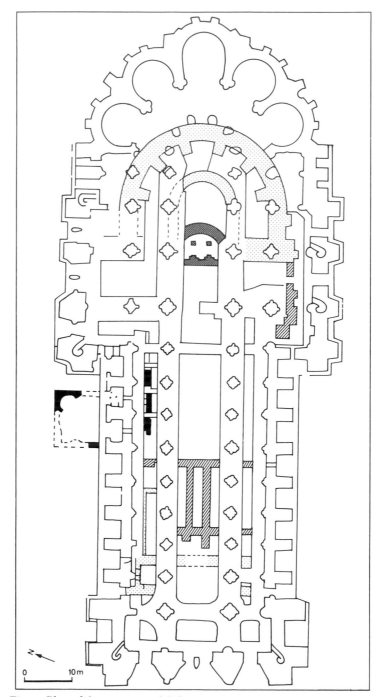

Fig. 44 Plan of the sequence of different cathedrals at Reims (after Deneux).

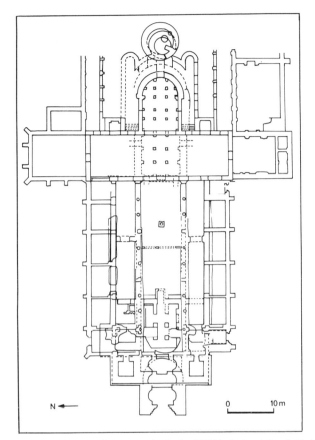

Fig. 45 Plan of the Carolingian cathedral of Hildesheim (after J. Bohland).

a freedom of action that was all the greater for his being distant from the sovereign, not so much in geographical as in familial terms, in the broadest sense of the word.

The Carolingian period, as we have recently come to realise, was a period of frenetic architectural activity. It resembled a vast building-site, which, with the conquest of areas in the east, was still further enlarged, since in such territories everything still remained to be done. If one considers the available statistical information, while making allowances for the limited size of the sample, one is struck by the importance of the earlier legacy, and by the outright predominance of the monastic world. Of the 1,695 large buildings considered, 312 are cathedrals, 285 of which predate our period. There are 1,254 monasteries, of which 837 are pre-Carolingian, 232 are Carolingian and 185 post-Carolingian, and there are 129 royal palaces, of which 29 are pre-Carolingian, 65 are Carolingian and 35 are post-Carolingian. These figures confirm the hypotheses that have been formulated on the basis of written texts: Palatine architecture represents a distinct step forward, which reached its culmination under Charlemagne, during whose reign there were on average 14 new foundations every decade. The monastic world continued the remarkable proliferation of the seventh century, with 50 new monasteries being founded every decade. The markedly lower figure for cathedrals may be explained by the fact that so many were already in existence. Where new cathedrals (8) were built, it was due to the *Dilatatio christianitatis*, in Saxony in particular.

3
The Gregorian reform

✦

The cathedral

HISTORICAL INTRODUCTION

Was 987, the date of the election of Hugues Capet as king of the French, merely an episode in the long-term scheme of things, the only real consequence of which was to secure the future of a dynasty which would provide each generation a male heir, and so guarantee its own continued existence up until the fourteenth century? Or did it represent a profound change in national history, causing a rupture in the long-term development of France? As is invariably the case, one can invoke chance or necessity. Certain events which, in other circumstances, would have been judged to be of secondary importance, are vested with a particular weight, in which passions have their own part to play. The year 987 may be accounted one such.

Contemporaries were themselves probably conscious, as we ourselves certainly are, that the election of Hugues Capet was by no means a routine affair but in fact inaugurated a new world. Carolingian civilization, all but exhausted by its persistent attempts to combat the forces that threatened to undermine it, was disappearing; a new hope was on the horizon, bearing within itself an implicit condemnation of what had gone before. Nevertheless, how could one help but regret the failure of the remarkable attempt of the Carolingians to construct a world adapted both to society and to the faith which inspired it? Hincmar had imagined a marvellous balance between political authority and the needs of religion. How, in such circumstances, could one fail to understand those who believed that the balance of human existence should be based upon that which was established between its spiritual aspirations and its material requirements? As the tenth century drew to a close, however, such conceptions were shown to be merely nostalgic, for the world had changed. Yet Adalbéron of Reims, in his *Poem to King Robert*, still dreamed of such a thing, as was evident from his definition of the 'City of God', which was 'divided into three orders, the first of which prays, while the second fights and the third toils. These three orders live together, and cannot bear to be separated from each other. The services rendered by the one order allow the others to continue with their own tasks, each in turn supporting one and all'.

The world had altered in the most fundamental sense. Antiquity, which had survived by renewing itself, was now yielding to another civilization, which has been called the 'Middle Ages'. In the latter, persons were no longer defined in terms of law but rather through ties between men which had gradually been forged, in order to compensate for the disappearance of the central authority. Religion and its observances were no longer the concern of the sovereign's authority, but had to do with faith. This nascent society was characterised by a belief in itself and in its future, and its dynamism was soon to find expression in a demographic explosion which must be reckoned, as many others have observed, unique in history, and which was closely connected to trade, to wealth, to the birth, in short, of a new zest for life.

The chief characteristics of feudal society are so familiar that there is no need to restate them again here. One should merely bear in mind just how unprecedented it was, for history has been written against this backcloth, and is inseparable from it. A number of its features would seem incomprehensible if one was unaware of the strength of the feudal tie, as much in the private or public world as in the religious domain. Cluny and Cîteaux, for example, were imbued with it. However, in the context of the present work, it seems to me crucial to describe three especially important aspects, which allow us to grasp the sheer scale of the renewal, namely, the Gregorian reform, changes in the nature of the town, and shifts in the domain of architectural style.

THE GREGORIAN REFORM

The election to the Holy See of Hildebrand, known as Pope Gregory VII, in 1073, has been variously judged by historians. Some have regarded this event as a turning-point in the history of the Church, and even in that of the medieval West. Others have played down the importance of the election, noting that the pope failed to achieve all of the aims which he had set for himself. He was forced to flee Rome in 1083, with the troops of the Emperor Heinrich IV in pursuit and to surrender the Holy See to the Anti-Pope Clement III; he died, exhausted and disillusioned, at Salerno, in 1085. As always, the achievements had not matched up to the dreams, but dreams there had been, and they had forced the Church to change. Such changes, which had by then become urgent, were also welcomed, for they reflected an almost universally acknowledged need. It was not by pure chance that Gregory VII came to hold supreme power, for he represented a current of opinion which enjoyed the support of the most brilliant clerics of the day. For several decades, these men had sought to restore the Church to its proper role in the world, in short, to wrest it, in the phrasing of a title of a particular work, from the power of the laity. This reform, it should be remembered, was implemented in a Europe that was in full expansion, an expansion in which it took part, lending it its vitality and the strength of its conviction and, indeed, becoming one of its constituent elements.

The desire for renewal had already found expression in the monastic world, the most tangible evidence for which was the foundation of Cluny, in 909. In this domain, the example of the seventh century was heartening, for a number of prelates, who had left the Burgundian abbey, were marked forever by it, and became reformers. One of the most novel aspects of Cluny, or at any rate the feature which enabled it to be so effective, was its exemption from lay control. The monastery was answerable only to the pope: 'let the church of Cluny be free of the domination of kings, bishops, counts and even of any relatives of Count Guillaume [of Aquitaine]'. This was not a mere formality, for it was the sole means of safeguarding the spiritual life of the monastery. Indeed, the success of the institution was as rapid as it was exceptional, with its influence extending well beyond the boundaries of present-day France. The prominent role played by Cluny in Europe as a whole may be explained by the high quality of its abbots, the first of whom were oriented towards pastoral matters while, from the middle of the tenth century, their attention turned towards politics.

Cluny was not the only focus for the reform movement. There were other abbeys which, although not enjoying so far-flung an influence, were just as effective, for example, Gorze, near to Metz, from 953, which was mainly concerned with the Empire, and Saint-Victor of Marseille, from 977, which concentrated upon the south of France and Spain. In Italy, one should note the abbeys of Camaldoli and Vallombrosa, which became active in the first third of the eleventh century. This reform movement could not remain confined to the monastic cloister, at a time when the dismantling of political authority was bringing about a parallel dissolution of secular religious existence, which had been closely linked to it since the Carolingian period. There was a general distraint upon the power of the bishops, who were now appointed by the sovereign, both in the Empire and, after the Norman Conquest, in England. In France, the first Capetians were themselves accused of simony. In fact, the sale of bishoprics brought them the substantial funds which they were so cruelly lacking. The pope himself, though the head of the Church, was no exception to the general rule, for he was no longer elected by the people and the clerics of Rome, but was appointed by the emperor. Some even went so far as to buy their office.

Heinrich III's appointment of Brunon (1048), Bishop of Toul, who took the name of Leo IX, and who had been chosen because of his reputation as a reformer, marked the beginning of a new policy, which found welcome support among those within his equally reforming entourage, namely, Pietro Damiani and Hildebrand. An anathema was immediately declared against simony. Leo convoked a council at Reims, and immediately deposed a number of prelates, who were accused of such manoeuvres, and were told in no uncertain terms that 'none may arrogate to himself the government of a church unless he has been elected by the clergy and the people'. The Church went through a difficult period after his premature death, in 1054, but the reformers did not lose heart. Their greatest victory was at the Lateran Council, in 1059, when it was decided that the cardinals should have sole responsibility for the election of the sovereign pontiff. In 1073, Hildebrand, who would resume and extend the work first undertaken by Leo IX, was elected Pope Gregory VII.

Once the right to elect the pope had been wrested from the laity, the next step was to reclaim the right to elect the whole of the ecclesiastical hierarchy. The civil authorities interfered so much in such elections, however, that the task was to prove a delicate one. In 1075, Gregory VII promulgated the *Dictatus Papae*, in which he affirmed the primacy of the pontifical power over the temporal power and, as a consequence, prohibited all lay investitures. He sought justification for this radical measure in history, his argument being that originally the prince had not had the right to make any appointments within the Church. The repercussions of this step were especially serious in the Empire, giving rise to a bitter struggle between pope and emperor, which went by the name of the 'Investitures dispute'. The emperor was abruptly deprived of one of his key instruments of policy – the conferment of episcopal and abbatial benefices had long been a way of exercising command over his subjects. In France and in England, the outcome had been different. William the Conqueror, who had managed to invest his conquest with some of the aura of a crusade, came to an understanding with Lanfranc, who had been Archbishop of Canterbury since 1070, affirming on his part that he would pursue policies of reform. William therefore continued to enjoy the right to invest the bishoprics and abbeys of his duchy and his kingdom. Gregory VII had little choice but to yield, and the decree of 1075 was not promulgated.

In France, the pope tackled the problem by diplomatic means, sending in 1077 a legate, Hugues, Bishop of Die, who immediately took steps against the simoniac bishops, such as the bishop of Noyon, the newly elected bishop of Chartres and the bishop of Châlons, and against those who had never been properly elected, for example, the bishop of Auxerre. He even went so far as to suspend a number of archbishops, among them those of Bordeaux, Bourges and Sens. His tact was such that upon each of these occasions he avoided any direct confrontation with the king. It was not long before those bishops who had up until then constituted the king's council deserted it, in order to attend those councils at which their presence was obligatory. Yves of Chartres played a key moderating role, for he was conscious of the need to reform the Church of France. As Provost of the canons of the collegiate church of Saint-Vincent at Beauvais, in 1078 he bestowed upon it a rule of 'moderated spirituality'. Soon after his appointment as bishop of Chartres (1090–1116), he concerned himself with the collation of collections of canon law, so as to replace outdated texts which no longer corresponded to the new reality. The *Tripartita*, the *Decretals* and the *Parnormia* were composed between 1094 and 1096. The latter, a summary of the previous version, evinced the spirit of moderation of the bishop. Indeed, not a great number of texts were borrowed from Gregory VII, and the centralising policies of Rome, being deeply resented in France, were modified at will. Indeed, as far as investiture was concerned, the bishop of Chartres developed a particularly subtle theory, which goes by the name of '*chartraine*'. There was, so the theory went, a distinction between the spiritual function (*episcopium*), which was not then covered by lay investiture, and the temporal prerogatives (*feudum*), which were. Hugues, Abbot of Fleury, brought valuable assistance to the bishop of Chartres, in the analysis presented in his *De regia potestate et sacerdotali dignitate* (1103–4). His exposition was remarkably clear: 'After his election, the bishop will receive, not the ring or the crozier, but the investiture of secular things; he will receive from his archbishop, through the ring and the crozier, the care of souls.' The affair of the see of Beauvais should be seen in the context of this conciliatory policy. Through a series of manoeuvres, Yves of Chartres managed to resolve a long-standing conflict through the election of Philippe (1104), thereby satisfying both king and pope. The theories which he had developed were finally accepted tacitly and by common agreement by both parties. They even served as the basis of the settlement of the dispute between the king of England and the archbishop of Canterbury, Saint Anselm. Thus, Henry I renounced the right of investiture with ring and crozier. In the Empire, these same positions were employed at the time of the drafting of the Concordat of Worms, in 1122.

In France, Gregory's retreat from his final positions had made it possible to safeguard at least the core of the reform. Thus, elections were to remain free of interference on the part of the political authorities, but 'after the canonic election, the apostolic authority has never debarred the kings from granting bishoprics' (Yves of Chartres). As for the election, which harkened back to the practices of the early Church, it was the responsibility of the people, that is to say, the Christian people, and the clerics. Lay participation in elections was gradually eliminated in the course of the twelfth century. At the same time, clerics on the king's council were replaced by laymen. In establishing the supremacy of the sovereign pontiff, the Gregorian reform could not help but undermine the ecclesiastical hierarchy in relation to the pope. The archbishops were now obliged to go to Rome to receive the *pallium*, and decisions regarding geographical circumscriptions were resolved there and nowhere else. Thus, in 1092, the former bishopric of Arras, which had been combined with that of Cambrai, was restored, while that of Noyon was detached from the bishopric of Tournai in 1146. In order to consolidate his new powers, the pope reinforced the position of his legates. They were now above the hierarchy, were responsible for the running of the church councils and, during the papacy of Gregory VII, their appointment tended to become permanent. Urban II, who was still concerned to make conciliatory gestures towards the temporal authority, tended to send them on more temporary missions. His long journey across France, in 1095–6, was to allow him to settle a great many problems, but above all else to renew links with the Church of France.

The spirit of reform was to have an impact upon the canonial order also. There had been particularly violent attacks upon those clerics who had become landowners and who had as a result grown much wealthier. In 1059, at the Council of Rome, Hildebrand had preached the common life and the sharing of goods, once again referring to the example of 'apostolic times'. One can well understand the hesitations of the canonial chapters when faced with such a brutal assault upon their well-established prosperity. A number of them in the south of France renounced their prebends, for example, at Toulouse (1077), Carcassonne,

Narbonne, Cahors, and Saint-Bertrand-de-Comminges. Everywhere else the status quo was maintained.

THE EMERGENCE OF THE TOWNS

At the end of the tenth century, the great towns of Antiquity were little more than a shadow of their former selves. Within their imposing walls, which had been hastily and clumsily repaired, there was desolation. From the middle of the ninth century, the collapse of the civil authorities had led to the abandonment of a startling number of sites, especially in the north. The counts had tended to fall back on the countryside, where at least they would be assured of life and subsistence. In other areas, the situation was less clearcut. In the west, for example, at Le Mans, Tours and Rennes, the counts still resided in their city castles, but they had also managed to lay hands upon the episcopate in such towns, and so to combine the two powers. South of the Loire, yet another picture emerges, for there the counts resided in the towns; up until the tenth century, they even held their courts there (Narbonne, Nîmes), or else were represented by their lieutenants (Arles, Marseille). In Aquitaine, a substantial administration still existed. In the course of the tenth century, however, these traces of an administrative system could not avoid becoming more tenuous, or even disappearing. Where institutions did survive, they had usually lost their former meaning. The Norman invasions merely served to accelerate a process that had begun long before, thereby delivering the town up to the episcopate, which then attempted to define it. This was not always the case, however, for as had happened in the particularly disturbed Merovingian periods, there were gaps in the episcopal lists. The west was especially badly affected in this respect. Of the seven dioceses in Normandie, only two, Rouen and Coutances, would seem to have had bishoprics in 911. In Bretagne, such lists are interrupted everywhere, save at Nantes and Alet. The Hungarians had an equally devastating impact on Bourgogne, as did the Saracens in the south. The bishop of Grenoble was forced to abandon his see and to retire to Saint-Donat, while the bishop of Aix fled to Reims. There were gaps in the episcopal lists at Nice, Antibes, Toulon and Vence up until the end of the tenth century. Dramatic though this period was, no town of Gallo-Roman origin actually disappeared off the map. This fact is of some importance, for it suggests that the institutions must have had considerable strength to survive so many assaults.

In a great many towns, the bishops thus remained the sole authority. Some of them took advantage of this situation, and either increased their power or secured it more effectively. Local circumstances would seem to account for the astonishing range of situations encountered, with no one town resembling any other. At Reims, in 940, the archbishop won the right to mint coin for the town, as well as for the whole county. At Tournai, the bishop took possession of the count's rights. At Langres, Tournai, Beauvais, Le Mans, Autun, Reims, Châlons, Mâcon and Paris, the bishops won significant financial concessions from the king. In those bishoprics which formed part of the Empire, such as Cambrai, Strasburg, Nancy, Toul and Verdun, the counts maintained their customary powers. In the kingdom of Bourgogne, Rodolphe III was forced in 1023 to concede the county of Vienne to the archbishop. In 1041–2, the emperor Heinrich III yielded the seigneury of Besançon to its archbishop. Some prelates took even more advantage of their situation. Thus, at Laon, the bishop was able to exercise the prerogatives of a sovereign, while at Noyon and at Châlons, they ascribed regalian rights to themselves, the bishop of Noyon actually assuming the title of count. Indeed, so weak were the local authorities during this period, that a number of documents were drawn up attesting to the venerable nature of the powers ascribed to the bishop. Such documents were clever forgeries produced in the episcopal chancelleries.

This power was wielded in towns that had been emptied of their inhabitants. As is usually the case with early medieval Europe, statistics are difficult to establish, but the balance-sheet is generally dramatic. At Beauvais, in the tenth century, mention is made of only 50 hearths, which would give a figure of around 300 persons, in addition to the clerics and knights (who would not have been counted). After this period of steady decline in population, the end of the tenth century onwards witnessed a tremor, which was to generate from the eleventh century a sharp upward trend. This trend was to continue through the twelfth century and to level out in the thirteenth century before falling again in the last third of that same century. The ancient towns, along with certain other urban centres, were reborn in the course of the eleventh century, thanks to this renewed population pressure. This advance on all fronts, demographic, economic and commercial – which worked chiefly to the advantage of the towns – is one of the most characteristic features of the West. The new towns which emerged during this period, by contrast with those of Antiquity, could best be defined in terms of their conviviality. They served as a meeting-place for people who had come from quite different places but who were prepared, so as to ensure that the efforts of each would work to the advantage of all, to live together. This represented a radical change in function, for notions of trade and exchange now supplanted that of administration. Whereas the ancient town had been the capital of the *civitas*, it now became an in–itself which set out to be a for–itself, a location whose links with the surrounding milieu became extended to a remarkable degree. It was no longer pressure but the price paid that brought produce from the country to the town. Another characteristic feature of the new towns, and one which would grow ever more intense, was their patriotism. This term may perhaps seem a little inflated, given the nature of the reality it is supposed to describe, and here it must include the notion of belonging to a community which established new relations between people – namely, urbanity. The twentieth-century town is a distant relative of the eleventh-century one, which from the start contained a vast potential for future development. Admittedly, the economic aspect should be kept well to the fore. The town was indubitably a centre of production and exchange, symbolised by the market, or even by markets. However, the essence of the town lay elsewhere. In a number of episcopal towns, there was a sort of doubling, which involved the creation, around an abbey located *extra muros*, of an agglomeration which would be subsumed when the restructured enceinte later encircled both the ancient city and the *suburbium*.

The phenomenon of urbanisation was so overwhelming that it gave rise, from the last third of the eleventh century on, to a new reality, which has been termed the 'communal movement'. Up until very recently, it has been accorded a crucial importance in the definition of the medieval town. Recent historical criticism has tended not so much to scale down the importance of this movement as to give a more subtle account of its consequences, to specify just what its objectives were and to emphasise its extraordinary diversity. Between 1070 and the middle of the twelfth century, only about twenty agglomerations, all of them located between the Loire and the Rhine, were affected. The origin of the communes was in fact quite diverse. At Le Mans, for example, the inhabitants entered into a sworn agreement, which they called a 'commune', the purpose of which was to put a stop to the exactions of Geoffroy of Mayenne. The bishop lent them his support, but the venture nevertheless failed. At Cambrai, in 1106, the inhabitants tried to impose a communal organisation upon the bishop, whereas at Noyon, in 1108–9, it was the bishop who was the founder. At Laon, in 1122, the communal movement was ranged against the bishop, who was himself put to death. The burgeoning of the towns had given rise to new relations between the inhabitants and the civil and religious authorities.

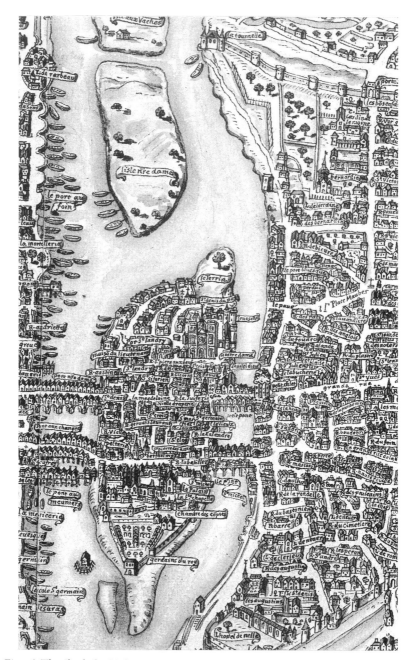

Fig. 46 The Ile de la Cité in Paris, in the first half of the sixteenth century, after the plan 'de la Tapisserie' (detail).

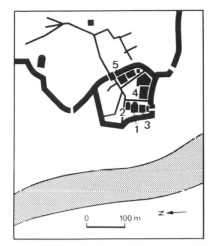

Fig. 47 Plan of the town of Béziers in the twelfth century (after Pelletier). 1. Saint Nazaire; 2. Notre-Dame-de-la-Sed; 3. The cloister; 4. The episcopal palace; 5. The viscount's palace.

The urban castle

Within the new town, the influence of two very ancient elements, namely, the urban castle and the holy town, still lingered. The former served as a focus, during this period, for the tensions which were emerging in the cities.

With the revival of its fortunes, in many different domains (including finance), the town represented a noteworthy prize. It had been deserted by the authorities, and was now suddenly the prey of too many disputing powers, each of which claimed the right to govern. In the towns of southern France, where governmental authority had fared somewhat better than elsewhere, the end of the eleventh century witnessed a growing partitioning of urban space. Strictly delimited zones thus became the preserve of a particular seigneur. At Marseille, the seigneurs fell back upon the castle (before 1069). At Narbonne, such a division was only accepted in 1122, by the viscounts who had to pay homage to the archbishop. There was a comparable partitioning of urban space at Aix, Arles, Avignon, Agen and Cahors, while at Le Puy, Mende, Lodève and Viviers the bishops wielded all of the counts' powers.

The situation of the seigneurial castle, within the ancient city walls, served as a visual emblem of authority, for it was clear that its owner wielded considerable power. Such castles were generally located where the ancient palaces, which had been rebuilt from time to time, had been, and some of their walls would date from that period. From the substantial building programmes undertaken at the very end of the eleventh century and throughout the twelfth century, one may fairly conclude that the seigneur was once again in residence. The castles were also redesigned, with more emphasis being placed upon their defensive function. Although the presence of the royal palace makes Paris into something of a special case, it has the particular advantage of being fairly well known, and dated. King Robert le Pieux (996–1031) undertook the rebuilding of the castle towards the end of his reign, turning it into a fortified quadrilateral defended by towers, with a stone 'keep'. Its surface area *intra muros* measured from around 110 to 135 metres on each side. Although none of the counts' castles were on such a large scale, the majority of them underwent a similar transformation. One should also note that castles stood very near to the cathedral complex, whose mass they were designed to counterbalance. This configuration is apparent in many towns founded in Antiquity, for example, Angers, Orléans, Tours, Auxerre, Dijon, Toulouse, Poitiers and Senlis. On the other hand, in a number of towns, such castles were built from scratch. This was the case in Laon, for example, where Hébert of Vermandois began to build a castle in 928. Herbert did much the same in Amiens, as did Thibaut le Tricheur (Thibaut the Trickster), Count of Blois, in Chartres, Richard I, Duke of Normandie, in Rouen, and an unspecified figure in Bordeaux. The information we have on such matters is in fact extremely vague. However, the castle of the counts of Anjou, in Tours, has been excavated. Built between 1044 and 1068, against the ancient wall, it would seem to have had a fairly simple ground-plan, with a large, rectangular hall and a square corner tower. We can judge how important the edifice was from the high standards of its execution.

THE NEW ARCHITECTURAL VISION

Technical mastery

It was only to be expected that so complete a renewal of values, both spiritual and worldly, touching every aspect of the Church and, in a still more intense fashion, the monastic world, should have had a profound influence upon artistic creation, not only in France but in the rest of Europe also. The Gregorian reform was accompanied by the emergence of a new style, that of Romanesque art. It was not an accident that a new art should have appeared, indeed, the two phenomena were so closely related that it is impossible to dissociate one from the other. Both reflect the dynamism of a society which was evolving along Christian lines. The Carolingian world, and its theocratic dream, had faded, in part because it had been subjected to violent attacks from the outside, but in part also because it no longer measured up to the prevailing realities. Carolingian art, which is essentially aulic in nature, was swept away at the same time. Romanesque art represented a response to a new set of questions, and by the same token a definitive breach with Antiquity. If one can discern links between Carolingian architecture and that of the Roman period, it is because of the overwhelming presence of ancient monuments, which had necessarily to be taken into account. The new generation of architects, faced with commissions from sponsors who would not be satisfied with mediocre constructions, had to learn how to build all over again, the tradition having been dramatically interrupted. Admittedly, there were still some remarkable examples, analysis of which might serve to inspire others to emulate them, but the masons had to learn again how to cut stone in order to lay it at right angles and could no longer settle, as had been usual in the recent past, for breaking it with a hammer. Tools had to be more responsive to the hand, and had to be hardened more effectively, so that they would not wear out too rapidly; they had to be given a keener edge, so that the metal would not be crushed. A slow-setting lime had to be redeveloped in order to guarantee the stability of the monument. The skill of digging foundations had to be relearnt, in order to prevent subsidence.

This technical mastery was quickly acquired, indeed, within the space of a single generation, and not, as has often been argued in the twentieth century, slowly and tentatively. Genius is not known for its hesitancy. The new mastery of technique represented a break with past experience and, in particular, with that of the 'Lombard masons' who had built a number of religious monuments in northern Italy, northern Spain and, more specifically, in Catalonia and in that part of France which is Rhône country. They relied upon the same tried and tested formula, involving small-scale monuments which were therefore vaulted, built of stones broken with the hammer, their sole decoration being *lésènes* or Lombard bands. Romanesque architecture was not the heir of Roman architecture either; it sought, rather, to rival it. Bishops, abbots and architects wished to build monuments that were as vast, as beautiful and as well-built as those which they had in such quantity before their eyes.

So strong a lesson could not help but be understood: it was applied only to monuments which served the other world. Yet a purely technical explanation will not account for the effort invested. At the same time, the approach employed during the Carolingian period, which reflected the theocratic

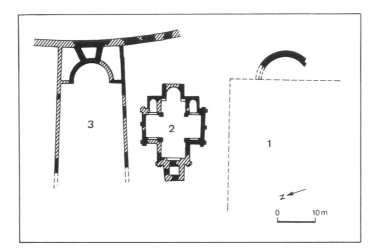

Fig. 48 Plan of the cathedral complex at Lyon in the eleventh century (after H.-F. Reynaud). 1. Saint-Jean; 2. Saint-Etienne; 3. Sainte-Croix.

aspirations of the court, was challenged. The attempt was therefore made to define a plan which was better adapted to the new requirements.

The reduction in the number of places of worship

Nevertheless, although the desire to implement religious reforms led to a fundamental renewal, the past continued to weigh very heavily in all areas, especially as regards architecture. The episcopal complex was no longer appropriate. Now that baptism entailed dipping rather than total immersion, a separate building was no longer necessary, for the catechumens no longer had to be immersed in a piscina. Where before there had been a wide range of different places of worship, the emphasis was now upon concentration, so that bishops, canons and the congregation might all assemble in the one place. The whole problem had to be rethought. Various solutions were adopted, each of which must be seen in the context of an immediate past which is obscure to us, in relation to contingencies which must necessarily elude us and under financial constraints which we are incapable of estimating. A further factor, certainly of equal importance, was the personality of the prelates involved, some of whom were no doubt more dynamic than others, together with the strength of the cathedral chapters which, like any other group, might either support or obstruct such ventures. In the course of this period, the cathedral complex, if it had not already undergone substantial alteration during the Carolingian period, was radically transformed. Although a large number of the monuments were preserved, they were now either cast in a different role or else quite quickly marginalised.

This necessary reduction in the number of places of worship, which had proliferated to such an extent under the Carolingians, was a general feature of the period, the architectural implications of which were to have an impact upon the whole of the religious world, both regular and secular. Recent foundations furnish especially compelling evidence for such changes. If you consider, for example, the plan of the Cistercian monasteries, where the church was designed to receive abbot, monks, lay brothers and the congregation, it was the position allocated to each of these elements within the edifice which led to its being partitioned. In the case of already existing monasteries, any number of expedients were resorted to. Older monuments might be preserved but necessarily used to a much lesser extent, as was the case at Cluny, or several different buildings might be merged. The latter would have been a complex operation, and the examples extant in medieval architecture, such as Metz cathedral, are particularly difficult to analyse. As far as monasteries are concerned, the most remarkable example is that of Saint-Benoît-sur-Loire, for the current, very beautiful church is actually a fusion of two perfectly integrated monuments, namely, an eastern rotunda which has been turned into a chevet with ambulatory and radiating chapels, and a western church. It was no easy matter for the architect to render these buildings 'Romanesque', but he nevertheless succeeded in creating the illusion of a homogeneous monument.

English cathedrals

For those concerned with episcopal architecture, England offers much that is of exceptional interest. One consequence of the Norman Conquest in 1066 was the general upheaval in religious affairs, with the Anglo-Saxon tradition being supplanted by Roman orthodoxy. Such changes occasioned a renewal of ecclesiastical personnel and significant changes in the location of sees. Such shifts were especially numerous in the aftermath of the rebellions of 1069–70. The king resolved gradually to replace the Anglo-Saxon clergy. From 1075, a new policy was adopted towards sees, with those bishoprics which were situated in places of minor importance being moved to towns, while a number of others were subdivided. This new geographical division led to the building of many new cathedral complexes. The king was as much of an authoritarian in aesthetic as in political terms, for the first generation of cathedrals, in Canterbury, Lincoln, Old Sarum and York, plainly reflect their Norman inspiration. The second generation of such buildings, in Gloucester, Rochester and Worcester, were less thoroughly permeated by Norman influence, however, and some account was taken of regional factors. The third generation of cathedrals, in Durham and Norwich, had a certain originality, while the fourth (1100–20), represented by buildings in Exeter, Hereford, Peterborough, Ramsey and Southwell, prove that the English architects of the day were capable of striking a balance between modernism and original creation. In all of these modern constructions, the 'ancient' part of the double cathedral and of the baptistry were condemned out of hand, so as to create a single edifice. There was no longer any trace of the sort of hesitation that had been evident in, for example, Rochester cathedral. Excavations have revealed that the rebuilding of Saint Andrew's cathedral by Bishop Ernulf (1114–26) had occasioned the destruction of the earlier Anglo-Saxon complex, which no longer answered to the worshippers' needs and reflected a by then outmoded state of affairs.

However, it should be emphasised that there was some hesitation shown in the decisions taken on the larger sites, and choices made were often revoked fairly rapidly. Some edifices show traces of a thinking which gained in maturity as time passed, with high-ranking prelates seeking an answer to questions posed by their island diocese. This was the case with Canterbury cathedral, the original elements of which can all be ascribed to Archbishop Lanfranc. This Italian, born at Pavia, had an intimate knowledge of the great Norman abbeys, for he had embarked upon the rebuilding of Le Bec (Bec-Helloin) and had launched the works at Saint-Etienne of Caen. His choice of 'Norman' architecture was a matter not only of taste but also, primarily, reflected his deepest religious aspirations. Although he could have copied the grandiose lay-out of Rouen cathedral, with its ambulatory and radiating chapels, he opted instead for that of Caen abbey, which featured a harmonious facade and an apse preceded by two straight bays. On the continent, there were usually canons, but in Canterbury there were Benedictine monks, and this may well have been the deciding factor. Building work ended in 1077, only to be resumed in the course of the following decade. Prior Ernulf, in accordance with the wishes of the new archbishop, Saint Anselm, took the decision to demolish the chevet, even though it had only just been constructed, and to build another, which would be much further to the east, and which would be better suited to liturgical requirements and to the worship of relics. Ernulf also erected a second eastern transept and an ambulatory, on to which three radiating chapels opened.

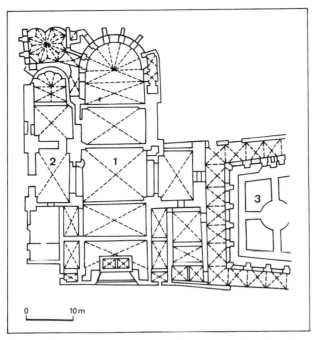

Fig. 49 Plan of the cathedral complex at Béziers (after P. Lablaude). 1. Saint-Nazaire; 2. Notre-Dame-de-la-Sed; 3. The cloister.

At Norwich, to which the see of North Elmham had been transferred in 1094, Bishop Herbert immediately adopted this new formula for the building of the new cathedral. He kept the single transept but adopted the plan with an ambulatory extended by means of three radiating chapels. This plan, which seemed at the time to be of French inspiration, was very quickly challenged and rejected, in favour of a flat chevet. The new design would seem to have been the invention of Bishop Roger, used by him at the cathedral of Old Sarum (1125).

The single cathedral in France

Since France never underwent a comparable revolution, and since, therefore, no one advanced modern solutions on fresh terrain, we cannot identify precisely what the ambitions of prelates were in this regard. Politics played no part in the decision-making process, and the prelates therefore enjoyed considerable leeway in the adaptation of a burdensome past to the new circumstances which they were doing their utmost to exalt. Although a wide range of different solutions

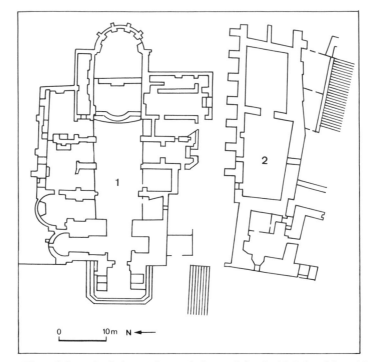

Fig. 50 Plan of the cathedral complex at Avignon (after L.-H. Labande). 1. Notre-
Dame-des-Doms; 2. Saint-Etienne.

was adopted, they all reflected a desire to expand one of the two edifices of the
double cathedral at the expense of the other. In the north of France, this
movement assumed its full weight during the Gothic period, when it was usual
for only one of the two buildings to be rebuilt, with the other remaining
relatively restricted in size. Sometimes, the second building would actually
disappear altogether, thereby releasing the ground needed for the prosecution of
such ambitious plans. There are traces of such a development as early as the
Romanesque period, when the episcopal complex at Meaux was reduced. When
Bishop Nicolas Saveyre (1045–82) was rebuilding the cathedral, he decided to
eliminate the second building, so as to focus his attention upon Saint-Etienne.
Both in the Romanesque and the Gothic period, the south of France was subject
to a quite peculiar development, with both buildings generally being preserved,
the purpose of each then being defined very precisely. In some cases, one
building was reserved for the use of parishioners, as was the case with the north
church at Fréjus, or with Saint-Paul of Nice. One could tell by the use of the

definite article which was the main building, the actual cathedral, which was generally consecrated to the Virgin, for example, Notre-Dame-de-la-Sed (or du Siège) at Aix, Apt, Nîmes, Nice, Riez and Saint-Lizier, and Notre-Dame-des-Doms at Avignon and Marseille.

However, it is as well to bear in mind that the church dedicated to the Virgin did not always prevail, and that other names may also be found, for example, Nazaire at Béziers, Pierre and Siffrein at Carpentras, Trophime at Arles and Sauveur at Aix. Such choices were not deliberate, but rather the result of chance. The north of France was no exception to this rule, for there numerous cathedrals were dedicated to the first martyred deacon, Etienne (Auxerre, Meaux, Paris, Sens and, in the south, Toulouse). The case of Paris is still more remarkable, inasmuch as the name of Saint Etienne was gradually abandoned in the course of this period, to be replaced by that of the Virgin.

It thus seems plausible to argue that where the double cathedral still existed, it was nothing more than a relic. It no longer formed part of the dynamic of the episcopal city, but bore witness instead to an illustrious past, justification for which was provided by giving it a new role.

The Romanesque cathedral

We may thus regard the Romanesque cathedral as single rather than double, its purpose being to allow the bishop to assemble the canons and to welcome the faithful. When the time came to rebuild an obsolete edifice, architectural considerations would be dictated by this threefold function, to which a fourth, the cult of relics, would soon be added. If we bear in mind that the monument, though it served many different functions, was essentially single, we are better placed to appreciate the innovations which the Romanesque architects were obliged to introduce. If we are to arrive at some understanding of the originality of the period, we would do well to look more closely at a number of such innovations.

I shall begin by discussing the ambulatory with radiating chapels. This was a long annular corridor which encircled the sanctuary and which, as the name implies, opened out on to a series of radiating chapels. It would seem to have been one of the most important creations of Romanesque architecture, both the invention and the development of which have been quite rightly linked to the emergence of the cult of relics, which had assumed great importance in the West. As a number of studies have shown, the cult of relics had many

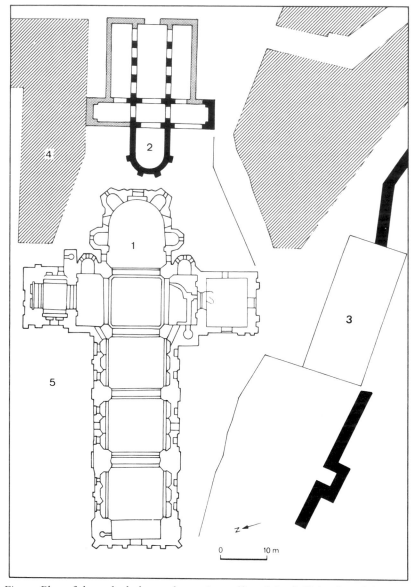

Fig. 51 Plan of the cathedral complex at Angoulême (after J. Hubert). 1. Saint-Pierre cathedral; 2. Notre-Dame; 3. Saint-Jean; 4. The episcopal palace; 5. The canonial precinct.

repercussions, especially as regards religious monuments. The earliest evidence for such an impact on this side of the Alps is supplied by the ambulatory, which appeared at Saint-Denis, during the Carolingian period (754–5), and took its inspiration from the lay-out of the Roman basilicas. The annular corridor allowed worshippers to process around the shrine of the three martyrs, who were buried beneath the apse. One of the consequences of the Norman invasions was to disturb the jealously guarded relics and, in order to ensure their safekeeping, the monks showed no hesitation in fleeing those regions that were endangered and taking refuge further inland. One can judge from the famous case of Saint Philibert the quantity and scale of such migrations. He had been buried at Noirmutier, and his relics were carefully preserved there. In 836, his body was transported inland, to Deas, which was then renamed Saint-Philibert-de-Grandlieu. The religious community was soon to resume its wanderings, carrying the venerated saint with it, proceeding in turn to Cunault in Anjou, to Messay in Poitou, to Saint-Pourçain-sur-Sioule and, finally, in 875, to Saint-Valérian at Tournus, which soon assumed the saint's name. Relics of diverse origin were likewise deposited in a number of cathedrals, for they offered better protection than the isolated, poorly defended monasteries. However, it was vital that the piety of the believers should be respected, and appropriate acts of worship be celebrated. It was soon realised that the ambulatory (its role in the circulation of the faithful during the Carolingian period was noted above) might readily be adapted to this purpose. The earliest recorded and accurately dated case of such a usage comes from Clermont cathedral, where the external wall of the ambulatory is pitted with rectangular niches, which were designed, as has been pointed out, to hold relics. The third stage in this sequence was marked by the joining together of relics and an altar, investing this space with the volume of a chapel. The ambulatory would thereby be endowed with radiating chapels. The date at which Clermont cathedral was built, indubitably at some time between 946 and 1027, is of crucial importance here. The differences between the crypt and the upper church, which have often been noted, do not justify the inference that one is concerned with two distinct monuments. This supplies us with a probable date, since the plan (Fig. 52) must have served as a reference. The nun Helgaud avers in her *Life of Robert le Pieux* that the architect responsible for the abbey-church of Saint-Aignan of Orléans was inspired by Clermont (*in similitudinem*). Since the abbey-church of Saint-Aignan of Orléans was consecrated in 1029, we have a *terminus ante quem* for Clermont cathedral.

Be this as it may, the third stage, namely, the creation of an ambulatory with

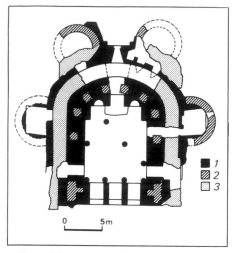

Fig. 52 Plan of the crypt at Clermont (after Du Ranquet).
1. First period; 2. Second period; 3. Third period.

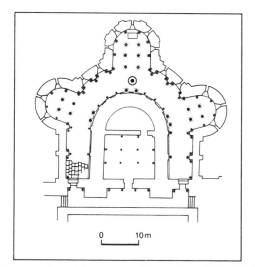

Fig. 53 Plan of the crypt at Rouen (after G. Lanfry).

radiating chapels, was soon reached. There are at least three contemporary sources, and it is worth emphasising that all three cathedrals, Rouen, Auxerre, Chartres, are situated in the north. In addition, all three have been dated very precisely. Rouen, the oldest of the group, is noteworthy also for its sheer size. Excavations have brought to light the original lay-out of the crypt, featuring an

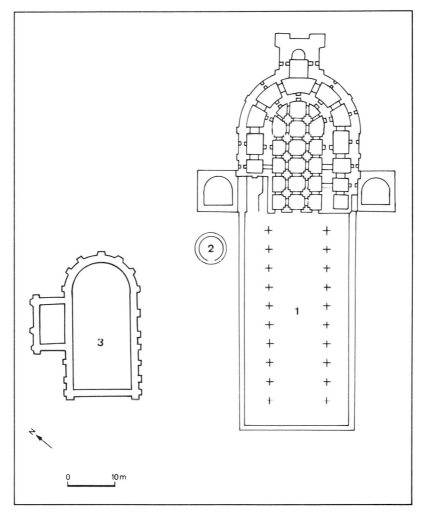

Fig. 54 Plan of the cathedral complex at Auxerre (after J. Hubert). 1. Saint-Etienne;
2. Saint-Jean-le-Rond; 3. Notre-Dame.

ambulatory and three radiating chapels, an arrangement which also characterised
the Gothic monument. The surviving historical documentation enables us to
resolve problems of chronology. We know, for example, that Archbishop
Robert (987–1037), son of Duke Richard I of Normandie was responsible for the
rebuilding, and that he embarked upon the task prior to the death of his father
(996). At Auxerre, a somewhat different arrangement was adopted for, if one
inspects the crypt preserved beneath the edifice, one finds an ambulatory, but

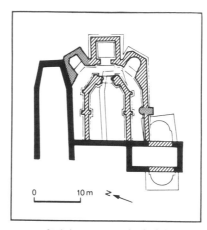

Fig. 55 Plan of the crypt of Thérouanne cathedral (in grey) (after H. Bernard).

with just one chapel. The building had been gutted by fire, and Hugues of Chalon (999–1039) devised an ambitious plan for reconstruction. Unfortunately, we lack a precise date for the catastrophe, although tradition has it that it took place in 1023. As for the third monument which was raised in this generation, and which evinced great ambition, reliable sources inform us that Bishop Fulbert launched the rebuilding of Chartres in the aftermath of the fire of 1020, which had ravaged the monument. There was an ambulatory with three radiating chapels, each of which was exceptionally deep (13 metres).

Other cathedrals may well have adopted a similar arrangement for their chevet at an equally early date. Thérouanne cathedral, which has been excavated, features a very similar arrangement, although the three chapels opening out on to the ambulatory were in fact rectangular. However, given the lack of an agreed chronology, we are obliged to reserve judgement, until such a time as fresh archaeological or archival discoveries are made.

The attested examples of Clermont, Rouen, Auxerre and Chartres force us to reconsider the question of the origins and history of this architectural arrangement. Scholars have generally accepted that an ambulatory with a significant number of radiating chapels was originally a feature of the large abbey-churches. Saint-Martin of Tours, Saint-Martial of Limoges, Saint-Sernin of Toulouse and Santiago de Compostela (in fact a cathedral) are so obviously linked that it has been argued that the architectural form was invented at these sites. The occurrence of major pilgrimages lent further weight to the hypothesis, which soon appeared incontrovertible. It was not long before the theory of 'pilgrimage churches', later demolished by scholars, was advanced. Closer inspection shows that the problem is in fact a very delicate one. Sainte-Foy of Conques, for example, combines a staggered ground-plan with an ambulatory with chapels. Of graver import, perhaps, is the challenge that has been mounted to a supposedly erroneous chronology. Once a genuinely scientific excavation has been undertaken, archaeologists tend to argue that a monument is of a more recent date than had previously been supposed, but prudence dictates that we withhold judgement. This is true of Saint-Martial of Limoges, for example, the destruction of which requires that we reserve judgement as regards the interpretation of historical documents. Analysis of Sainte-Foy of Conques has shown that, far from being a revolutionary monument, it is in fact a traditional, even an archaic one, which cannot be dated before the second half of the eleventh century, and may perhaps even be as late as the end of that century. As for Saint-Martin of Tours, which had long been regarded as the pioneering example of this type of building, recent excavations leave us no choice but to bring forward the dating of the ambulatory and radiating chapels to the last years of the eleventh century. These revised chronologies may seem less startling if one thinks of Saint-Sernin of Toulouse and Santiago de Compostela, since work on the former did not begin before 1082, while the latter is dated 1075 (?).

If, as there is every reason to suppose, the above picture is accurate, we are the better able to appreciate just why prelates around the year 1000, faced with the massive demographic expansion of their dioceses, should have been so concerned to build monuments on a sufficiently large scale to accommodate their flocks. In the east, it was a matter of allowing the worshippers to demonstrate their piety towards the cathedral's relics by guaranteeing them free passage around the building, and by associating such passage, by means of altars, with the celebration of Mass. As was still more markedly the case in the cathedrals of Chartres, Le Puy and Compostela, the prelates endeavoured to resolve the awkward problem regarding the double function of their building. For such churches both answered the needs of those residing within the diocese, and were reliquary churches, which aspect the bishop, anxious to check any drift of his diocesans towards other places of pilgrimage, sought to reinforce. The invention or, at any rate, the utilisation of an ambulatory with radiating chapels was part of a more general policy regarding the faithful.

The spectacular dimensions of the nave in such cathedrals reflected this same concern. Admittedly, it is not easy to comment upon the early Romanesque cathedrals in the north, for they disappeared during the Gothic period. However, as chance would have it, evidence from both Rouen and Chartres confirms what

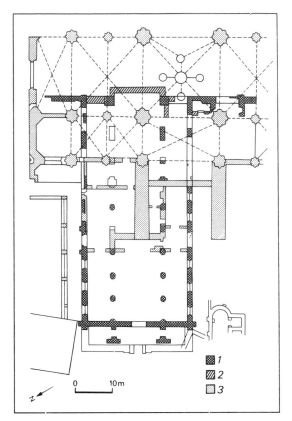

Fig. 56 Plan of the *Basse-Oeuvre* at Beauvais (after E. Chami). 1. End of the tenth
century; 2. Provisional chevet; 3. Gothic period.

their chevets suggest. In the Romanesque period, the naves of these two
buildings were already as long as those of the Gothic period, measuring 103
metres in the case of the former, 110 metres in the case of the latter. Such gigantic
dimensions, which appeared so suddenly at the beginning of the eleventh
century, would seem to have been a necessary response to the sharp rise in
population. They were to become a regular feature of Gothic architecture in the
course of the second half of the twelfth century, but it should be borne in mind
that, even before this date, they were to be found in Norman England. The nave
of Ely cathedral, for example, has no fewer than twelve bays, while Norwich
cathedral has fourteen.

Finally, I would like to comment upon the actual execution of the work, a
topic which deserves extended treatment, but which would be out of place here.

It goes without saying that the quality of a monument depends as much on the skill with which it is realised as on the merits of the architectural plan. The slightest lapse in this domain may damage the effect that was sought. Contemporary chroniclers were so struck by this aspect of things, which seemed to them to be in breach of customary practice, that they invariably emphasised it very strongly. The author of the *Gestes des évêques d'Auxerre* took care to point out that the cathedral had been built with stones cut at right angles (*quadris lapidibus*). Analysis of the crypt, a relatively easy matter given its good state of repair, bears out the chronicler's claims. From the evidence of stone cut and laid at right angles, of traces of coffering of the groined vaults, and of stones laid in the corners to support such vaults, we can conclude that the ambition of the architectural plan was matched by a technical mastery at odds with the customary practice of the period. The two other monuments described above, Chartres and Rouen, give one the same impression.

Harmonic facades

The second great innovation of the Romanesque period concerned the treatment of the western part of the church. The Carolingian period proved especially inventive in this respect, endowing it with complex constructions, such as a counter-choir, a tower with a tiered gallery, a western mass or *Westwerk*, whose effect in visual terms was to produce a perceptible increase in the heaviness of the western front. Under the Ottonian empire, architects persevered with this approach, their efforts culminating in a sort of bipolarisation of the monument, with a balance being achieved between masses on the east and the west. This aesthetic effect was accompanied by a functional change, which concerned the access of the congregation to the building. Indeed, a problem arose, for the western entrance was no longer necessarily guaranteed, and might well be relocated on one of the flanks. Prelates therefore sought as far as possible to challenge the new arrangement, by reverting to the conception of early Christian architecture, where facades offered generous and unambiguous access to the faithful. Where, however, buildings had already been erected, their demolition was out of the question. One had to be satisfied with introducing such modifications as would re-emphasise the role of the western front as facade. The reader will appreciate how hard it is to analyse this question, given the fact that this part of the building has either disappeared altogether or else has been wholly transformed by improvements whose precise sequence can only with difficulty be disentangled. Thus, in the case of the four edifices mentioned above, only Chartres and Rouen lend themselves to any sort of interpretation whatsoever. The western parts of Auxerre and Clermont cathedrals have wholly disappeared, and have not as yet been excavated. The situation at Chartres is very complex, as we shall see below. In the case of Rouen, it seems that, prior to the building of Saint-Romain tower in 1145, on the northern flank of the first bay of the nave, the cathedral featured a western facade pierced with portals. If so, this may be reckoned to have been a facade which was no longer encumbered with adventitious constructions.

It is worth emphasising that the Norman architects had, in the second half of the eleventh century, arrived at a formula that was so clear that it was very swiftly adopted, not only in the monastic world, its place of origin, but also in episcopal architecture. Its composition earned it the title of 'harmonic facade', for its schema was based on a rectangle divided into three parts, the central one being wider than the lateral sections, which were themselves surmounted by towers located in the extensions to the walls. This flat front was pierced by portals, the central one once again being more substantial than the two others. A resolution was thus found to the double problem of the facade, and therefore of the access enjoyed by the faithful, and of the towers. The latter were designed to house the bells, the ringing of which imparted a rhythm to the religious life to which the faithful were invited.

Relations between the abbey-churches of Caen, La Trinité and Saint-Etienne, allow us to retrace the refinement of the formula, which found its most perfect expression in the latter. It was destined to be much studied by others. One can gain some impression of the ground that had been covered by comparing it with Jumièges, which dates from a slightly earlier period, and which still featured a frontispiece, although admittedly in a reduced form, but projecting across the plan of the towers, which contained a huge tiered gallery. There was only a single portal, which was not itself a disadvantage in a monastic monument. Difficult though it is to analyse such buildings, the Romanesque architects responsible for building the cathedrals seem not to have embraced this principle immediately. In France, at any rate, one would have to wait until the Gothic period to see it applied. The same is not true of England, where the harmonic facade was immediately adopted, in Canterbury and Chichester cathedrals, which belong to the first generation, and as quickly abandoned in favour of a wide range of formulae originating in the Anglo-Saxon tradition. Among these formulae, one should mention the facade tower more or less integrated into a western mass, expanded width of the facade framed by towers, and suppression of the towers and the hollowing out of high niches starting from the bottom, as was the case in Lincoln.

The frons non occidentalis

The problem of the handling of the western front could be put in quite different terms, once it was not directed towards the town or towards the active centre of the town. It is no easy matter to judge just what the topographic relation between town and cathedral originally was, for disturbances have been especially numerous in the immediate vicinity of the latter, to such an extent, indeed, that they have sometimes even obliterated the main axes of the city, which had once served as its thoroughfares. Furthermore, a number of edifices with blind western fronts were given a western facade during the Gothic period, thereby overturning their original characteristics. Cahors cathedral provides in this respect a particularly instructive example of such a dialectic between cathedral and town, the consequences of which are evident today. Vigilant scrutiny of the urban topography and of the monument enable us to unravel this complex history and to grasp the original disposition of the monument, access to which today is achieved by way of a gate located to the south. At the end of the nineteenth century, scholars and amateur enthusiasts, astonished at finding, on the north wall of the first bay of the aisle of the nave, a splendid Romanesque portal, refused to believe that it could originally have been located there and therefore insisted that it must have been moved from the western facade, for which it had at first been intended, and subsequently, for the sake of preserving it, moved northwards. Opinions varied as to the precise date at which the portal had been moved, with some arguing that it must have been shortly after it had been built, at the end of the twelfth century, while others opted for the end of the thirteenth century, when the Gothic facade was realised. Not one of these nineteenth-century observers ever considered the possibility that access to the edifice might not have been planned from the very beginning to be from the west. Yet this was in fact the case in the twelfth century, for the western front was not accessible to the congregation; a number of structures rested against the cathedral, and no path led up to it. It was not until 1309 that substantial improvements were made. The canons permitted the demolition of several shops belonging to them, so as to define a space which up until then had not existed and to broach a passage to the facade. The latter was then added onto the blind wall of the monument. The Romanesque portal served from that time on as a secondary means of access, which gradually fell into disuse, being walled up in 1731 and rediscovered in 1841. It had therefore served up until the beginning of the fourteenth century as the preferred means of entrance for the faithful. This explains its elaborate decoration, which made of it one of the most impressive achievements of the Romanesque period. The location of the portal is easily explained: it in fact faced the nerve centre of the thirteenth-century town, the lay-out of which had changed relatively little since Antiquity, and it was close to one of the most important squares (today Clément-Marot), which occupied the northern part of the ancient forum. The *cardo* and the *decumanus* crossed there. As we shall discover in the case of numerous examples even as late as the Gothic period, patrons and architects invariably sought to ensure that the cathedral with whose construction they were concerned was turned towards the town, towards the faithful, thus abandoning a western means of access, which would only be realised subsequently. This concern accounts for many arrangements which today seem somewhat surprising.

Reliquary cathedrals

From our analysis of a number of different cathedrals, it becomes clear that neither the clerics nor those in charge of the site were obliged to follow a specific plan, and that the architectural complexity of such buildings may be accounted for in terms of their varying functions. Some cathedrals were not only diocesan churches but also, and most importantly, pilgrimage churches. We have already remarked upon the importance of the cult of relics during this period in western Europe. The bishops sought in this respect to compete with the abbey-churches, which housed the remains of particularly renowned saints. They needed both to retain the faithful of their own diocese and to attract others from further afield. In order to allow the pilgrims to perform their devotions, they were sometimes forced to adopt particularly original architectural solutions, at least three of which merit something more than a cursory glance, namely, Le Puy, Santiago de Compostela and Chartres. In two of these cathedrals, the introduction of an ambulatory with radiating chapels failed to meet the demand.

LE PUY

There can be no doubting the antiquity of the pilgrimage to the Virgin of Le Puy, even if the earliest mention of the statue of the Virgin is as late as 1094. In the famous *Pilgrim's guide to Santiago de Compostela*, Le Puy is mentioned as the

Fig. 57 Western facade of Notre-Dame of Le Puy in the eighteenth century.

first sanctuary along one of the major thoroughfares leading to Compostela. The reputation of the Virgin of Le Puy was such that it redounded to the credit of the bishop, who was authorised by Pope Leo IX (1049–54) to wear the *pallium*. As a consequence, he was no longer answerable to his metropolitan but took his orders directly from Rome. When the decision was made to rebuild the cathedral, prelate and architect had no choice but to take into account the attested success of the pilgrimage, which drew a particularly large number of worshippers. The architect, faced with this factor and exploiting the steep slope on which he had to build, devised a very original plan, the interest of which the reader will appreciate once he knows that the famous statue of the Virgin was located to the west of the rood-screen. Admittedly, the original design has been so profoundly altered that it is no easy matter to envisage the path taken by pilgrims, but a particularly attentive archaeological study has reconstituted it very accurately. The pilgrim would climb a flight of steps until he came to the western facade, whereupon he would continue his ascent, passing beneath the actual edifice and so arrive, by another flight of steps, at the eastern edge of the fifth bay of the nave, a few metres away from the statue which he wished to venerate. After he had said his prayers, the pilgrim would leave by one or other arm of the transept, each of which was pierced by a door. This curious circulation inside the edifice itself had given rise, during the Classical period, to a witty popular saying: 'One goes in by the navel and leaves by the ears.' The canons were well aware of the advantages of this arrangement, which allowed them to lead their communal life of prayer without being disturbed by a large and inevitably boisterous crowd. Their stalls were located in the apse and in the square of the transept, and both arms were left free. The architect had thereby discovered a way of resolving the problem posed by a pilgrimage without having recourse to an ambulatory with chapels. During this first stage, at the end of the eleventh century, he had reckoned upon having only four bays for the nave, but the pilgrimage flourished to such an extent that the original monument had to be expanded. Around 1200, the decision was therefore taken to extend it towards the west, by launching a further four bays into the void, which would be supported by a huge porch. In this way the by no means negligible slope was put to good use.

SANTIAGO DE COMPOSTELA

The church of Santiago de Compostela is equally exemplary. There should be no need to emphasise the extraordinary success which the pilgrimage to the tomb of the apostle enjoyed, attracting visitors from every corner of Europe.

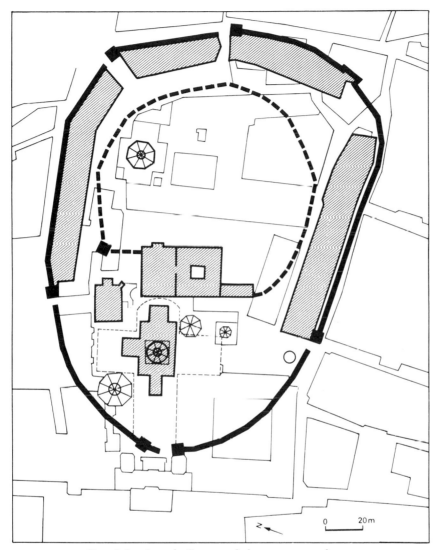

Fig. 58 Santiago de Compostela between 900 and 1040.

Indeed, it is clear that Compostela, second only in this respect to Rome, drew especially huge crowds, on a scale that it would be quite foolish to try and quantify. The remarkable dimensions of the edifice, on which work began in the last third of the eleventh century, reflect what must have been a genuine triumph. In 1078, Bernard le Vieux, described from this period on as 'admirable master', conceived a particularly ambitious plan, which took a long time to realise but was in large measure adhered to. As work on the church advanced, the medieval custom was followed of demolishing the earlier building, so as to make room for the new construction. The plan was for what is generally known as a 'pilgrimage church', with the radiating chapels connected to the ambulatory being five in number. In order to facilitate the movement of pilgrims within the building, the architect chose to put side aisles on each of the arms of the transept, and to furnish it with two east-facing chapels, thus creating a particularly vast surface area. The French author of the *Pilgrim's guide*, who wrote his book around 1130, included in his text some useful details, which give a clearer idea of the monument and of the approaches to it. The cathedral had no less than ten portals, three of which were large, facing to the west and towards both arms of the transept, with two gates in each. There were also seven other portals on a much smaller scale. The pilgrims who took the 'French road' would arrive by the portal facing the north arm, which therefore came to be known as the 'gate of France'. In front of the cathedral there was a parvis.

NOTRE-DAME OF CHARTRES

The plan for Chartres cathedral devised at the beginning of the eleventh century by Bishop Fulbert (960–1028), although less spectacular than that of Le Puy and Santiago de Compostela, was equally original. It was in the wake of the conflagration of the night of 7–8 September 1020, which wreaked havoc upon the old cathedral, that the bishop decided to rebuild it totally. As at Le Puy and Compostela, the architect's instructions were to build a monument that would serve both as a diocesan church and as a pilgrimage church. The pilgrimage was itself already famous and drew large crowds to Chartres, but the prelate sought to reinforce the Marian cult upon which it was based, and thereby to extend it even further. The feast of the Nativity of the Virgin, which fell on 8 September, was therefore celebrated as solemnly as that of the Assumption (15 August). So successful did the pilgrimage become, in the course of the twelfth and thirteenth centuries, that in the end it became the most important in the whole of northern Europe. This supposition is borne out by remarks made by Pope Alexander IV in 1260, when he referred to 'innumerable multitudes of the faithful' at Chartres. The pilgrims were attracted by the famous statue of the Virgin, by her Tunic and, finally, by the Saints-Forts well. If the engravings are to be trusted, prior to its disappearance in the course of the Revolution, the wooden statue representing the seated Virgin with child would seem to have formed part of a group, many examples of which still exist in the Auvergne, and for which we have evidence dating back to the twelfth century. The Chartres statue, which

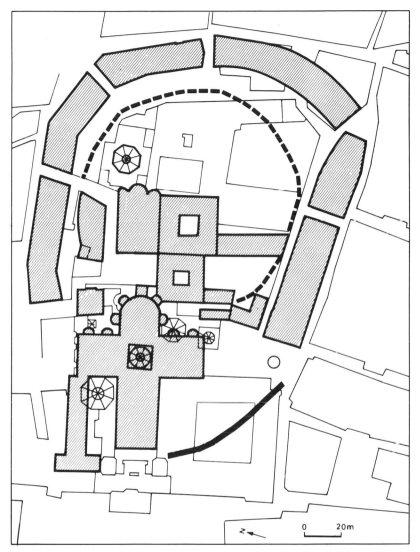

Fig. 59 Santiago de Compostela circa 1150.

very probably belonged to this same period, had undoubtedly replaced another, older statue, which served as the focal point of the Marian cult. At the time, the wooden statue was believed to have dated from before the Christian era, and druids were thought to have worshipped it under the name of the *Virgo paritura*. A precious relic had become associated with the statue, known as the 'Tunic of the Virgin', which was held to be the dress that the Virgin had been wearing on

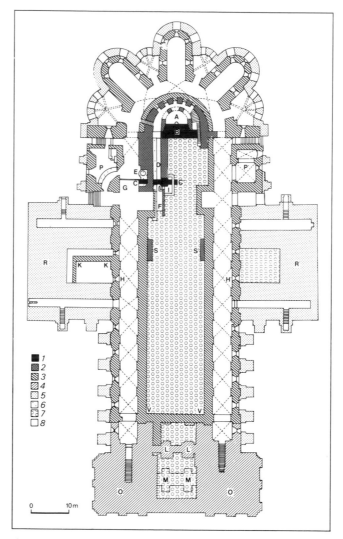

Fig. 60 Plan of the crypt of Chartres cathedral (after Merlet). 1. Gallo-Roman; 2. Ninth century; 3. Eleventh century; 4. Twelfth century; 5. Thirteenth century; 6. Seventeenth century; 7. Infill; 8. Modern. A. Saint-Lubin cellar; B. City wall; C-C. Gallo-Roman wall discovered in 1904; D. Vaulted corridor, ninth century, leading to Saint-Lubin cellar, discovered in 1904; E. Well of Saints-Forts, discovered in 1901; F. Northern side-aisle of the ninth-century cathedral, discovered in 1904; G. Chapel of Notre-Dame-sous-Terre; H-H. Original crypt windows, built in 1024; I. Main entrance to the ninth-century choir, discovered in 1904; K-K. Foundations from the end of the eleventh century, discovered in 1893; L-L. Foundations of the facade or of the western porch, built around 1145, discovered in 1901. Facade

the day of the Annunciation. Whatever the actual origin of the relic, Charles le Chauve had given it to the cathedral in 876, and in a short space of time it had become a symbol of its identity. The Saints-Forts well, on the other hand, was a part of pre-Christian tradition that had subsequently become christianised, as was the case in many places throughout France. Water drawn at the well was believed to have the power of working miracles, and to cure ergot poisoning. Its virtues were so well known that there is mention as early as 858 of a highly popular pilgrimage, indeed, so successful was it that a reception centre for the sick was established in the vicinity. The cathedral rebuilt by Fulbert featured an actual hospital, situated in the northern side aisle of the crypt, not far from the famous well. Monks would take good care of the sick for the space of nine whole days.

With these various requirements in mind, the architect hired by Fulbert conceived an edifice of a truly gigantic length (105 metres), the eastern part of which, as we have seen, consisted of an ambulatory with three radiating chapels. He proposed, at the bishop's request, a topographic distinction between the two main functions of the building, effecting a clear separation of the diocesan congregational church from the pilgrims' church. In this way it was hoped to avoid any conflict. The upper church, which was on the same level as the city, was to serve as the cathedral, while the lower church was to be reserved for the use of the pilgrims. The former was traditional in design, whereas the pilgrimage church was reduced to two long corridors – achieved by preserving a Terreplein beneath the nave – which joined up again in the east on the ambulatory. The architect had taken some trouble to differentiate between the entrances to the two buildings. Thus, the pilgrims were able to reach the statue, the Tunic and the well by means of either of the two corridors, which were pierced by doors at their westernmost ends, while the congregation entered the cathedral from the west. The later development of the western part of the building would be conditioned by this crucial separation. As we shall see below, the building programme culminated in the middle of the twelfth century with the siting, at the western perpendicular of the two towers, of the 'royal portal', which resolved once and for all the question of the access of the faithful to the diocesan church.

---

unfinished and rebuilt at M-M at the end of the twelfth century; O-O. Foundations of the two towers; P-P. Eleventh-century transept; R-R. Thirteenth-century transept; S-S. Lateral walls of the ninth-century cathedral, discovered in 1891; V-V. Facade of the eleventh-century cathedral, discovered in 1901.

THE CHURCHES WITHIN THE CATHEDRAL

The three cathedrals of Le Puy, Compostela and Chartres have such a strongly marked identity that one is tempted to regard them as exceptional. What would seem in fact to be exceptional are the pronounced features which have arisen out of their relationship to pilgrimages. When they were first built, the majority of Romanesque cathedrals had a number of characteristics reflecting the originality of their role and of their meaning. When prelates and architects launched their rebuilding programmes, they had to take into account the traditions of their church, the customs which had grown up over the years and any peculiar features of ceremonies celebrated there. It is not easy, given the form in which the buildings are known to us, to perceive what it was that originally differentiated them from each other. History has generally tended to erase whatever seemed unique, and to reinforce an increasingly dominant typical schema. The first major assault upon the internal appearance and organisation of the monument was precipitated by the Tridentine reform.

The screens

The wish to bring the congregation closer to the altar, and to allow them to participate in the eucharist, led to the various existing screens being demolished, so as to create a unified space in which both priests and congregation might pray together. The restoration of these monuments, so long abandoned, in the nineteenth century, made this homogenisation still more pronounced. Many details had become incomprehensible and were therefore suppressed, so as not to distract from the overall vision. The example of Le Puy cathedral is especially telling in this respect, for there the architect in charge of restoration decided to demolish the huge staircase which had allowed access to the middle of the edifice and to bring it round to the front of the facade. Admittedly, the majority of Romanesque cathedrals in France have not undergone such major surgery, yet many of them no longer feature their original internal organisation. Yet the manner in which they had been constructed had often been dictated in the first place by what took place within them. Without lapsing into a reductive functionalism, it is crucial that we achieve a better understanding of the religious functions which unfolded in each of these edifices.

The question was of some significance in the Romanesque period, for, as we have already observed, the wish to reduce the double cathedral to a single

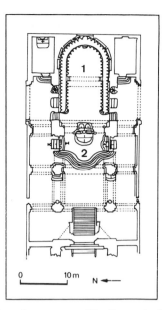

Fig. 61 Plan of the choir and sanctuary of Le Puy cathedral, prior to the changes effected at the end of the eighteenth century (after R. Gounot). 1. The canon's choir; 2. The high altar.

monument had certain consequences for its architecture and its organisation. A redefinition of the interior, guaranteeing complete independence to each of its divisions, had become necessary. We can more readily imagine what was involved if we consider the case of monastic architecture, which was not subjected to the same liturgical requirements, such as had been imposed at the Council of Trent: the abbey-churches have often kept their original screens and therefore allow us to perceive how circulation within the building might have been achieved. In the Romanesque period, the internal space of a cathedral was divided into three parts, namely, the presbytery, the canons' choir and the congregational nave.

The presbytery

The presbytery, from now on invariably on the eastern side of the cathedral, was the bishop's exclusive preserve. It therefore contained the episcopal throne and the high altar, at which the prelate alone could officiate. The high altar was still accorded the importance it had known at earlier periods, for it was held to be the site at which the alliance of God with the faithful of the diocese was renewed. No pains were spared in the treatment of the high altar, and its rich decorations were of great symbolic importance. At Apt cathedral, for example, the altar was on a considerable scale, measuring 2·45 metres in length, 0·96 metres in width and 1·08 metres in height. A very fine marble had been utilised in its construction, and its main surface featured inlaid statuettes, which had originally been placed in niches. In the middle there stood a recently identified representation of the Virgin and Child, for the cathedral was in fact named after both the Virgin and Saint Castor, the name of Sainte Anne only featuring at a later date. Nor was this an isolated case, for there are a number of equally remarkable altars in the south of France. In Marseille, for example, also preserved because of its facade (1·94 metres long), there is the same Marian iconography, on either side of which Saint Lazare and Saint Cannat can be seen. Conversely, Avignon high altar, which is also made of marble, no longer has any figurative decoration.

The same is true of the *cathedra*, which was the symbol of the bishop's power on earth. This accounts for its generally acknowledged role and for the privileged place which it occupied, which was intended to be symbolic. One should bear in mind here the shifts that had occurred since Antiquity. Originally, the members of the clergy who formed the prelate's entourage took their places on a stone bench leaning against the wall of the apse, on either side of the cathedral. Since the Carolingian period, the canons had occupied the stalls located in the choir, being joined there by the bishop. However, in some cathedrals in the south of France, the original arrangement had been preserved, with a stone or marble seat being placed at the end of the apse, raised up on one or more steps. At Vaison, for example, the seat, a thing of monumental simplicity, stood on two steps, whereas at Avignon it was made of a very beautiful white marble and featured on its outer surfaces symbolic representations of Saint Marc and Saint Luc. It was only very rarely that the prelate was supposed to take up his place there. The tradition survived up until the thirteenth century. Thus, at Vienne, when Jean of Bernin (1218–66) set about renovating the chevet of the cathedral, he put the old episcopal throne back against the wall of the apse.

This sort of traditionalism may perhaps account for the lay-out of the presbytery in Le Puy cathedral, such as it was prior to the upheavals mentioned above. The high altar stood in the central area of the sanctuary, as was only appropriate, but the monks' choir was moved to the east, occupying with its stalls two rows deep the apse and the greater part of the bay situated to the west, leaving only the customary two side gates. It is worth recalling in this respect the difficulties the architect faced in tackling the staircase, which ended up in the fifth bay, thus making it impossible to situate the canons' choir to the west. The bishop's stall occupied the upper central area, as was the rule.

The canons' choir

The canons' choir was located immediately to the west of the sanctuary, from which it was separated by a low or light screen, beyond which access was possible from north and south. This choir extended more or less towards the west, depending upon the size of the chapter, with stalls on two levels, which came back round again to the west in order to close off the choir. This arrangement was a direct consequence of the reform of the canonial chapters and was plainly inspired by similar lay-outs in monasteries. Bishops took great care over such arrangements, as a number of texts testify. This was the case with Bishop Gui at Auxerre (933–61), and with Bishop Notger at Liège (977–90). They were responsible for the communal existence of the monks inside the cathedral, and had therefore to ensure tranquillity. The massive influx of worshippers from the eleventh century onwards made a more solid partition necessary. Where stone walls did not yet exist, they were therefore built. When the edifice was rebuilt, provision was made for such walls from the start. Excavations carried out in recent years at Cimiez have thrown some light on a question which remains somewhat obscure. The old cathedral, which was situated on the top of the hill, alongside the 'castle', and turned into a citadel in 1388, consisted of a cathedral complex of three edifices, namely, Notre-Dame, the bishop's church, Saint-Paul, the congregational church, and Saint-Jean, the baptistry. The bishop had decided to organise a canons' community, which was subsequently placed under the rule of Saint Augustine, and which is first mentioned in 1022. In order to cope with the demands of a communal existence, he was obliged to provide, as we shall see below, a canonial precinct and to build a new edifice (1018), consecrated to the Virgin in 1049. This building has just been uncovered, and excavations have revealed how it altered over time. It was a small monument, 36 metres long by 20 metres wide, framed on either side by an apsidal chapel situated within the extension of each of the side aisles; the stone screen which has recently been brought to light ran between the last two bays, and then returned towards the east; at the centre of the western screen, the gate has been found, a relatively narrow example which is 91 centimetres wide.

The choir thus occupied a rectangle measuring 8 metres long by 6 metres wide, an area sufficiently large to hold the dozen canons of which the chapter then consisted. When their number increased, however, at some date prior to 1148, there was no longer sufficient room, and Bishop Pierre took the decision to restrict the size of the canonial precinct, which had been enlarged in order to make room for the new monks. Extraordinary though it may seem, the choir was extended eastwards: the three apses were demolished, only to be rebuilt 4 metres further east, to avoid disturbing the position of the original screen.

The congregational church

The rest of the cathedral, that is, the nave with its side aisles, the transept and the ambulatory, was reserved for the congregation. It goes without saying that, when services were being celebrated, as is the case nowadays, access to the eastern parts of the building might be prohibited, so as not to disturb the monks in their meditations. The congregation had no access to the high altar, and were thus unable to see the bishop's celebration of the office. The clergy, and more particularly the prelates, had been conscious of this problem from the start. So it was that the construction of the screen, which I will discuss again at greater length in the context of the Gothic period, was vested with a particular significance, for it was intended both to serve as a screen for the canons and to open up the act of worship to the congregation. The transformation in the liturgy, begun in the tenth century and consolidated in the course of the Romanesque period, allowed a solution to the problem. Prior to this date, the priest had celebrated the office while facing the congregation, a practice that has been revived since Vatican II. From that time on, he was to face the east, and so to turn his back upon the congregation. The earliest testimony we have regarding this innovation appears in a work by Abbot Reginon of Prüm, written in 906, the *Libri de synodalibus causis*. The Romanesque practices described above yielded to new customs, which came to prevail in the course of the eleventh century, and gave rise to the drawing up of new *ordines*. Celebration of the office with one's back turned to the people, although it had no repercussions for the high altar, facilitated the positioning of the secondary altars, which might now be placed against a wall, either that of an apse or that of a choir screen. So it was that altars were set up in front of the screen, in order to allow the congregation to participate in the celebration of the Mass. Bishop Gui of Auxerre (933–61) gave assurances that both he and his successors would celebrate Mass, whether for the congregation or for the dead, as often as they could on the altar which had just been built, with this in mind, at the foot of the screen. The latter was thereby invested with a new meaning. Its bare walls were used, from this period on, for decoration of a pedagogic nature, both painted and carved. Some cathedrals, Vienne for example, featured carved flotsam which might originally have served such a purpose.

THE BAPTISTRY

The intended purpose of the third element in the cathedral complex, the baptistry, was still more fundamentally altered. It should be emphasised that the majority survived during this period, but suffered particularly drastic alterations. The example of Nevers would seem to have been exceptional in this regard, for, after a fire either in 953 or in 996, it was restored. The entrance gate was then raised up and a staircase added; the piscina was filled in and a new floor laid. The building still served as a place of baptism, a rite which was performed in a cistern. In Paris, baptism was still being solemnly administered at this period by immersion, either at Easter or at Pentecost. At Rouen, Archbishop Jean II of Bayeux (1069–79) was buried in the baptistry.

The south of France, however, was all but untouched by the changes affecting the north, and a wide range of different formulae were adopted. The majority of baptistries there were preserved, some even undergoing significant restoration, with the piscina usually being eliminated in the process. Riez baptistry has survived up until the present day, but stands all by itself. The ancient city, which was abandoned, lay on the plain, while the townspeople took refuge in the eleventh century on the hill of Sainte-Maxime, beside the cathedral and the canonial chapter. The baptistry in fact remained on the plain and its upper parts were significantly restored in the course of the twelfth century. At Aix, the baptistry was in large part rebuilt and altered both in its superstructure and in its signification. Two entrance ways were created, one lying to the north, towards the cathedral, the other to the west. The baptistry was thereby oriented. The floor was also raised, but there is some doubt as to whether the piscina was filled in or not. At Marseille, the baptistry was apparently still being used for the rite of baptism, but it was performed in a cistern. However, from the eleventh century, it is known under the name of the church of Saint-Jean, which implies that by then it was serving another purpose. At Valence, the baptistry, which was discovered in 1846, to the south-west of the cathedral, had been completely rebuilt in the course of the eleventh century, with the original plan being altogether disregarded; subsequently it became a church. The baptistry of Le

Puy, which we mentioned above, was rebuilt during the Romanesque period. At first, the piscina would seem to have been kept in operation, but it fell into disuse, being replaced by a cistern located in a niche hollowed out of the north wall of the second bay.

The holy town

THE EPISCOPAL PALACE

As the episcopal complex was being redefined, in the course of the Romanesque period, significant alterations were made to the palace and to the canonial precinct. The aim of Chrodegang's reform, successfully implemented, had been to persuade the monks in the bishop's entourage to quit the *domus* and to live as a community within the precinct. The prelates had cause to fear that they would then have room to spare, in a building originally designed to house both themselves and their priests, but this was very far from being the case. Indeed, in order to meet the urgent need for additional living space, they had to enlarge the buildings which they had inherited, to organise them in a different fashion and, finally, to introduce into them the relative comfort that their new responsibilities required. It was in fact during this period that their residences assumed a precise architectural form and, in addition, a specific symbolic significance. This important development was reflected in a lexical shift, with the term *domus* generally being replaced by 'palace'. The palace, the bishop's residence, was supposed to express his responsibilities in both the spiritual and the temporal sphere. Indeed, it had become of crucial importance to assert his prerogatives in temporal terms as against those of the count. It is a telling fact, moreover, that the earliest recorded use of the term 'palace' in relation to such a residence dates from the time of Bishop Notger (972–1002), in Liège.

The history of this episcopal see, although somewhat exceptional, serves to illustrate the sort of power that a bishop might acquire during so turbulent a period. Its transfer, during the eighth century, from Tongres-Maastricht to Liège, to what was at that time a mere *vicus* (market-town), was in time to turn the latter into an important agglomeration, which grew up in the shadow of the cathedral. Bishop Hortgar, in the ninth century, spared no pains in building a magnificent residence, as is apparent from the enthusiastic account of it given by the Irish monk Sedulius. Nevertheless, in 965, Bishop Eracle showed no hesitation in transferring both cathedral and *domus* to the mountain of

Publémont. This exile was, however, to prove merely temporary, for Bishop Notger brought them back to Liège, making them the centrepiece of an ambitious political programme, which Imperial generosity had enabled him to launch. He had gained the use of regalian rights and the privilege of immunity, to such an extent, indeed, that he avowed himself to be both lord of the town and of the temporal domains which he had acquired beyond it. This was how the principality of Liège, which was closely associated with the diocese while remaining distinct from it, came into being. The bishop was its spiritual head but the temporal prince also. Notger would seem in fact to have been the real founder of the town; he designed a new city wall, tried to populate specific quarters, built a number of churches, but devoted his best energies to the cathedral complex: he built a new religious building which was only to be finished after his death and, most important, embarked upon the construction of his residence, which was afterwards called a palace. The *Life of Notger*, written at the end of the tenth century, placed special emphasis upon the meaning he attributed to the building, which was raised in the image of his ambiguous power. Notger's palace in fact established a formula which was from that time on to prevail in the West. The choice of site served first of all to emphasise the weight of willingly respected traditions, for it was located on the north flank of the cathedral and integrated into the defensive system of the town. As we have seen, this customary location in the cities of Gaul dated back to the origins of Christianisation; here, however, a quite deliberate choice was being made. The building was meant to play an active part in protecting the town, and was placed in a particularly strategic site. There was a second aspect to this choice, which provides intimations of future developments: Notger embarked upon the building of cathedral and palace at one and the same time, employed the same workmen on both sites, and invested equally large sums of money in both projects. To his mind, it was not a double but a single operation. Cathedral and palace were closely associated with each other, the implication being there were intimate links between the spiritual sphere and temporal responsibilities. The latter were given architectural expression in the *aula*, which became the chief element in the palace, for there the famous 'court of the ring' was held. The third, equally innovatory element concerned choice of materials. Up until this time, episcopal constructions, apart from the cathedral, had been, for obvious reasons of economy, made of wood. Notger, however, built his palace of stone. This initiative represented a break with the past, for in its underlying meaning it was an aspiration towards eternity. Since symbolism in the Middle Ages was as important as material reality, the use of stone was highly significant; an

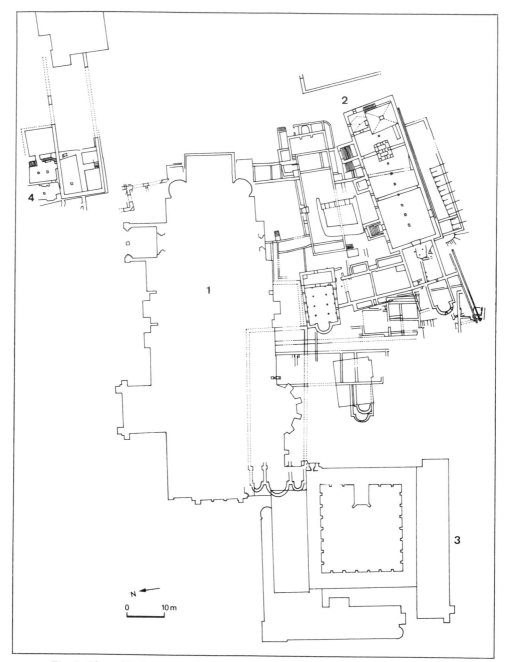

Fig. 62 Plan of Paderborn in the eleventh-twelfth century. 1. The cathedral; 2. The imperial palace; 3. The canonial precinct; 4. The episcopal palace.

authority was being asserted which would endure over time. A similar choice was made all over the north of France so that, when reconstruction was embarked upon, use was now made of non-perishable materials. These reconstructions were not invariably, in material terms, strictly necessary, but were carried out for the sake of prestige. Chroniclers, while emphasising the enhanced quality of the new buildings, were adamant on this point. Thus, at Cambrai, Bishop Erluin (995–1012), when he rebuilt his *domus*, would seem to have used hard materials for the purpose. The buildings were at any rate described as superb. At Le Mans, the chronicles emphasise that Bishop Avergnon took good care to build in stone, and this was true at Chartres also. It goes without saying that the very notion of a palace could hardly be said to sit very well with the use of perishable materials.

Most of these reconstructions also witnessed, contrary to what one might at first have supposed, a perceptible increase in the surface area of the buildings and of the grounds in which they stood. The prelates inevitably came into conflict with customary rights. Yves of Chartres, for example, had to buy a neighbouring plot, at that time owned by the vidame. We do not know what sum was paid, but it was probably substantial. This was not always the case, however. Thus, at Auch, Raymond II of Padirac (1098–1118) built the *aula* on a plot of land which had been given to him, and which lay near to his own residence. We cannot hope to give an idea of the exact dimensions of the new buildings, for texts and chronicles are as a rule very vague on such matters, and such graphic documents as survive from so early a period are difficult to interpret. Nonetheless, one has the general impression that certain palaces were at this time built on a considerable scale; some had even attained their ultimate size already, with later alterations being designed solely to provide more living space. If a recent study is to be believed, the palace of Beauvais, rebuilt by Henri of France, brother of Louis VIII, already covered its present-day surface area. The palace at Laon, rebuilt after 1122, already featured a ground-plan in π, which was subsequently to become its characteristic feature. Within the three wings, there was an inner courtyard. The palace at Reims was already known as le Tau, at any rate after 1138.

The lay-out of the Romanesque palaces

Analysis of both texts and graphic documents will give us some notion as to how episcopal palaces looked at this period. They were generally surrounded by a protective wall, which was made of stone. It was not an enclosure but a screen, which lacked any defensive elements, and yet it was sufficiently thick to shield the palace from surprise attack, a thing always to be feared, given the frequently riotous disposition of the urban population. To have reinforced the wall further would have been impolitic. Indeed, the bishops refrained from doing so, being concerned not to provoke an active and dynamic population already resentful of the count's residence, which during this period assumed a more dissuasive, not to say defensive character. The palace was sufficiently well defended from the town, but it was more vulnerable to external attack, being located close to the old city walls, and generally in fact adjacent to them. It played a part in the defence of the town, as we have already noted in the case of Liège, but this was not without its difficulties, either during this period or subsequently. Contemporaries thus conceived of the palace as a closed space within a town that was itself shut off also. The space that was thereby delimited was occupied in various different ways, by buildings, as we shall see below, but also by vegetation. The bishops would seem to have reserved certain areas within their dwelling places not only for gardens designed for recreation and relaxation, a standard feature of medieval towns, but also for cultivated fields. They had to live off their own resources, including the produce of the soil. When Geoffroi, Bishop of Coutances (1069–93), decided to renovate his *domus*, he planted both an orchard and a vineyard. Others were concerned to create well-ventilated spaces. Thus, in the course of the rebuilding of the palace of Lyon, Hugues of Bourgogne (1085–1107) and Josserand (1107–8) stipulated that several inner courtyards should be created. Unfortunately, we know neither how large they were, nor how they were arranged or decorated. Some were no doubt designed to serve as extensions to the stables, which are so often mentioned in contemporary accounts, while others were for recreation. At Reims, Archbishop Gervais had a bronze stag placed in the entrance court, above the gateway, which did not disappear until the Revolution.

The chroniclers were invariably struck, in their descriptions of the actual buildings, by the care taken in their construction, as well as by a new concern with comfort. At Lyon, mention is made of the different kinds of chamber, of what was known as an *atrium* and, more particularly, of a *loggia*, which was located on the ground floor, was supported by marble columns and decorated with paintings. It is probable that the latter were not merely decorative but in fact depictions of religious scenes. This was at any rate the case with Notger's palace at Liège. If one examines what survives from this period, one cannot help but be impressed by the quality of the execution and the decoration. At

Beauvais, remnants dating from the time of Henri of France are especially telling in this respect, with the capitals and gateways boasting fine carvings.

We can judge the degree of refinement of the work of this period from Auxerre, where a large part of the Romanesque palace has survived. Bishop Hugues of Montaigu (1116–36) had pursued the policies of aggrandisement embraced by his predecessors. He made the most of an already impressive site, encouraging the spectator to look past the religious edifice towards the river Yonne and the superb landscape beyond. A contemporary chronicler responded in lyrical terms to the construction, which was, moreover, in stone: 'In that part of the episcopal dwelling which faces east, Hugues of Montaigu built upon the city walls a covered walkway (*statio*), popularly known as lodges (*loggiae*), a construction that is most pleasing to look upon, being decorated with very beautiful columns, the view from which takes in both the river which flows below and the vines and the fields.' This gallery still exists, being located within the buildings which today constitute the prefecture. So marvellously placed is it that it still allows the prefect and council the privileged vista which Hugues was already able to enjoy in the twelfth century. Admittedly, the building was subject to a fair amount of restoration in the nineteenth century, for it was then in a parlous state, and many of its architectural features were renovated, and its sculptures replaced, but invariably by identical ones. The gallery was 22 metres long and 6·3 metres wide, resting upon the ancient wall, which had been truncated to allow the view to the east. The handling of the eastern facade made the vista possible: the arches of the bays, intended to be kept open, culminated in small columns, single or paired. Below, the wall had been maintained unbreached, for security reasons, the openings there not having been made before the fifteenth century.

The gallery at Auxerre was one of the very first examples known from the Romanesque period, although there are contemporary instances of the same feature recorded in civil architecture. It is worth emphasising the name by which they were popularly known, namely, lodges, a term which was also employed at Lyon, and which was to be revived in the still distant Renaissance. This taste for comfort was evident in many other episcopal palaces, as well as at those already described in Beauvais, Liège and Lyon, for example, at Senlis and Angers. The latter was rebuilt in the course of the first half of the twelfth century. Situated between the north arm of the cathedral transept and the ancient city wall, it contained the body of a lodge attached at its north end to the ramparts, with a long hall divided into two chambers by columns. If one then retraced one's steps towards the transept, one came across another building

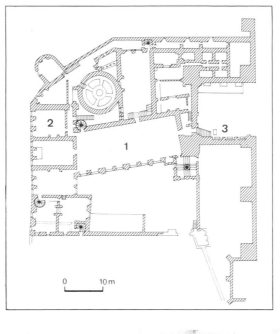

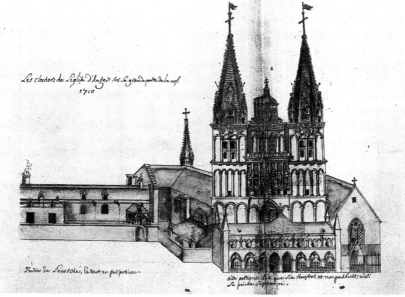

Fig. 63 (Top) Plan of the episcopal palace at Angers before 1643. 1. The great hall; 2. The chapel; 3. The northern arm of the cathedral transept.

Fig. 64 (Bottom) Angers cathedral, episcopal palace (on the left) and parish church (on the right), in 1710.

whose lower hall had originally served as a refectory, and, on the ground floor, the great hall or *aula*. The latter was large, being 26 metres long by 10 metres wide, lit by numerous bays and covered with a timber-framed roof; it was linked to the first hall by three arches.

The great hall or *aula*, the importance of which has already been emphasised for the earlier period, was generally rebuilt during the Romanesque period, the aim being to adjust its dimensions to fit the prelate's responsibilities. It served as a meeting place, where bishop and canons, or bishops and diocesan administrators might assemble, and, most important of all, where law courts might sit and the most important legislation be signed. Such a hall had, therefore, to be both large and well lit; it was generally also cleared of superfluous struts and covered with a simple timber-framed roof. In this respect, there was a curious resemblance between episcopal and seigneurial halls. The hall of the palace of Poitiers, which was contemporary with that of Angers, has many features which are similar, a fact that may be explained by their common origin and shared purpose.

The second element of crucial importance to an episcopal palace was the oratory, which during this period became a chapel of at times quite substantial size. This size too was linked to the fact that the canons had assumed an increasingly prominent place within the cathedral. The bishop had tended to return to his palace if he wished to pray, and it was not long before his entourage likewise became accustomed to taking part in the religious ceremonies that were celebrated within the palatine chapel. Following a process the precise nature of which is obscure to us, but which very probably entailed imitation of civil, royal or seigneurial architecture, episcopal chapels were now built on two floors, with the ground floor being reserved for the bishop's entourage and the floor that was on the same level as the apartments being for the use of the bishop and his circle. At the time, this chapel was generally located within one of the towers of the precinct, an arrangement which had the advantage of giving the eastern part the rounded form of the apse (Senlis). Subsequent reorganisation of the palace led to the chapel being moved, but it was always situated close to the residential quarters. At Laon, Gautier of Mortagne rebuilt the chapel on two floors. Elsewhere, the chapel's decor is mentioned, with paintings and pavement being featured at Lyon.

As well as these two significant elements, one should also mention the presence of two constructions, one of which continued to be exceptional, while the other would become an obligatory feature in the following period. At Besançon, Pietro Damiani, in his description of the residence of Archbishop

Hugues (1031–70), remarked upon the existence of a cloister within the chevet of the cathedral, intended for the use of the bishop, whereas a second, reserved for the canons, was on the flank of the cathedral. Our knowledge of this highly original lay-out derives from an eighteenth-century plan, which shows the three galleries hemming in the chevet and the traditional garden. This circumstance would seem nonetheless to have been fairly exceptional.

On the other hand, the tower, the second construction, which became a quite general feature in the subsequent period, was already common. Its first appearance cannot have been much before the eleventh century, which was when the earliest testimonies were recorded. This circular construction, wooden to begin with but stone from the twelfth century, was described from this period at Liège and Reims. At Liège, the Irish poet who described the *domus* built by Bishop Hortgar averred that the tower there was 100 cubits, which would be 45 metres high (?), although he would seem to have used poetic licence here. The important point to note is that it was much higher than the other buildings of the palace and that, when one climbed up by way of a staircase to the upper part, one was granted a view across the rooftops. At Reims, the tower mentioned in the eleventh century may be identified, from its position, with the one that survived up until the seventeenth century, but it was built of stone, and stood at the entrance to the palace. It was circular also.

The palaces in the south

In the south, episcopal palaces remained on very much the same scale as they had been in the past, in part because of the position of the bishops. At Grasse, the surviving wing of the palace is more reminiscent of a city dwelling than of a prelate's residence. At Aix, excavations of the archbishop's palace in 1984–5 have brought to light the fact that the buildings had grown up around a courtyard measuring 350 square metres, at any rate to the south and to the east, and probably to the north also. The southern wing served as living quarters. Analysis of the foundations provides evidence for an ambitious, but never completed architectural programme. As in the north, so too here, mention should also be made of the famous towers. At Arles, it was first mentioned by the name of 'tour Gioffredi', then 'the bishop's large tower'. It consisted of three or four floors, one of which contained a chapel. There was also a square tower at Fréjus, with a chapel, but it would seem not to have predated the fourteenth century. At Viviers, the tower, measuring 10·5 metres on each side, was 19 metres high. It would seem to have contained the bishop's chamber, the treasury, the archives and the prison. The *aula* would seem to have been in a building located in its extension towards the north-west and above the chapel.

THE CANONIAL PRECINCT

The reforms

The efforts made by the Carolingian sovereign to impose a communal life upon the canons were not entirely successful. The political upheavals of the tenth century led to a general relaxation of mores which, once habit had taken hold, was difficult to reverse.

However, this period witnessed a number of attempts to restore order. The chapter of Le Puy, for example, was reformed in 932, and a number of especially rigorous constraints were imposed, among them a ban on the canons having property of their own. The Gregorians went on the offensive again. Pietro Damiani drew up a document criticising land-owning clerics; Hildebrand also attacked them at the Synod of Reims, in 1059, and one of its articles therefore prescribed the communal life and the sharing of property, the only path to evangelic perfection. A distinction thus arose between regular canons, who were prepared to respect the rules of the communal life, and secular canons, who refused to give up their prebends. This was too much to ask and, all in all, the cathedral chapters in France refused to submit to a rigorous rule. The same was not true of the south-west. There, under the influence of Isarn, Bishop of Toulouse, a number of chapters embraced the reform: 'The canons possessed nothing of their own, and would not even go so far as to say that something actually belonged to them; they would have common dormitories and refectories and would all wear the same clothes; finally, they would acknowledge the authority of their prior.' The reform was introduced at the end of 1072 or at the beginning of 1073, by the canonial chapter of Toulouse cathedral and, thanks to Bishop Frotaire, by that of Albi. At Cahors, it was introduced somewhat later by Bishop Géraud (1083–1112?), upon the authority of Saint Hugues. The chapters of Carcassonne, Narbonne and Saint-Bertrand-de-Comminges followed suit.

This spiritual reform, which in the end was merely of local significance, was paralleled by a material reorganisation, which was sooner or later to affect the whole kingdom. The canonial patrimony had become severely depleted in the course of the tenth and eleventh centuries and, to ensure the livelihood of the monks, some steps had to be taken. Large donations made by bishops were the crucial factor in this reorganisation. At Cahors, for example, Géraud bequeathed a generous endowment in his will of 1090 to the reformed chapter. In a letter addressed to the chapter, Urban II confirmed the donations, taking due note of the restoration of discipline. He forbad the canons to leave the precinct without the authorisation of their prior; he also took the canons' property under his protection, and even confirmed what had previously been granted to them, and had since then fallen into the hands of the *milites* (knights). A policy of recuperation was then pursued. The organisation of the chapter was itself tackled and, after collective debate, a new hierarchy (provost, archdeacon etc.) was established. This reconstitution (or, in some cases, constitution) of the canonial patrimony affected every diocese in France. A crucial distinction should, however, be made between those dioceses in which the canons kept their prebends, and so won a degree of independence, and those where they did not. Where canons had maintained their prebends, their greater independence would find its most obvious expression in the fact that they lived, not communally, but in individual houses.

Canonial organisation thus appeared to have been placed on a firm footing, in accordance both with rigorous principles and with highly diverse circumstances, with traditions varying from one diocese to another. In general, a canon was appointed by his bishop or elected by the chapter, after verification in the latter case that he fulfilled the conditions stipulated by the law and the customs of the chapter in question. From the end of the twelfth century, moreover, there was a marked increase in the number of nobles taking up canonial offices, which were in fact very lucrative, owing to the income generated by some prebends, especially in the north. I shall return to this point below.

The dean, himself sometimes a provost, was elected by the chapter, and served as its head. He dispensed justice in the name of the chapter, was responsible for the surveillance of the precinct, represented the chapter and received homage from vassals. He had himself to pay homage to the bishop, but to remain loyal to the chapter. The cantor, originally responsible for choir rehearsals, served as the dean's deputy in his absence. There was often an *écolâtre*, as at Chartres, who was responsible for the running of the episcopal school. There might also be a chancellor, a penitentiary, a treasurer and a sacristan, but not all of these posts were invariably filled. It depended upon the importance of the chapter in question. In this regard, canonial organisation was not as rigorously defined as was that of the monasteries. The canons' duties varied from diocese to diocese.

One of their chief responsibilities, however, was the election of the bishop. Developments in this area only reached some sort of conclusion in the thirteenth century, and there were therefore serious conflicts between the two institutions. It was not uncommon for the chapter's material wealth to be a factor in such disputes. In order to administer such resources, which often derived from the land, a provost was appointed, with a team of deputies at his disposal. The capitulary revenue was divided into prebends, each of which guaranteed a canon a living. Soon, and at any rate in the twelfth century, the chapter would often assert itself as a rival authority to that of the bishop. The time had long since passed when canons had been responsible merely for helping the bishop, in spiritual matters, in the celebration of liturgical services, and in the temporal domain, in the administration of the diocese.

Finally, it is worth noting the often very high number of canons. There were as many as seventy-two at Chartres and at Santiago de Compostela, sixty at Nevers and at Noyon, and fifty at Auxerre. The usual figure lay somewhere between thirty and forty but might at times, towards the end of the twelfth century, become even more inflated. At Lyon, there were ultimately as many as eighty-four canons.

One may readily understand, therefore, the substantial building programmes embarked upon in this period, which should be related to the reorganisation of chapters and the restoration of places of worship. No diocesan capital would seem to have been unaffected by a renovation of this sort. In the eleventh century, the bishop would have been responsible for such a decision, and he would have both reformed the chapter and undertaken substantial building work there, even assuming overall responsibility for it. Thus, at Angoulême, under Bishop Gérard (1101–36), Itier Archambaud built a dormitory, a refectory, a storeroom and some gateways. At Le Mans, Hildebert of Lavardin (1096–1125) embarked upon the building of the chapter-house. At Maguelonne, Gautier built the tower of Saint-Sépulcre, the storeroom, the refectory and dormitory; his successor, Raymond (1133–46), was responsible for the precinct, which featured wash-rooms and a mill. At Rouen, Guillaume Bonne-Ame (1071–1110) restored the canons' residence. At Cimiez, Bishop Pierre marked out an area to the south of the cathedral, as we have already seen, which was to serve as the precinct. At Vienne, it was a layman, Altar, a doctor by profession, who was responsible, around 1050, for the embellishment of the canons' residences.

In the twelfth century, the chapters would seem to have taken their own destinies in hand, and to have rejected episcopal interference. In 1112, the chapter of Orléans was authorised by the king to build houses against the city walls, which would be made of stone and wood, but it was denied the right to make a breach in this same wall. In 1127, the same chapter came into possession of 'Tanuz' square, together with the authorisation to install a gate in the town wall, and to rest whatever constructions were necessary against it.

Archaeology merely serves to reinforce the impression one gains from studying the documentary sources. The canonial precincts underwent substantial modifications in the course of this period, being either merely renovated, expanded or even shifted. All such operations involved addressing the delicate issue of terrain, in a town whose fabric was just then shrinking in a characteristic fashion. Where expansion was concerned, all means were deemed acceptable. Thus, at Le Mans, Bishop Gervais (d. 1047) gave the canons his father's *aula*, which stood in the eastern corner of the city, together with all the adjoining plots of land on either side of the enceinte. Analysis of plans drawn up prior to the Revolution serves to show just how varied were the positions of such plots, because it was always difficult to purchase land in the built-up areas around cathedrals. The canonial precinct would therefore often be highly irregular in shape.

A written source survives to this effect regarding what was soon to be known as Saint-Bertrand-de-Comminges. Bertrand of l'Isle-Jourdain, first bishop of what was then known as *Lugdunum Convenarum*, who was enthroned in 1083 and canonised after his death (1123), set out to build a cathedral in the upper town, which was later named after him, and a precinct for the canons. His biographer, Vital, emphasised the difficulties which he had faced: 'Near to the church, he built a cloister, though hampered by the narrowness of the plot and in spite of the sheer nature of the rocks, and he established there a precinct for the canons, who were to lead an ecclesiastical life under the rule of Saint Augustine.' As a consequence, the cloister had to be designed in a very particular fashion, being built to the south of the cathedral, in the middle of the twelfth century. It consisted of only three galleries, the northernmost one having been abandoned in order to gain more space.

The canonial precinct was generally situated on the north or south side, facing the episcopal palace. This opposition had not come about by chance, but was very probably due to both parties wishing to maintain a degree of independence from each other. This geographical division, usually dating from this period, was to have serious consequences, as we shall see below, for the building placed in the middle and for the gates which allowed access to it. There are records, however, of precincts located on the east, in the chevet of the cathedral, and not

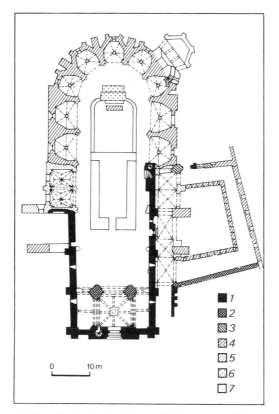

Fig. 65 Plan of the cathedral and cloister of Saint-Bertrand-de-Comminges. 1.
Romanesque period; 2. Second half of the twelfth century; 3. Thirteenth century; 4.
Beginning of the fourteenth century; 5. End of the fourteenth century; 6. Fifteenth
century; 7. Sixteenth century.

solely in collegiate churches, as one might more readily anticipate. These are
chiefly to be found in Imperial domains, for example, in Avignon, Köln,
Hildesheim and Strasburg.

The actual lay-out of the precinct could be as diverse as the various
communities of canons themselves were. It was still a strictly closed space, shut
off by walls which served to define it, and pierced by a reduced number of gates
which were, as we have seen, strictly supervised. This screen, which had
originally been wooden, was now built of stone; it seemed not to have a
defensive character, although one must be circumspect here, since certain
elements had assumed a less civilian appearance. The wall at Viviers, for
example, which has been studied in recent years, was plainly built with defence

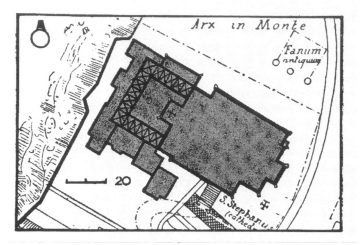

Fig. 66 Mass-plan of the cathedral and eastern cloister of Saint-Etienne of Besançon
(after J. Gauthier).

Fig. 67 The cathedral and eastern cloister of Saint-Etienne of Besançon in 1667,
by J. Gauthier.

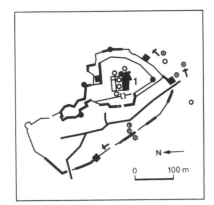

Fig. 68 Plan of Viviers (after Y. Esquieu). 1. The cathedral.

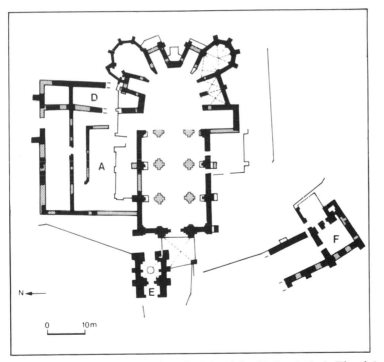

Fig. 69 Plan of the cathedral complex of Viviers (after Y. Esquieu). A. The cloister;
D. The chapter-house; E. The bell-tower; F. The episcopal palace.

in mind. The holy town occupied what the texts call the 'castle' (*castrum*), as opposed to the lay town (*civitas*), a spur which overlooked the Rhône on one side and the town on the other. To this natural defence a second, artificial line of defence was added. A bell-tower still survives, in front of the western facade, which is in fact the defensive tower placed at the entrance to the canonial precinct. It was turned into a bell-tower as late as the end of the twelfth century, and raised to the height of 38·5 metres in 1318. Originally, it had been a more or less square building (9·3 metres by 9 metres), 16·6 metres high, with a gate on its eastern side and an annex to the west which served as a porch. This element of material, and essentially passive, defence was matched by one of a spiritual order, for the first floor contained a chapel dedicated to Saint Michel. There are other examples in the south of equally passive and symbolic forms of protection.

A case can be made for differentiating between those precincts which, owing to the presence of a cloister, are perfectly organised, and those which remain inorganic and are characterised by a somewhat anarchic juxtaposition of buildings. The former are less commonplace than the latter, for canons generally refused to sleep in dormitories, especially in the north. A precinct would therefore have to contain a number of small, two-storey houses with gardens. However, at Langres, as early as 1214, we learn of eight such houses located outside the precinct. At the end of the eighteenth century, they were scattered across an area measuring 500 square metres. Shared sites did exist, however, in the eleventh century, and are often referred to in the texts. The most frequently mentioned was the refectory (Amiens, Bourges and Saint-Jean-de-Maurienne). It too would later fall into disuse, however. As in the previous period, communally used places still existed.

It was during this period that what is generally known as a cloister for the particular use of the canons made its first appearance, consisting of galleries and looking out on to a garden. There was a fairly large number of them, most of which were destroyed during the Revolution. Our knowledge of such cloisters derives either from documents or from plans or even from excavations, which have proved an especially valuable source of information.

Cloisters

Cloisters first appeared during the Carolingian period, if the plan of Saint-Gall, drawn up between 816 and 817, is to be trusted, for one can clearly make out, on the flank of the abbey-church, a regular quadrilateral, consisting of four galleries leading by way of arcades into a garden. The success of this arrangement in the context of monastic architecture is well known. Indeed, such cloisters became the crucial element in the lay-out of monasteries, and, if a written description of Saint-Florent at Saumur is reliable, it was deemed perfectly acceptable, from the beginning of the eleventh century, to decorate them. It was in the south, and more particularly in the area around Toulouse, that this sculpted decoration was to become obligatory, at the very end of the eleventh century at Moissac. Links between the abbey and Cluny, forged in the middle of the eleventh century, were instrumental in establishing this interest in decorative art, the success of which was guaranteed by the beginning of the twelfth century (the Daurade of Toulouse). Cluny could not help but look favourably upon the spread of the cloister, for it was a place both for prayer, whether collective or individual, and for the relaxation that a balanced life required; it was also a place of meditation or reading, for books were generally kept in an *armarium* placed in one of the walls. The Gregorian reform favoured the building of cloisters, although no attempt was made to impose them. One may readily understand why the bishops and canons in the south should have wished to repeat, in the shadow of the cathedrals, an architectural form which had proved so successful in the monasteries. Thus, around 1124, Diego Gelmirez took his inspiration for the cloister of his cathedral at Compostela from what he had seen in his travels in France, and placed it in the south-east corner of the transept. Shortly afterwards, numerous other Spanish cathedrals, for example, Gerona or the Seu d'Urgel, featured cloisters. When the cathedral was renovated or rebuilt, during the Gothic period, these cloisters were sometimes preserved (Gerona).

Cloisters had become a feature of French cathedrals at a still earlier date, although, for want of documents, it is difficult to be precise. In the early stages, they were wholly undecorated, save perhaps for some ornamentation of the capitals upon which the galleries rested. This would seem to have been true of the cloister at Viviers, which lay to the north of the cathedral. It consisted of an irregular rectangle measuring 26 metres by 15·6 metres, and was probably a very austere construction. The existence of a cloister must necessarily have entailed a lay-out of the precinct similar to that featured in the monasteries, and subsequently in the Cistercian abbeys. This lay-out took the exigencies of the terrain into account, as we have already noted in the case of Saint-Bertrand-de-Comminges, together with the requirements of the chapter and the financial constraints. Excavations at Viviers have proved especially informative in this respect. The refectory, which was relatively large (25·8 metres by 6·4 metres), extended over the north gallery, while the chapter-house protruded over the east wing. It was there that canons and bishop would meet, and there too they would wash the feet of the poor. The canons' residences were destroyed during the Huguenot sack of the town, in 1567. There was a somewhat similar lay-out at Saint-Bertrand-de-Comminges, where one can readily identify, in the middle of a number of other buildings, the chapter-house. At Avignon, mention is made in 1123 of a chapter-house, a refectory and some dispensaries. The same is true of Arles, Le Puy and many other episcopal sees.

From the end of the eleventh century, particular care was taken with the decoration of the monastic cloisters. The capitals were now carved, and marble plaques featuring figures, as at Moissac, were the rule. In the course of the twelfth century, these forms of decoration were introduced into the canons' cloisters, especially in the south of France. Some of these cloisters have disappeared, and are known to us solely through slabs in museum collections or lapidary storehouses (Avignon, Toulouse). Others have survived in their original context, and with their decoration intact, as at Aix, Arles, Elne, Le Puy, Saint-Lizier or Saint-Bertrand-de-Comminges. One of the largest, the exceptional positioning of which, on the east side, was remarked upon above, was that of Notre-Dame-des-Doms in Avignon. It occupied a surface area of 294·72 square metres, with fifty-two arcades, the capitals and pillars of which were marble. The scenes in the sculptures referred to the life of Christ, but there was also a combined statue and column, featuring a lay figure, who could well have been a benefactor. The dimensions of the cloister at Arles were equally imposing (28 metres by 26 metres), and could vie in this respect with the monastic cloisters. The construction of this cloister, rendered all the more difficult because of subsidence, took a long time. Work on the north gallery had begun around the 1180s, and had continued with the south gallery around the 1220s, being completed in the course of the fourteenth century. Such delays had not jeopardised the iconography, which had remained exceptionally coherent; on the north side were the apostles, on foot, evoking the communal life, together with Saint Trophime and Saint Etienne, the titulars of the cathedral. The cloister at Aix would seem not to have been so ambitious, and it was at any rate less than half the size of those at Avignon or Arles. At first, it had been smaller still, and rectangular in shape, before the western gallery was moved eastwards. However, the extraordinary quality and profusion of the decoration make it one of the most remarkable ensembles. The cloister at Aix, like that at Avignon, features a combined statue and column. The iconographic programme is, however, less clear than the one at Arles, although the north gallery, devoted to the life of Christ, is an exception in this respect. The cloister was very probably built without interruption between 1190 and 1210. At Le Puy, there is an equally impressive number of capitals (154), but the iconographic programme is less sophisticated. Indeed, the majority of capitals are merely decorative. At Elne, the cloister begun by Guillaume Jourdain (1172–80), in marble, with the north gallery, was continued along the west gallery in the course of the thirteenth century. The south and east galleries were completed in the Gothic style. At Saint-Bertrand, it is worth noting the presence, in the western gallery, of a pier formed of four combined statues and columns representing the evangelists. At Toulouse, the cloister leaned against the choir of the cathedral of Saint-Etienne, on the eastern side, and before its destruction featured a particularly remarkable series of carved decorations, which was extended to the portal of the chapter-house, with its ledges and statues of the apostles.

The existence of these sculpted cloisters raises a number of difficulties which have not yet been satisfactorily resolved. It would be wrong to leap to the conclusion that, wherever they are to be found, the clergy had embraced the Gregorian reform and, as a consequence, the communal life. Admittedly, a cloister could not help but facilitate such an existence. Moreover, the inscription engraved upon a capital in the southern gallery of Elne cloister, borrowed in part from the first verse of Psalm 132, celebrates the sweetness of the common life. There are other places, however, where the setbacks of the reform movement are well documented, for example, at Aix, and where the existence of a sculpted cloister therefore cannot be interpreted in these terms.

It is worth enquiring as to the exact dates at which particular architectural elements appeared. It is possible that many galleries, whose decoration suggests a relatively late date, were merely renovated at that time, and that they had been preceded by other, more crudely built versions. Only thus can one account for the building of the cloister at Arles, which seems to have been spread out across a relatively long timespan. It has been claimed that the interruption of the building work was linked to the canons' rebellion against the archbishop in 1194, and that the resumption followed the agreement reached in 1204, after the prelate had declared his readiness to increase the number of canons. The old buildings must have been demolished as progress was made on the site, and a permanent area for prayer thereby guaranteed the canons.

The north of France lacks such remarkable ensembles, for the communal life was rejected virtually everywhere, whereas the south, as we have seen, was far more receptive to the Gregorian reform. Furthermore, it was in southern regions, for example, in Italy and in Spain, that decorated cloisters were successful, as the most spectacular example, that of Gerona, proves. In spite of the rebuilding of cathedrals in the Gothic period, the canons tried to preserve the Romanesque buildings, not least because they boasted highly coherent iconographic cycles.

England

In England, the existence of regular canonial chapters imposed a markedly different lay-out upon the precincts. The Norman Conquest did not represent a wholly new start, since Canterbury, Winchester and Worcester had already been organised in that fashion. However, with the Conquest, the formula prevailed everywhere. Thus, in 1130, eight dioceses were granted a regular chapter, four being endowed with both a regular and a secular chapter. This is why the holy town seemed so surprisingly large by comparison with contemporary French sources. Buildings satisfying the needs of communal life were huge, whereas, once the chapter had embraced the reform, canons' residences ceased to exist altogether. Life within such institutions had a curiously monastic quality to it, for it was profoundly autarchic, as much in religious as in financial terms. This accounts for the isolation of the cathedral within the town, an isolation which has lasted up until the present day and which offers the astonishing spectacle of 'cathedrals in the country'. The buildings which made up the cathedral precinct merely reinforced this impression, in part because of their number, which had risen significantly as the body of monks had increased. At Rochester, for example, such buildings increased in number from fifty to sixty. The new monarch could not help but favour such a development.

At Canterbury, where Lanfranc had been appointed archbishop (1070), having previously been prior at Le Bec and abbot at Saint-Etienne of Caen, there can be no mistaking the concern to draw closer to monasticism. Within this town, the kernel of which dated back to Antiquity, Lanfranc decided to found a genuine monastery. In order to obtain the land which such a foundation required, and which was ultimately to cover almost a quarter of the ancient town, Lanfranc was forced to raze a whole district, destroying twenty-seven houses in the process. The 'holy town' was surrounded by its own enclosing wall, which enclosed the cathedral – the plan for which had been inspired by that of the abbey-church of Caen, ninety metres long – the archbishop's palace and the monastery, which lay further to the north. As was so often the case, a large number of buildings were then rebuilt, early in the thirteenth century, but a sufficient number of elements from the earlier period, together with a valuable drawing of the detailed working of the hydraulic system, allow us to form a clear idea of this ambitious project. Lanfranc had envisaged a precinct inhabited by 150 monks.

Circumstances in Norwich were similar. The bishopric of East Anglia had been founded in 1094, in a city whose economy was flourishing. To provide space for new construction, many buildings had to be demolished. In order to build his own castle, William the Conqueror had been obliged to raze some ninety-eight houses. Likewise, Herbert, the new bishop, bought a large part of the town, destroyed the existing houses and then built his cathedral, together with 'three large lodging-houses for the monks' (Robert of Torigni). The cloister, which was rebuilt at a later date, ran along the south flank of the cathedral; in the middle of the east gallery stood the chapter-house, which had been designed as an aisle culminating in a semi-circle. Several buildings survive from this period. At Ely, for example, to the south of the cathedral, the infirmary still stands.

The most original feature of the English ecclesiastical architecture of this period was its chapter-house. In the abbeys, it had been the practice of abbot and monks to meet daily in such rooms, not only for prayer but also to decide upon the activities for the day. The whole monastery would attend such meetings, with lay brothers remaining outside, in the cloister gallery. In episcopal architecture, whether in France or in England, such buildings had been relatively modest in size. In England, at the beginning of the twelfth century, chapter-houses were greatly expanded, as well as being redesigned. The new formula, featuring a chapter-house with centred plan, would seem to have been pioneered at Worcester, around 1110–15. As is well known, architects of the Gothic period were to use the design to good effect.

THE EPISCOPAL SCHOOLS

We have noted that the Carolingians wished every episcopal city to have a school, where young clerics, notorious for their lack of culture, might be trained. These institutions enjoyed only a moderate degree of success, and many of them survived only a short time. The point, however, was taken. Thus, in the Empire, Heinrich the Fowler, founder of the Saxon dynasty, adopted the same policy, surrounding himself with learned clerics and educated bishops, themselves capable of training clerics and of founding episcopal schools. Such traditions were maintained more successfully there than in areas further to the west. It should be noted, moreover, that the kings of Germany allied themselves with the bishops against the lay aristocracy, continuing to entrust the administration of the towns to them. The most brilliant schools were therefore located in episcopal palaces in a number of towns in Lotharingia and Franconia, for example, Trèves, Köln, Liège, Mainz, Worms, Wurtzburg, Speyer, Bamberg, Magdeburg, and Hildesheim. Verdun, Metz and Toul would seem to have been more modest centres, yet they were to play an important part in the revival of studies. Italy basked in the reflected glory of the Carolingian achievement, as for example at Ravenna or Rome. In France, intellectual life was still moribund. The only centre of any significance was Reims, which was anyway linked to the Carolingian tradition. It was there that Abbon of Fleury was trained. New lustre was added to the reputation of Reims by the presence, in the middle of the tenth century, of Flodoard, a prestige that was further enhanced by the arrival at the end of the century of Gerbert of Aurillac, later Pope Sylvester II. It was to remain an important centre up until the twelfth century, but had increasingly to reckon with the rivalry of the monasteries and crucially, from the eleventh century, with that of Chartres.

In this domain, as in so many others, there was clearly a shift from the Carolingian centres to others, that were now more innovatory. Chartres may be taken as a characteristic instance of this renewal, for it was to become one of the greatest intellectual centres of the period. As Pierre Riché has been at such pains to emphasise, 'if the monastic city represented the past, the town represented the future'. The development of urban space was to establish the optimal conditions for intellectual life. 'Town air makes one free', as the famous adage put it, and it did indeed liberate the mind. The crucial event at Chartres was the arrival of an Italian cleric, born in the vicinity of Rome, who had attended Gerbert's courses at Reims (984), before going to Chartres to study medicine (992). Fulbert soon became head of the school, with the title of *écolâtre*, and later bishop (1016). His influence was such that the greatest minds of the period flocked to study with him, and his disciples regularly likened him to Socrates. Yves, Bishop of Chartres (1090–1116) was also trained there. The reader will recall the important part which he played in the implementation of the Gregorian reform. Intellectual life was equally intense in the twelfth century, the rediscovery of Plato and his *Timaeus*, a work which was to have a lasting impact upon contemporary thought, being an event of the greatest significance. Neo-platonism made particular progress owing to the efforts of, among others, Bernard, who ran the episcopal school between 1116 and 1119, later becoming chancellor (1119–24). He too endeavoured to reconcile the thought of Plato with that of Aristotle. His brother, Thierry, appointed master in 1121, was responsible for the creation of the famous *Heptateuchon*, which was divided into the *trivium* and the *quadrivium*. He sought to reconcile intelligence and faith, his aim being to identify Platonic correspondences within the Christian dogmas. He engaged Abélard in debate, accusing him of having paid undue attention to intelligence, and of having consequently neglected the truths of faith. This debate in fact marks the moment at which Chartres went into decline, and Paris began to take its place.

There were other episcopal schools, but none was so famous internationally as Chartres. The Gregorian reform could not help but foster such schools, and numerous charters therefore featured a subscription for *écolâtres*, for example, at Cambrai, Rennes, Le Puy, Béziers, Albi, Cahors, Poitiers, Noyon and Le Mans. They were designed to give young clerics the necessary training in exegesis, liturgy and grammar. In some of these centres, a portion of the chapter's income was set aside to pay for the upkeep of the teachers, and for their fees. This was the case at Clermont, Liège and Albi. The influence exerted by such institutions was invariably linked to the personality at their head, with some enjoying merely a fleeting existence while others served to found a tradition. Thus, at Laon, Saint Anselm had revived the study of the Bible by gathering together earlier exegeses into the 'ordinary gloss'. One should not of course ascribe the whole of the intellectual upheaval of the twelfth century to the influence of these episcopal schools, but it must be allowed that they almost everywhere played a part in it, that they sometimes even led it, and that without a doubt they attracted the most brilliant clerics.

Although our knowledge of the material resources of these schools is incomplete, there is no doubt that they were generally very rudimentary. In France at any rate, teaching took place as a rule within the precinct. Since such teaching was chiefly based upon the gloss, it was vital to have a library close at hand. It is hard to judge just how many books such libraries contained, but, by contrast with the monasteries – where collections had been accumulated over the generations, and where the *scriptorium* had added still further to the stock – there cannot have been a very large number. An eleventh-century catalogue from Paris mentions 150 books, many of which were in fact profane.

I ought, however, to draw the reader's attention to the siting of the school at Châlons outside the precinct, a circumstance which was still unusual in the twelfth century, when it is first mentioned in the documents, but which became commonplace subsequently.

THE HÔTELS-DIEU

The repeated injunction to the bishops, during the Carolingian period, to succour the needy must have taken on a new meaning after the Gregorian reform. As we have already observed, the division of responsibilities defined during this period was gradually put into effect. In the course of the tenth century or, where the process had not been completed, in the eleventh, the canons became responsible for the running of the hôtel-Dieu. There are numerous testimonies to this effect, through the length and breadth of France, from Grenoble to Sens. At Angoulême (1063), very precise conditions governed the canons' responsibility for *hospitalitas*. One should bear in mind that, as we have already observed upon several different occasions, it was the bishop's initiative that was of crucial importance here. At Nevers, the hospital founded by Hériman benefited in 1074 from a legacy bequeathed by Bishop Hugues, for the care of pilgrims and widows suffering in the house of God. In 1080, the bishop made a large donation to the chapter, for the building of a hôtel-Dieu. At Cambrai, Bishop Gérard II was responsible for the renovation of the paupers' hospital. At Orléans, Dean Etienne of Garlande was the founder of a similar institution, whereas at Paris Bishop Renaud (1006) decided to make a gift of the second part of the hôtel-Dieu, the first part of which already belonged to the chapter.

It is unfortunately no easy matter to map more precisely these *intra muros* charitable institutions, the upkeep of which was the canons' responsibility. It would seem that in this domain, as in so many others, the north was more favoured than the south. Indeed, each diocese was very probably endowed with a hôtel-Dieu, although its size and importance might well vary. Where some sort of topographic information is available to us, it seems clear that there was almost always a cathedral in the vicinity. We saw in our treatment of the Carolingian period why this should have been the case, namely, that the charitable works which were every canon's obligation could be more easily performed if those deserving of succour were in close proximity. It is probable that, when many 'holy towns' were built, the desired or existing site gave rise to many difficulties. When Angoulême hôtel-Dieu was brought back into operation, in 1063, it was relocated in front of the canonial precinct (1097); the realisation of such a project must have caused problems in topographic terms, but there is no trace of them in the surviving documentation.

Although our information as regards the buildings themselves is equally scanty, the techniques employed in their construction clearly underwent a significant change. Prior to this date, they had been built of timber, a perishable material if ever there was one. The twelfth century, which saw so many changes of a more general nature, also witnessed the replacement of wood with stone. It is not easy to discern the various stages of the process, but it would seem to have affected the hall first of all, before being extended to the other buildings, some of which were still built of wood at a very late date. At Le Mans, the residence for the use of older monks and nuns was partly built of stone (probably the ground-floor), partly of wood (the first floor).

The scale of a hôtel-Dieu would seem to have been directly related to the importance of the diocese; some of them appear already to have been large, because of the aspirations of the bishop responsible for founding them. At Nîmes, where the hôtel-Dieu was founded in 1080, records mention not only the *mansio elemosinaria* (*elemosina*: alms), that is, the hall, but also the different rooms set aside for the reception of the poor, the pilgrims or the sick.

One may readily appreciate that it began to seem increasingly hard to run such institutions, for they required both substantial sums of money and a permanent staff. Indeed, some canons became specialists in certain areas. In Paris, for example, the chancellor was responsible for the hiring of such experts.

4

Gothic construction

✦

THE GOTHIC WORLD

The fourth decade of the twelfth century would seem to represent a turning-point in the history of form, for it was then that the western facade of the abbey-church of Saint-Denis was finished, and the first stone of its chevet laid. This stylistic revolution, which affected architecture as deeply as it did sculpture, stained glass and the decorative arts, was accompanied by a number of other, equally important, shifts of emphasis.

First of all, the general framework had altered. Where Romanesque art was mainly situated outside the cities, having its chief impact in the monasteries, Gothic art was primarily urban, and found expression in the cathedrals. The movement which arose in the dioceses around Paris, in the second half of the twelfth century, was to continue and to be extended, in the course of the thirteenth century, to the periphery, so as to exert an influence upon neighbouring countries, whether England, the Empire or Spain. The revival of the cathedrals and Gothic art were so closely linked that it is hard to imagine one without the other. We think of abbey-churches as Romanesque, and cathedrals as Gothic. The rebuilding of the cathedrals was to result in the development of projects that were on a truly gigantic scale, in terms of height and length and width. In this regard, the Gothic world heeded the early church, which had likewise been prepared to contemplate ambitious schemes. There had, admittedly, been remarkably large buildings in the Carolingian and Romanesque periods, but they had been the exception rather than the rule. In the Gothic period, however, largescale buildings

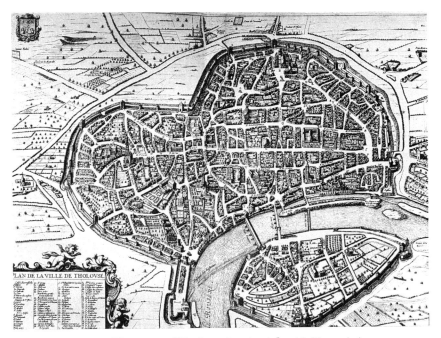

Fig. 70 The town of Toulouse in 1631 (after M. Tavernier).
Paris, Bibliothèque nationale.

sprang up everywhere, a phenomenon which is admittedly not easy to account for, but which may have been no more than a response to changing needs.

As is so often the case, the reasons advanced for such changes, in this area as in so many others, seem reductive, insofar as they invoke a materialist conception which is inappropriate here. This tendency should in fact be related to the condition of cities as they were then: the urban boom was fully evident to those who lived through it. How could it have been otherwise? In the space of a few generations, formerly deserted towns had become densely inhabited. This spectacular growth was felt at the time to be potentially limitless. Between 1000 and 1328, the population of the kingdom of France is reckoned to have doubled. It is invariably a delicate matter to hazard a precise figure, but numbers would seem to have risen from 6 million to 13·5 million. It is important to note that towns benefited far more from such increases than did the rural areas, and that the urban population would seem in fact to have tripled. This was a fairly widespread phenomenon, which was still more pronounced in the north, and which had a number of immediate consequences. Thus, the city walls, which

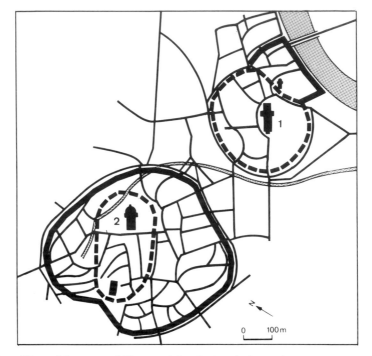

Fig. 71 Plan of the town of Limoges (after P. Lavedan). 1. The ancient city and the cathedral; 2. The borough and abbey-church of Saint-Martial.

had survived from Antiquity, and which had sheltered the population up until that time, were no longer large enough to hold it. The suburbs grew so rapidly that the original town was soon submerged. New city ramparts had to be raised, and these became particularly massive during the thirteenth century. With their rigid high walls, they enveloped the various suburbs and so reunited the town. This drastic reordering served to move the holy town away from the centre, so that it was no longer an important part of the urban territory. Such changes could not be said to constitute a marginalisation; it was simply that the relation between town and 'holy town' was from then on based on new criteria. The image of the town was by the same token profoundly altered.

The town may itself have expanded, but contemporaries were struck by what they saw as a shrinking in the distance between the chief monuments. Indeed, the cathedral and the count's castle, which had originally stood at opposite ends of the city, now seemed disturbingly close to each other. This was plainly the case with Paris, but the same was true – even if the evidence has generally disappeared – of numerous other towns, for example, Chartres, Laon and Rouen.

Fig. 72 Plan of the town of Arras (after P. Lavedan). 1. The ancient city and the cathedral; 2. The borough and the abbey-church of Saint-Vaast.

The ancient city was thus regarded as being designed to house great monuments, and its symbolism was further reinforced by changes taking place in this period. The suburbs, as economic activity there grew more intense, were becoming active and dynamic centres. Town-plans record this shift quite clearly, as Toulouse acquired the suburb of Saint-Sernin, Tours, that of Saint–Martin, Limoges, that of Saint–Martial, and Arras, that of Saint-Vaast. There plainly was a risk, perceived as such by contemporaries, of marginalisation. A

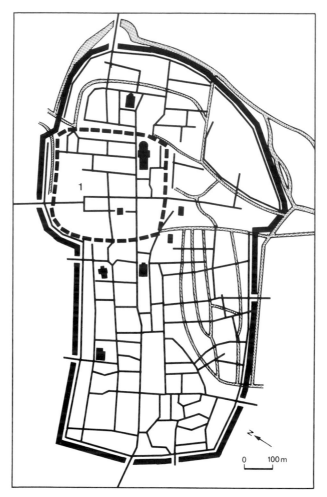

Fig. 73 Plan of the town of Troyes (after P. Lavedan).
1. The ancient city and the cathedral.

final reason for the building of monuments on a larger scale may perhaps be advanced: new conditions were increasingly incompatible with the ancient city, and the need was felt to respond to changed circumstances by erecting an edifice whose dimensions would impress. A cathedral served to dominate the town, and was without question the most powerful image known to its inhabitants. Finally, it should be emphasised that the building of the medieval ramparts was not necessarily contemporary with the construction of the cathedral; generally

Fig. 74 Plan of the town of Metz (after F. L. Ganshof). 1. The ancient city and the cathedral (A); 2. The town circa 1150; 3. The town prior to 1329; 4. The town prior to 1444.

they came later. The demolition of the old city walls was therefore not precipitated by the erection of the new.

The new structure of the town clearly established a religious and urban bipolarity. The importance, as much physical as spiritual, of the abbey-church, around which the new agglomeration revolved, risked fostering rivalries. The institutional relation was not so much cordial as strained, and it is this that

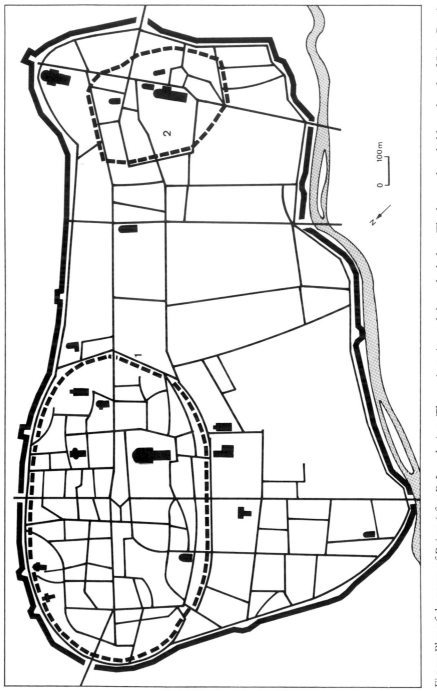

Fig. 75 Plan of the town of Reims (after P. Lavedan). 1. The ancient city and the cathedral; 2. The borough and abbey-church of Saint-Remi.

EVREVX.

Fig. 76 The town of Evreux (after Mérian).

Fig. 77 The town of Narbonne (after Mérian).

163

Fig. 78 The town of Orléans (after Mérian).

Fig. 79 The town of Rouen (after Mérian).

164

Fig. 80 The town of Sens (after Mérian).

Fig. 81 The town of Nevers (after Mérian).

explains why many towns hesitated over which seal to choose, with some keeping the silhouette of the abbey-church, which thus served as a pendant to the count's castle (Toulouse), while others opted for that of the cathedral (Bayonne).

One should also take account of the motives of those responsible for commissioning the edifices, who very probably wished to give still larger scope to their ambition, while at the same time fostering civic pride. Both a resident's and a stranger's perception of the town could thus be overturned by its recentring around a major building, which was felt to be a unifying factor in an increasingly fragmented urban reality. By these means, the cathedral might once more enjoy a highly symbolic position within these thriving towns.

The building of a cathedral had serious repercussions for towns in the Gothic period, first of all because the advent of such edifices was so sudden that it disrupted the pattern of the already existing buildings, secondly, because the size of the ground-plan had a strong impact upon the existing monuments and upon the urban fabric. The shock wave sometimes travelled very far before dying away. As a consequence, monuments were in many cases rebuilt, while old thoroughfares were suppressed and new ones created. In short, the religious quarter was thoroughly restructured.

Salisbury

To appreciate just how ambitious a Gothic project might be, we need to consider a newly founded episcopal town. As chance would have it, thirteenth-century England furnishes us with a unique example, one which gives us some idea of a prelate's ambition in such circumstances.

In 1219, Bishop Richard Poor was authorised by the pope to move his bishopric from Sarum to Salisbury. Since the land was his own, he had a free hand in the planning of the new town. It was divided into two sections, virtually identical in area, the episcopal city and the lay city. The episcopal city, situated within the close, lay to the south, in the southern part of which stood the episcopal palace; to the north were the individual canons' residences, which stood at a radius of 120 metres from the building, so as to be out of its shadow. The lay town, the other area mapped out by Bishop Poor, immediately prospered, as the creation of three parishes, Saint Thomas's, Saint Justin's and Saint Edmund's, proves. Royal permission to hold a market and a fair made Salisbury even wealthier. Closer analysis of the original ground-plan suggests that much thought had gone into it, for it consisted of a trapezium measuring

Fig. 82 The town of Soissons (after Mérian).

Fig. 83 The town of Troyes (after Mérian).

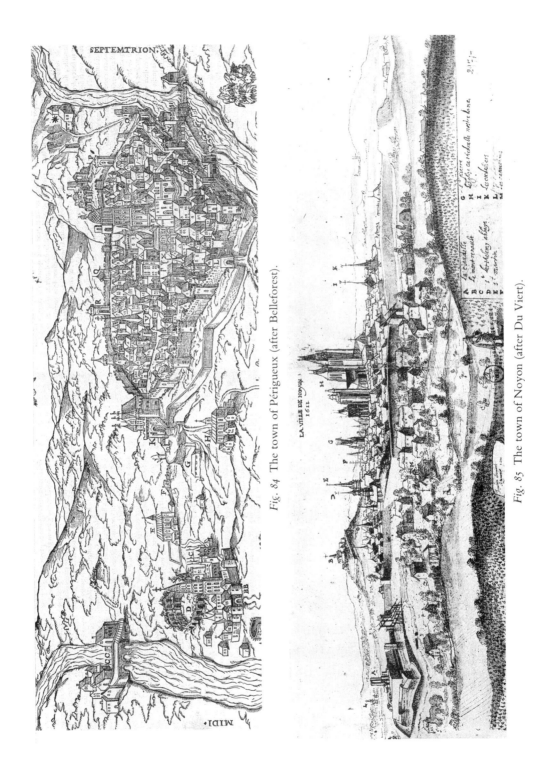

Fig. 84 The town of Périgueux (after Belleforest).

Fig. 85 The town of Noyon (after Du Viert).

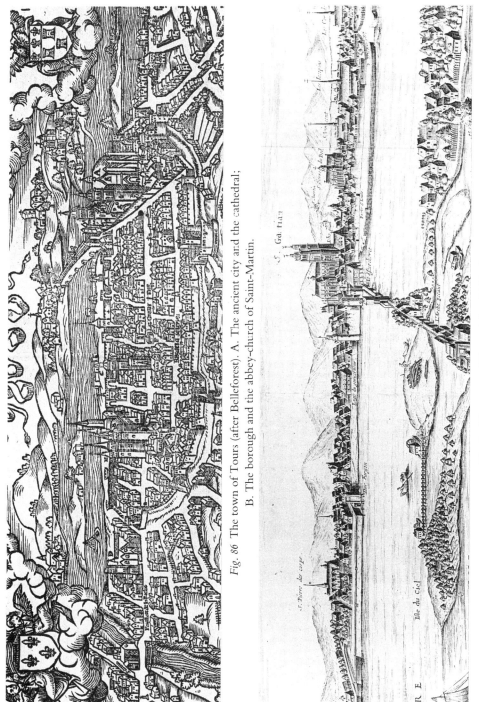

Fig. 86 The town of Tours (after Belleforest). A. The ancient city and the cathedral;
B. The borough and the abbey-church of Saint-Martin.

Fig. 87 The town of Tours (after Mérian).

169

Fig. 88 The town of Tours after Dumachy (1787).

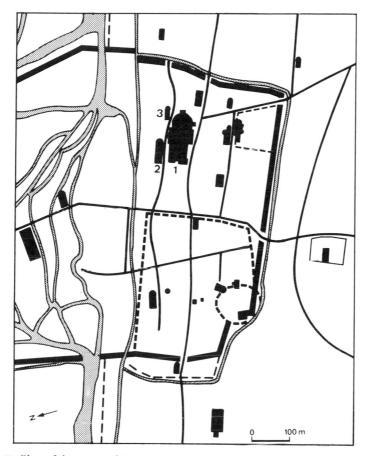

Fig. 89 Plan of the town of Amiens circa 1250 (after Guillerme). 1. The cathedral; 2. Saint-Firmin; 3. The palace.

440 by 675 by 850 metres, enclosing a surface area of 50 hectares, divided into blocks. Furthermore, the positioning of the constituent elements had not been left to chance. Thus, the main roadway served to link the market-place, which occupied a block lying between Saint Martin's and the town hall, and the cathedral. Indeed, the ground-plan of the holy town in Salisbury was one of the most regular of the period, as regards both the edifice itself, the cloister situated to the south and the chapter-house located on the eastern gallery.

The case of Salisbury is unique, as I have already noted, and reflects both a general tendency and something uniquely English. One of the characteristic features, already fairly pronounced in the earlier period, was the decision to isolate the holy town. This led to the creation of the close, which obviously

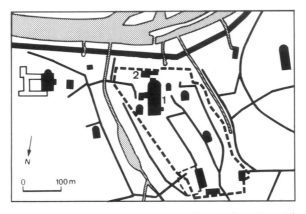

Fig. 90 Plan of the town of Auxerre circa 1250 (after Guillerme). 1. The cathedral;
2. The palace.

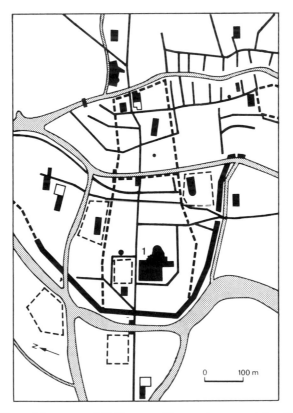

Fig. 91 Plan of the town of Châlons-sur-Marne, circa 1250 (after Guillerme).
1. The cathedral.

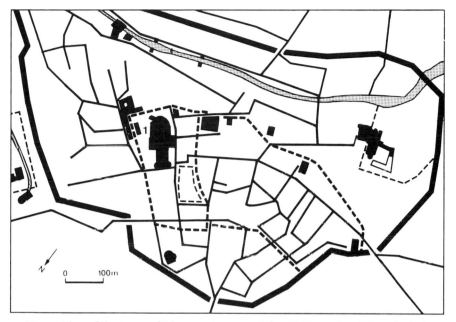

Fig. 92 Plan of the town of Chartres circa 1250 (after Guillerme). 1. The cathedral.

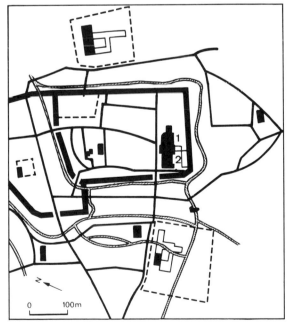

Fig. 93 Plan of the town of Evreux circa 1250 (after Guillerme).
1. The cathedral; 2. The palace.

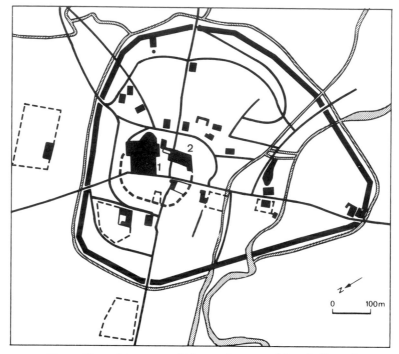

Fig. 94 Plan of the town of Noyon circa 1250 (after Guillerme).
1. The cathedral; 2. The palace.

served to emphasise the clearcut separation between holy town and town, the link between the two being established by the cathedral, in which the whole of the Christian community of the diocese, clerical and lay, assembled. The holy town existed in close union with its bishop, creating a unity which was ultimately to become an autarchy. This offered the communal life of the canons some protection. All of these arrangements would have a number of repercussions for both the internal and the external treatment of the religious buildings, as we shall shortly see. Externally, a new conception of the facade arose; internally, various spaces came to be treated in a new fashion. The English cathedrals should therefore be distinguished in many respects from those built in Latin countries, and not long afterwards in the Empire, which were characterised by close links between the urban fabric and the cathedral.

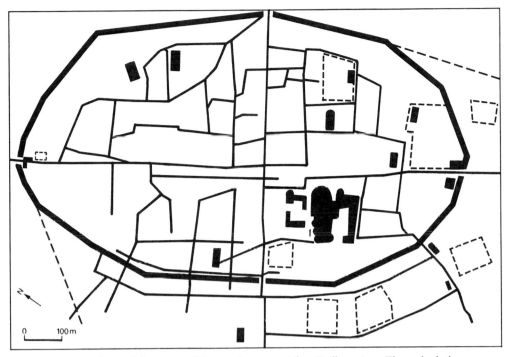

Fig. 95 Plan of the town of Reims circa 1250 (after Guillerme). 1. The cathedral.

The gigantic cathedrals

As the cathedrals were rebuilt in the Gothic style, they came to assume truly gigantic proportions. The phenomenon may have begun on the Ile de France, but in the course of the thirteenth century it affected every Christian country, including England, where builders had been predisposed since the Norman Conquest to build on a large scale, southern France, Spain, the Empire and even Italy (Firenze, Siena and Milano). This development assumed a particularly striking form in northern France. The surface area occupied by the cathedrals provided compelling proof of this fact, with the plot measuring 5,500 square metres in Paris, 6,200 square metres in Bourges, 6,650 square metres in Reims, 8,000 square metres in Amiens and 8,900 square metres in Köln. The other dimensions of such monuments were no less gigantic. Thus, although observers have always been most impressed by the vaults of Beauvais cathedral, which are forty-eight metres high, there is statistical evidence for an equally impressive increase in the size of the transepts. The external dimensions are no less striking, although the frequent absence of spires, which have either disappeared or else

175

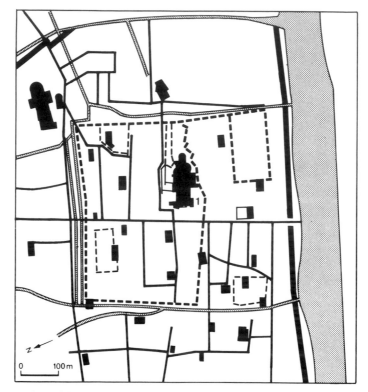

Fig. 96 Plan of the town of Rouen circa 1250 (after Guillerme). 1. The cathedral.

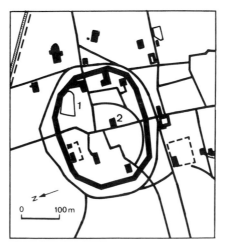

Fig. 97 Plan of the town of Senlis circa 1250 (after Guillerme). 1. The cathedral; 2.
The hôtel-Dieu.

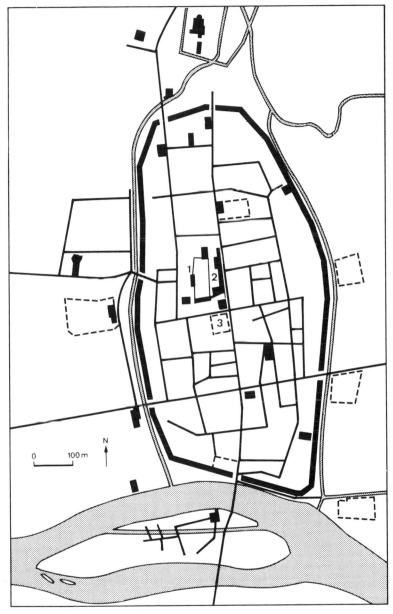

Fig. 98 Plan of the town of Sens circa 1250 (after Guillerme). 1. The cathedral; 2.
The palace; 2. The hôtel-Dieu.

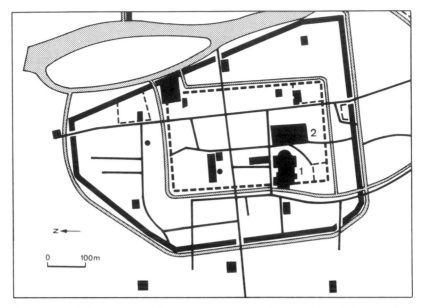

Fig. 99 Plan of the town of Soissons circa 1250 (after Guillerme). 1. The cathedral; 2. The hôtel-Dieu.

were never built, means that our calculations are necessarily arbitrary. While conquest of the skies only involved technological problems, the tackling of the ground-plan posed difficulties, the importance of which has only very recently been appreciated. Solutions to a wide range of unanticipated problems were invariably arrived at, and these bear witness to the remarkable ingenuity displayed by the architects in coming to grips with the existing structures. What has since become a banal reality was at the time a genuine novelty.

The organisation of the site

Before trying to weigh up the impact of such constructions, I shall try, in the light of recent, pioneering studies, to evoke the manner in which the site was organised. As today, the first step was to define one's programme; the second stage involved the choice of architect and the third, the choice of a plan. A project concerned the monument as a whole, and not merely one particular element. In other words, once a scheme had been decided upon, all of the various people involved, whether clerics, bishop, canons, laymen or architect, would have a clear idea of the probable consequences. In topographic terms, for example, no one disputed the fact that, for the successful implementation of a project, much would depend upon demolition programmes and upon town-planning.

Yet we cannot help but be struck by the characteristic indifference displayed by those who took such decisions. Indeed, it was as if they tended to leave it to their successors to tackle problems as and when they arose, their own concern being simply to address those which were most pressing. To appreciate the scale of the difficulty, we have to bear in mind that medieval religious sites differed in one crucial respect from modern ones, whether civil or military. Our technology necessitates a complete clearing of the terrain, with our machines being deployed once there is a *tabula rasa*, and profound knowledge of the subsoil. In the Middle Ages, however, the ground was never completely cleared of the previous place of worship, which was actually destroyed as progress was made on the site, bay by bay, element by element. The stonemasons were capable in this respect of truly remarkable feats, which are only discernible to us after we have subjected the monument to close scrutiny. If demolition followed construction, it was because it was deemed vital not to interrupt worship. Rites could be moved from one spot to another within the monument, but they could never leave it. Care had therefore to be taken to ensure that work on the site did not disturb religious ceremonies. From the start, the clergy were aware that they would have to hold services inside sites which would invariably be in existence for longer than had at first been anticipated.

The building works were therefore separated off from the area reserved for worship by a temporary screen, examples of which have actually survived until very recently. Consider the case of Köln. For those generations which had some experience of such huge sites, there was something truly monumental about the image of the cathedral, as I shall try to show. In the second half of the twelfth century, and the first half of the thirteenth century, such edifices would seem to have been divided into two parts, consisting of two opposed elements. The first element, generally the choir, was conceived on a gigantic scale, and was Gothic in style; the second element, the nave, looked small, cramped, obscure and inappropriate. So imposing was its mass that the choir overwhelmed the nave, which was therefore condemned both physically and intellectually. Even today, at Beauvais cathedral, one may readily discern an equally curious contrast between the thirteenth-century choir, whose style was extended to the transept in the fifteenth and early sixteenth century, and the nave, which belongs to the late tenth and early eleventh century, and is aptly known by the name of 'Lower Works'. The situation is less clearcut at Le Mans, because the eleventh-century

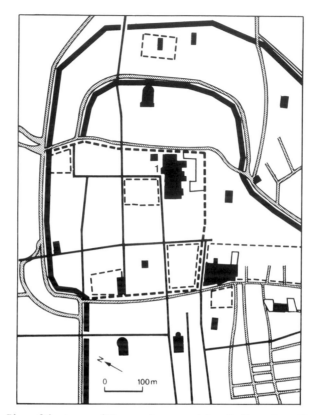

Fig. 100 Plan of the town of Troyes circa 1250 (after Guillerme). 1. The cathedral.

nave was possessed of more majestic proportions, and one has to use one's imagination if one is to grasp that the same situation applied in the cathedrals of northern France, at Paris, Laon, Chartres, Bourges and Reims. At all of these sites, clerics, foremen and congregations were faced with similar brutal distortions of scale in their monuments. For the best part of a century, this image was a familiar one throughout northern France; to such an extent, indeed, that this was what a town was assumed to look like.

The crossing of the ancient wall to the east

As a rule, the building of cathedrals, and also of a fair number of other religious buildings, was begun from the east side, that is, from the presbytery. There are, however, many exceptions to this rule, the most illustrious being Amiens, a case that is fairly difficult to account for. There were other instances, however,

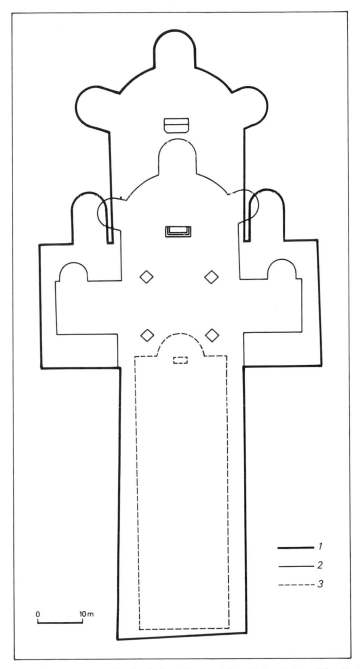

Fig. 101 The sequence of cathedrals at Rouen (after G. Lanfry). 1. The Gothic cathedral; 2. The Romanesque cathedral; 3. The original cathedral.

Toulouse among them. Work was begun on the eastern side for a number of different reasons, foremost among them the fact that it was common sense to do so. A second factor was the religious significance of the presbytery, the place in which the daily miracle of turning the bread and the wine into the body and blood of Christ was performed. This sacred place was the object of the most particular attentions. Thirdly, the terrain to the east was invariably free of structures, and it was therefore easier to commence building on that side. Many cathedrals had been built in close proximity to the ancient city walls, and therefore all the land to the east of the chevet and as far as the walls was usually the undisputed property of the clergy. Beyond the walls, the land was privately owned, and usually on a lower level. This situation did not favour construction, and there was anyway an obligation to preserve a ramp. Both sponsors and architects could thus envisage an extension towards the east. One merely had to obtain authorisation from the king, where one expected to touch the walls, to build in the moats or on the ramp. Walls, moats and ramp were in fact supposed to belong to the king, even though their maintenance was now by and large the bishop's responsibility. Since towns had already spread far beyond the walls, and had so overwhelmed them that their usefulness was no longer apparent, it was not hard to obtain such authorisation.

Royal authorisations are of the utmost value to us in our attempts to date work carried out on monuments, often a delicate matter. Thus, at Troyes, Bishop Hervé had the ancient wall demolished, and then, in October 1208, had to request Chrétien le Pécheur to move a communal oven so as to make room for the axial chapel of the chevet, which was dedicated to Our Lady. In return he was offered another plot, which was adjacent to the hall of the episcopal palace. At Le Mans, the crossing of the city walls was to prove, legally speaking, somewhat complicated. Philippe Auguste had given Bishop Maurice permission. In November 1217, he informed Queen Bérengère, wife of Richard I Lion Heart, that he had given the canons authorisation both to build and to close the moats running alongside the canons' precinct. This would seem not to have sufficed, for in 1221 it proved necessary to purchase a plot located within the chevet.

Other such agreements must have been reached, but no written evidence for them has survived. One of the earliest crossings, if not the earliest, was effected at Noyon. The chevet was built, outside the city walls, from 1145 to 1150 onwards. A number of towns then followed suit, Senlis a little later, Paris during the 1160s, then Bourges, Angers, Tours, Nantes and Köln. The sequence would seem to have been somewhat different at Limoges. From the discovery in the

Fig 102 Limoges cathedral: the chevet and the bell-tower, after a photograph from the photographic archives.

nave, in the nineteenth century, of a wall which may well have been the ancient city wall, we may conclude that the crossing was effected in Roman times. This was, however, an exception.

When the cathedral was too far away from the moats, it proved necessary to acquire the plot of land located on the chevet of the edifice. There were difficulties at Châlons, however, because of the presence of a church dedicated to Saint Sauveur and to Saint Nicolas, which had been consecrated by Bishop Roger III in 1076. Around 1200, the chapter set about demolishing this church, in order to clear the land for construction. A lengthy law-suit ensued, which resulted in the merging of the two chapters of Saint-Nicolas and La Trinité. Events assumed a less dramatic turn at Meaux, but there too they demonstrated just how difficult it was to alter the original plan of the chevet. When the Gothic cathedral had first been conceived, in the twelfth century, provision had been made for only three radiating chapels opening out on to the ambulatory. This at any rate is the plan which features in Villard of Honnecourt's famous notebook, a drawing which dates from the first half of the thirteenth century. At the beginning of the fourteenth century, the decision was taken to add two more

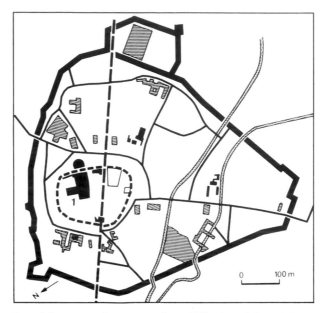

Fig. 103 Plan of the town of Noyon in the Middle Ages (after M. Laporte). 1. The
ancient city and the cathedral.

chapels, on either side of the axial chapel. Since the land belonged to the town
rather than to the church, Bishop Simon Festu saw fit to put his case before the
pope. Papal involvement forced the king's hand and, in 1317, Philippe V
released the land for the south chapel. In 1322, Charles IV yielded the land that
was required for the building of a second chapel, to the north.

By extending the monument to the east, it was possible to preserve the chevet
of the old edifice while the new one was under construction. Demolition
generally only occurred when the new chevet could be used as a place of
worship. The condemned building would then be razed. The site was
undoubtedly organised in this fashion at Alet, when a new chevet was built for
the cathedral there. When John XXII created a number of new bishoprics, it
became necessary to turn various abbey-churches into cathedrals, so that the
buildings in question would have a dignity befitting their new status. Thus, at
Alet, the former abbey-church of Sainte-Marie was rebuilt as a cathedral in 1318.
Bishop Barthélemy (1318–33) took the decision to renovate the choir by adding
an additional three bays to the east, together with an apse with ambulatory and
radiating chapels. To begin with, he preserved the apse, while building the new
one to the east, at some distance from it. Demolition would only have taken

place after the completion of the new apse, had work not in fact been interrupted at an early stage.

At Chartres, the architect entrusted with the task of rebuilding the cathedral after the fire of 1194 was faced with an edifice built on a considerable scale. A chevet already existed, with an ambulatory, on to which had been grafted three particularly evolute radiating chapels. The architect therefore did not have to enlarge the existing edifice. He chose to keep the lower level of the chevet, which he surrounded with a new casing, adding two more radiating chapels so as to give the new chevet a more Gothic appearance. In the crypt at any rate, worship had never been interrupted, and this economy had helped to cut the cost of the building work.

One should, however, emphasise that, in some cases, development on the eastern side, although desired, ran up against insuperable obstacles, so that sponsors and architects had to abandon any hopes of enlarging the building. The case of Carcassonne is indicative of the constraints under which clergy wishing to renovate their cathedral laboured. In 1267, Bishop Bernard of Capendu (1266–78) and the canons had obtained royal authorisation to extend Saint-Nazaire cathedral, which was situated within the city. They refused to touch the Romanesque nave and, as a consequence, were forced to keep the western alignment of the building. It had proved impossible to enlarge the chevet because of a roadway on the eastern side of the cathedral, and it was therefore necessary to find another solution. The decision was taken to increase the width of the transept, which appeared disproportionately small on the plan, to a spectacular degree. We know from the example of the architect of Poitiers cathedral, that other solutions, involving a better use of the available space, could have been adopted. Since at Poitiers the existence of an urban thoroughfare made it impossible to extend the chevet further to the east, the architect built a flat chevet, which faced directly on to the thoroughfare and, indeed, dominated it in a quite vertiginous fashion. In order to create a more familiar image, he planned an apse and two apsidal chapels inside the new chevet.

The disruption of the urban fabric to the west

The difficulties experienced in placing the chevet were generally overcome, by recourse to solutions which were, as we have just seen, both highly various and ingenious. The enthusiasm and the dynamism of those involved in ventures that were both exalted and new, together with the financial resources available at recently opened sites, made it possible to resolve such problems, which would otherwise have brought building work to a halt. However, as time went on, the projects lost momentum and, as funds ran low, problems were less easily resolved. Plans were advanced with great ardour in the early stages of a project, and at first nothing on a site seemed too ambitious, yet as time went on the original designs might come under discussion once more, be challenged, altered, transformed or even abandoned. When the western facade was finally completed, a moment which usually marked the end of the process, one almost invariably found that time had worked a significant change in the plan. Furthermore, the facade generally had to be situated in the dense urban fabric. Purchase of land, which was possible, as we have seen, on the eastern side, was an altogether trickier affair on the west, for the ground might well be built upon already, and belong to several different proprietors. For want of any of the legal procedures which have emerged since the Revolution, among them the declaration of public utility, one had to enter into negotiations knowing full well that talks might well be protracted, and that one could not guarantee a successful conclusion. Such difficulties were far more common than has generally been supposed, for they come to light through study of documents, not through analysis of a monument.

The documents refer to difficulties of every kind, some of which were so skilfully overcome that the monument bears virtually no trace of them. The Reims affair, which has been studied in recent years, suggests that we ought to be circumspect in our analysis of the western facade of many other monuments. We know that the cathedral was wholly rebuilt after 1210 and, given the homogeneity of the monument, it was generally allowed that the site had been managed with great dispatch. The subsequent discovery of a number of documents has brought to light the fact that the western facade was actually built at a later date. It could not have been in existence in 1230, for example, the date at which two charters record that the hôtel-Dieu rented out two or three small houses situated on the parvis, on the east-west alignment of Samson's facade, in short, at the very spot where the Gothic facade was later to be. These houses were demolished in 1252, and the ground was at last free. The slow pace of construction had caused a delay in the building of the western facade. It is worth noting, on the other hand, the concern to reap some advantage, for as long as was feasible, from the renting-out of the small houses.

The architects in Amiens had to tackle difficulties of a wholly different order. In the nineteenth century, Viollet-le-Duc remarked upon the curious nature of the facade, noting that the towers were not built on a square plan, as was the usual practice, but on a lopsided quadrilateral. After analysing their foundations,

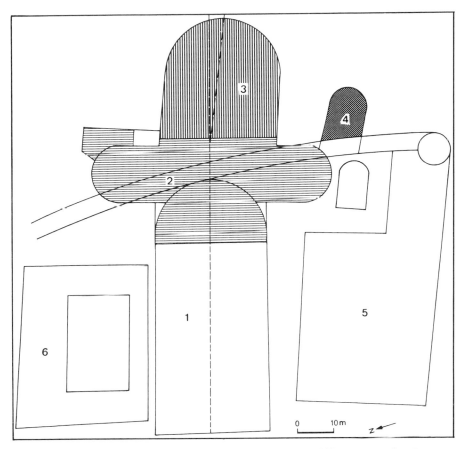

Fig. 104 Mass-plan of the complex at Noyon in the twelfth century (after C. Seymour). 1. The original cathedral; 2. The ancient wall; 3. The choir of the Gothic cathedral; 4. The episcopal chapel; 5. The episcopal palace; 6. The canonial precinct.

he formulated the hypothesis that they had first been conceived in the customary fashion, and he bolstered his theory with a diagram representing the original scheme. For want of soundings, Viollet-le-Duc was unable to prove his hypothesis. Nonetheless, the unusual placing of the towers demands some sort of explanation. In addition, facade and nave appear to be ill-matched, both inside and outside: the western towers do not seem to be built on the same scale as the magnificent nave. Analysis of the various documents concerning the placing of the facade furnishes still more evidence for the difficulties encountered by the architect. For the venture to succeed, it would have been necessary to demolish a number of the hôtel-Dieu's buildings. When, therefore, the architect,

Robert of Luzarches, had responded to Evrard of Fouilloy's commission, and drawn up a plan for the cathedral in 1220, he had obtained permission to have the hôtel-Dieu moved and a number of its buildings demolished. However, there was fierce opposition to the move, to such an extent, indeed, that in 1236 the architect had to abandon his original design for the facade and substitute a second plan, which did not extend so far to the west; he had, therefore, to scale down the size of the towers. In spite of this significant reduction, he did not have sufficient land to provide some means of access to the cathedral on the western side. The congregation therefore had to enter the building as before, by a door into the first bay, on the southern side, which faced on to the major highway running from east to west through the town. It was not until 1304 that the canons obtained authorisation from the municipal magistrates to build a parvis, apparently on a particularly reduced scale, on the western side. The chapter undertook, moreover, not to make any attempt to extend it subsequently.

The municipality frequently imposed such restrictions, but they were rarely so extreme as was the case at Narbonne. The cathedral had originally been conceived in 1272, according to a highly ambitious plan, in the south-west part of the city. The architect, in all probability Jean Deschamps, had envisaged placing the chevet inside the ancient walls, and the transept and nave with the facade on the outside, the crossing of the ancient walls leading ultimately to their disappearance. It was relatively easy to envisage, in a period of peace and tranquillity, Narbonne being transformed into an 'open town'. This was no longer the case, however, in 1345, when work was begun on the transept. In this period of unrest, the old city walls had recovered their former meaning and offered some protection to the city. The consuls therefore opposed the slightest breach in the city walls. A long lawsuit ensued, which ended in victory for the consuls, in 1361. The cathedral was therefore never completed, and the choir was closed off by means of a temporary wall, which became permanent in the course of time. The town walls were not demolished until the sixteenth century.

There are probably other examples of a similar kind. In Tours, for instance, the elements of the cathedral are deployed in a similar fashion, with the western facade being built *extra muros* in the twelfth century.

The elaboration of the plan would sometimes leave one with no choice but to position the cathedral on the west, as must have been the case at Bordeaux. Thus, the architect who, around 1280, conceived the new cathedral, beginning its construction with the choir, opted for a different plan, taking into account the clergy's desire to preserve the Romanesque nave. It had no facade, but rested against the archbishop's palace, which was itself squeezed between this nave and

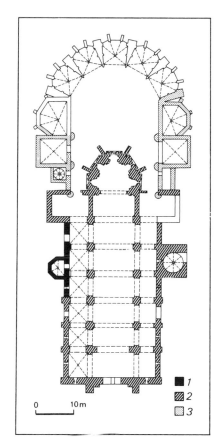

Fig. 105 Plan of Alet cathedral (after G. Leblanc). 1. First period;
2. Romanesque period; 3. Fourteenth century.

the ancient wall. It would have been out of the question at that period to demolish the wall; nor was the notion of moving the palace ever considered, or was at any rate not embraced. The architect therefore planned to allow the congregation access by way of the north arm of the transept, which was to be conceived and treated as a harmonic facade. As in the case of Cahors, this location had the advantage of fronting the street leading to the city centre. At Metz, likewise, the nave rested against the palace, which could not be demolished, and access to the various parts of the edifice was therefore arranged at the side.

Faced with equally awkward problems, the architect at Lausanne adopted a particularly ingenious solution, which had not been anticipated when the

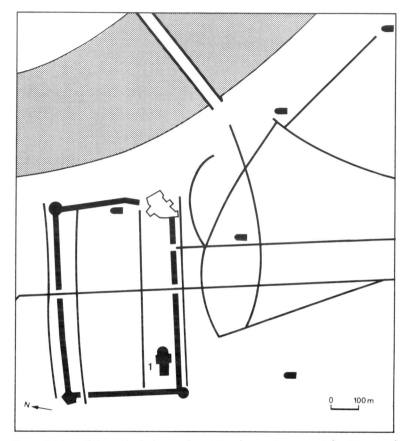

Fig. 106 Plan of the cathedral complex at Bordeaux circa 1430 (after Renouard).
1. The cathedral.

original plan was drawn up, around 1170. The western part of the cathedral was located on the main north-south axis linking the two sides of the town, namely, the Upper City and the Lower City. At the time of building the *massif occidental*, the existence to the north of a canon's residence, whose demolition was prohibited, made it impossible to divert the road in front of the western facade, for there was in fact insufficient space between the western facade of the house and the north-west buttress. Thus, in order to allow free circulation of traffic, and with the agreement of the chapter, the architect resolved to keep the north-south axis as it was and to run it across the cathedral. He planned an especially wide bay, which formed a kind of vestibule, closed off in the direction facing the nave, on the east, by walls which extended as far as the triforium, and covered

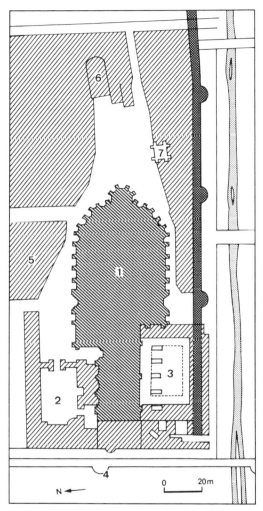

Fig. 107 Plan of Bordeaux cathedral (after J. Gardelles). 1. The cathedral; 2. The palace; 3. The cloister; 4. The ancient wall; 5. The deanery; 6. Notre-Dame-de-la-Place; 7. The Pey Berland.

by a flat roof at the same height as the gallery. A large arcade was added to both the north and south walls, to ensure adequate access. This roadway, revealed through close inspection of the monument, disappeared in the course of the sixteenth century, when major alterations impinged upon both the architecture and the town-plan. Demolition of the canon's residence enabled Bishop Aymon of Montfalcon to divert road traffic westwards and to create a square (1502). He

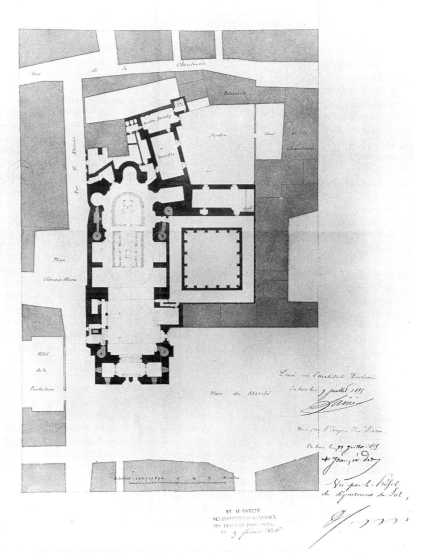

Fig. 108 Plan of the cathedral complex of Cahors prior to restoration
(after C. Laisné), 1856.

was thus able to integrate the former roadway into the nave, block off the large
arcades, knock down the walls separating roadway and nave, and demolish the
roofs covering it and the gallery above. The redesigned building now conformed
more exactly to the usual image of a cathedral. The work was executed both

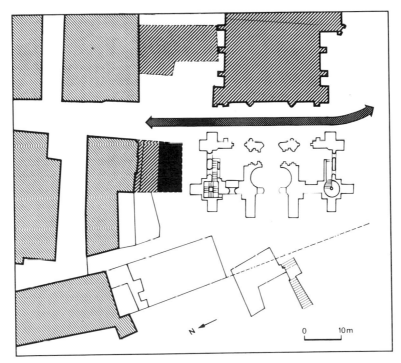

Fig. 109 Plan of east-west traffic in the town of Lausanne up until 1504
(after M. Granjean).

admirably and swiftly, and was completed in 1505. The problem then arose of access, which had previously been on the west. There was great hesitation as to which plan to adopt, as we learn from the surviving texts, but in 1515 the decision was finally taken to opt for a harmonic facade.

Paris presents us with a unique example, which contrasts with everything described so far. When work had commenced, in 1160, a very different solution had been adopted, and one which settled in advance the question of the location of the western facade. Admittedly, one should be wary of making excessively strong claims when one is undertaking a topographic analysis of the Ile de la Cité, for many points remain obscure, especially as regards the still controversial eastern passage of the ancient wall. It had once been thought that this passage ran across the entire edifice, and that the wall discovered in 1711 formed part of it, but this hypothesis has now been abandoned and the passage is reckoned to have been situated much further to the east. This is not the place to rehearse this thorny problem in all its detail. However, in the light of our present knowledge,

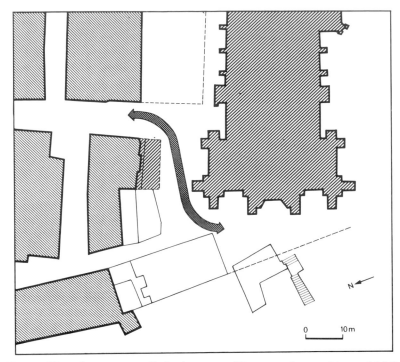

Fig. 110 Plan of east–west traffic in the town of Lausanne from 1586 to 1786 (after M. Granjean).

the traditional hypothesis would seem in fact to be more convincing. Maurice of Sully, having at his disposal a plot of land *extra muros* that was not built upon, decided to move the monument further to the east, thereby releasing some ground to the west, which became a parvis. Finally, to arrange for access to this parvis, he cut a street running from east to west across the island, and ending up at the bridges situated further to the west. This 'rue Neuve-Notre-Dame' has been uncovered on two different occasions, during the excavations of 1867 and of 1965. It would seem to have emerged at a distance of forty metres from the Gothic facade and fifteen metres from the original cathedral. The bishop would thus seem to have been concerned to ensure that the congregation enjoyed easy access to the cathedral.

As time passed, it became increasingly difficult to obtain land, both on the west and on the east, for the realisation of architectural programmes. Administrative obstacles grew more serious, a new preoccupation with town-planning emerged and, more generally, the available land simply grew scarcer.

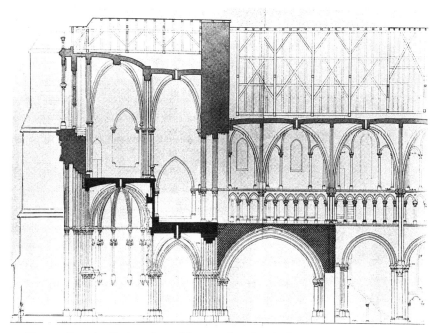

Fig. 111 Longitudinal section of the *massif occidental* of Lausanne cathedral, with superimpositions indicating the location of the galleries and of the former path of the 'great bay' before the beginning of the sixteenth century (the existing galleries are marked in black; the restored part in oblique lines).

We have already seen an instance of such difficulties in the case of Meaux cathedral, when two radiating chapels were built; similar problems arose with the construction of the facade. The monarch himself had to intervene, at the chapter's behest, but before giving an answer he sent his foreman, Nicolas of Chaumes, together with a number of other advisers, to consider the question on the spot. Nicolas drafted a particularly detailed report, dated 6 October 1326, his response in the end being a positive one. Authorisation was therefore given in January 1327 by Charles IV, and this decision was confirmed in November 1335 by Philippe V. Work could then proceed with the present-day facade.

Extensions to the north and south

The gigantic scale of the cathedrals must be measured as much in terms of their width as their length. It should further be noted that the arms of the transept were especially wide. The case of Chartres is particularly illuminating in this regard, for there the architect showed no hesitation in surrounding it on its three

Fig. 112 The 'roadway' through Lausanne cathedral (after G. Lavor and P. Margot).

sides with an aisle. The clergy could see the implications of this decision for land tenure and, consequently, for the amount of demolition that would prove necessary. A large number of texts concerning the construction of chevets and facades survive, but very few mention lateral extensions. One should not, however, jump to the conclusion that they were uncontroversial, but rather that differences were generally resolved in an amicable fashion. Indeed, in the

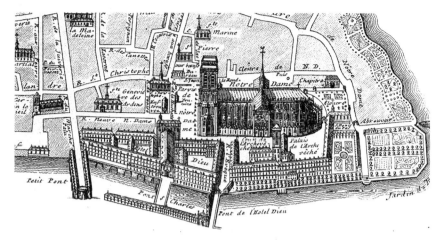

Fig. 113 Plan of the city of Paris, by Jean de la Caille, 1714 (detail)

majority of cases, the land belonged to the clergy, to the bishop or to the canons. Some sources testify that good will was withheld. We have seen what happened when one of the canons at Lausanne refused to let his residence be destroyed. Authorisation originally requested at the end of the twelfth century was only granted, centuries later, in 1502.

The policy adopted by the chapter of Reims sheds some light on the way in which land was acquired for the siting of the thirteenth-century cathedral. On the south side, where the palace extended, the ground belonged to the archbishop himself, who raised no objections. The canons were especially concerned to pay homage to him in their obit, which suggests that this was not always the case. Problems arose on the north side, because of the stance of the treasurer, a church dignitary who had been in conflict with the chapter for some years. He refused to sell a crucial strip of land, necessary for laying the foundations of the north wall of the cathedral, and only yielded after protracted negotiations, and, more especially, after the prelate had agreed to arbitrate, in 1221. The treasurer demanded compensation for damages.

There was an equally delicate set of problems to resolve at Amiens, a solution to which was only found after protracted haggling. In the northern corner of the ancient city, as in the western part, the urban fabric was particularly dense. Since the edifice was supposed to measure 145 metres long by 75 metres wide at the transept, substantial demolition work would be necessary. Three sets of buildings would seem to have been affected, namely, the palace, the church of Saint-Firmin and the canons' precinct. Unfortunately we have no information as regards the

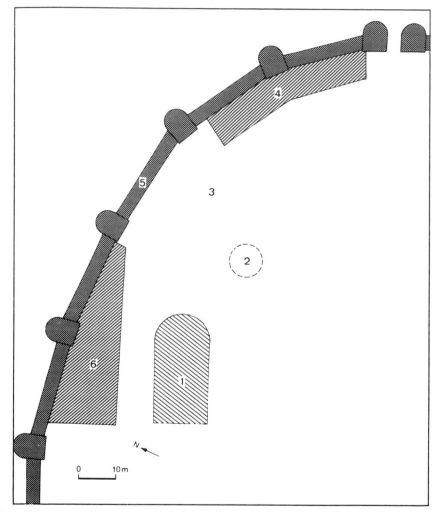

Fig. 114 Mass-plan of the cathedral complex at Senlis at the end of the tenth century (after Vermand). 1. Saint-Gervais – Saint-Protais; 2. The baptistry (?); 3. Notre-Dame; 4. The episcopal palace; 5. The ancient wall; 6. The chapter buildings.

first, but its present location, to the north-east of the Gothic cathedral, suggests that it was shifted in the course of the Middle Ages, since it now lies outside the ancient walls. One may reasonably infer that this transfer was effected in the thirteenth century, through the good grace of the bishop, Evrard of Fouilloy (1211–22), who was responsible for initiating the whole enterprise. Saint-Firmin, a canonic church, was condemned, for it very probably stood on the site

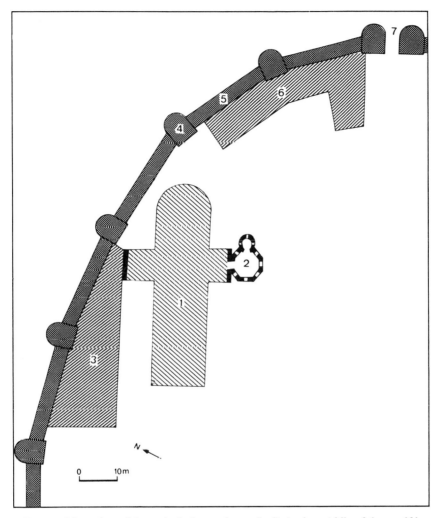

Fig. 115 Mass-plan of the cathedral complex at Senlis in the middle of the twelfth century. 1. Notre-Dame cathedral; 2. Saint-Gervais – Saint-Protais; 3. The canonial precinct; 4. Saint-Michel; 5. The ancient wall; 6. The episcopal palace; 7. The Reims gate.

of the thirteenth-century transept. No sooner had work begun than it became necessary to consider moving the church, and lengthy negotiations were therefore entered into. Agreement was reached at some point between 1238 and 1241, that is, over eighteen years after work on the site had begun. The decision was taken to rebuild the church on the northern flank of the cathedral, with its facade being brought up slightly closer to the latter. This choice forced the builders to abandon the notion of shifting the canons' precinct, which was to have been located to the north. It was therefore situated on the south side, but separated from the cathedral by one of the larger roadways running through the town along the east-west axis, the present-day Rue de Cormont. This thoroughfare was so busy and so noisy that the canons could enjoy no peace, nor were they able to shut off the precinct very effectively. This had occasioned major altercations between the canons and the municipal magistrates, who were unable to countenance the idea of the slightest threat to what was in fact one of the town's most important thoroughfares. All of these problems would have been resolved by a shift northwards. Yet pressure from the curé of Saint-Firmin and his parishioners caused the plan to fail, and the canons' precinct was destined to remain on the south.

In order to build the thirteenth-century nave at Rodez, the bishop's palace standing on its future site had to be demolished. A number of transactions, listed in a bill of sale of 12 April 1289, were necessary: the bishop purchased from Canon Béranger of Arpajon, for the sum of 30,000 Rhodanian *sous*, the tenancy of Corbières, so that he would have another plot of land upon which to build the new bishop's palace. At Clermont, two bills of sale drawn up between the chapter and the bishop in 1273 serve to show that at this date the plot upon which the edifice was to stand was not yet free. The bishop authorised the chapter, on payment of the sum of 300 *livres*, to take from those houses and courtyards in the bishop's possession whatever land was needed for the building of the cathedral. At Rouen, Archbishop Guillaume of Flavacourt proved just as understanding with regard to the construction of the north gate. In a charter dated 1281, he made over to the dean of the chapter, Philippe of Ambleville, a part of the palace and the land running from Rue Saint-Romain to the cathedral, on the one hand, and from the archbishop's palace up to the close, on the other. Two canons' residences were given in exchange.

It is impossible to envisage the construction of such gigantic transepts without many other buildings having been demolished, purchased or moved. The creation of a site must have been in this respect a particularly sensitive issue. No sources survive, but with transept arms the size of those at, for example, Chartres, there must have been conflict. I have a suspicion that the demolition, in 1906, of the *Chambre des comptes*, which was located near to the north arm, had already been broached in the thirteenth century.

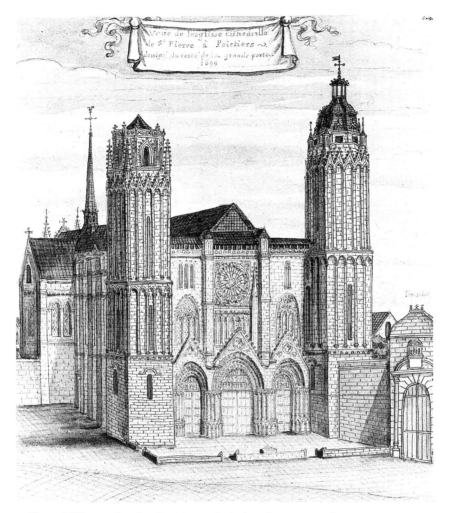

Fig. 116 Western facade of Poitiers cathedral, and its parvis, after Gaignières (1699).

The parvis

I have just remarked upon the difficulties involved in assessing the impact of such constructions upon the immediate environment. Nonetheless, it is possible to imagine what they might have been. The indirect consequences would seem to have been equally important for, like a shock wave, the repercussions would generally affect a large part of the city. This impression is further reinforced by a study of access to the edifice. One had to do more than simply erect luxurious and attractively decorated facades. Indeed, the crucial point was to ensure that the congregation could readily find their way, which, given the labyrinth of streets around the cathedral, was not always easy. One also had to create a small square, which was called a parvis, in front of the edifice. This term was first used at a very early date, but with a different meaning, for it referred to a strictly circumscribed space, outside the building, in front of the main entrance. The parvis therefore did not have to be on the west. At Bordeaux, Cahors and Metz, for example, it was located to one side. Such spaces clearly dated back to Antiquity, and enjoyed privileges which had originally belonged to temples, then to early Christian sites. In the Middle Ages, they came under the jurisdiction of either the bishop or the chapter, but never under that of the civil authority. It is easy enough to see how the term should rapidly have acquired significance, and have come to be regarded as a necessary element in a cathedral. Both clergy and architects therefore made sure that it would have the requisite dimensions; subsequently they sought to expand it, though at the same time safeguarding its original meaning; it was never regarded as simply a square. When Maurice of Sully decided to move Notre-Dame of Paris further east, he set out to create a parvis, which consisted lengthwise of all of the western part of the original cathedral which had not been subsumed within the new edifice. Documents from the period emphasise the manner in which ground was thereby obtained on the western side.

I noted above, in the case of Amiens, that the chapter had to wait until the beginning of the fourteenth century to acquire a narrow strip of land in front of the western facade; they promised the municipal magistrates that they would not try to expand it. It is very much in this spirit that one should interpret a document from 1340 concerning Agen: Archbishop Guillaume of Auch and the seneschal of Toulouse and Albi gave the consuls of Agen some houses that were to be demolished in order to enlarge the market-place situated in front of the cathedral. It was necessary to ensure that the market-place did not prevent the congregation from gaining access to the cathedral.

If one scrutinises plans that predate the redevelopment of towns in the eighteenth century, one finds that the parvis was generally quite small. At Reims, Viollet-le-Duc found traces of one such, the boundaries of which were marked by stone posts. The area had to be precisely demarcated, for legal reasons, but it had to be easy to cross, for the public had to have right of access. This feature was particularly important in medieval towns, where there were so many closed spaces, and was still more so in the 'holy town'. The parvis was thus a space which opened out on to the city, and which was meant to serve as a buffer, prior to entering the house of God.

Fig. 117 Western facade of Angers cathedral and its parvis, after Gaignières (1699).

As we have already observed, the clergy were particularly concerned to ensure that the cathedral, more than any other building in their care, should be 'legible'. It was vital to ensure that there was access to the cathedral, so that it might play a full part in the life of the city, and, indeed, be one of its most prominent elements. The clergy was well aware of the risk of marginalisation.

We have already mentioned Maurice of Sully's creation, in Paris, of the Rue Neuve-Notre-Dame. Admittedly, we are none too clear about matters of detail and we do not know, for example, who granted the bishop permission to create, along an east-west axis, a thoroughfare which would cut so deep into a very dense urban fabric. It has always been claimed that his aim was to allow convoys easier access to the site, but this hypothesis fails to take into account the existence, when work began, of the western part of the original cathedral, which would have served as a barrier, whereas the site itself was located on the eastern side. It would have been easier to supply it by water, and on the eastern side, where the land was not built upon. The prelate had a quite different set of concerns. Indeed, Rue Neuve-Notre-Dame, which ended up at the parvis, was meant to join up in the west with the north-south axis, which served to link, through the Ile de la Cité, the left bank and the right bank, and thus to allow the faithful easier access to the cathedral. At this period, the thoroughfare running from north to south was still the ancient roadway which crossed the Seine by means of the Grand Pont to the north and the Petit Pont to the south. Judging by the sheer number of texts which discuss it, it must have been a massive enterprise. Three bills of purchase survive, regarding houses belonging to Leonellus and his wife Pétronille; the first in 1163, the second in 1164–5, and the third in 1173. Negotiations with each owner must have been particularly delicate, and the building of the thoroughfare must therefore have advanced rather laboriously, in stages, with a very high price being paid for those houses that had to be purchased.

GOTHIC DESIGN

The harmonic facade

The architecture of Gothic cathedrals was conceived in terms of a number of basic assumptions, regarding, for example, plan and elevation. It was perhaps of even greater importance to consider how the edifice would be viewed from the outside. The latter preoccupation represents a clear break with Romanesque art, where choices had been so diverse that it had been impossible to summon up a mental image of the building. Gothic art played a crucial role in imposing a structured reality upon an imaginary. The architectural innovations of the Ile de France thus represented a turning-point in our perception of urban space, achieved by means of two elements described above, namely, the harmonic facade and the ambulatory with radiating chapels. A large number of 'Gothic' sites in Europe thus took their inspiration from the models first elaborated on the Ile de France, and featured these two motifs in combination.

Prosp: der Kirche de Noſtre Dame

Fig. 118 Notre-Dame of Paris and its parvis, after Mérian.

Once Gothic art had emerged, the earlier reluctance to employ the new architectural elements all but disappeared. Gothic art was altogether opposed to the formula established during the Carolingian period, which Romanesque architects had found it so hard to abandon, namely, the western mass or *Westwerk*. Gothic architects showed no hesitation, on the other hand, in embracing the clear definition which this Norman invention from the Romanesque period offered them. The clergy could not help but be in favour, as we shall discover below. Refinement of the formula had not been altogether straightforward, and the architectural record bears the trace of hesitation, and of architects groping to find their way. However, their overriding preoccupation was plainly to offer a warm welcome to the congregation.

Two edifices allow us to appreciate what was, from the start, at stake, namely, the abbey-church of Saint-Denis and the cathedral of Sens, examples which have the additional advantage of being close together in both space and time.

The altogether exceptional nature of the architectural programme realised at Saint-Denis may be attributed to the personality of Abbot Suger, to the political role which he played, and to the fact that he was concerned to keep the public informed of what he had done, and of his reasons for adopting the forms which he had chosen. He had drawn up a plan to rebuild the Carolingian abbey-church from scratch, a venture which involved the demolition of the *Westwerk* and the addition, in front of the abbey-church itself, of two bays ending in the west with a facade. He opted for a harmonic facade. This feature was not in itself novel, for its invention went back some three-quarters of a century, but this was the first time it had been used on the Ile de France, a site which would play a crucial part in the emergence of a revolutionary new style. The harmonic facade was intended to be quite striking, and so it was perceived. The clarity of the composition quickly became apparent, for the three gateways cut into its base assured the faithful of a welcome. Furthermore, the gates themselves were enhanced by an equally remarkable group of sculptures, in the tympanum and, above all, in the piers. The statues of the Old Testament kings and queens foretold the New Covenant, symbolised by the Church into which the faithful entered. It must have struck people very forcefully, but one was left with a more confused impression once one had crossed the threshold, for one then came upon the two bays of the three naves which preceded the Carolingian nave. The latter was soon to be demolished, only to be replaced by another, built a century later.

The design adopted for Sens cathedral represented a successful solution to the same problem. The facade had been built long after work on the chevet had begun, which was in the 1140s. Guillaume of Champagne (1169–76) was responsible for the work, but he was obliged to take into account the original plan, conceived by the first Master of Sens, which involved a harmonic facade, admirably balanced in both its design and its volume. There was an equally extensive programme of sculptures also, which gave the edifice its full meaning. In this case, the progress of the faithful through the portals to the main body of the cathedral was not interrupted by any other architectural element. They must have been deeply impressed by the manner in which they made their way so directly, from the outside, terrestrial world into the Temple of the New Covenant, having been invited to cross the threshold by the statue-columns of the Old Law.

We are concerned here with a moment of great importance, both in the history of architecture, and in that of the Church, which had thereby established a new set of relationships between congregation and monument. The solution adopted so promptly at Sens could not readily be used in existing monuments, nor could their demolition be contemplated.

It is with these considerations in mind that one should reflect upon the 'royal portal' at Chartres, which has proved so difficult to interpret. The architect working on the cathedral in the years between 1145 and 1155 had to turn the western parts of the monument into a harmonic facade. The existing elements, among them two bell-towers providing access to the lower church, belonged to several different periods, and had therefore to be homogenised. Since demolition

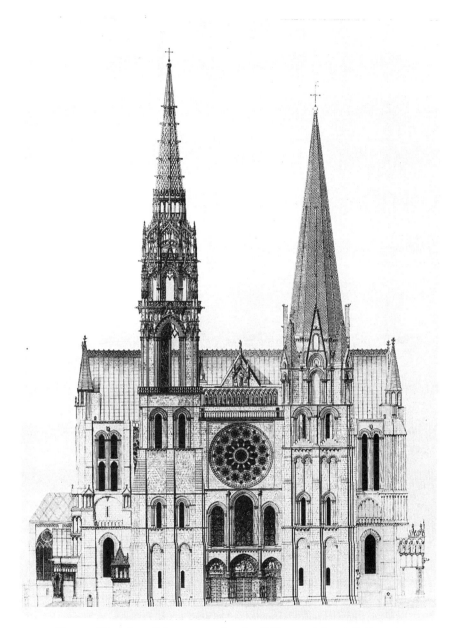

Fig. 119 Elevation of the western facade of Chartres (after J.-B. Lassus).

was out of the question, they had to be integrated into a general composition. The architect envisaged joining them together with a wall extending along their western alignment. This wall was pierced by three portals, divided by slender buttresses, the formula for them being derived from the harmonic facade. Notwithstanding its ingenuity, this plan did not solve the question of the space located on the other side of this wall, which lay between the facade and the nave. In 1195, when the 'Master of Chartres' proposed his plan for the rebuilding of much of the cathedral, he ran up against the very same problem. We do not know precisely how he resolved it, but the schema that was ultimately adopted, and that has survived until the present time, was established at some point between 1220 and 1230: the two towers were kept, together with the 'royal portal'. The wall above was pierced with a rose window, and the upper part of a gallery was furnished with kings of Judah. The finishing touch concerned the treatment of the other side of the facade, where a number of architectural elements encumbering the volume were eliminated and these two bays were rendered uniform with those of the nave. The arrangement thereby achieved, although it took three quarters of a century, was the one with which we are familiar today, when we enter by way of the facade and proceed directly into the central aisle. One has to have a practised eye, however, to discern that the attempt to achieve uniformity was not wholly successful: the side walls of the towers still feature decorative elements from the Romanesque period, which were supposed to have been eliminated when the ogival vaults were launched and their springing sunk into the already existing walls.

Many half-hearted attempts were made during this first period, before a solution was found. Such delays were due to the habitually conservative traditions involved. In some cases, moreover, solutions were found when the work was actually in progress. The period of time generally separating the original elaboration of a project from the actual completion of the work accounts for the fact that, with changes in personnel, new teams of workmen were liable to challenge the plan which had first been adopted. This revision was not necessarily complete, and might entail keeping the plan but modifying the elevation.

It is in such terms that the treatment of the western side of Noyon cathedral should be understood. The overall project had originally been elaborated during the 1150s, and work on the western part began in 1205. The present-day porch extends across the whole width of the cathedral and crosses the facade with its powerful horizontal, to such an extent, indeed, that the plan of the harmonic facade is obscured. Behind the latter, there runs a bay of three naves, clearly longer than the width of the aisle. The arches of the aisle are the same height, and form a sort of transept, with which it has often been compared. There is no doubt that substantial alterations were made to the original elevation. Indeed, the architect from around the middle of the twelfth century must have intended to build, in this position, a forenave, as was still common practice at the time, but would have made no sense at the beginning of the thirteenth century. In order to avoid creating a breach on the other side of the facade, the new architect decided to treat it as a transversal aisle.

The generation of architects after those at Noyon had to resolve this awkward problem in the appropriate fashion, both at Paris and at Laon (1160). Neither at Laon cathedral, where the facade was finished in 1215, nor in Paris, where construction had already begun in 1218, do there seem to have been important alterations made to the original plan. Both architects, notwithstanding their different, indeed opposed sensibilities, elaborated projects based upon the harmonic facade. At Laon, the hollowing out of the walls and the breach in the horizontals gave the facade a Baroque quality; at Paris, on the other hand, its simplicity and its lack of any plastic effects lent it a Classical aspect. In either case, emphasis was placed upon the breach of the reverse side of the facade with the nave. At Laon, the first two bays, and at Paris the first bay alone, were given a special treatment. It was not until 1210 that the problem was solved, at Reims cathedral, where the nave was continued up to the other side of the facade.

At Amiens, the clumsy solution was adopted of introducing a semi-bay on the other side of the facade. However, the architect succeeded in concealing it within the central aisle by making the semi-pillars on the same side exceptionally wide; he failed, however, to find so pleasing a solution for the side-aisles. From this period on, I would allow that architects had fully mastered the harmonic facade with its two bell-towers, and had so arranged things that the eastern pillars designed to support them from the inside did not subvert the homogeneity of the nave. The faithful thus seemed to be assured of a still warmer welcome.

It is easy enough to understand why the clergy should have wished to make the cathedral more accessible to the population of the diocese and, more specifically, to the inhabitants of towns which were, as we have seen, growing at a rapid rate. Most edifices would subsequently feature the close link first established at Saint-Denis between the western front and a programme of sculptures, for it represented an additional encouragement to enter the building. This same aim found expression in the actual movement of the piers, which were larger near the outside and diminished as one proceeded through the doorway. Finally, the two towers on the harmonic facade made it possible to install a belfry. The rhythm of city life was dictated at this period by the ringing of bells, which announced ceremonies rather than the precise hour. Public, secular time did not yet exist, and municipal clocks, in the open air and visible to one and all, did not make their appearance before the middle of the fourteenth century. The first such clocks would be located on a royal or a count's palace; in Paris, for example, it would be installed, after the reign of Charles V, on the tower which bears his name. The belfry, located in one of the western towers, therefore addressed itself to the faithful in the town rather than to the clergy. Developments in the course of the thirteenth century are very clear in this regard, if one takes account of what occurred at Reims, and subsequently at Chartres. The original plan had been to build the transept and then frame it with towers, which would themselves house the belfries. This scheme was abandoned somewhat belatedly at Reims, where the arches located beneath the towers were pierced with holes to allow the bells to be hoisted into position, whereas at Chartres it was abandoned almost immediately, and the ogees rested upon the keystone. From this period, those bell-towers whose peals were for the ears of the monks were clearly differentiated, primarily by size, but also by their position. We then have evidence that the different sorts of bell-tower were distinguished one from the other.

The harmonic facade, which had gradually come to fruition on the Ile de France, subsequently spread throughout Europe, together with Gothic art. The process began in France, starting with the conquest of provinces further to the south, which had either elaborated a Gothic art quite different to that of the Ile de France (the West, with its 'Plantagenet Gothic'), or else had remained loyal to Romanesque traditions.

At Poitiers, work on the monument was finished and the facade all but built when the original design was challenged. The originality of the plan first conceived by Bishop Jean Belmain (1162–82) lay in the form of the edifice: a rectangular box on the outside, handled on the inside like a church-hall, with its three aisles by and large open to each other and covered with ogival vaults rising to the same height. We do not know what the plan was for the design of the facade, which must have been conceived in terms of the tradition of the screen-facade, customary in the region since Roman times. In the middle of the thirteenth century, however, when building began, this twelfth-century schema was set aside in favour of a harmonic facade, which had to be adapted to fit the existing structures. Two projecting bell-towers were erected, linked by a wall pierced by three portals. The existence of buttresses thus created a tripartite division. The rose-window pierced above the central portal, and the adoption of a programme of sculptures, make it plain that the formula had been borrowed from the north of France. The actual style of the sculptures suggests that the sculptors had themselves been trained in the north, as had the new architect. One's surprise is therefore all the greater when one crosses the threshold and finds oneself in a huge hall, when one had been anticipating a church with side-aisles.

The harmonic facade continued to be the norm until a relatively late date. At Toul, for example, the plan could not have been earlier than 1460. At Lausanne, the attempt to harmonise the facade was still more telling, because it concerned an already existing monument. The construction of the western part of the cathedral had proved especially difficult, and it is this which accounts for the adoption of a plan whose originality has often been remarked upon. As early as the thirteenth century, texts betray an awareness that the design was indeed exceptional, for they refer to a *magnum portale*. It was, in fact, a covered parvis, which had not been intended for specifically religious purposes. Thus, in the fifteenth century, the ground floor of the towers still served as a workshop. Moreover, it was separated from the main body of the church by the 'thoroughfare' linking the upper and lower towns. Finally, the western front rested against the city walls. The congregation therefore entered through a portal pierced in the south wall, to the west of the transept. Whereas the ground floor of the *magnum portale* was given over to profane activities, the first floor contained a western sanctuary, directly connected, at this level, to the church itself. Between 1499 and 1505, Bishop Aymon of Montfalcon had eliminated the north-south thoroughfare and integrated the western part of the church by extending it up to the other side of the facade. He then decided to rebuild the western front, and to make it the chief means of access. A portal was therefore added to the facade, so as to give it the more conventional appearance of a harmonic facade with two towers.

Harmonic facades in the south of France

Prior to this period, the south of France, which had long remained loyal to Romanesque tradition, was influenced by the new Gothic aesthetics, in the form known to art historians as 'rayonnant art'. Thus, a number of cathedrals were taken in hand in the last third of the thirteenth century, at a time when the great sites of the north were being wound down. There were plainly links between developments at each of the southern cathedrals, and connections of the more indirect kind with the art of the north. The custom has thus arisen of associating work executed at Clermont, Limoges, Narbonne, Rodez and Toulouse cathedrals with the name of a particular architect, Jean Deschamps, who had been trained in the north. These edifices are in fact characterised, as regards both the plan of the chevet and their elevation, by a dramatic breach with regional tradition. The ambulatory with radiating chapels was adopted, albeit with one peculiarity, namely, their length was increased to a spectacular degree by means of straight bays. The choice of an elevation with three levels was equally innovatory, and here the original feature was the triforium, which was not pierced with bays leading towards the exterior, as had been the practice in the north, but was blind. For various different reasons, none of the southern cathedrals were completed, and we therefore have no information regarding the plan for the western facade. However, the northern inspiration was so powerful an influence that we can safely assume that a harmonic facade had been planned for each and every one of the edifices. The architect summoned to the site at Bayonne in the sixteenth century would therefore seem to have been altogether justified in so handling the western facade, to which Boeswillwald was to put the finishing touches in the nineteenth century, by adding spires.

The desire to conform to what was held to be the 'ideal facade' assumed a symbolic meaning at Bordeaux. Since it was impossible to locate the cathedral portal on the west, architect and clergy resolved to shift it to the side. No sooner had the first stone of the chevet been laid than the decision was taken to build the portal on the northern arm of the transept. Bertrand Deschamps, the architect who replaced the person responsible for the original plans for this part of the edifice, designed an elevation based upon the 'harmonic facade'. He reduced it in length, keeping just one portal instead of the usual three. The strong vertical lines of the two towers framed an elevation that was northern in inspiration, and therefore faced the town. The portal faced the main axis linking the edifice and the heart of the city, which spread out towards the north-east. Fourteenth-century congregations in Bordeaux must soon have come to terms with the challenge to the imagination posed by this unusual facade.

Harmonic facades in Spain

Spain proved much more receptive to the harmonic facade than southern France had been, and it was adopted, and adapted, there from the thirteenth century onwards. Some cathedrals were probably conceived or even built by architects who were French or who had at any rate been trained in France.

Burgos cathedral, begun in 1220 or 1221, is one of the most remarkable of such monuments, and the inspiration of models from northern France may readily be discerned. Here too, adoption of the northern Gothic style set in motion a process which had various consequences for the design of the facade. One may readily understand why Catalan architects, whose conception of Gothic art was quite different, should have renounced it of their own accord. A harmonic facade was not obligatory.

Harmonic facades in the Empire

Similar alternatives arose within the Empire. The choice there was more awkward, and resulted in many hesitations, traces of which may still be discerned in the monuments. Those tackling the building of the nave at Strasburg, for example, were faced with this problem in a particularly acute form. The eastern parts of the cathedral were based upon the plan of 1190, inspiration for which came from the Rhineland, but the construction of the transept entailed some modifications. Around 1240, a new architect, who had been trained in France and who was therefore aware of the most important innovations that had been introduced on sites within the Parisian region (Saint-Denis), designed a nave in rayonnant style with fasciculate pillars, illuminated triforium, and bays that were as wide and as high as the wall. Such strongly defined features required a harmonic facade with its two towers, its three portals and its rosc-window. The Musée de l'Oeuvre Notre-Dame contains several drawings of the facade, one of which, 'Plan A', plainly takes its inspiration from the elevation of the south arm of Notre-Dame of Paris. However, when work began in 1277, this plan was not implemented. Analysis of the facade of Strasburg cathedral, in relation to the various plans, shows that the architects found it hard to choose between a harmonic facade and a block-facade, which had been traditionally employed in the Empire. In its present form, the monument may be regarded as a remarkable compromise between these two tendencies, and one which reflects each generation's questioning of what had gone before. In the middle of the thirteenth century, Köln cathedral, like Strasburg, chose the 'French option'. After the fire of 6 April 1248 had gutted the monument, and the decision had been taken to rebuild it in the Gothic style, a harmonic facade was adopted.

Faced with the very same problem, the clergy and architect of Metz cathedral arrived at an especially ingenious solution, the precise nature of which is obscured by the substantial alterations effected since the fourteenth century. Modifications continued right up until the beginning of the twentieth century, when a western facade, permitting access to the cathedral from the west, was added. In the thirteenth century, the building in fact consisted of two separate churches: the cathedral to the east, which was oriented in the customary manner, and the collegiate church of Notre-Dame-la-Ronde, which lay on a north-south axis, with the cathedral resting against it, at the fifth bay from the crossing of the transept. Up until 1380, a partition, albeit a fairly low one, gave material expression to this duality. A harmonic facade was therefore not suitable. An ingenious compromise was reached, with the towers being shifted back to the side-aisles of the first western bay of the nave (at present, the fourth), the chapter tower to the north, the Mutte tower to the south. The congregation gained access to the cathedral by way of the former, through a portal consecrated to Saint Etienne.

The rejection of the harmonic facade

We are able to learn as much from the rejection of the harmonic facade as from its acceptance. Those areas which rejected it, tended to reject Gothic art also, as we have seen in the case of the south of France.

In the case of the harmonic facade, as in so much else, England once again proved the exception to the rule, for, where this architectural element existed, it never served, as had been the case in the French cathedrals, to welcome the faithful. English facades in the Gothic period presented themselves as independent elements, and their external design was not intended to express the internal organisation of the monument. They were supposed to be partitions rather than openings. The two western towers were, admittedly, a commonplace feature, but they were dissociated to a startling degree from the western front. Their base might even disappear beneath a continuous horizontal decoration, as is the case at Salisbury and Wells cathedrals, or they might on the other hand be driven back behind the facade (Lincoln) or located at either end of the edifice (Peterborough). The wall took the form of a horizontal screen, in which the portal only played a secondary role. There was thus a pronounced difference between the English and the French designs, for in the case of the latter the overall composition was organised around the means of access, with the portals being the crucial determinant. In England, the portal was not directly apparent, and might in fact be driven back on to one of the flanks of the building. At Peterborough, the architect launched three huge arches, which opened out on to a partly blind wall. A relatively small door was cut into the lower part. Finally, it should be noted that the piers were free of all carved decoration.

Ambulatories with radiating chapels

The link between ambulatories with chapels and cathedral design dates back, as we have already seen, to the huge edifices of the early eleventh century. After a brief period of hesitation, such ambulatories became an obligatory feature in the majority of the large constructions in the north of France. Thus, Sens cathedral, in its earliest form, would seem to have had only one axial chapel. The original plan for Notre-Dame of Paris had provided for an ambulatory without any chapels. When the chapels were designed, this layout was adhered to, and, in order to preserve the semi-circular form of the chevet, they were placed between the buttresses. A similar arrangement was adopted at Laon cathedral, which was greatly enlarged around 1200, when the clergy and the architect took the somewhat original step of abandoning the traditional layout and opted for a long rectangular choir instead. There was, admittedly, an ambulatory which broke off at the corners and opened out on to three square chapels, a highly original plan for which no-one has yet provided a convincing explanation.

Subsequently, the ambulatory with chapels came in general to be closely associated with the type of plan adopted for cathedrals.

The case of Bourges cathedral typifies this frame of mind. Thus, in the first plan, drawn up in 1195, the architect designed a chevet which, as was the case at Paris, had only one ambulatory. The form of the crypt reflected this plan but, in a second stage (around 1200), a number of excrescences were added to the ambulatory, being mounted upon the outside buttresses, which had never been intended for such a purpose. Bourges thus reverted to a more traditional schema. It should, however, be borne in mind that, strictly speaking, it was not a question of chapels, since no provision was made for altars. The architect would seem to have added them in order to increase the area of glass, since each of these excrescences was breached by three bays with stained-glass windows.

The same situation applied at Châlons. Thus, when the decision was taken, in 1285, to renovate the chevet, built in 1231, the new architect designed an ambulatory with three chapels, which effectively subsumed the earlier chevet.

This feature was especially successful, as we have already observed, in those cathedrals in the south of France which have traditionally been ascribed to Jean Deschamps, and which were conceived in the last third of the thirteenth century. There was also a particularly high number of radiating chapels. The formula was also employed in other southern cathedrals, for example, at Bordeaux. This is all the more surprising if we consider the case of specific buildings, such as Albi and Saint-Bertrand-de-Comminges. Planned as single-aisled monuments, they were furnished with chapels; the ambulatory, which previously had not existed, was placed within this huge space thanks to the closing off of the choir, around which the faithful could circulate.

The case of Spain was similar. For, where such an arrangement was lacking, steps were clearly taken to remedy the situation. Thus, Bishop Raymond (1311–17) took the decision to graft a new chevet on to the Romanesque nave of Elne cathedral. The plan stipulated an ambulatory with seven chapels that were pentagonal in form, located between the buttresses. The construction work reached a height of ten metres before it was abandoned, for lack of funds.

Likewise, at Alet cathedral, a plan which was too ambitious for the period, and which was without adequate funding, was soon abandoned.

There is no need to discuss the case of England yet again, for the chevet had always fulfilled a different purpose there. Whereas in France the chevet had served to welcome the faithful, the same was never true of the English cathedrals, none of which therefore had ambulatories with radiating chapels.

The picture was much the same in Italy and Germany also. The plan of Köln cathedral, however, drew its inspiration from the French cathedrals, as we have already observed, and an ambulatory with radiating chapels was therefore featured. Yet the case of Köln is exceptional, if not unique.

There was also an ambulatory with chapels at the cathedral of Saint-Guy in Praga, but there too the inspiration had quite plainly come from a French cathedral. The emperor Karel IV had commissioned a French architect, Mathieu of Arras, who had begun work in 1344.

The transept

In the medieval imagination, the cathedral, like the parish church, was supposed to have a transept with protruding arms. This tradition, which dated back to the origins of the Church, allowed of no exceptions. So bold were the first Gothic architects that, with the support of specific prelates, some of them actually dared to break with this custom. Thus, there is no transept at Sens, Senlis or Bourges. Paris is a case apart in this respect, for the transept exists in elevation, but is not marked out on the ground.

The suppression of the arms of the transept was meant to unify the internal volume of the monument and to simplify its external masses. This bid for independence was soon sanctioned, first of all at Laon, where the transept was affirmed on the inside of the building and sublimated on the outside through the presence of the towers, and then at Chartres. On this point as on so many others, the Master of Chartres took the opposite view to that of the Master of Bourges, and chose therefore to extend both arms of the transept, with its two bays and side-aisles, to a quite spectacular degree. As at Laon, so too at Chartres he was prepared to add bell-towers to each of its facades, although their construction soon lapsed.

The absence of transept arms must have shocked the successors of these pioneering figures, for several of them were added in later years to edifices which had previously lacked them. The quest for conformity found expression around 1240 at Senlis, where the side walls of the second and third bays of the nave were knocked down and pillars removed, so as to permit the building of a transversal aisle. The same process was embarked upon at a much later date at Sens, after a first attempt, at the beginning of the fourteenth century, had proved abortive. In 1490, Martin Chambiges was asked to design the new crossing of the transept. That same year, the architect undertook the construction of the south arm, which he completed in 1500. He immediately embarked upon the north arm, which was finished in 1518. Such works had a considerable impact, as one would expect, upon the architectural environment. I shall consider the case of Senlis below. In Paris, this question is harder to analyse. The transept undoubtedly existed in elevation, but its affirmation at ground level hardly seemed adequate; in addition, the placing of chapels between the buttresses created a new external casing which, in visual terms, engulfed it. When rebuilding was in progress, around 1250 on the north side, and at some point before 1258 on the south side, the decision was taken to preserve weak external projection, but to sublimate it by installing a genuine facade, pierced in its lower part by a large sculpted portal, and above by a huge rose-window. Both portals were reserved for the solemn entrances of the clergy, with canons entering by the north side and prelates by the south side.

THE MAJOR DEBATES

Throughout recorded history, largescale monuments have always precipitated major, and often astonishingly heated, debates between sponsors and architects. Whether knowingly or not, the architectural environment has been a source of real concern. The controversy over the Louvre pyramid shows clearly enough that a choice, even where it is a personal one, cannot help but involve the city. In an earlier period, the controversy over the eastern facade of the Louvre was equally intense, and there too the choices that were made had repercussions for those who were not themselves specialists. To what degree was this also the case in the Middle Ages, when the building of such immense cathedrals often resulted in a drastic and irreversible disruption of the urban fabric? Did the public feel indifferent to the construction of such monuments? Or were they rather the object of general fascination? Did people keep a close watch on the progress of the site? Unfortunately, it is hard to give a clearcut answer to these questions, for the situation varied from country to country, or even from town to town. Analysis of monuments over the last hundred years or so has shown that the original plans for a number of such monuments were modified to a significant degree. Some of these modifications may be accounted for in terms of the wish to take account of new circumstances, or of constraints which had not been fully appreciated before. Explanations in terms of style, and by implication the drafting in of a fresh team of workmen on to the site, cannot account for major changes. Some choices led to an exchange of views before a solution was adopted and executed, and sometimes such exchanges were so heated as to occasion fully fledged conferences. If a prelate came up against a difficulty, he would rather ask advice of others than risk revising a plan that had already been agreed upon, and that was already being implemented. There were grave repercussions, whichever decision were taken. To persevere with a project while blithely disregarding both changes in attitude or taste and formal developments was to fence oneself round with what could easily appear to be an absurd traditionalism. However, a challenge to the original project might sometimes entail demolishing parts of the monument in order to start again in a different way; greater expenditure would be incurred, and one would also risk offending public opinion. Prelate and canons had to stand firm when under pressure from new workteams, which, being young and dynamic, were prepared to question the whole endeavour and reluctant to be trapped within a static perspective.

Some monuments, Strasburg cathedral among them, allow us to imagine the debates that might have been occasioned by the continuation of the building work. Texts confirm this superficial impression. To arrive at a sufficiently informed decision, some debates became international in character, as the prelate wished.

This was indubitably the case at Canterbury, in the aftermath of the fire. The monk Gervaise gave a very detailed account of subsequent events at the cathedral. The clergy immediately asked a number of architects, some from the Ile de France, some from England, to assess the scale of the damage. The monks, being anxious, in a state of distress and quite unable to judge what the consequences would be for those parts of the monument which had been affected by the fire but which still stood, would seem to have called for corroborative evidence. They refused to place their trust in the usual professionals, not wishing to credit their own alarmist analysis. Finally, they entrusted the site to a French architect, Guillaume of Sens, so impressed were they with the clarity and decisiveness of his response. Guillaume had already produced a scrupulous analysis of the damaged masonry, and had compiled a list of those areas of the building which could safely be preserved. He took a less pessimistic view than his colleagues had done, and was therefore commissioned to restore and rebuild the eastern parts of the edifice. It goes without saying that, together with a technical analysis, he had drafted a plan for the restoration of the cathedral, which had satisfied the sponsors, as regards both the architectural design, with the famous 'Becket's Crown', and the financial estimates, which were lower than those produced by the other, more pessimistic architects.

The conference which met at Gerona, in 1416, was more ideological than technical in tone. The rebuilding of the cathedral, according to an inordinately ambitious plan, began with the chevet. In 1416, the monument had the appearance of a characteristic medieval cathedral, with a gigantic Gothic chevet and a smaller Romanesque nave. The latter was also in an alarming state of disrepair, which could not be accounted for in terms of age alone. A number of earthquakes had shaken it so severely that rebuilding was out of the question. In order to agree upon a design, Bishop Dalmau summoned the twelve most prominent architects of the region, and asked them three questions. They had in fact to address the various problems which the canons faced, and over which they could not reach agreement:

First question: Would it be safe for the cathedral to have a single nave?

Second question: If a single nave is impossible, what do you think of the type with three aisles?

Third question: Whatever solution one adopts, what form of nave would be 'the most suitable' and the best-proportioned in relation to the already completed chevet?

The various questions, the manner in which they were formulated, and their order plainly indicate the solution which the bishop, and in all probability a part of the chapter, would have preferred. Since it had been impossible to arrive at a consensus, a commission had been set up, whose debates would then have to be adroitly steered. Discussion lasted for four days and, because the minutes happened to survive, we are able to follow the arguments as they unfolded. Pierre Lavedan has published the minutes, together with an expert commentary, and I shall therefore reproduce his text here, at the same time summarising the opinion of each of the architects:

Paschasius of Xulbe, stonecutter and foreman at the cathedral of Tortosa:

(a)   the single-nave system would, '*en science et conscience*', be perfectly safe for Gerona;

(b)   the three-nave system is also very good, but its construction would occasion more difficulties of a strictly technical nature;

(c)   the three-nave system is more suited to the apse in its present form.

Jean of Xulbe, his son and collaborator:

(a)   one nave would be good, and there would be no danger;

(b)   three naves would be better;

(c)   the three-nave system is better suited to the apse in its present form.

Pierre of Vallfogona, stonecutter and foreman at Tarragona cathedral:

(a)   one nave would be good;

(b)   three naves would be better;

(c)   three naves, 'without a doubt'.

Guillaume of la Mota, stonecutter and assistant foreman at Tarragona cathedral:

(a)   a church with a single nave would be none too safe, because of earthquakes;

(b)   the three-nave type is better;

(c)   three naves, 'without a doubt'.

Barthélemy Gual, stone cutter and foreman at Barcelona cathedral:

(a)   the single nave is dangerous;

(b)   the three-nave system is completely safe;

(c)   three naves, 'without a doubt'.

Antoine Canet, sculptor of the town of Barcelona, foreman for the bishop of Urgel:

(a)   the single-nave system is altogether safe;

(b)   the three-nave system likewise, but it is not so 'noble' as the one with a single nave [*no tant honorable com la de una*]; besides, it would cost much more.

(c)   the single-nave system 'would be much more suitable and better proportioned to the chevet', and it would cost a third less.

Guillaume Abiell, stonecutter and foreman at the churches of Notre-Dame-du-Pin, Notre-Dame-du-Mont-Carmel, Santiago of Barcelona and of the hospital of Sainte-Croix:

(a)   according to '*son intelligence et bonne conscience*', the single-nave system is altogether safe;

(b)   the three-nave system is good, beautiful and safer than the other;

(c)   three naves, 'without any doubt'.

Arnaud of Valleras, stonecutter and foreman at Manrèse cathedral:

(a)   the single nave system is 'good, safe, stable and without risks'.

(b)   the three-nave system is 'good, suitable and applicable';

(c)   the three-nave system is 'beyond question more suitable' [*competible*] and better proportioned as regards the existing chevet.

Antoine Antigoni, foreman at Castillon d'Ampourias:

(a)   the single-nave system presents no dangers;

(b)   the three-nave system 'is not suitable' [*no es congrua*] and, no matter what one did, one would never arrive at a thing of beauty;

(c)   'Without any doubt, beyond all question, the single nave would always be the most beautiful, the most suitable and the best proportioned as regards the chevet of the church.'

Guillaume Sagrera, foreman at Saint-Jean of Perpignan:

(a)   the single-nave system is 'good, stable, safe'; earthquakes would pose no dangers;

(b)   the three-nave system is bad;

(c)   the single-nave system is 'beyond all question more compatible and better proportioned with respect to the chevet'.

Jean of Guinguamps, stonecutter, of Narbonne:

(a) the single-nave system is good, stable, safe;
(b) the three-nave system is bad;
(c) the single-nave system is 'beyond all question more suitable [*competible*] and better proportioned with respect to the chevet'.

The last day was reserved for Boffy, the actual architect of Gerona cathedral:

(a) he was prepared to guarantee the stability of the single nave;
(b) he condemns the three naves;
(c) he ends up by declaring that, beyond all question, the single nave was best suited to the chevet, and that a single nave with large windows 'would be a very beautiful and noble thing'.

Of the twelve who offered an opinion, seven found in favour of the nave with three aisles. Five, however, opted for the single nave, among them the cathedral's actual architect, who defended his own plan with the utmost vigour. Pierre Lavedan has observed that the architects' pronouncements tally with their geographical origins, with the supporters of the single nave coming from the vicinity of Gerona, and their opponents from areas to the south of the town. After this lengthy process of consultation, which should by rights have made it possible to resolve the matter, the canons themselves voted. They opted for a single nave, at the same time justifying their choice. Some of the reasons which they advanced drew upon the experts' observations:

1) while just as safe as the other, the single nave had the advantage of being more solemn and possessing more clarity;
2) it would radiate more light, which would be more pleasing and more joyful;
3) it would be much less burdensome to realise;
4) the work would be less lengthy.

The single-nave scheme was therefore adopted, but the work, though begun immediately, lasted longer than had been anticipated. The reader will perhaps know the extraordinary outcome of the joining of the chevet, which had originally been designed for a nave with three aisles, with the single nave. The architect succeeded in harmonising the whole, by means of a subtle play of light, achieved by piercing the wall located above the great arcade of the sanctuary with a rose window and two oculi.

Such combinations were by no means exceptional. If the stakes were especially high at Gerona, it was because a challenge had been mounted to a plan which had been delineated long before, and, above all, because there was a breach with the traditional feature of cathedrals, namely, the nave with three aisles. It may seem strange that the clergy, in the course of their discussions, took no account whatsoever of their congregation.

The debate launched in Milano in 1391 was likewise aesthetic in nature. A plan had been adopted for the cathedral, but the elevation was a source of controversy. In an attempt to resolve it, architects from a number of different countries were summoned, together with technicians, and a mathematician, Gabriele Stornaloco, from Piacenza, a specialist in the art of geometry, who sent his own opinion. The decision was taken, in May 1392, to appeal to the council of fourteen masters, among them Henri, of the famous Parler family, who had for several years been engineer for the vestry in Milano. The assembled experts had to answer eleven questions, one of which concerned the finishing of the edifice: should it be conceived *ad quadratum* or *ad triangulum*? Without rehearsing the various interpretations of these two phrases which have been advanced, I want simply to note that contemporaries saw it as a matter of judgements of an aesthetic nature concerning the internal perception of the monument. Such terms were concerned with the relations between the width and the height of the building.

The case of Siena may give us a clearer idea of the importance of such conferences. There should be no need to remind the reader of the rivalry between the neighbouring cities of Firenze and Siena, which was especially pronounced in the artistic domain. The construction of a cathedral, being a communal enterprise, could not help but involve both towns in fierce competition. In 1317, the Siennese decided to enlarge their cathedral, and the plan which was adopted involved extending the existing edifice to the south. The inhabitants of the town were, however, so reluctant that in 1322 the government '*dei Nove*' decided to convoke a commission of five masters. They turned down the plan which had been submitted to them and proposed building a new monument instead. Since the controversy refused to die down, a further twelve masters were consulted. As no progress was made, the decision was then taken to execute two drawings, representing the plans under discussion. Finally, the republic chose that of Lando di Pietro, a goldsmith, at that time based in Napoli. The terrible plague of 1348 led to the abandonment of this ambitious project, traces of which still survive, in the shape of the unfinished walls. Throughout this whole period, the local population exerted such pressure, that their opinions had to be taken into account. It was they who were in large part responsible for the abandonment of the project, after serious faults had been discerned in the construction.

Analysis of the monument serves to confirm the documentary evidence as regards such hesitations, which were also evident in the case of many other edifices treated in a similar fashion.

The facade of Strasburg cathedral was subjected to a number of modifications, as we have already noted, although there is no mention of them in the documents. There must have been protracted debates, with bishop, chapter and vestry expressing divergent opinions down the generations. A number of archaeologists have tried to identify the sequence of events at Strasburg, basing their accounts on the various drawings now in the keeping of the Musée de l'Oeuvre. The oldest drawing, which has been given the name 'Plan A', features a harmonic facade inspired by the scheme employed at the Ile de France, which owes much to the elevation of the south arm of Notre-Dame of Paris. An erudite interplay of verticals and horizontals creates a fairly remarkable harmony. We again encounter the three portals, the central rose-window and the bays on the side towers, as well as the traditional emphasis upon the correspondence with the internal elevation. The plan was not adopted, however, and recourse was had to a second design, 'Plan B', which was elaborated in 1275. Here the correspondence between facade and nave was rejected, and the decision was taken to have an independent facade instead. The rose-window was placed so high that, in order to illuminate the interior of the monument, the vault located behind it had to be raised to an equivalent height itself; the towers tended to be isolated from the facade, thus assuming an importance which the architect took special pains to emphasise. In front of the wall of the facade were stretched a network of mullions, which resembled the strings of a harp. Work began on Plan B in 1277, in the north-eastern corner, but substantial modifications were soon introduced, perhaps on the part of the famous Erwin of Steinbach. The rose-window was once again lowered, and other modifications to the plan were made in later years. In 1382, Michael of Freiburg fundamentally altered the whole spirit of the facade by abandoning the idea of towers. He put his plan into operation in 1384, by filling the gap with the belfry. In 1399, Ulrich of Ensingen reverted to the idea of a facade with two towers, but left the belfry alone; in the end, only the north tower was built.

These countless changes in the conception gave rise in the end to a truly unique edifice, a work of such startling beauty that one ends up by forgetting that it was the unexpected fruit of abandoned schemes, and that it had been the object of fierce criticism. There can be no doubt that the debate was held in public. The rejection of the French plan, which featured a harmonic facade, reflected a clear desire for independence, and similar motives underlay the choice of the architect. Thus, the appointment, in 1382, of Michael of Freiburg was itself part and parcel of an essentially Germanic vision. He belonged to the Parler family, of whose members one, Henri, had revolutionised Gothic architecture by realising the choir of Schwäbisch Gmünd, in 1351, whereas another, his son Peter, was summoned in 1354 to the most prestigious site in the whole of the Empire, that of Praga cathedral, inheriting the post formerly held by the architect Mathieu of Arras. The choice of architect represented a challenge to the original programme, and Michael of Freiburg rose to meet it.

A similar debate must have been entered into at the cathedral of Saint-Guy in Praga, when Peter Parler inherited the post of Mathieu of Arras. If one bears in mind how important the city of Praga, subsequently an archiepiscopal see, was to Karel IV, it is easy to understand why he should have paid such meticulous attention to the choice of architect. When the venture was first launched, in 1344, he summoned a French architect, Mathieu of Arras, from Avignon. This choice served to determine the plan which Karel IV wished to adopt, namely, a cathedral of the French type. The monument would certainly have been an exception in the Imperial domains, and must have occasioned some surprise. However, with the accidental death of the architect, in 1352, the work was left incomplete; only the chevet was in place, while the walls had reached the height of the triforium. Four years later, Karel IV chose Peter Parler, who could not help but embark upon a drastic revision of the parts of the cathedral that had already been built. He showed no hesitation in this respect, justifying what was regarded at the time as a genuine aesthetic revolution, and taking steps which were soon to prove wholly irreversible. The choice of a successor to Mathieu of Arras was very probably contentious, for the process took the best part of four years, and the plan adopted twelve years before was no doubt contested at the same time. The emperor certainly played a crucial role in the proceedings.

A number of great monuments – in the period under discussion, cathedrals – were clearly the object of discussions, polemics and violent clashes between specialists, sponsors and, in addition, amateur enthusiasts and the general population of the town. To disregard such disputes would be to accept an impoverished account of the historical process. As well as recriminations over the excessive cost of operations, there were aesthetic differences of opinion as violent as any we have known in subsequent centuries, which serve to demonstrate how passionately concerned the city was with such matters. The fact that the cathedral was also the house of God in the diocese added a further dimension to the debate.

THE NEW DIOCESES

When new dioceses were created, either through the dismemberment of those deemed too large or for other reasons, it became necessary to build new cathedrals. Analysis of such creations allows us to perceive more clearly what the contemporary notion was of building an edifice of this nature from scratch. However, one should proceed with some caution here, for the majority of such creations involved the transformation of an existing monument into a cathedral. These creations, which were non-existent in the thirteenth century but frequent in the fourteenth, were very diverse. As regards the thirteenth century, mention should in fact be made of Salisbury, although one should bear in mind that it was not so much a matter of creating a new diocese as of moving an episcopal see.

In Praga, the elevation of the town to the status of episcopal see, and subsequently to that of archiepiscopal see (1344), resulted in the creation of a cathedral. We know, in the context of the emperor's policies, what such a demand meant. He wished to turn the capital of the kingdom of Bohemia into the capital of all his Estates. In order to give symbolic expression to this desire, he transferred the *imperialia* to the castle of Karlstein, a few kilometres from the town and, with the construction of an impressive number of religious buildings, Praga was turned into a building-site. The emperor created a new quarter. In such circumstances, one might have expected him to build his new cathedral in the heart of the town which was a thriving centre, as much on the economic, as on the political and religious plane. Instead, he decided to turn the ancient seigneurial church of Saint-Guy into a cathedral. The church was not located within the town boundaries, but on the hill overlooking the other bank of the river Moldau. Furthermore, it was enclosed, together with the palace, within the castle walls. It must be allowed that the building programme was in fact an especially ambitious one, for the church contained the mausoleum of Wenceslas – the patron saint of the country, murdered by his brother in 929 – and of the royal family; it was used for coronations and held the treasures and the crown of Bohemia. In order to execute this ambitious plan, the emperor appointed a French architect, Mathieu of Arras, who was instructed to build a monument that would rival the great cathedrals of his native land. Praga cathedral therefore features an ambulatory with radiating chapels, an architectural element that is wholly uncharacteristic of the Empire. The entrance to the cathedral lies not to the west, but towards the south, in the direction of the town, and Mathieu planned a huge porch, which was to face the faithful, and which would be realised by his successor, Peter Parler.

An identical sequence of events unfolded at Aix. For reasons of an eminently political nature, the elevation of the town to the status of a bishopric, which had long been requested, was obtained by Karel IV. The palatine chapel, an edifice with many historical associations, could easily have been demolished, so as to make room for a new monument. However, the decision was taken to turn the octagon into a nave for the use of the congregation, and to build, on the east side, a relatively small-scale sanctuary.

In France, the creation of bishoprics never had a very great impact upon episcopal constructions, and yet they were particularly numerous. The decision taken by Pope John XXII in 1317–18 had several motives. Chiefly, it may be regarded as a consequence of policies pursued by the king of France in the aftermath of the Albigensian Crusade. Pope John XXII sought both to consolidate his own authority and, at the same time, to reassert that of the Church by curbing heresy. We are concerned here with the most substantial reorganisation of ecclesiastical administration since the constitution of bishoprics at the origin of Christianity. One might have expected such a policy to result in constructions expressing ambition in the clearest possible terms, but this was by no means the case. The clergy either did not know how to, or were unable to embark upon architectural ventures which measured up to the new juridical status of places of worship, or to the role which they were supposed to play. The bishoprics were installed in already existing centres, for the most part Benedictine abbeys, some of which were justly celebrated. The monuments of the Romanesque period, with the exception of Luçon, the rebuilding of which had been undertaken in the thirteenth century, seemed to require substantial work if they were to match expectations. These projects turned out either to be of secondary significance, or else, in those cases where they had been planned with a degree of ambition, remained unfinished. This is what occurred at Alet. John XXII had located the dismembered episcopal see of Toulouse at Limoux prior to transferring it to Alet. The abbey-church was immediately promoted to the rank of cathedral, and its abbot to that of bishop. The decision to rebuild the beautiful Romanesque church, on a scale befitting its new function, was taken on the spot. The chevet was to be shifted eastwards, and was to have an ambulatory

DIOCESES CREATED BY POPE JOHN XXII IN 1317–18

In first Aquitaine:

    Castres, dismembered from Albi
    Saint-Flour, dismembered from Clermont
    Tulle, dismembered from Limoges
    Vabres, dismembered from Rodez

In second Aquitaine:

    Condom, dismembered from Agen
    Luçon, dismembered from Poitiers
    Maillezais, dismembered from Poitiers (La Rochelle)
    Sarlat, dismembered from Périgueux

In first Narbonnaise:

    Alet, dismembered from Toulouse
    Lavaur, dismembered from Toulouse
    Lombez, dismembered from Toulouse
    Mirepoix, dismembered from Pamiers
    Montauban, dismembered from Toulouse
    Rieux, dismembered from Pamiers
    Saint-Papoul, dismembered from Toulouse
    Saint-Pons-de-Thomières, dismembered from Narbonne

with five radiating chapels. Yet work was soon abandoned, leaving only a few traces of what had clearly been a highly ambitious plan.

There was an equally striking failure at Maillezais, where the sole element actually to be built, the north arm of the transept, testifies to the grandiose nature of the project.

Some of these ventures, however, were brought to a successful conclusion. At Mirepoix, a diocese created through the dismemberment of that of Toulouse, the new bishop, Pierre of Lapérarède (1317–48), launched an equally ambitious project, featuring a single nave, the largest in France (21·4 metres).

The same design featured at Vabres in the fifteenth century.

At Saint-Pons-de-Thomières, an apse with radiating chapels replaced the Romanesque chevet at the end of the fifteenth century. At Rieux, Jean Tissandier embarked upon largescale building works in 1330, incorporating the sanctuary of the old abbey-church into the new structure. At Sarlat, the first bishop,

Raymond of Roquecor, started building a chapter-house, and Pierre Itier (1346–59) was probably responsible for initiating work on the idiosyncratic chevet. At Lombez, the cathedral was taken in hand from 1346 onwards, with a plan inspired by that of the Jacobins in Toulouse. At Lavaur, the old chevet was demolished, and a new one built on a large earthworks.

There is every reason to suppose that these abbots turned bishops and these monks turned canons were highly ambitious, but circumstances were not in their favour. The new cathedrals were not situated in the heart of busy, thriving and wealthy towns, but in small market-towns which had sprung up around the abbeys, and were parasitic upon them. They stood outside the important economic centres, and far from the major thoroughfares. Wars, plagues and epidemics had also worked to the detriment of ventures requiring substantial resources. Indeed, all of these dioceses were relatively small in scale and had a low level of financial resources, which meant that still less money could be devoted to the building of cathedrals. Times had changed since the twelfth and thirteenth centuries. It was no longer 'the Age of Cathedrals'.

5

Men, finance and administration

✤

THE PRIME MOVERS: THE SOVEREIGN, THE
GREAT LORDS, THE PRELATE

Only quite exceptional characters could ever have imagined, conceived and executed such immense constructions. No matter how great their powers of persuasion may have been, the countervailing forces were powerful also. It needed boldness to confront or to deflect such forces, and to ensure that the work did not get bogged down and that the original ambition prevailed. It also needed minds that were resolute enough to overcome another difficulty intrinsic to such projects, namely, that of securing the financial means at the start, and for as long as the site was in operation. As we shall see below, the available documentation suggests that the decision-makers tackled such questions head-on, and with a clear awareness of their implications.

One should dismiss out of hand the theories current in the nineteenth century, which attributed the realisation of the cathedrals to a spontaneous upsurge of popular energy, of sufficient strength both to inaugurate and to see through such a project. This argument stands condemned by its vagueness alone, even if we have proof that certain people, although not directly involved in the venture, were favourably disposed towards it and lent their strength to the task. It was common enough, for example, to put one's shoulder to a cart, to extricate it from the mud, and thus to give concrete expression to one's enthusiasm, but very little more than this was done. Nothing in the medieval period may be compared to the building of the Orthodox cathedral of Saint-Sava in Beograd, where, notwithstanding interruptions on site occasioned by the grave economic crisis of recent years, the work has gone to plan. The financing of the project has been achieved entirely through gifts from the faithful in Yugoslavia, and from Serbs living abroad. Once the cathedral is finished, it will measure some 6,400 square metres, and will have space for some 15,000 people.

If we therefore reject the 'spontaneous' theory of cathedral-building, we are obliged to find some other answer to the fundamental question posed by the existence of the many, huge sites of the medieval period, namely, how were funds raised to realise, within the relatively short space of around a century, constructions which, in scale and number, may be said to rival the grandest ventures in the history of humanity?

The study of this phenomenon, which has by no means reached any sort of conclusion, points to a significant difference between the pattern in France and that characteristic of other countries during the same period. This difference derives from the fact that solutions were invariably improvised in response to ever varying problems. As so often in the Middle Ages, a highly pragmatic attitude was generally adopted, with men disposed to take account of specific contingencies. Nonetheless, notwithstanding these variations, general tendencies were at work during the twelfth, thirteenth and early fourteenth centuries in France, which contrasted quite strikingly with parallel developments in the Empire, Italy, England and Spain.

First of all, one should note that, by contrast with England or Spain, the French sovereign was not involved in the process. He was responsible neither for the decision to build, nor for the raising of funds. On the other hand, if we consider Rouen – which, though a part of the national territory, came under the sway of the duke of Normandie, at the time King of England – we find that Jean sans Terre played a crucial role. It had been the custom of the dukes of Normandie, from as early as the end of the tenth century, to involve themselves in such matters, and the Plantagenets wished to honour it. Thus, Jean sans Terre, in a charter of 24 September 1200, donated 2,000 *livres* for the repair of the cathedral, which had been damaged by fire. Nor did he settle for a gift alone, albeit a substantial one, but promulgated another charter on 13 January 1201 authorising a number of collections.

Spain provides some even more conclusive examples, since the sovereign there acted as '*décideur*'. Thus, in 1160–2, Fernando II, King of León, elevated Ciudad Rodrigo to the status of dependent diocese of Compostela, against the express wishes of the inhabitants of Salamanca, who even took up arms in defence of their cause. As a mark of the king's concern for the construction, a decree of 1168 awarded funds to the value of 100 *maravedis* to Benito Sanchez, the master of the fabric fund. Royal interest continued throughout the thirteenth and fourteenth centuries. In 1230, Fernando III of Castilla raised funds to the value of 200 *maravedis* for the same site, and, in 1359, Queen María assumed responsibility for the salaries of seven workmen and raised funds to the value of 500 *maravedis*. In Majorca, the situation was more complicated, because King Santiago I had decided that the cathedral would house his tomb (1306). In the codicil to his will of 1306, he set aside a legacy of 2,000 *livres* for the building work. Three years later, he authorised the taking of collections in the island of Minorca. Subsequently, in June 1343, Pedro el Ceremonioso donated 1,000 *sous*. At Pamplona, in 1397, King Carlos el Generoso donated one-fortieth of his revenues. Financial involvement was, admittedly, not permanent, but it contrasts strikingly with the situation on French sites.

Indeed, the king of France never regarded the building of cathedrals as being in any sense his responsibility. When he was involved, as we shall see, on a number of different sites, it was always indirectly. At Le Mans, for example, he facilitated the venture and, when it proved necessary to breach the ancient wall, which was regalian property, he gave the requisite authorisations. In the case of the cathedral of Saint-Etienne at Meaux, he twice intervened on behalf of the clergy, as we noted above. At Senlis, the king played a larger part, addressing letters patent in 1155 to the archbishops, bishops and clerics of his kingdom to inform them of the imminent rebuilding of the cathedral. He invited them to help defray the cost, and consigned to their care the alms-collectors who were to travel around the kingdom, bearing both the royal message and relics. This was no more than a small gesture of courtesy on the part of Louis VII. The case of Paris is still more striking, for there Louis VII, and after him Philippe Auguste could not help but be involved in a venture which concerned them even more directly. They had resolved to make the town the capital of the kingdom, and the work on the site was unfolding no more than a few hundred metres from their palace. We know, moreover, of the particular interest shown by Philippe Auguste in the monument, in which, in 1186, he buried the son of Henri II of Plantagenet, Geoffroi II, Count of Bretagne, and, four years later, his wife, Isabelle of Hainaut, who died giving birth to twins. That same year, he increased the number of churchwardens, whose responsibility it was to see to the security and maintenance of the edifice. There is no record, however, of any involvement in construction. The only act of generosity on the part of the royal family was due to Queen Adèle, who bequeathed the sum of twenty silver marks to the cathedral, in 1206. Other instances of bequests included, for example, endowments for lamps (Senlis), and the creation of chaplaincies (Paris), but in no case was the structure of the building involved. It was altogether as if the boundaries had been very precisely drawn, and as if the policy of royal non-intervention was generally accepted.

The monarchy had a wholly different attitude, however, to monastic foundation. The thirteenth century, in particular, saw an especially high level of activity in this domain, which was only to die down towards the end of the Middle Ages. At the beginning of the Gothic period, a change in attitude is discernible, and, as the sites ran into increasingly serious difficulties, involvement in such projects grew, with the pope, the towns, the clergy and the faithful all playing a part. Louis XI contributed the sum of 1,500 *livres* to construction work at Toul cathedral, while in 1475 the pope made a gift of 100 gold florins.

The great lords merely followed their sovereign's example, proving especially generous, in every period, towards monastic foundations, but showing little or no interest in contributing financially to the cathedral sites. I would not wish to underestimate the importance of the building of chapels inside many of the cathedrals, but it should be emphasised that they were for personal use, and as a rule were built long after the edifice had been completed.

While in France the sovereign played no real part, at any rate in the decision-making and the execution, the prelate's role in both these areas was taken for granted.

In the Romanesque period, the prelate was the chief '*décideur*'. The historical records suggest that in almost every case he took the initiative. In the Gothic period, the situation was very much the same. There might be a number of different reasons for deciding to build a new cathedral. The monument might, for example, be very old, and therefore too small for the congregation. One should also take into account the influence exerted by the construction of Saint-Denis in 1140, and by the subsequent progress at Sens. The old French cathedrals seemed to both clergy and laity to be ill-suited to the rapidly changing conditions in the cities. It was not fitting for the house of God to seem archaic. It is in these terms that the rebuilding of Notre-Dame of Paris, begun in 1160, should be seen. The texts imply that, some twenty years earlier, the ancient cathedral had already been subjected to a significant degree of modernisation. It was thus in a satisfactory state of repair, and provided with an up-to-date decor, namely, the portal of La Vierge with its statue-columns, which was to become, after its modification and enlargement at the beginning of the thirteenth century, the portal of Sainte-Anne. A stained glass window, also dedicated to La Vierge, was added, and its fame was such that it was preserved with the utmost care until the end of the eighteenth century.

It is a trickier matter, on the other hand, to pronounce upon the condition of the other cathedrals which were rebuilt, Senlis, Sens or Laon, for example. We know why some monuments were rebuilt. In the case of Chartres, Rouen and Bourges, the damage and destruction wrought by fire was so extreme that renovation seemed impossible. These were often 'miraculous' fires which probably occurred when rebuilding was already on the cards and then became a necessity. Only in these terms can one account for the speed with which the projects were elaborated, the site cleared and the construction begun. The chroniclers would seem to have been under some obligation to exaggerate the degree of damage in order to win acceptance for the principle of rebuilding, for there was in all likelihood opposition to these projects, which some would have seen as unreasonable.

Be this as it may, the prelate had to shoulder the burden of the responsibility for so momentous a decision, just as his predecessors had done before him. We have already observed how, at Chartres cathedral, ravaged by a fire during the night of 7–8 September 1020, Bishop Fulbert (1007–28) immediately embarked upon the rebuilding, enlarging the monument considerably, and with a vigour that is reflected in the letter which he addressed to Guillaume IV, Duke of Aquitaine, in 1024. The work was completed by his successor, Thierry, after the timber frame had also caught fire.

At Cambrai, Archbishop Girard displayed equal determination in the rebuilding of his cathedral, which was to be consecrated in 1030. He would seem to have played an even more prominent role than Fulbert had done, for the conception was wholly his own, to such a degree indeed that he was described as an 'erudite architect'. He also spearheaded the whole operation, raising the funds, recruiting the workforce and seeking out haulers as close as possible to the site so as to reduce the difficulty and the costs of transport. Girard would seem to have assumed an extraordinary degree of responsibility, but the text is itself exceptionally clear and precise on this point.

The prelate's role would seem to have been scaled down subsequently, and this was certainly the case in the Gothic period, because of the complexity and technical nature of the site. Nonetheless, Abbot Suger at Saint-Denis, for example, was still the '*décideur*', and was at great pains to explain his own position. The same is true of Maurice of Sully in Paris, Gautier of Mortagne in Laon, Guillaume of Seignelay in Auxerre, Evrard of Fouilloy in Amiens, and Milon of Nanteuil in Beauvais.

Much the same pattern is discernible in the last third of the thirteenth century, among the bishops of the south of France, who, even though circumstances were still more precarious, succeeded in launching equally ambitious projects. They would no doubt have seen their own image mirrored in that of Guy Foulques, Archbishop of Narbonne, who was to assume the tiara in 1265, and who announced his wish to imitate the cathedrals of northern France. How could it have been otherwise, when a large number of them had links, either longstanding or recent, with the north: the family of Bertrand of l'Isle-Jourdain had rallied to the crown, Bernard of Capendu was descended from Simon of Montfort, Guy Fourquin was clerk to the king, and the family of Pierre of Roquefort had switched sides? Each and every one of them sought to rival these extraordinary structures, the majority of which had already been completed.

Men of the same temper might be found among those abbots promoted all of a sudden to the rank of bishop in 1317–18, when John XXII took the decision to elevate their abbeys to diocesan status. In the latter case, admittedly, the majority of projects failed, but there is no disputing the will of the prelates involved in such ventures. It was simply that the times were against them.

FINANCIAL BACKING

The personal patronage of the bishop

Nowadays, we tend to organise financial backing for a venture when it is already under way. A '*décideur*', however, had to be sure that he was in a position both to launch a site and to bring it to a successful conclusion. He was aware that there was a direct correlation between the amount of funds available and the speed with which work might be executed. This fact would lend weight to his attempts to persuade his partners in the enterprise, not all of whom were necessarily convinced of its timeliness, of the merits of the plan or of the choice of architect. It should need no emphasising that activity on the site mirrored very exactly the sums invested in it. If Château-Gaillard, the Sainte-Chapelle and Westminster Abbey were completed very rapidly, given the sheer scale of the ventures – in two years, six years (?) and twenty-four years respectively – this was because Richard Coeur de Lion, Saint Louis and Henry III had invested huge amounts of money in each.

Since a prelate never had at his disposal anything like the same resources as the Exchequer could place in the hands of the sovereign, episcopal projects necessarily took longer to complete. A bishop never had the funds to inject an especially large sum at the very start, so as to spur the site into action. Moreover, his revenues were vulnerable to chance factors, and could therefore drop quite suddenly. As we shall see below, drought or torrential rain could easily have an adverse effect upon episcopal revenues and bring work on the site, which always required fresh supplies of cash, to an immediate halt. Irregularity thus seemed to be the rule; the site was at the mercy of systolic and diastolic rhythms, with all the obvious repercussions, for human relations in particular. Prelates were especially concerned to come to grips with such fluctuations, and therefore to marshal the appropriate resources. They could not accept the idea that a miracle would resolve problems as and when they arose.

A number of prelates had substantial liquid assets, which may be accounted for, as much in the south as in the north, by their family origin. They thus had sufficient freedom of manoeuvre to enable them to launch a site on the scale required. One has only to consider what sort of sums might have been needed to pay for the recruitment of the workforce, their lodgings, and for raw materials, to appreciate just how large the original investment would need to have been.

We have no idea, however, of the precise sums involved, and it would be rash even to hazard a guess. Since accountable receipts have for the most part disappeared, our assessments cannot help but be highly approximate. As chance would have it, however, the few surviving testimonies suggest that one of a prelate's chief preoccupations was invariably with finance, and that, if need be, he was perfectly prepared to draw on his own funds. The chroniclers, who were at pains to remark upon the efforts of Maurice of Sully, Bishop of Paris (1160–96), emphasised that he was not only responsible for initiating projects but, in addition, was one of the chief purveyors of funds. In his will, for example, he bequeathed one hundred *livres* for the lead roofing of the cathedral.

Guillaume of Seignelay, Bishop of Auxerre, who was likewise the initiator of the rebuilding programme, acted in a similar fashion. At the outset, he made a gift of seventy *livres* and, from 1215 onwards, ten *livres* per year. Here too, there was a longstanding tradition, for in the eleventh century, Geoffroy, Bishop of Coutances, had ensured the completion of the edifice inaugurated in 1056 by paying the masons, carpenters, sculptors, goldsmiths and other guild members out of his own pocket.

The bishops of southern France behaved in exactly the same fashion, and drew from their own revenues as and when they chose. Thus, the bishop of Béziers made a gift in 1215 of 1,000 Melgorian *sous* for Saint-Nazaire. Pierre Amiel, in Narbonne, bequeathed 15,000 Melgorian *sous* in 1238. Raymond Calmont of Olt, a member of an especially wealthy family, lavished gifts upon Notre-Dame of Rodez, the most substantial being the legacy of 10,000 *sous* earmarked, admittedly, for the building of the cloister. At Limoges, Aimeric of la Serre (1246–72), who had dreamed of rebuilding the Romanesque edifice, left for the purpose such huge sums that seventeen years' worth of building costs would have been covered. Bertrand de l'Isle, at Toulouse, in his will dated 1285, bequeathed equally large sums, namely, 1,000 *livres tournois* for the chapter, 1,000 *livres* for the fabric of the cathedral and 1,000 *livres* for the building of a chapel.

Such figures are, as always, hard to assess. Nonetheless, if we compare them with the total cost of certain buildings which had been priced up, we are the better able to appreciate their value. Admittedly, such buildings are by no means as large as those under discussion here, but their dimensions allow us to make a genuinely useful comparison.

If we look first at the middle of the twelfth century, we find that calculations of the cost of building the chevet of the abbey-church of Saint-Denis, begun on 14 July 1140 and consecrated in 1144, come to a figure of some 2,100 *livres*. This is a minimum estimate, but in all probability an accurate one.

At the end of the twelfth century and the beginning of the thirteenth, Philippe Auguste erected a number of towers, modelled upon that of the Louvre, in the north of the country, nineteen of which have so far been recorded. Prices ranged from 1,400 to 2,000 *livres*, with the tower of Orléans costing 1,400, that at Villeneuve 1,600, that at Laon 1,900, and that at Péronne 2,000. Three of these towers have disappeared, but the one at Villeneuve is in a sufficiently good state of preservation for one to be able to assess the quantity of stone used, the external diameter being 16·5 metres with the walls being 4·95 metres thick. At present, the tower measures 27·28 metres in height, but, like those at the Louvre and Laon, it was supposed to have been 31 metres high.

The Sainte-Chapelle in Paris provides a yardstick for the middle of the thirteenth century. The enquiry into the canonisation of Saint Louis stated that he had spent 40,000 *livres tournois*, but this figure obviously ought to be treated with some circumspection since it was not supplied by an institution which kept accounts, but by a necessarily biased witness.

The bishops would seem to have played such a role up until the end of the Middle Ages. In the north, on 26 September 1477, Louis of Harcourt, Bishop of Bayeux between 1460 and 1479, informed the chapter that he wished to proceed with the construction of the square tower, located at the crossing of the transept, which had been begun long before. He agreed to assume sole responsibility for the work, which lasted from 1 October 1477 to 1 August 1479, and which cost as much as 4,092 *livres*, 12 *sous* and 6 *deniers*. At Toul, bishop after bishop proved especially concerned to finance building work. Thus, in 1460, Guillaume Fillâtre offered a large sum of money for the erection of the portal; Antoine of Neufchâtel (1460–95) bequeathed some silver for the fabric of the cathedral. In the south, at Condom, Bishop Jean Marre (1496–1521) made a handsome contribution to the construction of the cathedral; at his death, he left 1,500 quintals of lead, which he had just purchased, for roofing the edifice, together with 1,000 *livres* and the wood that was needed for the construction of the canons' choir. In addition to the above figures, which were to be spent on structural work, one should add the money set aside for furnishings, the sum total of which is unknown, together with a further 60 marks.

A cathedral could obviously not be built solely out of the funds at the personal disposal of the prelate. Before embarking upon such huge ventures, the bishop would generally begin by imparting a degree of order to the temporal possessions of his church, as can be seen in the historical records regarding a number of them. Here again, the example of Abbot Suger at Saint-Denis was crucial. It has, moreover, the added advantage of being well known to us, for the abbot took care, at the request of his monks, to explain his approach to administration. With this in mind, he drafted the *De rebus in administratione sua*, in the course of 1148. He recounts, in chapter 9, how he managed to win back the abbey dues, and to achieve a perceptible increase in revenues. His overhaul of the general budget was spectacular, because achieved in the space of a few years. It enabled him to embark upon the venture that was closest to his own heart: 'After having put the situation to rights, I had my hands free for proceeding with construction'. The abbot had deployed his financial resources to such good effect that the budget for 1140 was not merely adequate, but in fact more than sufficient:

We persevered to such good effect with a venture that was on so large a scale and so onerous that, whereas at the start we found our modest budgeting was scarcely adequate, when later on our investments became more substantial, we never found ourselves running short, and an actual abundance of resources caused us to admit: 'Everything that comes in sufficient quantities comes from God'.

Gautier of Mortagne, in Laon, and Maurice of Sully, in Paris, followed in Abbot Suger's footsteps. Both men pursued financial policies of such consummate skill that they succeeded, by reorganising their administration, in boosting the incomes of their respective dioceses to a significant degree. Bishop Arnoul (1142–82) followed the same course of action when he set about rebuilding the nave at Lisieux. These procedures did not meet with universal approbation. Thus, whereas Maurice of Sully and Evrard of Fouilloy won general approval for their reforms, the same cannot be said of Lisieux. In 1181, the canons went so far as to file a lawsuit against their bishop, charging him with having squandered church property. The pope's initial response was to suspend the bishop of Lisieux, but he later revoked his decision. The harassment was such that Arnoul resigned, but later, between 1182 and 1184, drafted a long letter seeking to justify what he had done:

I who have won for the church over 12,000 *livres*' worth of revenue in perpetuity, who have paid 500 *livres* into the treasury, who have spent 10,000 *livres* on buildings that are now standing, who have had the cathedral built, in large part at my own expense, who have increased by the sum of 600 *livres* in revenue the common income of the canons, who have further added some 500 *livres* to that of the bishopric.

At Lisieux, too, the adjustments would appear to have been drastic in the extreme, and there is therefore nothing particularly surprising about the canons' strong response. The monks of Saint-Denis were to react in like fashion after the death of Abbot Suger. A fairly violent conflict within the community divided those who remained faithful to his memory from those who sided with Eudes of Deuil, who was himself accused of squandering the abbey's resources and of persecuting the family of the former abbot.

The crucial role played by the bishops appears still more evident in the south, at the end of the thirteenth century. The building of the southern cathedrals, during the last third of the century, had been made possible by sweeping reforms introduced in the aftermath of the Albigensian Crusade. The power of the bishops was thereby consolidated, while the patrimony of the churches was put on a firmer footing. In addition, those tithes which had been wrongfully in the possession of laymen were, from 1210 onwards, in large part restored to the church, an important development which led to a substantial increase in resources. At the same time as income was considerably increased, its management became more methodical, thereby opening up possibilities which had previously not existed. The final aspect of this revival in the power and authority of the bishops concerned their standing within the towns. Thus, at Béziers, Clermont, Narbonne and Rodez, the bishop enjoyed the status of lord. Only Limoges continued to be an exception to this rule, until the end of the thirteenth century, the date at which the relationship between bishop and viscount was put on a regular footing.

At Albi, recognition was taken to such lengths that the bishop in fact became lord of the town. The situation was in every respect exceptional, and is worth scrutinising, not least because Albi has been the object of a monographic study. The rebuilding of the cathedral, as was often the case, had been mooted some time before. Thus, in 1275, Sicard Alaman had bequeathed a substantial legacy of fifty *livres* to the vestry. No sooner had Bernard of Castanet been appointed to the episcopal see, in 1276, than he embarked upon the construction of the new cathedral. On 19 January 1277, the day after the first Mass which he had celebrated within the old edifice, he reached an agreement with the canons. In order to implement this decision, he immediately set about putting his diocese to rights, his policy being to restore tithes to the church. During the first six years of his episcopate, revenues increased to a marked degree. At the time, it was reckoned that his policy of evicting laymen and of the generalisation of the episcopal deduction of two-thirds had helped to increase annual income from 2,000 to 20,000 *livres*. Careful study of the evidence produces approximately the same figure. At the beginning of the fourteenth century, prior to the dismemberment effected under John XXII, the net income of the bishopric stood at 4,605 *livres*, whereas that of Bernard of Castanet fluctuated between 15,000 and 20,000 *livres*. If one bears in mind that the movement of funds through the royal treasury during the reign of Philippe le Bel did not exceed 220,000 *livres*, it will be realised that Bernard of Castanet had a substantial sum at his disposal. An additional factor was the agricultural prosperity of the Albigeois in the second half of the thirteenth century, which had a direct impact upon the amount of tithes collected. The wealth of the district was also reflected in the creation, again in the second half of the thirteenth century, of thirteen blockhouses. When Bernard left to take up his appointment in Le Puy, he could claim, without fear of contradiction, that he had left a rich church behind him. The chapter also benefited from this spectacular reorganisation, for it gave every appearance of being the wealthiest religious community in the Albigeois. At the beginning of the fourteenth century, the bishopric of Albi was ranked fourteenth out of the 120 bishoprics in France, Flandre and the Tarentaise, for it possessed 11,000 florins, whereas Bourges had 13,000, Chartres and Reims 12,000 and Paris 10,500.

We are now in a better position to understand the real meaning of the creation by John XXII of the new bishoprics in 1317–18. It led to a drop in revenues which, in the case of some of the dismembered dioceses, was dramatic. Toulouse, the hardest hit, fell by 80%, Albi by 40% and Rodez by 28%. A further disaster, in 1340, was the collapse of agricultural production. However, in a fair number of the dismembered dioceses, the construction of the cathedral was already under way. To compound the other problems, financial difficulties brought work to a halt. At Narbonne, for example, it is clear that the clergy was no longer able to oppose the will of the consuls.

Meeting of costs

It was out of the question for a prelate to assume sole responsibility for a project, whether by drawing upon his own funds or by allocating a part of the episcopal income for the purpose. Both popes and councils had decided against such a solution, for they had already stipulated how the contribution of each should be allocated: a quarter of the goods of each church were earmarked for the upkeep and repair of places of worship. The bishop was appointed the trustee and dispenser of such goods, which were supposed to be drawn from the episcopal revenues or from the offerings of the faithful. In fact, there would seem to have been no general rule, and the various contributions were defined afresh by the bishop, when the occasion arose. A chance mention in a text suggests that the decision was generally taken when the site was set up, but we cannot be certain that this was also the case in the second half of the twelfth century. The limited information we have on this topic would lead one to suppose that the bishop's involvement was still particularly important, just as it had been in previous periods. In the following century, the situation had altered, for by then it is clear that canons had a part to play.

The charter of Milon, Bishop of Beauvais, promulgated in 1225, sheds some light upon the difficulties of such an enterprise, and upon the need to define the rules of the game in advance. This charter contained a formal statement of the joint decisions taken by bishops and canons as regards the rebuilding of the cathedral, which had been damaged by fire. They agreed to fund the building work with the annates from all the vacant benefices in the diocese, together with the tithe from their revenues, for a period of ten years. They also made various gifts to the vestry. In order to lend the agreement yet more dignity, Milon immediately requested the papal legate to ratify it. Milon had taken every precaution to ensure that the site was well run. As a consequence, work began at a breakneck pace. Milon's two successors did their best to sustain the momentum. Thus, Robert of Cressonsacq (1238–48) showed particular generosity, and Guillaume of Grez (d. 1267) was still more lavish, bestowing a huge gift of some 6,000 *livres*. After this period, the site seemed to run out of steam. When the vaults collapsed, in 1284, an incident which caused a severe psychological shock, the site had already ground to a standstill.

Whereas the bishops would seem to have played a crucial role on the majority of cathedral sites, the part played by the canons in the process is less easy to evaluate. The judgement of historians on this topic has varied from period to period, although in general the canons have been ascribed a leading role. Some studies have even gone so far as to include a chapter bearing the title 'The canon–builders', whereas others have arrived at a negative judgement, and have argued that the canons acted as a curb upon such activities; still others have taken the view that they were a force for stability. Dioceses, regions and periods were so diverse that it is not possible to arrive at a generalisation that applies to one and all. A second difficulty concerns our appreciation of the action taken by communities, for personalities tend to merge into the whole and are therefore less easily judged.

In the earliest sites from the Gothic period, the canons were probably not responsible for initiating the process, but were won over in the course of time. At Notre-Dame of Paris, Maurice of Sully did not entrust the supervision of the site to a canon but to a layman, his nephew Jean, who married Gila, the daughter of the nurse of Philippe Auguste. When, however, the decision was taken in 1204 to implement the reform, decreed in 1190, to increase the number of churchwardens, a number of priests were appointed.

The canons would seem to have become more deeply involved from the beginning of the thirteenth century onwards, not only on a financial level but, as a consequence, in the actual running of the site. They were to be saddled with such onerous responsibilities that a specific institution emerged, namely, the vestry, which had a fundamental role to play on some sites, at any rate in the north. To grasp the full meaning of this development, it deserves to be discussed separately.

In the north, as in the south, a distinction should be drawn between rich and poor dioceses, Senlis being the most noteworthy instance of the latter. Bishop Thibaut, taking cognisance of the poverty of the chapter, bestowed upon it, when the cathedral had been completed, half of all the surplus offerings intended for the construction of the cathedral. His successors, Henri in 1184 and Geoffroy in 1186, had no choice but to renew this concession. There should be no need to labour the fact that the canons had no hand in the construction of the cathedral.

The canons could hardly be said to have played a more substantial role on the other sites of the same period. After the fire of 1194, which devastated Chartres cathedral, bishop and canons agreed, at the prompting of the legate Melior, to pay a 'by no means modest share' of their revenues in order to undertake the rebuilding of the damaged edifice. The information that we have is in every respect vague, since neither the respective shares, nor the amounts, are specified, yet to the author of the text they plainly seemed considerable, by the standards of the time. They found no difficulty in paying because the revenues derived from the land were substantial. In addition, the management of the temporal possessions of the chapter had just been placed on a new footing; where formerly it had been in the hands of the provosts, who could do as they wished, in 1171 Guillaume aux Blanches Mains decided to entrust the task to the canons. The transfer had been completed by 1193. The bishop's obit stated that, as a consequence, the prebends' revenues had been doubled. The exceptional speed with which the work was completed suggests that huge sums were spent. The site was opened in 1194, shortly after the fire, and work on the nave was finished by 1200. In 1221, the chevet was completed, and the transept around 1230–5. The financial resources employed were mainly local, the involvement of other parties being of secondary importance, as we shall see below. The canons were not invariably so co-operative, but it should be borne in mind that the situation in many chapters differed markedly from that of Chartres. So difficult was it in some cases for bishop and canons to reach an agreement, that the pope himself had to intervene. At Châlons-sur-Marne, Innocent IV had thus to fulminate a bull (1249) obliging each canon to pay the vestry the sum of one hundred *sous*, and the dignitaries ten *livres* for the upkeep and repair of the edifice. In the north of France, it became difficult around this time to secure ready cash in order to keep the sites in operation. In order to compensate for this serious shortfall, the bishop of Meaux, Jean of Poincy, and the chapter decided in 1268 to use, for a ten-year period, the annates from those parish churches which had just fallen vacant and various other benefices, together with special subsidies and the alms of the faithful. Attention had to be drawn to this ruling in 1282, presumably because it had rapidly fallen into disuse.

In the course of the thirteenth century, bishop and chapter generally arrived at a formula for the joint financing of sites, although proportions would vary from one diocese to another. The original ruling had stipulated that one half of the annual resources from the empty benefices, whether collected by the bishop or the chapter, should be earmarked for the vestry. However, a time limit was also agreed. Thus, at Limoges, the ruling applied for three years, and at Narbonne, in 1292, for five years. However, at the very end of the thirteenth century, this mode of financing became perennial. At Limoges, for example, Raymond of La Porte extended it, in 1294, for a further six years. The arrangement was continued up until 1327. In 1302, Pierre of Pleine-Chassaigne took the same decision, with very much the same consequences. In the case of Albi, we are better informed. It would seem that Bernard of Castanet and the chapter guaranteed the financing of the site at the going rate, advancing one-twentieth of their annual income for a period of twenty years. They further added a year's revenue from all the churches which had recently fallen vacant, to be collected by the bishop or the chapter.

Other formulae were adopted in the south. The revenue from particular ecclesiastical benefices was earmarked for the vestry, when the occasion arose, in 1256, in Narbonne, and in 1295, at Limoges. At Rodez, from 1281, the vestry was endowed with a fixed income levied from some parishes; it obviously proved insufficient to sustain the site. When the bishop and chapter ran into problems at Narbonne, they committed themselves to an annual *pro rata* contribution of 200 *livres* and 50 *livres* respectively. At Saint-Bertrand-de-Comminges the pope was obliged to intervene, as at Châlons, and bishop and chapter were obliged to pay the sum of 1,000 florins.

A similar pragmatism was in evidence at the end of the Middle Ages, when certain cathedrals were nearing completion, for example, Toul, and when work on others was beginning. It is important to realise, however, that, as time went on, the canons' commitment grew stronger. This process is clearly in evidence at Toul, where capitulary deliberations show that they took the initiative throughout the fourteenth and fifteenth centuries, having set their hearts on the completion of the edifice. They subsidised the site to a considerable extent, and, to overcome any economic problems which arose, had no hesitation in adopting new financial techniques. In 1382, we find the first mention of a debt, actually mortgaged on a religious treasure, the pieces of which were to be redeemed at a later date. In order to face up to the demands of the moment, the canons conceived of the most ingenious solutions to the problems of fund-raising.

Not every chapter displayed such audacity in the running of its vestry. When Jacques of Amboise, for example, became aware in 1507 of the deplorable state of the roofing of Clermont cathedral, he abandoned his own rights to a joyful advent and requested all the benefice-holders of his diocese to make a gift proportionate to their own resources. It is probable that he was paid little heed, for one of his canons, Jean of Lugny, was made responsible for the collection of this compulsory tax, and for keeping the records of it. Disciplinary penalties were actually stipulated for those who reneged upon their original commitment to pay. The gesture made by Jean of Marcilly (d. 1510), Canon of Meaux, who provided the funding for the north portal of the western facade, was exceptional in this regard.

In the south, the financing of Condom cathedral was to prove equally problematic. Thus, Jean Marre (1496–1521), who had decided to rebuild the edifice after the bell-tower had collapsed, on 10 December 1506, was faced with similar financial difficulties. He set aside a third of his income, which amounted to around 6,000 *livres*, and he defrayed the cost of three harnessed carts, used for transporting stones and other materials. The canons, for their part, promised to contribute each year the tithe from their benefice, together with a prebend's income. They also offered to supply whatever timber was needed, which might be taken from a wood belonging to them.

The site at Condom was not marked by the fervour characteristic of a number of cathedral sites established around that time in Spain. In 1402, work was begun, to a truly gigantic plan, on Sevilla cathedral. A canon, somewhat taken aback by his own boldness, ventured to say: 'We shall build so large a cathedral that those who see it in its finished state will think that we were mad'. It was, indeed, the largest edifice built in the Gothic period.

EMERGENCY RESOURCES

Ordinary sources of funding generally proved inadequate, and prelates and canons had therefore to think up other ways of providing for the vestry's requirements. Their imaginative approach is reflected in the wide range of different options pursued. Sometimes, indeed, recourse was had to several approaches at once. First and foremost, however, appeal was made to the generosity of the laity, both when they were alive and, after their death, through gifts, legacies, collections and the granting of indulgences.

In France, as we have already noted, the sovereigns were rarely involved in cathedral-building in the north, and what they did in the south was of little significance. We mentioned the case of Louis VII, who made a gift of 200 *livres* to Notre-Dame of Paris, and of Philippe Auguste, who gave the same sum, for an unspecified purpose, to Chartres cathedral, in 1210. Other members of the royal family were none too generous either. There are occasional references in passing to the involvement of persons close to the court in building projects. Thus, it was very probably his wish to follow the example of Louis VII which prompted Barbedor, his secretary, to bestow a gift of 15 *livres* upon Notre-Dame of Paris. The cantor Albert also made a gift of 15 *livres* to the same edifice. Laymen in fact showed little enthusiasm for such projects. Mention is made in the texts, however, of one Pierre, custodial of Sainte-Croix, who contributed the sum of 10 *livres* towards a pillar in Lyon cathedral, and of one Robert of Blavia, who, in 1214–15, gave 25 *livres* towards the construction of a pillar in

Chartres cathedral. Early in the thirteenth century, at Lyon, mention is made of some gifts, earmarked for specific purposes.

These gifts are proof of a generosity for which there is abundant evidence in the historical records. Donors tended not to remain anonymous. Thus, at Chartres, local guilds or confraternities gave forty-two stained-glass windows. The other windows were donated in a similar fashion: the inhabitants of the town of Tours offered three, while several great families connected in various ways to the region, took it into their hearts to present one. Every donor was concerned to mark their gift, either by having the life of the patron saint of their guild represented, or by reproducing their coats of arms. None of these gifts therefore remained anonymous. Many clerics were responsible for comparable donations, from an early period. Thus, at the beginning of the eleventh century, the sacristan Pierre had the choir of Chartres cathedral paved. Again at Chartres, some monks, associated to some degree with the chapter, donated sixteen stained-glass windows. At Lyon, the archives tell of priests donating stained-glass windows for the chevet between 1200 and 1256.

The situation was not markedly different in the south of France. Thus, Cardinal Godin gave, at some point prior to 1335, 3,000 *livres tournois*, valued at 5,000 florins, on condition that this offering be used to build the vault to three bays of the transept of Bayonne cathedral. He later bequeathed 3,000 *livres* for three vaults for the nave. In this respect, Pope Clement V (1305–16) would seem somewhat out of the ordinary, but it should be borne in mind that, before donning the pontifical tiara, Bertrand of Got had been Archbishop of Bordeaux. He showed a marked interest in what was then generally known as the *novum opus*, lavishing privileges and favours upon it. In February 1307, he bestowed indulgences upon it, and in November 1308 the first-year fruits of all the vacant benefices in the diocese. Most important of all, he bequeathed the sum of 20,000 florins for work on the cathedral, where he had resolved to be buried. When Bertrand opted for Uzeste instead, the sum was reduced to 10,000 florins (9 April 1314). The amount was obviously linked to his choice of burial place and, having changed his mind, he did not dare to lower the sum any further, although, in order to give a more generous endowment to Uzeste, he had probably contemplated doing so.

There was a particularly dramatic situation at Meaux, when the western facade was under construction, for, though the terrain was at last free, the financial means were wanting. In 1390, Charles VI launched an appeal to the townspeople, who responded by giving 260 *livres* in 1393, and 200 the following year.

A radical change occurred when the great cathedral-building programmes were revived, in the wake of the Hundred Years' War, for the ordinary sums placed at the vestry's disposal by the prelates and the canons no longer seemed adequate. Desperate appeals were made to all and sundry. The chapter of Toul, which was still well endowed, even went so far as to appeal to the pope and to the king, obtaining 100 florins from the former and 1,500 from the latter. In other places, the town itself became involved. Thus, when Châlons council met, in 1462, it granted 100 *livres tournois* for the bell-tower (?) and for the roofing of the cathedral. Likewise, at Meaux, the town granted subsidies in 1495, 1505 and 1510.

Legacies also played a part in the process, but it is difficult for historians to assess just how important they were. It is crucial to identify burdened legacies, for example, for the conditions governing their use were so precise that they could not form part of the common fund, which served to finance the work as a whole. We should therefore disregard chaplaincies, the endowment of masses and bequests for the building of tombs or even of private chapels. In the twelfth century, legacies were in fact chiefly made to religious orders and, quite explicitly, to the Cistercians, while in the thirteenth century the mendicant orders were favoured. This was particularly the case in the south of France, as documents from the period show. Once the mendicants had begun, around 1230–40, to concern themselves with the dead, they attracted numerous, substantial legacies, not only from burghers but also from lords and from the most eminent figures of the period. The case of Jeanne of Toulouse, daughter of Raymond VII and wife of Alphonse of Poitiers, sole heiress of the powerful counts of Toulouse, is indicative of this trend. She died in 1271, when Toulouse cathedral was a site of frenetic activity, and bequeathed 10,000 silver marks to various religious institutions but left nothing to the cathedral; her father likewise bequeathed 10,000 marks yet earmarked only 100 for the site of Saint-Etienne. Another, equally telling example is that of Sicard Alaman le Vieux who, in 1275, bequeathed 1,000 *livres* for work on religious buildings, 10 *livres* of which were earmarked for Toulouse cathedral and 50 for Albi cathedral. In 1280, his son's will followed the same ratio, although the overall sum had risen to 1,025 *livres tournois*. We have already noted the case of Cardinal Godin, who bequeathed 3,000 *livres* for three vaults for the nave at Bayonne, and that of Clement V, who reneged upon his decision to bequeath 20,000 florins to Bordeaux cathedral, opting instead for the lower figure of 10,000.

The fairly detailed sources we have for Bordeaux merely serve to confirm this negative picture, for there donations to the monks were particularly numerous.

This pattern was to have dramatic consequences for the nobility, which was left as a consequence in an especially impoverished state. The '*obre de Sent Andriu*' was frequently named in wills, but because bequests were often divided up between several institutions, the sums in question usually turned out to be quite small. Pierre Aumanieu of Albret, the Lord of Buch, gave 15 *livres* in 1500; Amanieu, Viscount of Tartas, gave 50 *livres* in 1324; his wife bequeathed some 2,500 *livres* to pious institutions, but of this sum only 10 went to the cathedral. Likewise, in 1368, Jean of Grailly bequeathed 40,000 old gold *écus* to religious institutions, of which 300 were earmarked for the cathedral. The religious themselves were not markedly more generous. We hear, for example, of Archbishop Arnaud of Canteloup bequeathing a rent of 11 *livres* in 1331, of Canon Arnaud Garsia leaving a legacy of 20 *livres*, in 1353, to purchase some rents, and of Guilhem of Médeville bequeathing 100 *livres*.

These exceptional funds were so exiguous that they could hardly be said to be adequate for such gigantic ventures, the importance of which prelates and canons were trying to communicate to the population at large.

Indulgences requested of the pope should by rights have prompted the faithful to display more generosity. From the middle of the thirteenth century onwards, such interventions were commonplace, and they could have made resumption of work, and eventual completion, possible. The repetition of bulls testifies to the failure of this policy. Thus, Innocent IV and Alexander moved in favour of Besançon, in 1245 and 1257 respectively; Innocent IV intervened on behalf of Bayeux, in 1243, 1245 and 1254. In the south, such intervention was required if a site were to be opened, or even got ready. Such bulls proliferated to a spectacular degree, but were so ineffectual that they had to be renewed at regular intervals. Clermont was a special concern of the popes, with Innocent IV, Urban IV and Clement IV, in 1296 and 1297, involving themselves in the matter. Narbonne was similarly favoured. Clement V was especially concerned with the fate of Bordeaux, his first bull dating from 1307, but being fulminated again the following year.

The success or failure of such grants of indulgences might be measured by the anonymous yield of collections, if we were able to assess the amount accurately. The relevant documents are, however, so scarce, that here too our judgements needs must be circumspect.

At this period there were chests, much like those still in existence in present-day churches, which are distantly related to those of the Middle Ages. Their purpose was to hold alms given by the faithful. In the bulls of 1286, 1289 and 1297, Pope Nicholas IV had granted indulgences to those who gave alms while visiting the new sanctuary of Clermont. However, chests were also distributed throughout the diocese, at markets or in shops. Records state that, in 1294–5, there were ten such chests, both in churches and in private dwellings, in the town of Autun. In addition to the chests, there were collectors, who used to work in strictly defined areas. This ancient tradition took on a new dimension, from the end of the twelfth century onwards, as the numbers of collectors grew. Jean sans Terre gave some thought to this development and, on two separate occasions, on 13 January 1201 and 16 October 1202, authorised collections in the duchy of Normandie. Bishops and archbishops could not help but be in favour, but were only able to grant authorisation within the bounds of their own diocese. Thus, we hear of Guillaume, Archbishop of Reims, exhorting both clergy and congregation to help with the building of Senlis cathedral, which was hampered by a lack of funds. Likewise, Guy of la Tour, Bishop of Clermont, solicited Urban IV and was granted authorisation, in 1263, to have his collectors traverse the kingdom. They did not appear empty-handed, but bore relics, which they would put on display. Such objects served as the focus of religious ceremonies designed to encourage the faithful to be especially generous. The realisation soon dawned that, once the cost of the necessarily arduous journeys had been met, the yield of such collections was mediocre. In 1403, at Toul, the collectors were only able to hand over one-third of what they had harvested. The collections were not so productive as had been hoped, and measures were quickly taken to reinforce them. This is what happened at Clermont in the fourteenth century, when money was needed fairly urgently. Bishop Aubert Aycelin of Montaigu issued a pastoral letter to his clergy, instructing them to exhort the faithful of the diocese to contribute to the building costs of the cathedral. Collectors bearing these precious letters were immediately sent to every corner of the diocese. Funds trickled in so slowly that the bishop resolved to grant, in certain specified localities, collection contracts to licence-holders, who would levy such sums at their own risk. It is hard to gauge just how widespread this mode of collecting became, but it undoubtedly featured in a number of other dioceses. At Toul, for example, the office was frequently rented out for a period of one to three years, indeed even from one to seven consecutive years. In 1506, Jacquot of Vaubécourt paid 5000 francs a year for the privilege, for a period of three years.

Collectors might be either religious or laity, but initially they would seem to have belonged more to the former category than to the latter. In the fourteenth century, the documentary evidence for Toul gives the names of a large number of such collectors, all of whom were laymen; some appear to have been held in high esteem, since they were interred with wife and children in the cathedral cloister. They were, in fact, genuine professionals. Conversely, some of the collectors turned out to be dishonest. Thus, at Toul, in 1381, the property of one such man was confiscated, so as to reimburse the vestry for what it was owed.

We do not know what such collections ultimately yielded. As chance would have it, the yearly accounts audited for the vestry at Rodez, for the year 1293–4, allow us to form a fairly accurate notion, although it would be hazardous to extrapolate from them. The sum was 232 *livres rhodaniennes*, which represents 34 per cent of the vestry's overall income for that year. This is plainly a considerable sum, although due allowance should be made for the fact that Rodez is in the south. In corroboration of these accounts, we know that, in 1311, the inhabitants of Collioure gave the collectors of Saint-Bertrand-de-Comminges cathedral 46 *livres parisis*, and the inhabitants of Argèles-sur-Mer, 6 *livres parisis*. If one takes into consideration the small size of these localities, one will appreciate just how generous these offerings were.

Recourse to this means of fund-raising and of supplying the vestry treasury with cash continued up until the end of the Middle Ages. The bishop of Meaux, Jean of Drac (1459–73), instructed his canons to journey through the diocese soliciting offerings from the faithful. Similar collections were repeated in 1493, although in neither case do we know what sums were involved. We know, however, the solution that was adopted, at the end of the fifteenth century, by Robert of Croix-Mare, Archbishop of Rouen, in order to procure funds for the building of the second tower for the cathedral façade. He used the alms raised through dispensations of butter and milk during Lent, which earned the new structure the name of 'Butter Tower'. As it turned out, the sums raised were inadequate, so, notwithstanding the *gourmandise* of the Normans, numerous gifts had to be devoted to the task also.

QUARRIES

Securing hard cash was one thing, cutting costs an altogether different, and equally important, consideration. Of all the financial preoccupations of the prelates and canons, that of raw materials was by no means the least. They had to keep the site supplied with a steady flow of wood and stone, at a price that was not too high, if expenses were to be kept within reasonable limits. Wood generally did not pose too much of a problem, for prelate and canons tended to own forests, the resources of which could meet the needs of both builders and carpenters. The same was not true, however, of stone. Up until the Gothic period, demand had not been so great, and prelates had not therefore had to concern themselves with this problem. During the Romanesque period, competition for this resource had not been fierce, and it was therefore possible to procure it at fairly acceptable prices. The case of Canterbury is especially telling in this respect, for, when Guillaume of Sens was entrusted with the task of restoring the cathedral after the fire of 1174, he demanded that he be allowed to use stone from Caen, upon which he could wholly rely.

Everything changed in the Gothic period, for the men of the twelfth century had rediscovered stone, which guaranteed the quality, stability and beauty of the construction. All monuments of any importance were supposed to be built of stone, whether they were religious, military or civil. In the countryside, castles were rebuilt; the same was true, in the towns, of municipal buildings, princely and seigneurial residences and even individual houses. Demand was such that it must have occasioned a significant increase in the cost price of best-quality building stone. Before embarking upon the construction of a cathedral, a prelate would therefore have to satisfy himself that he would be able to find an adequate and uninterrupted supply of dressing stone, for the coherence of the monument would depend upon it.

It is true that Gothic architecture favoured the use of voids, and that this cut down the use of stone, but this economy, substantial though it was, was largely offset by the scale upon which monuments were built. In order to guarantee a plentiful supply, bishops would acquire quarries in the vicinity of the edifice that they were rebuilding. Thus, in the first third of the eleventh century, we find the bishop of Cambrai, Gérard I of Florines, setting out in search of quarries for the purpose of rebuilding his cathedral. One had then to effect the transfer of quarries which yielded their rightful owners a by no means negligible income. This was the case at Laon, and subsequently at Troyes. Thus, in the case of the former, in 1205, Jean of Chermizy surrendered to Bishop Renaud Surdelle all rights over any quarries located within seventeen kilometres of the site, to be used for the rebuilding of the chevet. The transfer was ratified through a charter dated 1205. A similar agreement was reached, a little later, at Troyes, where Milon, Count of Bar-sur-Seine, outlined in a charter of 1218 the precise conditions governing his donation to the church of Troyes. Thus, he granted the right to extract as much stone as was necessary from Acrimont quarry until such a time as the building was completed. We lack any information as to how, in the process of building Lyon cathedral in the thirteenth century, the canons of Lyon acquired the Lucernoy quarries and the Saint-Jean quarry at Anse. At Amiens, a purchase effected by the bursars of the vestry, in March 1235, from the chapter of Saint Martin of Picquigny, won them the authorisation to extract stones from

Beaumetz quarry. At Meaux, on the other hand, it was Bishop Aleaume of Cuisy who, in 1263, authorised the chapter to use Vareddes quarry, located ten kilometres upstream from Meaux, near to the Marne. At Tours, it was Saint Louis who, in 1241, surrendered the right to use Choillé quarry to the chapter.

A handful of examples taken from other countries serve to underline the fact that, due to a difference of overall context, financial arrangements differed considerably from those in France. We have already remarked upon the involvement of the town of Firenze in the building of its cathedral. The Florentines in fact paid the vestry a salt-tax of four farthings per pound on all salt passing through the communal chamber, and a poll-tax of two *sous*. Regular incomings thus guaranteed an uninterrupted rhythm to the site. At Orvieto, the inhabitants were taxed according to their possessions as assessed by the cadastral survey of 1292, and this solution to the problem was as successful as the one adopted in Firenze. In Milano, a wholly different formula was adopted. Registers of gifts donated by the faithful, of widely varying social origin, show that they were very numerous and were generally in kind; a shop was opened in the vicinity of the cathedral to sell them, and thus to procure ready cash.

The building of Praga cathedral was, as we have seen, a royal and Imperial affair and, in order to guarantee the success of the site, Jan of Bohemia, and later, his son, Karel IV, set up a fund which was replenished by tithes from the Kutnà Hora silver mines.

It would be an easy matter to produce any number of other examples of the diverse solutions adopted to the problem of sustaining the flow of raw materials required for such edifices.

THE VESTRY

Recurrent financial difficulties, the range of resources available and the number of people implicated in these problems to do with money necessitated the creation of a centralising institution, which was to play a double role, namely, to collect the takings and to fund the work-site. With their habitual pragmatism, the men of the Middle Ages conceived of a wholly original structure, which was given the name of 'vestry'. It reminds one irresistibly of institutions created by the modern state when faced with a similar set of problems, and when about to embark upon largescale ventures: the *établissement public*, the role of which is to ensure a flexibility which excessively rigid administrative rules hardly allow for.

The vestry was responsible for a number of key financial operations, namely, cashing incomings, which were generally sporadic and of varying amounts;

ensuring the regular funding of the site; and setting a budget which defined an overall programme and filled in the detail as regards the various chapters. In a word, it was a crucial regulator for the inauguration and the prosecution of sites over and above a certain size. It was designed to bring order into a situation that was, as we have already noted, somewhat anarchic. It met a definite need, but it acquired original characteristics in different periods, countries and dioceses which are in danger of being obscured by the use of one and the same term in every case.

To understand an institution such as the vestry, we need to bear in mind the date of its first appearance. Nothing was known of this institution either in the Romanesque period or in the early Gothic period, when the prelates were themselves in charge of the works, seeking support where it was needed from their own administration. They also saw to the financial side of things. The advantage of such an arrangement was that, as well as ensuring a unified command structure, it provided a much-needed flexibility. With the prelate in control, it was as if one had a financial steering-wheel, by means of which one could deal with urgent situations, emergencies and difficulties of every kind, all of which eventualities were only too frequent. His personal decision could lead to a swift resolution of a budgetary crisis and to the desired resumption of activity on site. As we have already noted, the financial resources upon which bishops could call, thanks to a drastic administrative reorganisation, enabled operations to be brought to a successful conclusion. Notwithstanding the greater size of the cathedrals, for which funding on the appropriate scale had to be found, there was at first no sign of a transformation in administrative terms.

It was in fact in the early years of the thirteenth century that the vestry emerged as a financial institution. One should not be misled by the fact that the same term (*fabrique*) was already in use in the twelfth century, for at that time it referred to the building under construction. This is how Louis VII's gift of 200 *livres* for the 'fabric' of the church (*ad fabricam ecclesiae*) should be understood. Other texts support this interpretation, and this usage anyway survived until a relatively late date, and until the middle of the thirteenth century in the case of Saint-Germain of Auxerre. It would be a simple matter to demonstrate that, on those sites which lacked a financial institution of this sort, the term kept its original meaning. It features, for example, on a number of accountable receipts from the same period, and it is in this fashion that the site of Saint-Pierre-des-Arcis in Paris is referred to in the accounts of the Hôtel de Saint Louis, from February to June 1234. One may readily understand why the word should have ended up, through a semantic evolution proceeding from the particular to the general, by subsuming a much larger reality. The charter of the archbishop of Bourges to the canons, in 1195, sheds some light on the change that was in progress, for there, in order to make it clear that the construction work was being referred to, the expression *opus fabricae*, actually a pleonasm, was used.

Communities

Nevertheless, institutions concerned with the financing of cathedral sites had been in existence prior to the thirteenth century. We do not know exactly how these communities of laymen were organised, either in administrative or in human terms, but they would seem not to have lasted long. There is sufficient documentation, however, for us to be able to affirm that they met the needs of the moment, in a wide range of different regions in both the south and the north. Around 1120, Raymond of Mastres, Bishop of Bayonne, and the viscount of Labourd together founded a confraternity, the purpose of which was to lend support to work on the cathedral site. An annual fee of four *deniers poitevins* was paid to the *operarius*, for each pair of parishes from Labourd and from Arbesouc. At Lisieux, Bishop Arnoul (1142–82), whose difficulties we discussed above, decided to call upon priests from the diocese of Noyon to form pious associations, their task being to organise collections for the building of the cathedral. Some priests went as far as England in search of funds. At Bayeux, Bishop Henri II (1165–1205) founded a charitable confraternity, the sole aim of which was to contribute to the financing of the half-finished cathedral.

The practice would seem then to have faded out, but at Toul, a place characterised by a still intense imagination, a confraternity was founded in honour of the cathedral site. Such associations would seem not to have performed the services anticipated of them. More particularly, they seemed incapable of resolving any major difficulties that arose. The priests sent by Arnoul to England had to admit defeat, and others fell into debt and disappeared from view. One should, however, bear in mind that the chapter had played no part in the founding of such associations, and that they had been created at the bishop's prompting alone; they served in fact to relay his wishes, and were designed to confront the various problems occasioned by the financing of a cathedral.

In the thirteenth century

The picture changed radically in the course of the thirteenth century, when the canons, who, with very few exceptions, had played no part on the sites, became equal partners. Their financial involvement was now such that they wished to have a correspondingly greater role. A bicephalous command structure required financial unity, and although we are not certain how it happened, the embryonic vestry would seem to have come almost immediately under the control of the chapter. The 1201 charter, which mentions the vestry of Bourges cathedral (*fabrica ecclesiae*), was promulgated by the chapter. The vestry was at this stage run by a layman, and was therefore still a very tentative affair, but the canons would soon take charge. This was at any rate the case in 1231, when texts refer to the existence of *receptores*, whose precise role is none too clear, and to *provisores*, who were treasurers. The administrative staff grew in numbers as time went on, with *procuratores*, or stewards, being added in 1260, and *rectores* in 1266.

As the vestry grew, its role began to be defined more precisely. In 1212, it was empowered to receive money. It was in fact vested with the status of person in civil law, which enabled it, in 1231, to own land. Although it is hard to be altogether certain, there is a strong probability that it acquired a high degree of independence at this time. From the number of canons involved, and, insofar as one can judge from the flourishing condition of its landed property and the considerable sums of money at its disposal, the vestry was a powerful entity in the first half of the thirteenth century, during the period when the cathedral was under construction. One cannot help but conclude that, though we lack any detailed information on the subject, it played a key role in the building of the cathedral.

The link which we have observed at Bourges between vestry and chapter became the general rule. A canon was usually in charge of the vestry. Henri Albus, for example, was a canon at Lausanne, in 1226, who held the office of sacristan and that of 'guard of the vestry and of gifts made to the fabric fund'. At Bordeaux, the canon who was in charge of the vestry, before 1235, would seem to have played less of a financial and administrative role, and to have been concerned more with establishing close links with the site, at least if the epithet applied to him is anything to go by (*operarius*). The documents provide more information with regard to Toul, where, in 1263, the vestry was under the sole control of the chapter, one of whose members was elected to run it and was known by the title of 'master of the vestry' or 'master of the fabric fund'. His responsibilities were very probably administrative and financial, for he served for only two to three years. We are concerned here with an essentially pragmatic attitude towards a wide range of different situations, and it would therefore be ill-advised to draw any general conclusions, and so to depict a typical vestry.

The vestry and the master of the fabric fund

The canons responsible for the financial running of the vestry were not content merely to serve as treasurers. They were naturally led to extend their field of action from the handling of expenses to the site itself. They were responsible for setting an annual budget, defining the sums involved and checking the relevant work as it was done. The sites were on such a gigantic scale, and required the spending of such huge sums, that the canons had to adopt an especially rigorous approach to the task in hand. They soon grew dissatisfied with a responsibility that was merely administrative and financial, and began to involve themselves in the actual running of the site, so as to ensure that it did not go astray, for any mishaps would have immediate repercussions financially. They had to purchase the crucial raw materials, such as wood or stone, when they did not already own stocks of them, and they were also responsible for paying the workmen and, in most cases, the architects too. They kept an especially careful watch on the latter, and made sure that they did not modify their original plans, for scrupulous adherence to them not only guaranteed a coherence to the construction, as we shall see below, but also set a limit to the overall expenditure. The administrators of the vestry were well aware of the consequences of changing an 'artist', for his successor was only too inclined to challenge, to alter or to overturn the original plan, being convinced that his own ideas represented a marked improvement. The history of architecture is full of instances of this sort, and it would therefore be otiose to list them. Every alteration to the plan had momentous consequences for the site, for its rhythm and for the cost of the whole operation. The canons were therefore concerned to involve themselves as closely as possible, and to make their presence felt on the site. It is in terms such as these that one should understand the application of the epithet *operarius* to a canon, it being his particular responsibility to attend what in modern-day parlance would be known as 'site meetings'. He would thus create a link with the vestry, and would weigh up, and pass judgement upon, each new operation.

When Gautier of Varinfroy was put in charge of the site at Meaux, in the middle of the thirteenth century, yet another stage was reached. A contract was drawn up between bishop, dean and chapter. The involvement of the bishop would seem to have been unusual for the period, and here he was doing no more than ratify an agreement. Generally, only the chapter was involved, during the fourteenth century at any rate. At Rouen, Jean of Andeli took an oath in the presence of the chapter, in an agreement binding just the two parties. The same formula was employed at Toul, in 1381, with the chapter hiring Pierre Perrat as 'master of the stone fabric fund' by means of a contract.

The chapter had good cause to be anxious, for architects had often made drastic alterations to previously agreed plans. It was crucial to ensure that a project did not go astray, and to guarantee, by clarifying the terms under which the architect was hired, the coherence of the site. The chapter was therefore prepared in some cases to go into details, and their descriptions are a particularly valuable source as regards the organisation of the site. In the contract of 1381 between Pierre Perrat and the Toul chapter, the architect undertook to leave the church the *molles*, that is, the lengths of wood cut to the shape of the edifice, which the stonecutter used to fashion the bases, the abacuses and the ogives, and thereby ensured that the outlines of the edifice would be homogeneous. These markers were of particular importance to the site, and their preservation was therefore crucial. Analysis of Pierre Perrat's contract suggests that some architects regarded these templates as being in some sense their own property. They would therefore keep them in their workshop during their period of employment on the site and then take them away, without troubling to hand them over to their successor. The chapter wished to establish that it was the rightful owner of such things, and that it was entitled to the free use of them. There must have been countless difficulties of this sort, to judge by the case of Toul chapter, which was prepared to challenge the artist's proprietary rights over a by no means negligible element of the building. By an agreement of 9 May 1460, the Toul chapter bought the drawing of the cathedral from the architect Hattonchâtel, reserving the right to have it executed by an architect of their own choice.

The vestry as the site's memory

The vestry and those who managed it had both to ensure that the site ran smoothly and to avoid any mishaps, the financial consequences of which could easily be anticipated. They were therefore at some pains to preserve any documents referring to the construction. In this respect, I have little time for those unfortunately widely held theories which deny the existence, in both the Romanesque and Gothic periods, of drawings and models. Such documentation was, admittedly, found to be lacking until a very late period, and this fact served to reinforce the notion that a creation which existed only in the architect's imagination would have taken shape on site. Recent researches have shown just how absurd such theories are, for they display blithe disregard for the quality of the execution of the edifices, which undoubtedly required extremely detailed preparatory studies, as elaborate as those known to us from the Renaissance and Classical periods. This documentation regarding the work-site comes under two different, and necessarily opposed, headings. The architect was the nub of the matter, since he was the link between the sponsor and the men employed on site. His task, then as now, was to produce for both parties sets of drawings or representative plans, which were not interchangeable, one with the other. The great merit of the vestry was to have tried, not always successfully, to ensure the preservation of both sets.

There should be no need to emphasise that the choice of architect had an impact upon the style of the monument. One could even go so far as to say that he had been hired precisely because his earlier projects had proved convincing. Once this hurdle had been crossed, further clarification of the project, which was still somewhat hazy in the mind of the sponsor, became necessary. Further development of the scheme required discussion between these two partners, after they had agreed upon what bears a curious resemblance to our modern specifications, although they were never put in writing. It was obviously the case that such encounters, if they were to be fruitful, had to rest upon study of the graphic documents, covering plan, elevation and details. The architect could thus convince the sponsor, while the latter was in a position to understand the proposed project. As today, such documents functioned at several different levels, from the overall conception to the finest detail, and ranged from models enabling one to assess masses, to general plans allowing one to gauge the impact of the construction work upon the environment, all of which made it possible to grasp the style of the monument. Particularly important parts of the monument were elaborated in still greater detail. Acceptance or rejection of the proposed design of the facade was of particular importance in this regard. This is why there are so many documents of this nature, beginning with Strasburg cathedral at the end of the thirteenth century. Discussion focussed upon models or drawings, which were probably highly detailed, and which could be corrected or amended before reaching their definitive state. There must have been many heated exchanges before the final agreement was reached, and it is worth noting that the financial estimate was not arrived at until the agreed project had been clarified.

The definitive drawing was traced upon hides of stitched vellum, as at Strasburg, which served as reference documents once the site was opened. The success of the site depended upon the safe preservation of such drawings, and it was clearly understood that the addition of too many minor alterations would prove disastrous. The vestries took charge of such documents, and we may readily understand why a number of them were so scrupulous in this regard that several of the drawings have survived until the present day, at Strasburg, Köln, Vienne, Ulm, Siena, Orvieto, Milano, Firenze, Cambridge and Clermont. The majority of the other vestries were no doubt equally careful, but their archives disappeared when they themselves were suppressed.

When the partners were in dispute, these documents, being the record of their original agreement, served as a reference point. The sponsors would invoke them when they wished to guarantee a degree of homogeneity to the construction, the plans for which were frequently overturned by new architects dissatisfied with the original project. As is observed below in relation to Villard of Honnecourt's Notebook, it is circumstances of this sort which account for the startling coherence of Reims cathedral, which took over fifty years to build.

In addition to the architect's drawings, mention should also be made of those documents which were assembled at the chapter's behest, before it had actually embarked upon the construction of its cathedral. The chapter wished to be better informed regarding rival sites, before coming to a decision. Thus, the vestry in Strasburg assembled drawings from Praga, Freiburg, Ulm, Esslingen, Ratisbon, Paris and Bourges, the largest sites in Europe, both in France and in the Imperial domains, in the course of discussions which were, one imagines, somewhat tense. Although it is impossible to be absolutely certain, it is probable that the largest vestries had at their disposal extensive, diligently preserved documentation, to which they might refer whenever any contentious issue arose. Here too, Villard of Honnecourt's Notebook is instructive.

These especially precious drawings or models were not intended for use on the work-site, for communication between the architect and those in charge of construction was achieved by other, more disposable means. This is why, in the Middle Ages as today, such devices did not survive the winding-down of the site. In order to define his plan more precisely, the architect would communicate with the representatives of the various guilds – who nowadays would be clerks – by means of quick sketches drawn on perishable surfaces, with equally perishable materials, for example, chalk on wooden planks etc. Obviously none of this has survived, just as nothing has been preserved of the rapid drawings dashed off by an architect on his visits to the site and pounced upon by clerks and journeymen.

Finally, there was another documentary series of which some examples have survived, as recorded in texts, in their original form or in reproductions. So much did the successful running of the site depend upon the preservation of the templates, as we have noted in the case of Toul, in 1381, that the vestry was especially careful to save them. The preservation of these pieces of cut wood, made for the use of the stonecutters, would seem to have been the general rule. Since the templates were in constant use by the stonecutters, they would seem to have been portable. They are reproduced in the stained-glass window of Saint Chéron at Chartres, at the beginning of the thirteenth century, in the stonecutter's workshop. They might even have circulated from place to place, as numerous testimonies at the end of the Middle Ages imply. The oldest would seem to have been those used at Canterbury cathedral. Thus, Guillaume of Sens, the architect entrusted with the task of rebuilding the fire-ravaged cathedral, sent the various outlines to Caen, so that stones might be cut to specified sizes at the quarry entrance, thereby achieving a considerable reduction in the massive transportation costs.

Villard of Honnecourt's Notebook

Villard of Honnecourt's Notebook is a unique source in this regard, if one accepts the interpretation of it that has recently been advanced. Analysis of this manuscript, which is traditionally dated to the years between 1225 and 1235, and which was first published by the architect Lassus in 1858, has proved particularly contentious, with doubt being cast upon the ultimate purpose of the document. The album is in fact defective, with eight of the forty-one sheets mentioned in the fifteenth century being missing. It had previously been supposed that it was a sketch book, and that Villard was contemplating the drafting of a sort of treatise enumerating the various techniques used at the time. The drawings dominate the written text, which is brief, even perfunctory. Of the drawings which have survived, a number are concerned with architecture and with building techniques. The majority of monuments drawn are cathedrals, namely, Cambrai, Chartres, Lausanne, Meaux and Reims, with the exception of the Cistercian abbey of Vaucelles and the basilica of Saint-Quentin, both of which were close to Villard's home town, Honnecourt. Contrary to claims that have often been advanced, the drawings are not on-the-spot representations of plan and elevation, such as would have made the document a unique record of the state of sites at a specific moment. Villard had in fact merely recopied the various drawings kept by the vestry in the fabric fund hut. This was a markedly easier task, as one will appreciate if one considers what was involved, now as in former times, in the delineating of a plan or the tracing of an elevation. This accounts for the often noted differences between the existing monument and the drawings, as with the section at Reims, or the drawings of the rose-windows at Lausanne and Chartres. Since Villard was copying from an already existing drawing, he did not trouble to check to see if he had executed it accurately. It was architectural invention, not the reality of the monument, which interested him, and he probably selected from among the various documents the drawing which best served to illustrate his argument. We cannot therefore be sure how many sites he actually visited, for he could well have found all the documentation in one, particularly well-endowed place. If this was the case, Reims could well have been the source, for Villard's notebook contains a plethora of outlines of that edifice. In these drawings, he took particular care to distinguish what already existed from what was anticipated, and it is possible that he studied the plan in the fabric fund hut. Thus, on folio 32, he reproduced the 'toraus pillar' of the cathedral, which was to support one of the towers of the western facade, erected some thirty years later.

Not only did Villard find the plans, covering both ensemble and detail, for Reims cathedral, but he also came across the discarded elements made for the use of the stonecutters. Thus, on folio 63, he sketches the templates [*molles*] of the various supports for a radiating chapel built many years before. Although these templates were of no further use to the stonecutters, the vestry had shown great diligence in preserving them. This additional testimony casts a fresh light upon Reims cathedral, and upon the homogeneity of its construction, a characteristic which may be accounted for in terms of the quite exceptional wealth of documentation.

It therefore became absolutely necessary for the vestry to allocate a place which might serve both as a store for the conservation of documents and as an architect's office. The chapter calculated that the best way of guaranteeing such continuity was to place at the disposal of the architect and his team a location, which, so as to prevent any of the documents falling into private hands, would then be passed on to his successor. It is hard to say just when such a building was placed at the architect's disposal, or when his office came to be subsumed by the vestry.

The vestry as fabric fund hut

The aforementioned process had been completed by the thirteenth century, on the great sites of northern France, but the bishops may well have tried to set up such offices earlier, during the twelfth century, in order to avoid the difficulties mentioned above. The vestry was located in a building that was probably originally made of wood, but which would tend, from the thirteenth century onwards, to be built of stone. It was situated in the immediate vicinity of the cathedral, outside both the canonial precinct and the palace, for obvious reasons of convenience. The size of the building reflected the importance of the vestry. The vestry at Strasburg was in every respect exceptional, as we shall see below, its importance given material form in the fabric fund hut built in 1276 immediately to the south-west of the cathedral. A part of the building is still in existence, although it has been modified, enlarged and finally, turned into a fabric fund museum, a fitting outcome for an institution which played a major role in the process of construction and in the everyday life of the monument.

It is worth considering Strasburg vestry in greater detail, for it was a particularly original institution, and one which is far better known than many others, in part because a proportion of its archives have been preserved. It has survived until the present day, in a form which owed much to the Middle Ages, its present status dating from a decree of 1803, which made the town of Strasburg responsible for its administration. Its property and incomings, reserved for the upkeep and conservation of the cathedral, are managed by the town, but quite separately, so as to avoid any confusion. It owns a number of buildings, including the *Musée de l'Oeuvre Notre-Dame*, and heads a team of stonemasons, sculptors and specialist artisans, playing a part, therefore, in the restoration of the monument.

This situation represents the culmination of a long and turbulent history, closely linked to the turmoil and difficulty experienced on the site. In contrast to the other vestries, that of Strasburg was first mentioned in texts at a relatively late date, in 1246. It was known as 'l'Oeuvre de Notre-Dame' (*opus sancte Marie*), and was run by administrators, who, at the end of the thirteenth century, included a governor (*gubernator*) and a procurator (*procurator*), the former being a layman, the latter a cleric. From this period, the fabric fund was increasingly under municipal control. Like many Rhineland cities, the town of Strasburg was concerned to break free of episcopal authority, and therefore sought, from the middle of the thirteenth century, to involve itself in the administration of the vestry. The agreement between bishop and town, in 1263, was to give rise to a contract, one of whose articles recognised the right of the latter to appoint the priest in charge at an altar, any gifts he received being credited to the fabric fund. The magistrate was thus granted a preliminary right of inspection, which was to be extended subsequently and provoked numerous disputes. In the fourteenth century, the chapter managed to retain a right of supervision. Bishop Friedrich of Blanckenheim attempted to claw back rights from the town, which subsequently, in 1399, staged a minor revolution. The resulting reorganisation allowed the council to appoint three administrators, and provision was made for a chaplain authorised to receive ill-gotten goods, along with a lay tax-collector. The chapter thereby lost a large part of its responsibilities, since the tax-collector had previously been a cleric, and the chaplain became an employee of the fabric fund. In 1422, it was ruled that the vestry's resources were solely 'for the use of Notre-Dame'. At the end of the fifteenth century, the institution became a municipal foundation, to such an extent, indeed, that in 1501 the claim could be made that fabric fund and town were 'one and the same'. In 1648, the chapter's right of supervision, maintained until this time, was suppressed.

The fabric fund received gifts in cash but also, as we have seen above, in kind, each item being scrupulously recorded in a book, first mentioned in 1262 and referred to up until the sixteenth century. It collected rents in cash and in kind, and also managed larger properties. Finally, in 1351, it received the rent from 130 houses and shops in Strasburg. The extraordinary wealth of the institution is borne out by the balance of incomings. Its outgoings, if one disregards the, in fact substantial, administrative costs, were all committed to the building and its upkeep, no responsibility being assumed for objects of worship. The bitter controversy of 1451 between fabric fund and chapter regarding baptismal fonts reflects this fact, with the administrators refusing to fund them, it being their view that they were fixtures and fittings, and therefore the concern of the parish, not of the cathedral. The town's annexation of the fabric fund of Notre-Dame was to remain an isolated case, and may be explained by the urban context of the Rhineland, but also by the cupidity that such wealth aroused.

Municipal vestries in Italy

Municipal vestries existed in other parts of Europe aside from France. Italy, for example, provides several examples of such a phenomenon, which is itself intrinsically linked to the role of the municipality in the construction of cathedrals. Italian cathedrals, by contrast with the French, enjoyed a close relation with municipal life, contributing, much as the town halls had done, to the greater glory and independence of the commune.

At Firenze, when it was decided to renovate the church of Santa Reparata, they wished to build 'the most beautiful and the noblest church in all of Tuscany'. The Siennese, being equally proud of their own city, entertained a similar ambition. In 1248, the commune embarked upon the rebuilding of its cathedral, the facade of which was under construction in 1284. At the beginning of the fourteenth century, a time of peace and tranquillity, the Siennese suddenly decided to enlarge the monument to a considerable degree, even though it had only just been completed, their aim being to give proper expression to the independence of the commune. The baptistry was erected further down to the east, with the apse adjoining it. Once again, in 1339, the inhabitants of Siena changed their mind, judging that the nave was not large enough, and began to build a new one, grafted on to the south arm of the transept. They thereby transformed the monument quite radically, the choir of the nave becoming the transept of a gigantic edifice. The ill-executed venture was in the end abandoned.

If the Siennese changed their minds, vacillated and backtracked so often, it was in part because the executive authority was too unwieldy, being subject to a plethora of conflicting influences and therefore unable to fulfil its role effectively. In 1260, the administration of the fabric fund devolved upon nine *legales homines*, chosen in equal proportion by the bishop, the consuls of the various trades and the city priors. They had to present annual accounts to the Council of Bell and People, but the executive authority did not belong to them but to men appointed by this same Council, the *operarii*, who swore an oath to the *podestà*. The *operarii* were also responsible, among other things, for the choice of architect.

At Firenze, in 1296, it was the Calimala guild which was responsible for the fabric fund (*opera*). At the beginning of the fourteenth century, mention is made of three presidents elected by the bishop, the chapter and the commune. In 1321, an edict introduced a modification, whereby the running of the fabric fund was entrusted to five of the major guilds, namely, Calimala, Wool, Por Santa Maria, Doctors and Grocers, with a presidency rotated on an annual basis. The system was so unwieldy that it was suppressed in 1331, and management of the fund was entrusted to the Wool guild.

At Orvieto, the commune played a still more prominent role, appointing a notary. There were interminable disputes with the clergy, which the pope ended in 1420 by ruling that neither bishop nor clergy could interfere with the running of the fabric fund.

In Milano, the vestry council was 500 strong in 1387 and numbered around 300 people in 1401. It seemed indispensable to delegate authority, if the vestry was to be run efficiently. By contrast with the other cities, the clergy managed to retain some sort of role for itself, but it failed to heal its internal rifts. In the great debate of 1391–2, recourse was finally had to a council of fourteen architects, from all over Europe, to whom a series of famous questions was addressed (see above, p. 223).

The vestry as maintenance service

Surprising though it may seem, we lack any solid information regarding the mode of organisation and the role of the vestry when the northern cathedral sites were at the height of their activity, in the thirteenth century. Its function is more easily discerned in the fourteenth and fifteenth centuries, when the great constructions were completed and the tension had abated. All the signs are that their role had been not so much in construction as in the upkeep of the already completed edifice. The first mention of the vestry at Chartres does not predate the fourteenth century, when it gave every appearance of being a remarkable and perfectly polished administration. It was certainly already a seasoned institution, although it is impossible to specify a precise birth date. The treasurers, known as *provisores*, who were three, or sometimes two, in number, were canons, elected yearly and answerable to the chapter alone. They were assisted by an accountant, a clerk responsible for paying the workmen and the suppliers, and for meeting any expenditures. They drew up accounts, which were then submitted to the chapter. Working alongside was the 'master of the fabric fund' (*magister operis*), who was neither a clerk nor a technician, but a layman whose hereditary office was in the gift of a prebend. In 1384, the chapter managed to buy back the office, which was then held by a certain Jean of Ivry. In fact, this 'master of the fabric fund' functioned as a steward, who enjoyed only a limited degree of responsibility.

We do not know how such a situation arose, although it undoubtedly has its roots in the thirteenth century. There were other laymen involved, for example, master craftsmen contracted to the fabric fund, and the other workmen also. As it happened, all of this did not represent a very high level of activity; the vestry's resources were directed towards maintenance work on the cathedral, but also on the canons' residences. There was a somewhat similar situation at Autun, and at Toul, where the vestry's chief responsibility concerned permanent works required by such largescale constructions rather than any new works. One should further add that, as was only to be expected, the resources proved inadequate to the needs of a large site.

6

The churches in the cathedral

♣

When we contemplate a Gothic cathedral, what strikes us most forcibly is the fact that we are able, at a single glance, to take in the full extent of its long nave, which dissolves into the apse to the east, and into the penumbra of the side-aisles to the north and to the south. Our eye is then drawn to the altar, bathed in light supplied by the many openings in the apse. We are at the same time impressed by the regular and vigorous rhythms of the bays, which in French architecture are conceived as identical cells. This repetition establishes a first dynamic. A second dynamic, diametrically opposed to the first, is achieved by means of the verticality of the supports which meet up again on the keystone of the vault. We have the impression that this overall perspective was intended, and we are so entranced by this tension in height and in depth that we have no inkling of the technical expertise employed in the actual construction of the monument.

This was not at all how the men of the Middle Ages saw their cathedrals, for the huge nave then consisted of a series of volumes clearly demarcated by screens serving to divide up the central aisle. It is true, however, that they did not rise to the full height of the building, and that the worshipper, if he were to raise his eyes to the vaults, would recover the sense of spatial unity which so impresses us today.

Many cathedrals outside France feature such a fragmentation of the interior volume. This was not the case in Italy, however, which suffered the same upheavals as France had done, nor in Germany, but was true, rather, of England and of Spain. English architects disagreed sharply with many of their colleagues in this respect, and the quest for spatial unity was not of paramount importance to them; the twofold tension between depth and height did not strike them as fundamental. They did not conceive of the bay as a self-sufficient unit, whose

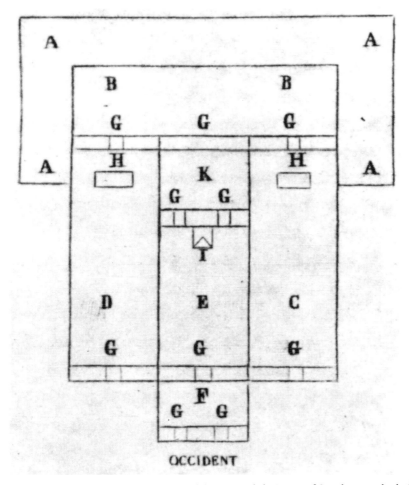

OCCIDENT

Fig. 120 Schematic representation of the internal divisions of Strasburg cathedral, published by Specklin in the sixteenth century.
A. The residences of bishop and monks; B. Communal courtyard; C. Part of the church set aside for the use of women; D. Part occupied by men; E. Middle part of the church, used for preaching and baptisms; F. Place outside the church; G. Doors and entrance-ways; H. Two altars; I. The throne; K. The choir reserved for the use of the clergy.

repetition would determine the interior volume, with the vaulting of the latter serving as its logical culmination. The roofing was, on the contrary, seen as a unity functioning as a kind of lid. The organic link between the vertical supports and the spring of the ogives was intentionally interrupted. By the same token, the interior fragmentation of the monument was integrated with the original design of the plan, the roofing being designed to unify the interior volume.

The Spanish Gothic cathedrals respected the rules of French aesthetics, and their interior volumes were conceived as fragmented ensembles. By contrast with the northern cathedrals, however, they have maintained their medieval lay-out. The subdivisions, if compared to those on the other side of the Pyrenees, could even be said to be sublimated. The 'coro', which generally occupied a significant part of the central aisle to the west of the arms of the transept, took the form of an entirely closed space, which the worshipper encountered upon first entering the edifice. The autonomy of the 'coro' was deliberately emphasised, by being separated from the sanctuary by the transept.

The French cathedrals had originally featured a somewhat different formula for the division of their interior, involving a close link between the sanctuary and the clerics' choir. We have already noted that the various screens had been suppressed across the centuries. The crucial factor had been the implementation of the rulings of the Council of Trent, which had called for a visual link between the priest celebrating the sacrifice of the Mass and the participation of the congregation. Some of the stone divisions disappeared altogether, or else were replaced by metal screens. A new harmony of a particularly felicitous sort was achieved between the monument and the decor of the seventeenth and eighteenth centuries, and one which restored the spatial unity of the monument as the architect had conceived of it in his original plans.

If one is to summon up an accurate picture of the lay-out of the French cathedrals in the medieval period, one has to use one's imagination. Many texts evoke such arrangements, and the ancient plans give us some of the details, especially the drawings seen from above, which give us a striking and quite unique image (Paris, Angers etc.). What stands out, in contrast to the Spanish conception, is the close link between the sanctuary and the clerics' choir. The French cathedrals would seem to have been divided into two ensembles. Thus, to the west stood the church used by the congregation; to the east was the priests' church, which was enclosed by a stone screen, which itself looped back to the west with the rood-screen. The second ensemble was subdivided into two smaller sections, with the sanctuary situated to the east and the clerics' choir to the west.

THE PRIESTS' CHURCH

The presbytery

The treatment of the priests' church depended upon the architectural conception of the whole edifice, for the presence or absence of an ambulatory had a profound impact upon its internal lay-out and, consequently, upon the access enjoyed by the faithful to this part of the building. In cathedrals with ambulatories, the dimensions of the priests' church were defined by the supports of the right-hand bays and of the apse, between which a screen could easily be extended. A worshipper was able to gain access to the turn in the ambulatory without disturbing the priests, who, on the other side of the screen, were assured the sort of calm that was propitious to prayer. In those monuments which featured a semi-circular apse rather than an ambulatory, the former was reserved for the use of the priests, and the congregation was excluded. For obvious reasons, the first type of monument was common in France, while the second type, though far rarer, occurred in a number of instances, at Angers and Besançon in the north, and at Carcassonne in the south.

The presbytery was organised around the high altar, whose position had not altered since the previous period. As a rule, the high altar was centrally placed, although Reims, where it was located at the crossing of the transept, was an exception. It was generally accorded the utmost care, and was sometimes very elaborately worked, as was the case at Köln cathedral, where it had been in place since the consecration of 1322. Its four faces dressed in alabaster were 4·5 metres long by 1·5 metres wide, and featured scenes from the life of the Virgin and from the childhood of Christ, its focus being the crowning of the Virgin, to the west. This altar was the object of general admiration right from the start.

The high altar was reserved for the use of the prelate, whether bishop or archbishop. There was a second altar, located further to the east, of lesser importance, upon which the daily Mass was celebrated.

The canons' choir

The western part of the priests' church was reserved for the use of the canons. This partitioning was emphasised by a screen, which was generally fairly low, judging by the evidence from numerous ancient plans (Besançon). At Le Mans, the dividing screen was made of copper, whereas at Toul a veil, which could be opened or closed at will, was used. The canons could thus participate in the

Fig. 121 The canons' choir at Notre-Dame of Paris, after Israël Silvestre (1699).

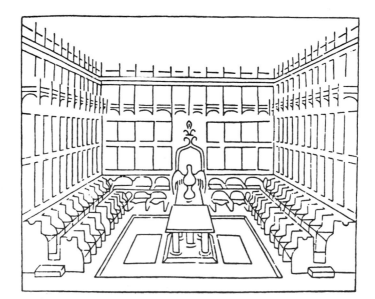

Fig. 122 Elevation of a canons' choir (Toul cathedral?), by Jean Pèlerin, known as the Viator (1505).

Fig. 123 Sanctuary and canons' choir at Angers cathedral, after Lehoreau (before 1699).

bishop's celebration of the act of worship. Their communal life, which, as we observed above, had been markedly reduced, recovered its meaning in the prayers which were recited in common at specified hours. Admittedly, there was a fairly high rate of absenteeism, in spite of the severe penalties imposed.

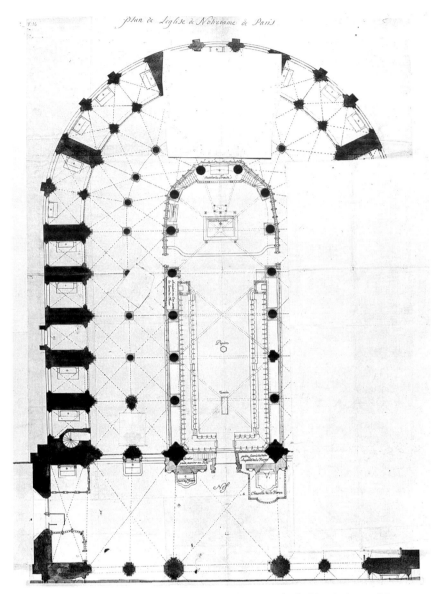

Fig. 124 Plan of the sanctuary and choir of Paris cathedral by Robert of Cotte (1700).

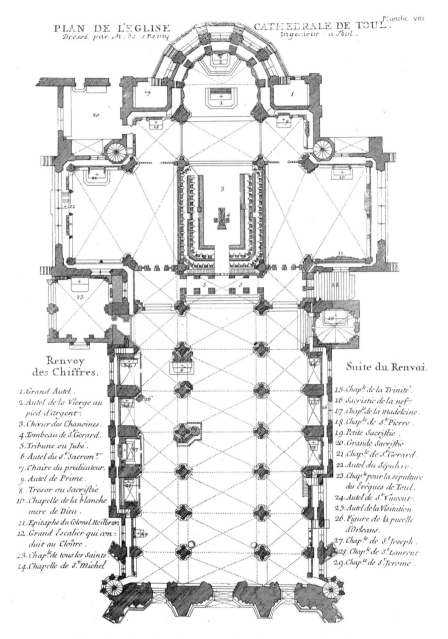

PLAN DE L'EGLISE   CATHEDRALE DE TOUL.
Dressé par M. de S. Rémy   *Ingenieur a Toul.*

Planche. VIII

Renvoy
des Chiffres.

1. *Grand Autel.*
2. *Autel de la Vierge au*
   pied d'Argent.
3. *Choeur des Chanoines.*
4. *Tombeau de S. Gerard.*
5. *Tribune ou Jubé.*
6. *Autel du S. Sacremt.*
7. *Chaire du prédicateur.*
9. *Autel de Prime.*
8. *Trésor ou Sacristie*
10. *Chapelle de la blanche*
    mere de Dieu.
11. *Epitaphe du Colonel Heilbron.*
12. *Grand Escalier qui con-*
    duit au Cloître.
23. *Chaple de tous les Saints.*
14. *Chapelle de S. Michel*

Suite du Renvoi.

15. *Chaple de la Trinité.*
16. *Sacristie de la nef.*
17. *Chaple de la Madeleine.*
18. *Chaple de St Pierre.*
19. *Petite Sacristie*
20. *Grande Sacristie*
21. *Chaple de St Gerard.*
22. *Autel du Sépulcre.*
23. *Chaple pour la sépulture*
    des Evêques de Toul.
24. *Autel de St Vincent.*
25. *Autel de la Visitation*
26. *Figure de la pucelle*
    d'Orleans.
27. *Chaple de St Joseph.*
28. *Chaple de St Laurent.*
29. *Chaple de St Jerome.*

Fig. 125 Plan of Toul cathedral in the eighteenth century (after de Saint-Rémy).

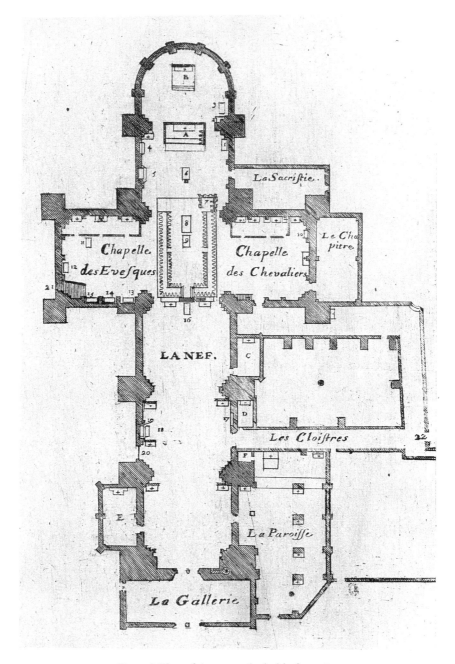

Fig. 126 Plan of Angers cathedral before 1699.

This was explained in part by the great age of a number of canons, in part by the onerous responsibilities assumed by the most gifted of them. There was some risk, indeed, of administrative duties taking precedence over the religious life. The number of stalls in the choir corresponded to the number of prebends, each canon having a place reserved for him. One may readily understand why it was that, when the plans for reconstruction were being elaborated, particular care was taken to ensure that the lay-out of the choir respected their need for silence, so that they could pray and meditate. The building of a screen along the sides, and its further extension to the west both reflected this need for isolation and at the same time supported the stalls, which were generally on two levels. The stalls were surmounted by screens, of varying heights, which shielded the canons from the rigours of the climate. Jean Pèlerin, known as the Viator, made a drawing of this arrangement in his *Perspective classique* (1505), with the stalls resting against a very high wall, and with the furnishings, consisting of a table and a lectern, also being represented.

The bishop's chair was placed at the easternmost extremity of the south stalls, thereby establishing a sort of link between the sanctuary and the canons' choir. In the choir of Angers cathedral, for example, such an arrangement served as a symbol of the participation of the bishop in the communal life of the canons. There should be no need to remind the reader that this choir did not have an altar, for the canons celebrated holy office at one of those located in the radiating chapels, in the main body of the church or even in the galleries.

This general approach had to be adapted to local customs, but also to the plan of the edifice. This accounts for the wide range of different lay-outs. Where there was an ambulatory, the western limit of this choir was generally located at the western pillars of the crossing, thus leaving both arms for the use of the faithful. This was the case at Besançon, Chartres, Le Mans and Paris, whereas at Lausanne, Metz and Toul, the choir extended further to the west before being anchored directly above the western piers, and at Reims it was situated on the west of the crossing.

Where there was no ambulatory, the lay-out proved a trickier matter. The faithful were debarred from the eastern parts of the edifice, while the canons' choir generally occupied the crossing of the transept, the boundary being fixed at the western piers. This was the case at Angers and at Strasburg. At Angers, prior to the reorganisation of 1699, the choir extended as far as the crossing of the transept; the presbytery occupied the apse, and featured some very beautiful fourteenth-century frescoes, which are now obscured by the stalls. Each arm of the transept, being isolated from the congregational church, served a different purpose : to the north, alongside the episcopal palace, stood the bishop's chapel, while to the south was the knights' chapel. At Lyon, the choir extended beyond the transept, occupying the last bay of the nave.

In the south, circumstances were much more various. The cathedrals of the French type adopted the arrangement used in the northern cathedrals. Thus, at Clermont, the fourteenth-century rood-screen was stretched between the eastern piers of the transept. This was also true of the sixteenth-century rood-screen at Limoges. At Bayonne, on the other hand, the lay-out more closely resembled that generally adopted in Spain, with the choir occupying the last three bays of the nave, leaving the transept entirely free. It was therefore separated from the sanctuary placed in the apse, to the east of the transept.

England

It is important to appreciate the particular qualities of the English treatment of their cathedrals, which derived above all from the communal life led by the canons and from the strong sense of community shared by bishop and clerics. There were a number of consequences, which enable us to assess the differences in the architectural treatment of cathedrals in England and France.

One should first of all recall that there was a greater degree of liturgical uniformity in England than in France. The customs of Salisbury had been gradually adopted, and indeed, in the fifteenth century, the majority of cathedral chapters, including the dioceses of Wales and Scotland, complied. Secondly, one should take account of the communal life of the canons : a number of cathedral chapters had adopted the regular reform, which had repercussions, not so much for the cathedral as for the plan of the building, which reminded one irresistibly of that of a monastery.

Finally, England offers the already mentioned example of Salisbury, a thirteenth-century cathedral established on virgin soil, where Richard Poor, dean between 1197 and 1215, had begun to reflect deeply on the question of ritual. The plan of the cathedral, like that of the close, was the consequence, the transfer from Sarum having been realised in 1220. The secular community now numbered some fifty canons, and occupied the three right-hand bays located between the two transepts, so that through this double transept the priests' church was given a cruciform plan. The second transept marked the separation of choir from presbytery.

The other original feature concerned the treatment of the eastern part of the edifice, with its chevet, which contained the chapel of the Trinity, and which welcomed the whole of the religious community, both canons and vicar. This accounts for its especially large dimensions, and for its church-hall plan. A daily Mass for the Virgin was celebrated there. The canons' association with the cult of the Virgin should need no emphasis, but it was especially pronounced in England. At Ely, for example, the Lady Chapel became an entirely independent edifice, erected on the northern arm of the cathedral.

THE CONGREGATIONAL CHURCH

The rood-screen

Cathedrals were congregational churches, and one of their functions was therefore to welcome the faithful. A large space had to be allotted to worshippers, even though parts of the edifice were out of bounds to them when services were being held; they could not then circulate around the ambulatory or, when the canons' choir was extended into the square of the transept, enter the transept arms. Railings, if plans of the sort drawn up in Metz in 1728 are trustworthy, made it possible to block access whenever necessary. During these ceremonies, the congregation would assemble in the central nave and in the side-aisles. To the east, the congregational church rested against the western screen of the canons' choir. The screen, as we noted above with regard to earlier periods, assumed a complex meaning, for it was meant to be both a closure, dividing worshippers from canons, and a link, because the wall was pierced by a door permitting circulation between the two spaces. The upper part of the wall featured a platform, which could be reached from the choir by either of two staircases. A priest would climb up there and read the epistle for the day, preach or lead the responses. It was known fairly early on as a *jubé* (rood-screen) – this name, which has stuck, being derived from *Jube Domine benedicere*, the words uttered by the cleric whose task it was to ask for the bishop's blessing. In this fashion, the congregation could follow the Mass celebrated by the bishop at the high altar, with the cleric serving as an intermediary. Altars specifically for the use of the congregation were stationed at the foot of the rood-screen, on either side of the central section.

At a very early stage, this rood-screen was given an especially complex decoration, on the side facing the congregational church. A Christ on the cross was placed on the platform, alongside a representation of a standing Virgin and

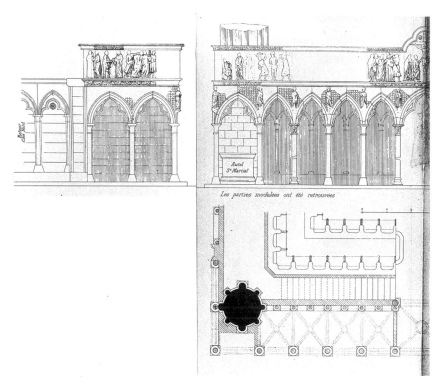

Fig. 127 Speculative reconstruction of the rood-screen at Bourges (after Gauchery).

Saint John. The wall itself, hung with arches containing altars and the door, was decorated with sculpted scenes, from the early years of the thirteenth century in the Empire, and from 1230 to 1240 in France. They generally featured the life of Christ (Chartres) or, more specifically, his Passion (Bourges, Laon, Paris etc.). The sculptures at Strasburg are particularly original in iconographic terms, with statues of the apostles between the sconcheons, of the Virgin with the rose bush in the centre and of sculpted scenes inside the choir.

The majority of the great northern cathedrals had rood-screens, but, from the seventeenth century until late in the eighteenth century, they were destroyed, in spite of strong opposition to this iconoclastic movement. At Noyon, where the decision to demolish the rood-screen was taken in 1753, recourse had to be had to the arbitration of the Conseil du Roi (1755), before the destruction could proceed. Some of the rood-screens were introduced very belatedly, at Auch, for example, which dates from as late as 1489; at Le Mans, which was erected at the end of the fifteenth century or at the beginning of the sixteenth; at Limoges,

Les parties silhouettées se trouvent mutilées

which dates from around 1533–4, and at Bordeaux, which was built in 1540. However, each of these screens probably replaced an earlier version.

These rood-screens, sculpted at a late date, replaced or completed older screens featuring on the original plans. At Toul, for example, there was a rood-screen as early as the middle of the thirteenth century, which was rebuilt at the bishop's expense between 1561 and 1568, and which featured walls seven metres high. At Le Mans, the rood-screen, first mentioned in 1245, was renovated at the end of the fifteenth century and at the beginning of the sixteenth, by Cardinal Philippe of Luxembourg. Many other examples could be quoted which would serve to show that, if the architect's original conception had taken the existence of the canons' choir and of the closure to the west into account, the decoration of the edifice could well have been an afterthought. At Notre-Dame of Paris, at the time of its original construction, there must have been a rood-screen immediately to the east of the piers of the crossing, which was renovated when both arms of the transept were extended, during the decade 1250–60.

In some buildings, this decoration was continued along the outside of the

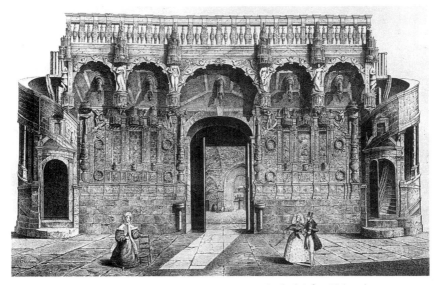

Fig. 128 The rood-screen at Limoges cathedral (after Tripon).

walls, against which the canons' stalls rested. These full partition-walls would seem to have been intended to receive such decoration, which was sometimes taken further still, beyond the doors located to the north and to the south which allowed access to the priests' church, up to the screen girdling the ambulatory. A different treatment was adopted at the turn, which generally involved, above a stylobate, a grating which enabled the faithful to glimpse the presbytery and the high altar, the focus, in religious terms, of the whole edifice.

Choir screens

One of the most famous choir screens was that of Notre-Dame of Paris. Not all the screen has survived, the revolving part having disappeared when Robert of Cotte was fashioning the Wish of Louis XIII, at the beginning of the eighteenth century. Above a high wall, which featured nothing more than a blind arcade, there unfolded to the north a number of scenes from the childhood of Christ; to the south, there were representations of various appearances of Christ after his resurrection; finally, the revolving part would have been devoted to scenes from the story of Joseph. The scenes ran in sequence from north to south, by way of the rood-screen, upon which were carved scenes from the Passion. As was so often the case, completion of the project was staggered across a period of time, the clerics having begun this highly ambitious programme at the western facade

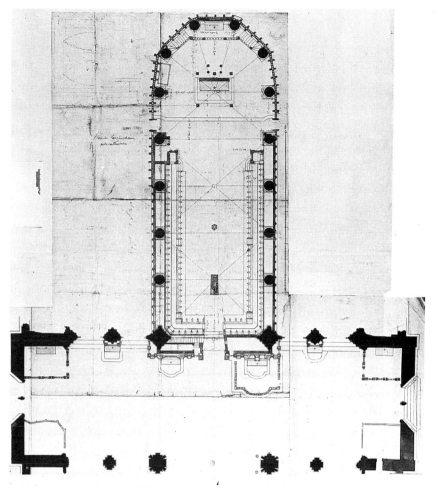

Fig. 129 Second plan of the sanctuary and choir of Paris cathedral, by Robert of
Cotte (1700).

during the decade 1250–60, before proceeding, at the end of the thirteenth
century, with the north, continuing with the south in the first third of the
fourteenth century and concluding a little later with the revolving part. The
iconographic homogeneity would lead one to suppose that the theme defined at
the start had been realised as and when funds permitted, without ever having
been challenged. This long sculpted band told the story of the New Covenant
and ended in a quite untoward fashion on the interior of the southern arm of the
transept, which featured a Last Judgement with the Christ of the second
Parousia, placed above the statues of Adam and Eve.

The iconography used in Paris was, as one would expect, much imitated in other cathedrals. It recurs at Reims, and again at Chartres. Thus, at Reims, Ferru of Cassinel made a gift, in 1390, of 1,000 *livres*, to fund the creation of a screen identical to that of Paris. As things turned out, the screen was never realised, and unadorned walls were erected in the right-hand part of the edifice, with perforated walls in the revolving part. At Chartres, in 1513, the canons decided to adopt an identical formula, and to demolish the old screen, which was very probably of stone. They entrusted the task to Jean of Beauce, who had just completed the new bell-tower. In fact, the documents suggest that Canon Manterne, who was responsible for defining the iconographic programme, changed his mind several times. At first, he had planned to represent sixty-eight scenes drawn from the Old Testament, but he opted finally for an iconography which took its inspiration from the New Testament. Work on the programme continued up until the beginning of the eighteenth century. In 1716, Simon Mazières finished the last groups.

Albi is a still more remarkable case, for there an edifice with a single nave and with no ambulatory was to be turned into a cathedral with a canons' choir ringed by an ambulatory. We do not know how the eastern part of the edifice looked when it was built. It was profoundly altered at the very end of the fifteenth century by Louis of Amboise (1474–1503), who built in the interior of this volume a closed space, all of stone, with a western door, some additional side doors and a polygonal chevet. The western facade, the rood-screen, was massive, both because of its depth and because of its two staircases, which gave access to the platform. The side walls, blind in that part which corresponded to the stalls, were then pierced with delicately worked galleries, providing a view of the altar, the stalls and the episcopal throne. The latter was almost merged with the walls, being distinguished from them only by its architectural development, at the easternmost end of the southern row. The sculpted programme, executed in a relatively brief period of time, displays a very clear iconographic coherence, with Christ, the Virgin Mary, prophets and figures from the Old Testament facing outwards, and the Virgin Mary and the apostles hooked on to the interior. As was so often the case in palatine chapels, the iconographic themes turned on the concordance between the two Testaments. The absence of any scenes referring to the Passion is explained by the presence of a huge Last Judgement, painted on the reverse of the western wall of the congregational nave. The figure of Christ was supposed to feature in the centre, but disappeared during the seventeenth-century refurbishment and the piercing of the door in 1693. On either side of the rood-screen were matching series of representations, with the lower section featuring the punishments meted out to the mortal sins and, above them, apostles and prophets. In fact, the bishop had compensated for the absence of a western portal and its sculpted decoration with a huge painting directly inspired by it. The worshipper was placed between these two iconographic ensembles, and he thus regained an image which had been a familiar feature since the middle of the thirteenth century.

Thus, in every cathedral, after having contemplated the facade, which featured the Christ of the Last Judgement separating out the good from the wicked, he would enter the Temple of the New Covenant, invited in by the prophets, the apostles and the saints, who provided him with an occasion to meditate upon scenes from the life of Christ, whose sufferings might bring about his redemption or even his salvation. The worshipper could readily grasp the implications of this double message and its complementarity. Stricken with dread at the sight of the Last Judgement, his hope was restored by a glimpse of the scenes from the Passion.

THE OTHER CHURCHES IN THE CATHEDRAL

Parish churches

The cathedral had a number of other functions, which deserve some discussion. For example, it was not uncommon for a part of the monument to be reserved for parish services. The curé and his clergy ministered to a parish, with the full range of responsibilities and tasks that the use of such a term implies. The cathedral was the diocesan church, and the parish served what was in comparison a very restricted area, although it enjoyed very particular responsibilities. Thus, baptism was administered by its priest in charge, and no longer by the bishop. When a baptistry was planned at Toul, the canons refused to assume responsibility for it, their pretext being that the parish ought to be responsible for its funding. However, the history of the parish in the context of the cathedral is complex, obscure and hard to interpret, occasioning different solutions in each case. At Angers, for example, the parish church was not integrated into the interior of the cathedral, but was built on it. Thus, the church extended along the south wall, its western facade being situated in the extension to the porch, and the nave continuing up to the second bay of the cathedral nave. Communication between the two monuments was achieved by means of a door. A similar arrangement had survived until as late as the sixteenth century at Condom,

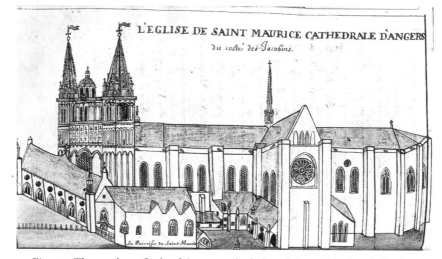

Fig. 130 The southern flank of Angers cathedral, and the parish church, by Jean Ballain.

where the bishop had responded to a request on the part of the consuls by authorising the community to erect a parish church on the south flank of the cathedral. The regulations stipulated that, on Sundays, Mass and the sermon would be given in the cathedral rather than in the parish church, so that bishop, chapter and faithful could listen to the word of God together. At Rouen, in the twelfth century, the ground floor of the Butter Tower was handed over to the parish.

By contrast with the no doubt numerous examples of a distancing between the two buildings, there are others characterised by a fusion within the same architectural ensemble; the reciprocal limits were precisely defined. At Amiens, Bishop Geoffroi of Eu authorised the curé of Saint-Firmin to celebrate parish services inside the cathedral, without however specifying the precise location. It should be noted that the Gothic rebuilding required the demolition of the parish church which was on the site of the future transept. Finally, Saint-Firmin was rebuilt to the north but was reserved for the use of the canons, parish services still being celebrated inside the edifice. The axis chapel, to which the faithful had ready access by way of the ambulatory, had therefore to be greatly enlarged. The same site was used for parish services at Narbonne, although there was no question there of enlarging the chapel.

Metz cathedral offers an original example, analysis of which is facilitated by study of documents and of the archaeological record. From excavations

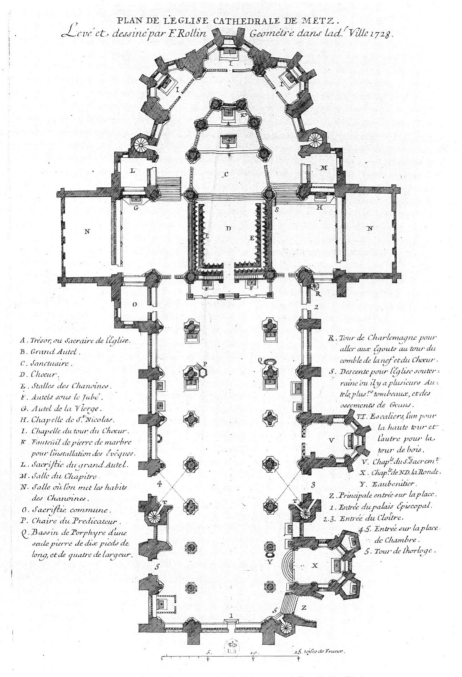

PLAN DE L'EGLISE CATHEDRALE DE METZ.
L'evé et dessiné par F. Rollin   Geométre dans lad.ª Ville 1728.

A. Trésor, ou Sacraire de l'Eglise.
B. Grand Autel.
C. Sanctuaire.
D. Choeur.
E. Stalles des Chanoines.
F. Autels sous le Jubé.
G. Autel de la Vierge.
H. Chapelle de S.ª Nicolas.
I. Chapelle du tour du Choeur.
K. Fauteüil de pierre de marbre
pour l'installation des Evéques.
L. Sacristie du grand Autel.
M. Salle du Chapitre.
N. Salle où l'on met les habits
des Chanoines.
O. Sacristie commune.
P. Chaire du Predicateur.
Q. Bassin de Porphyre d'une
seule pierre de dix pieds de
long, et de quatre de largeur.

R. Tour de Charlemagne pour
aller aux Egouts au tour du
comble de la nef et du Choeur.
S. Descente pour l'Eglise souter-
raine où il y a plusieurs Autels, plus.ª tombeaux, et des
ossements de Geans.
TT. Escaliers, l'un pour
la haute tour et
l'autre pour la
tour de bois.
V. Chap.ⁿ du S. Sacrem.ᵗ
X. Chap.ⁿ de N.D. la Ronde.
Y. Eaubenitier.
Z. Principale entrée sur la place.
1. Entrée du palais Episcopal.
2.3. Entrée du Cloître.
4.5. Entrée sur la place
de Chambre.
5. Tour de l'horloge.

Fig. 131 Plan of Metz cathedral in 1728 (after E. Rollin).

conducted in 1881, and again in 1914–15, we know that the facade of the Romanesque church stood at the alignment of the Mutte and Chapter towers. It rested against the collegiate church of Notre-Dame, which did not face east, as was the usual practice, but, like the churches and chapels of the Carolingian precinct, towards the south. When the thirteenth-century architect embarked upon his reconstruction of the cathedral, he was obliged to spare the collegiate church. Since the sloping terrain also precluded shifting his chevet further to the east, he adopted a highly original plan, incorporating the collegiate church into the general design of the monument, while at the same time respecting its architectural and functional independence. On his plan, he kept the north-south direction, providing access for the congregation from the north side and with an apse protruding from the wall of the south side-aisle, and he further enhanced the individual qualities at the alignment of those with the nave. A series of attempts to establish a homogeneity between the two monuments, one of which faces towards the east, the other towards the west, has almost wholly obscured the earlier lay-out.

Up until 1380, a wall running from north to south separated the nave of the cathedral from the collegiate church, and a difference in level served to reinforce the individuality of the two edifices. Access to the collegiate church had originally been by way of a door cut into the north side-aisle. The decision was soon taken, however, to add a second entrance, cut in a somewhat clumsy fashion further to the south in the side-aisle wall. It was embellished with a spectacular sculpted decoration, the richest in the whole cathedral. The western facade of the cathedral was itself pierced by a simple door, linking the bishop's palace, to the west, with the interior of the edifice. In 1380, the dividing wall was demolished, and a lowering of the floor of Notre-Dame-la-Ronde eliminated the difference in level between the two edifices. Only the apse preserved some trace of the original level. These improvements served, as was claimed at the time, to render 'the church more beautiful and more unified than it had been before'. With the suppression of the chapter, in 1761, it became possible to integrate still more the various parts of the interior volume. It was clear that the various means of access, of which there were two to the north – one lying to the west and serving the former collegiate church, the other, placed further to the east, beneath the tower, and leading into the cathedral – and two to the south, no longer made any sense. Furthermore, the size of each of the doors did not match the interior volume. As early as 1531, the creation of a means of access by way of the episcopal palace, by installing a portal in the west wall, had been mooted, although it was not to be executed until 1607. The turning-point was marked by the rebuilding of the whole of the south flank of the cathedral, which occurred after the canonial precinct had been replaced by the royal square. In an attempt to harmonise the decor of the square with that of the cathedral, Boffrand erected a Classical portal in the western facade. The final stage in this homogenisation, entailing stylistic modifications, was marked by the elimination of this portal, which could scarcely be said to be in keeping with the rest of the edifice, and the construction of a genuine Gothic facade. Various projects were put forward in the middle of the nineteenth century, but these were set aside in favour of the present plan, implemented by the occupying Prussian regime. Be this as it may, it must be admitted that the venture was largely a failure, access to the edifice today being by way of a door cut into the wall of the south side-aisle.

THE DOORS OF THE TEMPLE
OF THE NEW COVENANT

Doors for the congregation

As we have just observed, the division of the interior volume of the building could not help but have an impact upon its approach routes. When, therefore, the architect was defining his project, he had to ensure that the approaches were both independent of each other and at the same time interconnected. The ambulatory, where such a thing existed, played a crucial role here. The side-aisles established a connection between the congregational church and the arms of the transept, when the square was occupied by the clerics' choir. At Metz, they served as a link between the collegiate church and the cathedral. The independent doors were no less crucial, however, for they answered to a number of particular requirements, ranging from services to the needs of various categories of person – for bishop, canons, curé and congregation all required their own means of access. It is no easy matter to conduct an analysis of these doors, for there have been so many alterations to the building and its immediate environs, as well as changes in various functions. Some doors have in fact been abandoned over the centuries, even being walled up (Cahors), while others have been pierced for reasons that remain somewhat obscure (Laon, Metz). In general, we lack any real knowledge of the way people circulated when the cathedrals were first built, and yet this could be said to be a precondition for understanding their real meaning. Study of the problem is made the easier by descriptions or plans which predate the liturgical upheavals occasioned by the Tridentine reforms, or by accounts of particular ceremonies, but any firm conclusion on the subject must at present be judged premature.

The portals of the transept

The clergy of the Gothic period posed the question of the access of the congregation to the interior of the Temple of the New Covenant in a brutally frank fashion, and the architects were therefore obliged to respond with an equally frank solution. The admirable architectural formula arrived at was the harmonic facade, conceived by the Norman architects of the last third of the eleventh century. In the Gothic period, this formula served as a symbol of the cathedral. Indeed, when circumstances required, architects showed no hesitation in shifting this element to the arm of the transept, when the latter could serve as a means of access to the faithful. This was the case at Bordeaux, as we noted above. Once the chevet was built, the plan was to locate the access opposite the thoroughfare linking the holy town to the city.

There are many other examples of approach routes for the congregation being shifted onto a side better suited to welcome them. This tendency was especially pronounced at Le Mans, where, notwithstanding the existence of a facade to the west and of a portal, it was decided, around 1170, to pierce the south side-aisle and place a portal with statue-columns there. This portal was thus opposite the Grand'Rue, the central axis of the agglomeration, and was also visible throughout a town dominated by its cathedral.

Karel IV and the architect at Praga were prompted by the very same motives when they decided to place the access to the cathedral in the south arm of the transept. The edifice enjoyed such a prominent position that, from the other side of the river, the townspeople could see the Golden Gate.

The same was true at Lausanne, where the painted portal was placed to the west of the south arm. The congregation entered the building where it met the main north-south thoroughfare of the lower town, thereby avoiding the clerics' choir, which jutted forward into the central aisle.

The presence of the old city wall also made it impossible to contrive a facade on the west side at Albi. Since the palace of La Berbie ruled out any changes on the north side, use had to be made of the south flank. In order to stop the portal resting against the clerics' choir, it had to be shifted westwards, and, in order to eliminate the difference in level between ground and building, a ramp had to be constructed.

As well as being shifted to one of the flanks of the cathedral, the door reserved for the use of the congregation was often decorated. At Praga, the wall forming the extrados of the two archways was hidden by an extraordinary mosaic which, being on the south flank, caught the light. The same role was played at Le Mans and Lausanne by a sculpted portal with coving, spandrel and statue-columns. At Albi, Louis of Amboise designed the astonishing baldachin, which was completed at a later date, and which was reached by a monumental staircase. It was intended both to serve defensive purposes and, as its remarkable decoration suggests, to be an ornament.

For the bishop to gain access to the sanctuary, and the canons to the clerics' choir, other doors were used. The episcopal palace and the canons' precinct were often placed symmetrically on either side of the cathedral and therefore doors might be pierced opposite each other. From the middle of the thirteenth century, the decision was taken to decorate them with sculptures as grand as those used for the portals of the facade. These doors were reserved for the entrances made by the clergy during the more important ceremonies, which required a show of pomp. On routine occasions, more modest doors would seem to have sufficed, which accounts for the fairly frequent existence, on either flank of the cathedral, of a second means of access.

The cathedral of Paris may serve as an example. Each arm of the transept was lengthened, after 1250, and then pierced with a portal which was accorded a particularly intricate sculpted decor, the elevation of the transept being treated as if it were a genuine western facade, reduced to a single portal and surmounted by a huge rose window. This plan, delineated for the north part of the building by Jean of Chelles, was repeated on the south side in 1258, by Pierre of Montreuil, and further extended through the illusory creation of a triple portal. The close being located to the north, this portal was dedicated to the Virgin Mary, with the evocation on the spandrel of the miracle of Theophilus; in the palace, to the south, the portal was devoted to Saint Etienne, the first martyred deacon, to whom the original cathedral had been dedicated. The choice of the iconography was itself closely linked to the purposes of both means of access. There were two other approaches to the cathedral: one, on the north side, which is generally known as the Red Door, and lies further to the east; the other, on the south side, is a more modest door, reserved for the use of the bishop.

Prior to this date, a number of sources suggest that transept arms had sometimes served as means of access to, and therefore as passages through, the cathedral, each for this reason receiving the appropriate sculpted decoration. This was the case at Strasburg, around 1220. Since the episcopal palace was located on the south side, the bishop had to pass through the transept to reach the presbytery. Ever since the twelfth century, the bishop's court had been held on the small square in front of the facade of the transept. This passage was therefore partly closed in and covered by a hood near to the facade. The sculpted decoration of the two doors, known to us from an engraving by Isaac Brunn (1617), featured the representation of a king seated and drawing his sword from its sheath. He has been identified as the justicer king, Solomon. This juridical assertion of terrestrial order, on the outside of the cathedral, was complemented, on the interior, by the Angels' Pillar, which served to turn it into a Last Judgement of divine origin.

We know how important the treatment of each arm of the transept was at Chartres. They had originally been conceived as a harmonic facade with three portals and two spires. A huge porch was also added, which protected the three portals and permitted a further extension of the sculpted decoration. As we saw above, the decision not to build the four spires reflected a desire to maintain the western facade's signification as a sign to the faithful, and to avoid obscuring the message. Both arms were intended for the use of the canons, whose close surrounded the cathedral.

The hesitations mentioned above respecting the siting of both palace and close had a number of repercussions for the monument, as was the case, for example, at Amiens cathedral. In 1232, it had been proposed to shift the canons' close to the north and the episcopal palace to the south, so that the latter, being completely hemmed in to the north, might have more land at its disposal. In addition, the palace was separated from the new cathedral by what was, in purely commercial terms, one of the most important streets in the town, and this had occasioned a series of long-running disputes with the townspeople. The architect had therefore been instructed to design a portal on the north arm, dedicated to the Virgin. In 1241, this reorganisation was, for various reasons, abandoned, and the close therefore remained on the south. Work had already commenced on the pier of the north portal, together with the iconography devoted to the Virgin, since it was to house the statue of the Virgin and Child. A statue of Saint Firmin was placed there instead. The portal of the south arm kept the statues of the splays from the original project. After 1241, another, more traditional iconography was adopted, with the portals facing in the direction of the canons' precinct. The Virgin, the famous gilded Virgin, was placed on the pier.

Equally difficult decisions had to be taken at Rouen. In order to proceed from the canons' close to the cathedral, the canons had to make a long detour. In 1281,

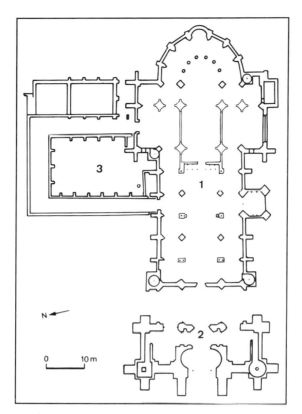

Fig. 132 Plan of Lausanne cathedral and cloister. 1. The cathedral; 2. The *massif occidental*; 3. The cloister.

Archbishop Guillaume of Flavacourt, himself a former canon, decided to surrender a strip of land to his former colleagues, so that they might create a more direct approach route. The canons restructured the whole of this area, entrusting the execution of the task to the architect Jean Davi. The Notre-Dame chapel, built a century before and extending along the north arm of the transept, was eviscerated; all that survives are the still visible remains of its chevet and portal. The north arm of the transept, the Portail des Libraires, was built as a means of access. Jean Davi adopted a bold plan, by extending the decoration, which could only be used on the facade, sideways. In fact, a small alley was created between a number of buildings, access to which on the north side was by a portal realised in 1482–4 by Guillaume Pontifs. The restructuring of the ensemble located on the north of the transept arm was immediately to entail the rebuilding of the south arm, the Portail de la Calende. The iconography was

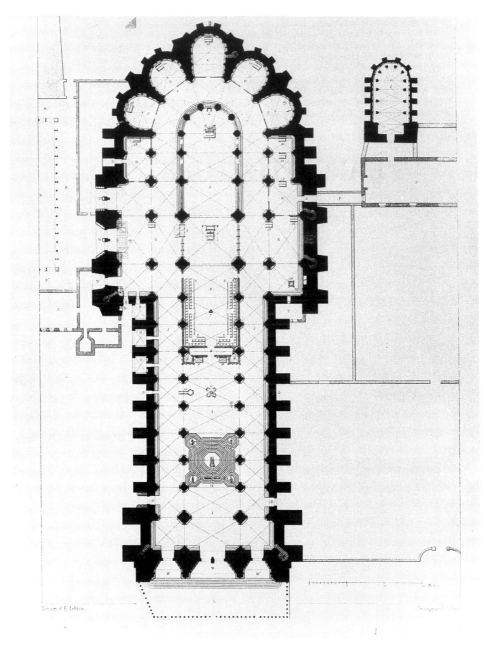

Fig. 133 Plan of Reims cathedral (after E. Leblan).

drastically revised from this period onwards. Thus, on the north flank, the unfinished portal, which lacked a spandrel, referred to the Last Judgement, while the theme on the south flank was the Passion.

Without lengthening this list unduly, one could quote many other examples of transept arms reserved for the use of the clergy. The case of Bordeaux was particularly original, with the north arm, facing the town, being for the use of the congregation, and the south arm, in the vicinity of the close, being reserved for the canons.

The restoration of the cloister, to the north of Lausanne cathedral, allowed the canons to circulate on the inside of the building. They entered by two doors, one of which stood on the west, opposite the painted portal, and gave on to the western gallery, while the other, to the east, in the centre of the transept, opened on to the eastern gallery.

It is worth mentioning Reims here, for it is a fairly well-known example. Without entering into an extended discussion of the three portals of the western facade, obviously intended for the use of the congregation, we should note the lack of any portal on the south arm of the transept, and the presence of three on the north arm. To the south, where the palace stood, the archbishop had to be satisfied with a small door cut into the east of the bay of the crossing. To the north, where the canons' close and cloister extended, the central portal, dedicated to Saint Calixte(?), opened on to the cloister; the western portal led by way of a passage to the chapter-house, and, as one might have expected, it was dedicated to the Virgin. The eastern portal, devoted to the Last Judgement, was also linked to the canons' close, but its precise purpose is more obscure.

7

The Gothic palace

✣

The rebuilding of the cathedral was to have repercussions for the holy town, which in general was totally restructured. The scarcity of available land gave rise to modifications in the buildings, which were transmitted like waves as far as circumstances allowed. The episcopal palace could hardly hope to escape unscathed. Its refurbishment could well have been occasioned by the enlargement of the cathedral, but such occurrences were in fact quite rare. Where there were modifications, they were generally due to the bishops' realisation that the palace had to match the standard of the place of worship. Since many of the palaces had not been rebuilt during the Romanesque period, the case for modernising them was all the more strongly felt. The balance between the various buildings was regarded as crucial, and the need to make the living quarters more comfortable also resulted in perceptible alterations. The palace also had, both through its mass and through its symbolism, to declare the somewhat ambiguous authority of the prelate. Every bishop who renovated his cathedral was likely, by the same token, to do the same for his own residence. Works on the palace were never very extensive, however, save in a number of exceptional cases, attributable to the personality of the prelate in question. The difficulties which they generally encountered were as much of a financial and psychological as of a topographic order.

Their financial difficulties were occasioned by the fact that the greater part of their available resources had been committed to the rebuilding of their cathedral. If, therefore, they diverted funds to their palace, they risked jeopardising the cathedral site, as the case of Albi shows. Yet there was great pressure on a prelate, simply by virtue of his office, to undertake the reconstruction of his cathedral. If he were to prove recalcitrant, while at the same time lavishing funds on his own residence, he might well be accused of selfishness or of unseemly luxury. Thus, in the twelfth century, Saint Bernard repeatedly fulminated against ostentatious display, and against what were, in his view, the outsize dimensions of the palaces. To this second difficulty, of a psychological nature, should be added the extreme scarcity of building land. In spite of the many problems, substantial building works were undertaken. The appearance of the episcopal palaces underwent a total transformation, the aim being to render them better suited to the circumstances of the time. They thus served to express what the bishop actually was and what he had to appear to be, both in the city and in the diocese. The palace had to express this, as much through the ground it occupied as through its architecture. It had to be the symbol of the prelate's twofold power, which was spiritual, insofar as he was responsible for the Church in his diocese, and temporal, in terms of the more or less important responsibilities which he had inherited. The drawing of any such distinction between the two was at the time inconceivable; indeed, it had never been drawn. As we shall see below, the halls whose presence was obligatory in the palace were themselves marked by this symbolic ambivalence.

In spite of the above difficulties, the bishop enjoyed a large degree of freedom in this domain. His actions went entirely unsupervised, save by the vigilance of his own functionaries. He was not obliged to follow a specific architectural schema and, since the vestry had no say in how funds were used, he was free to make whatever choices he wished. He showed a degree of discretion in this regard, as we shall see below.

THE SITING OF THE EPISCOPAL PALACES

The episcopal palaces enjoyed so privileged a situation with regard to the cathedral, that no one ever contemplated moving them elsewhere. As we have already remarked upon several occasions, their position dated back to the actual origins of Christianity, or at any rate to its official recognition. The prelate was therefore attached to the site, both for sentimental reasons, and also by the wish to remain in the vicinity of the cathedral. At the time of the rebuilding of Amiens cathedral, which almost occasioned one of the most drastic disturbances to urban topography in the whole period, the idea was at one time mooted of abandoning the episcopal palace, situated in the vicinity of the north arm of the new cathedral, and of rebuilding it further to the south. The plan was soon rejected, and palace and canons' precinct remained where they had always been, on the north and the south of the religious edifice. This was in fact the usual formula, with palace and precinct being aligned, although the precise lay-out would obviously vary with the topography. The custom was in fact so well established that it dictated the position of the new palace even when it was entirely rebuilt. At Albi, in 1236, Bishop Durand of Beaucaire persuaded the canons of Sainte-Cécile to surrender a number of houses on the banks of the river Tarn, so that he might build a new palace, which was soon erected, to the north of the future cathedral.

Nonetheless, the wish to create a bipolar structure could not overrule tradition. When, for example, the palace was located in front, and to the west, of the cathedral, there was never any question of moving it, in spite of the serious disadvantages such a lay-out had as far as access to the cathedral was concerned. Where such an idea was proposed, it was as quickly rejected. As a consequence, wherever the episcopal palace was situated near to the western flank of a cathedral, access routes at the site had to be planned from the very start. For a number of such cathedrals, the western entrance was realised very belatedly (Bayonne, Châlons-sur-Marne), sometimes even in the nineteenth century, after the palace had been demolished (Bordeaux, Metz).

One also had to take account of the privileged situation of the palace in relation to the ancient city walls, for it was often in close proximity to them, and sometimes even played a part in the defence of the town. It was thus shielded from attacks, the most threatening of which came from the town itself rather than from outside. This explains the relatively late date at which the problem of extending the constructions beyond the ramparts was addressed. Thus, at Senlis, it was not extended *extra muros* until around 1530; necessity had here proved the mother of invention, the building of the southern arm of the transept having occasioned the demolition of various buildings and therefore the construction of a number of new ones. Everywhere else, recourse was still had to the enclosure, which had certainly lost its defensive function, but which seemed adequate to guard against a surprise attack. This represented a further constraint, which those wishing to build extensions had to take into account.

As chance would have it, the bishop was fairly often the owner of estates inside the town, and was therefore in a position to undertake the construction required. The land occupied by the palace generally turned out to have plenty of free space and it was therefore possible to build additional structures without too much difficulty. This was the solution adopted by Gautier Cornut (1222–41) at Sens, when he embarked upon the renovation of his palace. He 'had it built in the courtyard of the officiality'. He thus avoided giving offence, or clashing with any particularly vigilant canons, some of whom, in 1331, wrung from Thomas of Bourlemont, Bishop of Toul, an undertaking that he would renew the commitment of his predecessor not to expand the palace in the direction of 'the church tower'.

In order to avoid unnecessary conflicts, the prelates were at pains to take the land to be built upon from their generally quite extensive gardens or cultivated fields, thus perceptibly reducing their surface area. A decision of this sort, for which it was very hard to see any alternative, could have a range of different outcomes. The most frequent result was for the palace to be extended westwards up to the western facade of the cathedral. This tended to be a gradual conquest, which lasted throughout the Gothic period and which had the advantage of placing all the buildings on one and the same alignment. There are many such examples, although it is hard to be sure quite how they evolved. The pattern was as common in the north (Paris, Reims) as in the south. At Arles in particular, the palace was extended southwards from the twelfth century onwards until it swallowed up the 'Gioffredi' tower, which up until then had been private. By 1616, it had come to be known as the 'great tower of the archbishopric'.

FORTIFIED PALACES AND RESIDENTIAL PALACES

The palace inherited by the prelates of the Gothic period resembled a random and uncoordinated collection of buildings, erected as and when they had been needed. The new generation set out to distinguish between the various functions, and so to impose a degree of order. Although such initiatives, as the case of Reims serves to show, were by no means unprecedented, they now became the rule, with the symbolism of the palace being asserted more forcefully. The greater the surface area available for building, the easier the task was. Thus at Beauvais, the western edifice was reserved for the residence, the other units being located to the north or the south of the strictly delimited plot of land. The same was true of Châlons-sur-Marne, where the demarcation was even clearer. The residential areas lay parallel to the cathedral, between courtyard and garden, while the areas in common had been shifted northwards, with their own separate, and clearly distinguished, points of entrance.

This necessary division acquired a particular colouring in the north, attributable to the social origin of the prelates. The latter had close links with the most important families, who sought to guarantee their own creature comforts by dividing their time between town and country, where they would build imposing residences. The bishops followed suit, being prepared to launch themselves into exceptionally ambitious rural ventures. In Normandie, the best instance of this is Gaillon, the oldest parts of which date from the thirteenth century. At the same time, the prelates strove to create palaces that might vie with the finest residences. They had therefore to reserve one wing of their palace for living quarters, and to place it in as agreeable a fashion as possible between courtyard and garden. They so much appreciated the light that they were prepared to pierce the walls with numerous bay windows. This was the excuse given by Guillaume of Seignelay (1207–20) at Auxerre, when he enlarged his own windows. Maurice of Sully had acted in similar fashion when he built his chapel, and the hall which extended it towards the west. It seems that he wished to take advantage of the southern light, but also of the equally beautiful view of the Seine. Similar care was taken over almost all such ventures. For example, the hall built by Guy of Mello (1247–69) at Auxerre is a thing of great beauty.

There can be little doubt that, during the closing years of the twelfth century and throughout the greater part of the thirteenth century, the residential aspect was the dominant preoccupation. Admittedly, all these palaces were ringed by buildings which already ensured their occupants a degree of protection, and the whole complex was anyway enclosed by a wall. As we have already observed with regard to the previous period, the defensive aspect was of so little importance as to seem all but negligible. However, circumstances were to change dramatically at the end of the thirteenth century, and in the course of the fourteenth century, as economic crises led to mounting tension in the cities. Soon the outbreak of war would necessitate a greater degree of protection. The scale of the change may be appreciated by considering the case of Beauvais, after the inhabitants of the commune had driven out Bishop Clermont of Nesles, in 1305. Immediately afterwards, two towers were added to the eastern side of the palace, so as to defend the approach routes. Now defence, not residential quarters, became the dominant concern. It is obviously in the south that one can best appreciate the scale of this change, reflected in the sheer number of palaces that were either renovated or built from scratch. The palace at Fréjus, realised around 1310–30, is an especially revealing case, for the building of a continuous external envelope had transformed it into a veritable fortress. Built of rusticated bossages, it was of sufficient height to ensure a passive defence. The prelates chose to enclose the lower courtyard, which had previously been outside the walls. As a consequence, various buildings were deliberately unified around an inner courtyard.

Tense relations between the archbishops of Narbonne and the viscount and the burghers had led the former to fortify the episcopal palace. The endless disputes that ensued worked to the ultimate advantage of the king and, from the end of the thirteenth century, the archbishop was forced to abandon the Old Palace. In addition, archbishop and canons fell out over the building work on the new cathedral, for they failed to agree over which buildings should be demolished. In 1271, the archbishop set about 'rebuilding the parts of the palace which had been destroyed'. He took advantage of the opportunity offered to bolster his own defences. Immediately after the building by Pierre of Montbrun of the Chapelle de la Madeleine, Gilles Aycelin embarked upon the construction of the *Turris Magna* (1290), in the south-west corner of the Old Palace, and the small tower which was later to be known by the name of Saint-Martial. Finally, he linked up the two towers by means of a wall reinforced with large arches, which continued further to the east. So imposing did such a fortress seem that, in 1356, the consuls raised the alarm, claiming that the new structure threatened the town and its traditional liberties. However, from the end of the thirteenth century, whenever a new palace was erected in the south, it invariably had a defensive aspect. This preoccupation is glaringly evident in the case of La Berbie at Albi, or in that of the Popes' palace at Avignon. Both structures are exceptional, but in either case may be regarded as a response to equally exceptional circumstances.

At Albi, the bishop had been engaged since the beginning of the thirteenth century in a bid to wrest the temporal power from the lay lords, the viscounts, his ultimate success in this venture being sealed by the agreement he had reached with the local population. A reversal of alliances occurred, however, in 1264, when the king of France recognised the episcopal usurpations but at the same time limited them. Once the king and the local population had arrived at an understanding, the bishop found himself isolated, and was obliged to lose no time in looking to his own defences. The task facing him was made all the easier through his having a huge income at his disposal, as much as 20,000 *livres* under Bernard of Castanet (1276–1308). Such wealth made it possible to transform the bishop's former residence with the utmost haste. The palace had been realised by Durand of Beaucaire (1228–54), who had built to the north of the Romanesque cathedral, on the slope which descends towards the river Tarn. It consisted originally of a hall and a tower that was square in plan, together with various houses surrendered by the canons in 1236, which the bishop had been prepared to run. Although the scheme had never been finished, it had been entirely without military qualities. His successor, Bernard of Combret (1256–71),

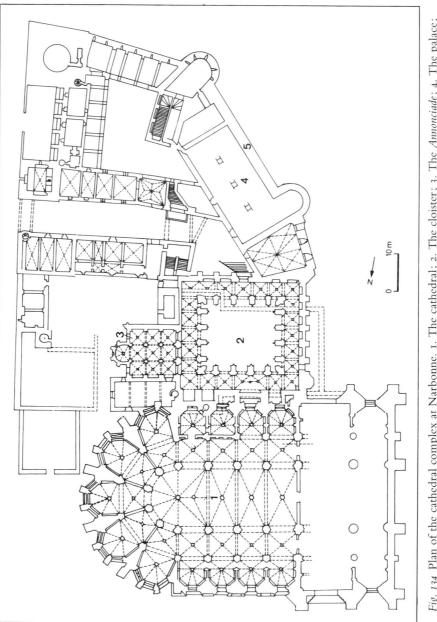
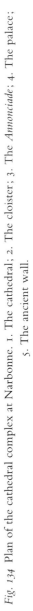

Fig. 134 Plan of the cathedral complex at Narbonne. 1. The cathedral; 2. The cloister; 3. The *Annonciade*; 4. The palace; 5. The ancient wall.

finding himself in a more tense situation, tried to unify the buildings at his disposal, and thereby to strengthen his defences. Bernard of Castanet, who had at first embarked upon the building of a new cathedral, turned his attention to the palace, which he had originally regarded as satisfactory. His chief contribution was the building of the Sainte-Catherine 'tower' (1286–1301), a mighty rectangular fortress, divided up into towers and protected by full, circular buttresses, one of which, being kept empty, was intended for the spiral staircase. La Berbie thus acquired the aspect of a wholly military fortification, which, through its massive and imposing character, appeared impregnable. Much as at Narbonne, the fortress was turned against the townspeople.

The Popes' palace at Avignon belonged to this same episcopal tradition. Given its altogether exceptional importance, however, this palace grew to a quite unparalleled size. Benedict XII (1336–42) had commissioned Pierre Poisson to rebuild the Old Palace, so as to give it a defensive aspect. He therefore reduced the openings, and strengthened the walls with mighty arches which were meant to support the machicolation, and the bases of which were sunk in the embankment underlying the walls. Clement VI (1342–52) entrusted Jean of Louvres with the task of building a second palace, maintained the external defences and reserved the comfort and luxury for the internal organisation.

The solution had been to build urban fortresses which concealed in their depths an altogether peaceful arrangement of buildings and a sumptuous decor. A number of prelates soon adopted the same formula, among them Pierre of La Jugie. Thus, at Narbonne, he preserved the 'New Palace' built by his predecessors, but modernised it, his task being facilitated by its powerful external defences. He extended the residence westwards, building the synodal hall along the ancient wall, which had been carefully preserved and which ensured shelter and protection. He likewise extended the palace southwards, in the direction of the cloister, which was then under construction. The archbishop's chief concern was to escape the din of the Place aux Herbes, which was then a thriving centre of commerce, and to withdraw to the inner part of the town. He had put to good use the space released by the demolition of the chapel, which had formerly housed the relics of La Madeleine, transferred to the cathedral in 1335. His palace now faced gardens, cathedral and cloister, and presented a strongly fortified aspect on the outside, although he had been prepared to cut huge bay-windows into the walls. The towers and the ancient walls, which retained all of their original width, were still sufficiently imposing to keep potential aggressors at bay. The archbishop's palace ended up occupying 4,000 square metres.

In these southern constructions, the massed plan remained the rule, for it was a lay-out which made defence easier. At Gerona, where in the course of the fourteenth century the bishops replaced the Old Palace, a similar plan was adopted, although the edifices lacked a defensive aspect. In this respect, the south differed from the north, which remained loyal to lengthy building units and extensive green spaces.

THE BUILDINGS

The chapels

As in the previous period, the episcopal palace consisted of a certain number of buildings and halls. In the Gothic period, however, they took on a new meaning. The greater importance of the chapel reflected the increasingly significant part played by the canons in the cathedral. The twelfth century was to see the bishop fall back on his palace, a tendency that was to be confirmed in the course of the thirteenth century. What had originally been the bishop's oratory became a generally ample chapel, whose two floors and often lavish decor were intended as a challenge to the royal and seigneurial chapels. Indeed, the likeness was so great in the thirteenth century that they could easily be confused. The bishop was soon left with little choice but to build on two floors, if he wished to withdraw and thus escape from the large palace staff. The main floor of the chapel was level with the bishop's own apartments, and was reserved for his own use; he would therefore assemble with his intimates and hold special ceremonies there. In addition to the episcopal chapel, the prelate had the use of a private oratory, which was likewise modelled upon those of the kings and the great lords; it was near to his own rooms, so that he could enter it whenever he wished.

The episcopal chapels were generally built at the same time as the cathedral, and were therefore often in a similar, indeed, an identical style. The bishop very probably called upon the architect who had drawn up the plans for the cathedral as a whole. A number of such chapels have since been demolished, and so this must remain a working hypothesis. However, where such chapels survive or where graphic documents contain a sufficiently detailed record of them, as, for example, at Albi, Laon, Meaux, Noyon, Paris and Reims, one can safely say that this was indeed the case. It is true that, where Laon is concerned, the chapel is somewhat more archaic than the cathedral, and yet the two buildings are close to each other in style. The archaism lies rather in the plan, which is characterised

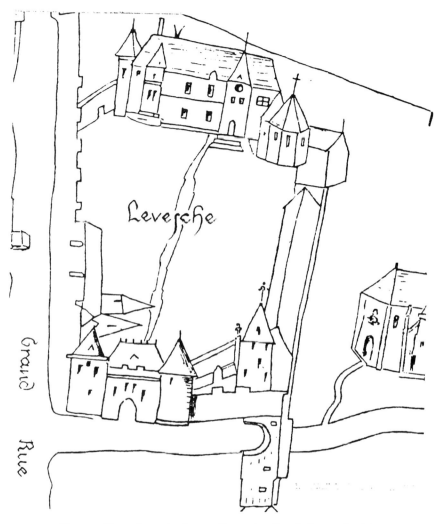

Fig. 135 The episcopal palace at Beauvais, after de Lorme (1569).

by the retention of side-aisles, on both ground floor and main floor. Such plans were to be abandoned not long afterwards.

Maurice of Sully, Bishop of Paris, would seem to have been responsible for the refinement of the new formula. At any rate, it proved so convenient that it was generally adopted. The Paris chapel was, as was to be expected, on two floors, but it had shed the side-aisles, whose usefulness was by no means apparent; it was terminated abruptly on the east side by the apse, while on the west it was preceded by a sexpartite bay. Its general situation was equally telling,

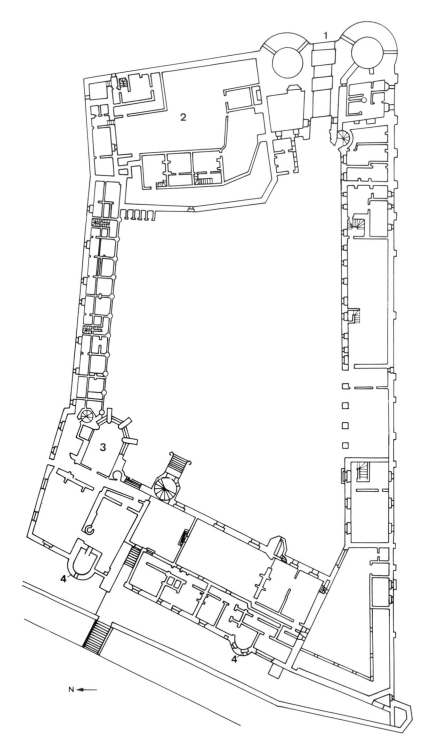

N ◄—

for it gave directly on to the hall located further to the west. At the same time as this plan was adopted, its palatine signification was confirmed. This point may be appreciated in the case of Paris, where the bishop did not reside at this period in his palace, but in town.

The bishop of Noyon, Renaud (1176–1188), espoused the Parisian formula as regards the plan and lay-out of the two floors, but he chose a different locale. Whereas at Paris the chapel, located parallel to, and on the southern flank of the cathedral, was therefore at some distance from it, Renaud attached it to the southern arm of his, so that it might serve as a link between palace and cathedral. In addition, the spiral staircase located in the arm of the transept served both the gallery of the cathedral and the upper level of the chapel. The link was equally close at Reims, where the chapel, on two levels, stood in the south-east corner of the transept.

Elsewhere, the topographic arrangements were fairly diverse, and may be accounted for in terms of specific local factors. At Beauvais, for example, where the palace lay to the west of the cathedral, running along the ancient wall, the chapel, also on two floors, gave on to the episcopal residence; it had been realised during the same period as the cathedral chevet. At Soissons the chapel stood parallel to the cathedral. If the two-floor formula seems to have been the rule during the Gothic period, there were noteworthy exceptions. Thus, at Senlis, the chapel was located on the main floor, above a building pierced with a blind arcade.

Finally, it is worth noting the care bestowed upon the decor of a number of such chapels, for example, at Reims, where the spandrel of the upper chapel featured a representation of the Adoration of the Magi. The stained-glass windows were likewise, if contemporary accounts are to be believed, as fine as those in the main body of the cathedral. There is no mention, however, of the sculpted representations of the apostles, a feature which was characteristic of the palatine *sainte-chapelles*, the much imitated model for which had been the Sainte-Chapelle of Paris.

Nothing in the south could match the architectural or decorative aspirations of those who built the northern chapels. As we have already observed, the prelates in the north, with very few exceptions, conceived their chapels as projecting constructions, which had the advantage, therefore, of being pierced by many windows. The southern prelates saw no need for such an arrangement,

Fig. 136 (Opposite) The episcopal palace at Beauvais after a plan of 1792. 1. The door; 2. The prisons; 3. The chapel; 4. The ancient wall.

and the chapels were therefore still integrated within the main body of the building. Their chapels were generally on one level, on the ground floor. They tended to stick to the formula of the oratory, although they might increase the scale, and the palatine symbolism, to which the northern prelates were so strongly attached, remained alien to them. This point is borne out in a particularly striking fashion at Albi, where, in spite of the substantial works realised at La Barbie, neither Bernard of Combret nor Bernard of Castanet ever dreamed of vying with the episcopal chapels of the north. The former restructured the hall which Renaud of Beaucaire had built, installing the Chapel of Notre-Dame within it; the latter built a new chapel, dedicated to Sainte Catherine, located on the same level as the eponymous tower. A somewhat similar formula was adopted at Narbonne, where Pierre of Montbrun built a chapel on a single level inside the palace. It was not until 1361 that Pierre of La Jugie was to realise a chapel on two levels, which was attached to a tower located to the left of the entrance.

At the Popes' palace, in Avignon, Benedict XII had built the chapel of Saint-Jean, which was on two levels and gave on to the northern gallery of the cloister. Innocent IV abandoned it, because it was on the north side and because it was too far from his own apartments. We know that he embarked upon the construction of a new chapel, on a truly gigantic scale, on the south side, below the Great Courtroom. In both of these chapels, only the Pope officiated. However, on the fourth floor of the Garde-Robe tower, an oratory dedicated to Saint Michel was also built.

This spectacular proliferation of episcopal chapels in the north was accompanied by a rebuilding, according to a formula which was soon very generally adopted, of the hall, the significance of which during the Romanesque period was discussed above.

The halls

Here too, we would seem to owe the basic conception to Maurice of Sully at Paris. Even if we cannot be sure that he was the inventor, there is no disputing the speed with which the formula became accepted as a model. As in the case of the chapels, the plan adopted was characterised by two original features, namely, size and number of floors. We can clearly see that the decision was taken to extend the hall, so as to be able to host larger gatherings, and to build on two floors. The ground floor was conceived with ogival arches falling back on to a row of supporting columns, thereby creating two aisles, whereas the first floor,

Fig. 137 The southern flank of the cathedral complex at Paris: the cathedral, the palace and the hôtel-Dieu, by Israël Silvestre.

which also featured ogival vaulting, was a single, unified space. One should note the evident preoccupation with the lighting of the latter, which benefited from generous bay-windows cut into the side walls. The hall ran the whole length of the residence. When it was oriented east-west, these openings seemed adequate, as indeed they were at Paris; when, however, it was oriented north-south, the attempt was made to increase the interior illumination. The long walls would then be pierced with bay-windows, and the southernmost wall would be entirely perforated.

As in the Romanesque period, the hall served a number of different purposes, for there was no difficulty in holding meetings, receptions and meals in an entirely unrestricted space. The bishop also dispensed justice there, or else delegated the task to an official. The courts, that is, the officiality, judged all cases that came within the bishop's jurisdiction, together with any appeals to the metropolitan bishop. In fact, from the time of Charles V, royal justice encroached to a marked degree upon the authority of ecclesiastical officers. The thirteenth century and the first half of the fourteenth century had represented the apogee of the bishop's judicial power, as the rebuilding of the hall on such an imposing scale suggests. Aside from its judicial functions, the hall could host the synod, a meeting of the main beneficiaries of a diocese. This consultative assembly, which was convoked and presided over by the bishop, often lent its name to the hall (Sens).

It is hard to generalise about the uses to which the lower hall might be put, although there was usually nothing very noble about its identity. Prisons are sometimes mentioned, with one or more cells. However, the lower halls have

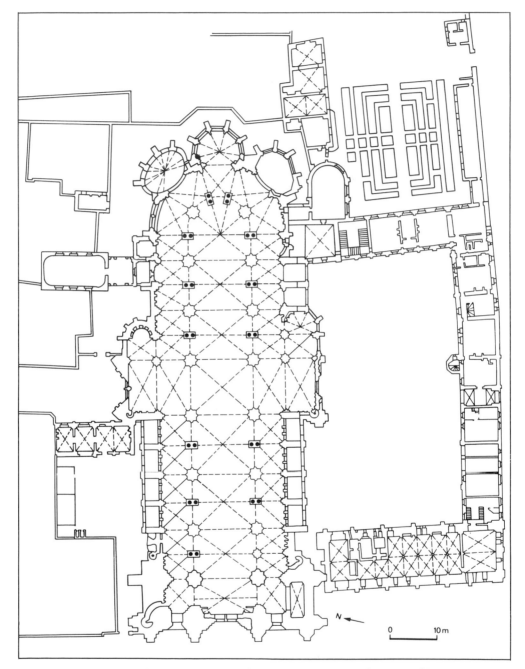

Fig. 138 Plan of Senlis cathedral and episcopal palace (after C. Porée).

suffered such drastic restructuring, from the earliest periods, that it is hard to be sure just what the original lay-out was. It is clear, however, that they offered a space that was sufficiently flexible, in spite of the row of supporting columns, to be adapted to meet a wide range of different purposes.

One of the best-known of such complexes, which has survived until the present day, stands at Sens. The hall there is quite unique, for it is aligned on a north-south axis, and serves to close off the palace courtyard on the western side. The building programme initiated by Gautier Cornut (1222–41) was meant to highlight the magnificent role which he played. A number of dioceses were answerable to him, including, to its deep resentment, Paris. The plan of the building had originally featured three floors, the first two being divided by the supporting columns into two aisles, with the third having just a single aisle. The first level, which was below ground and poorly lit, served as a dungeon. The second was divided into two parts, with the north allowing access to the inner courtyard, and the south leading to the gaols and the officiality. The third level, entirely unrestricted and bathed in light, was reserved for the use of the archbishop, who entered by a door in the eastern wall of the southernmost bay.

No other hall was so beautiful. Even at Paris, Maurice of Sully had simply wainscotted the hall which, as we have already noted, gave on to the chapel on the east side. At Auxerre, Guy of Mello (1247–69) built a new, oriented hall, the gable-end of which was also heavily pierced and which was merely wainscotted. The hall at Angers, which was 27 metres long, was wedged between the episcopal chapel and the oratory. Such halls generally measured between 20 and 30 metres in length, with the one at Reims being 27 metres, that at Beauvais, 24.

The most significant difference between the northern and the southern halls concerned their width. It should be realised that the use of the diaphragm arch permitted the boldest schemes. One of the most telling examples is the hall of the palace at Narbonne, for which Pierre of La Jugie was responsible. At the lower level, the vaults were borne by massive piers, while the great merit of the upper floor lay in the beauty of its space and its lighting. The southern halls generally featured two levels. At Albi, Bernard of Combret built two superimposed halls (25 metres by 7·6 metres), while at Gerona the hall was renovated in 1369 (22 metres by 13 metres), with diaphragm arches supporting the frame.

The towers

The third element, the tower, described briefly in the context of the earlier period, had become a widespread, even an indispensable, feature, with a clear symbolic value. Through its scale on the ground and its height, it served as a visual affirmation of the temporal might of the bishop; all the more so, indeed, given that, when it was first built, it dominated the lower town, even if, in the second half of the fifteenth century, it was swamped by an ocean of stone. The majority of the towers have disappeared, and it is therefore no easy matter to discern just what their various uses and their overall meaning were.

It is hard to discern precisely what the term 'tower' meant during this period, although in a material sense it referred to a stone construction that was circular in plan. In the Middle Ages, the word *turris* had a precise symbolic value, as the sources suggest. The tower seemed to be an expression of the feudal world, and formed an integral part of the pyramid of vassalage, for which it served as a visual emblem. The most powerful lords would build structures that were in general high, and which served as a concrete expression of their power. To begin with, the towers were wooden, but were rebuilt in stone in the course of the twelfth century; originally rectangular in plan, they tended to become circular, although not all did so. These structures were both residential and defensive.

Montgomery tower, in the Palais de la Cité, vestiges of which still exist, was built during the reign of Louis VII, and quickly acquired some of the symbolic associations described above. However, the situation grew more complex at the end of the twelfth century, when Philippe Auguste set about building the Louvre tower on the right bank of the Seine, at the very edge of the precinct. This mighty structure had originally been designed to serve as a defence against the alarming threat of the Plantagenets. However, once it was admitted that all the fiefs of France came under its jurisdiction, it came to be seen as tutelary and, shortly afterwards, as symbolic. At the same time, Philippe Auguste was building a number of towers, which were free-standing but closely linked to the town, and which immediately assumed this same symbolic signification, like the Grosse Tour of Bourges, upon which a certain number of fiefs were dependent. Finally, it may be worth recalling the famous Tower of London, invested with the same associations and symbolic significance.

It was in this context that a 'tower' arose, where it did not already exist, inside the episcopal palace, in the north as in the south. Like the hall, its existence added a new meaning to the residence; since the Carolingian period, it had been closely associated with the very definition of a palace. The 'tower' served to integrate the prelate into medieval society. It is of some significance to note that the towers were built on a considerable scale, as at Lyon. At Noyon, where the bishop was count, his fiefs were dependent upon the Roland tower. At Reims, one had to wait until 1595, the date at which the archbishop's former residence

Fig. 139 The Ile de la Cité, after Jean Fouquet, *Les Heures d'Estienne Chevalier.*

was destroyed, for the jurisdiction of the fiefs to be transferred to the palace of Le Tau. At Amiens, the tower, mentioned at a very early date, assumed a particular significance, the count having to swear homage to the bishop.

A number of such towers were built at the end of the twelfth century. Thus, in Jean Fouquet's *Heures d'Estienne Chevalier*, we see a representation of the tower in Paris, as if it were circular, although in 1658 Israël Silvestre was to

Fig. 140 The facade of Reims cathedral, the parvis and the palace of Le Tau, by N. de Son (1625).

depict it as rectangular. A circular plan was the rule in the north, for example, at Noyon, Laon and Beauvais. In the latter, Bishop Philippe of Drieux (1175–1217) had adopted the formula employed by the engineers of Philippe Auguste (the tower of Le Craoult) and had built the tower outside the ramparts, to the west of the palace. The siting of such structures was no less revealing.

Thus, in Reims the tower was placed at the western entrance to the palace, close to the hall; in Paris, it stood in close proximity to the hall and to the chapel; in Noyon, it was entirely independent, inside the palace. The tower of Beauvais would seem to have been exceptional in this respect.

The south, on the other hand, persisted with the rectangular formula until a late date. As we have already observed, the form had emerged during the Romanesque period, at Aix, Fréjus, Viviers and Béziers. In some cases (Béziers, Viviers), there is a close link with the hall. At Fréjus, the tower stood in the south-east corner of the palace. In some palaces, the rebuilding programmes of the Gothic period saw the towers grow to truly formidable proportions. At La Berbie, Pierre of La Jugie set about the construction of Sainte Catherine's tower in 1286, employing a rectangular plan enclosed within the corners of circular buttress towers. The dimensions of the tower were equally remarkable, with the buttress walls being 50 metres long and 7 metres thick. The defensive aspect was obviously of greater weight here than any symbolism. At Narbonne, around 1290, Gilles Aycelin undertook the building of the 'Grande Tour', at a time when relations with the viscount were at their most strained. This imposing mass of stone, being square on the outside and circular on the inside, perhaps because of the existence of an ancient turret, dominated the viscount's tower, which was much lower. Benedict XII adopted a very similar plan for the *Magna Turris* or Tour du Pape at Avignon (1335–7), located at the southernmost extremity of the Old Palace. He chose a square plan, the sides measuring 17·5 metres and the height of the walls being 46·5 metres, the defence of the structure being guaranteed by the thickness of the walls (around 3 metres), by buttress galleries and by reduced openings.

Loyalty to the rectangular plan may be explained by the ultimate purpose of the towers, there being a fundamental difference in this regard between south and north. For in the north, the towers were never meant to be inhabited, save at Reims, where an episcopal chamber is mentioned. Their symbolic aspect would seem to have been paramount. The same was not true of the southern towers, the contents of which were often listed. The contents obviously added to their symbolic value, but in addition account for the rectangular plan, which was more comfortable than the circular one. Mention is made, on the ground floor, of the bishop's chapel, as at Aix or Fréjus; more common still is reference to the episcopal chamber, for example, at Viviers and Albi. At Viviers, we also hear of the treasury and of archives. The popes would adopt the same formula at Avignon, where the lower storeys of the tower, in the basement, contained cellars and a 'Trésor bas'. This fortress held the most valuable objects, vestments and archives. There is mention also of a metal chest containing cash. These two storeys were also covered with stone vaults, so as to provide a second line of defence against theft or fire. The upper storeys, which were only planked over, contained the chamberlain's chamber, the pope's chamber and the 'Trésor haut', the latter being divided into the 'trésorerie petite' and the 'grande librairie'.

THE PRINCELY PALACES

Since the end of the Hundred Years' War, the building-sites, both religious and civil, had re-opened. The great lords vied with each other in the construction of new residences or in the rebuilding of their former castles. Peace allowed them to abandon austere, defensive structures and to create more pleasing residences, which served to express their love of life, recovered at long last. All the signs were that the movement launched at the time of Charles V and reined in for almost fifty years had finally come to fruition. The Maison Jacques-Coeur at Bourges, the mansion of the abbots of Cluny, and the Barrault residence at Angers certainly gave a foretaste of the future, but they owed much to the past also. The episcopal palaces of northern France were deeply marked by the advent of this new taste. They became princely residences, vying in this respect with the most beautiful structures erected by the various brothers of Charles V, and their religious meaning tended to be obscured by the taste for lavish display. It is no easy matter to give an accurate account of such buildings, for the majority of them have disappeared. Nonetheless, the handful of extant sources are sufficiently revealing for us to be able to grasp the radical change which occurred. The palaces were in fact extended further into the holy town, so that they ended up occupying a by no means negligible part of it and tended thus to become the most remarkable in the city.

The palace of Rouen, enlarged in the course of this period, is without question the most remarkable. Guillaume of Estouteville had embarked upon some substantial modifications in 1462, and Cardinal d'Amboise had taken them still further, spending what were for the period quite remarkable sums of money, between 1495 and 1507. He had quite exceptional funds at his disposal, and showed no hesitation in devoting a third of his incomings to his residences at Rouen and at Gaillon. Guillaume of Estouteville was responsible for the kitchens, the great spiral staircase and the hall, while Cardinal d'Amboise built the great residence, which faced the Rue des Chanoines. The apartments were fitted out in the most luxurious fashion possible. The palace assumed the form of a huge quadrilateral with galleries, which ringed a garden planted with rare flowers. To create what was, if one excepts the Palais de la Cité in Paris, the largest urban palace of its day, it had been necessary to purchase large tracts of land.

The case of Rouen may well have been exceptional, but a number of bishops had likewise sought to build magnificent palaces. The bishop of Evreux, Raoul of Le Fou, clearly shared this same preoccupation, for he asked the king for permission to use the wall of the town so as to build on its ridge. The affair was not without its difficulties, and led to the holding of an on-the-spot enquiry, led by the architect Pierre Smoteau, with the participation of the mayor, the captain and the representatives of the town. The palace was reduced to nothing more than a simple residence, flanked by a tower containing the spiral staircase. Equally substantial building programmes were prosecuted at Beauvais, by Villiers of L'Isle-Adam, at Besançon, by Charles of Neufchâtel, at Châlons-sur-Marne, by Geoffroy Soreau, and at Avranches, by Louis of Bourbon. In this respect, as in many others, the sixteenth century was in no sense a breach with the past. There was simply greater luxury and a shift in style.

8

The canonial precinct

✤

As the canons assumed a more prominent role in the holy town, the canonial precinct grew in size, from the twelfth century onwards, its enhanced significance complementing the spectacular development of the episcopal palace. It was in fact during the Gothic period that the precinct took shape, with a certain number of buildings being judged indispensable. This restructuring was due, as we have already noted, to the expansion in the surface area of the Gothic cathedral. In addition, provision had to be made for the increased number of canons, especially in the northern dioceses. In some cases, the increase was spectacular, and obviously linked to the correspondingly large rise in ecclesiastical revenues. The history of the process has been traced as regards Chartres, and it is clear that the church there flourished during this period. Its resources were mainly drawn from rural areas, for bishop and canons owned estates, chiefly in the Beauce, whose yield had increased to a significant degree. From the end of the tenth century, a highly efficient agriculture was established in the immediate vicinity of the town, and from 1080 to 1160, a remarkable amount of land was cleared, a process which continued up until the middle of the thirteenth century. The Perche, which had previously been entirely wooded, was brought under the plough. A polyptych from 1300 gives us a very accurate notion of the landed wealth of the chapter, which amounted to 3,500 hectares and yielded revenues of over 5,000 *livres*. As a consequence, the number of canons was increased to seventy-two, and the prebends' incomes were doubled in 1193. A number of virtually identical cases could be cited. Thus, at Laon, between the twelfth and thirteenth centuries, the number of canons rose from seventy-five to eighty-four. At Langres, likewise, the number rose to forty-eight.

During this same period, the authority of the canons within the holy town was consolidated, the bishop finally agreeing to a division of powers. As was only to be expected, the formulae differed from one diocese to the next. At Langres, it was not until 1179 that a specific capitulary domain was created, which was of gigantic proportions, and included the palace to the east of the cathedral and the hospital in the north-west corner. The cathedral itself, however, continued to be a disputed area, with the canons attempting to obtain jurisdiction over its interior. The conflict was so violent that in 1320 the bishop went so far as to order his hired men to storm the building, to batter down its door with axes and to occupy it. The interior was sacked, but at the last the bishop's standard flew again from the towers. In 1351, Guillaume of Poitiers recognised the canons' jurisdiction, not only over the cathedral but over the cloister and the hospital also. Only the palace was exempt.

At Toul, the chapter owned the cathedral. In Paris, its rights covered the eastern part of the Cité, the hôtel-Dieu, the Saint-Landry port and, of course, the precinct. At Laon, such rights extended over the cathedral, the precinct and part of the parvis. At Bordeaux, the canons' rights were so widely recognised that the quarter bore the name of Sauveté Saint-André.

THE FUNDING OF CANONIAL PRECINCTS

As is always the case with substantial building programmes, it is not easy to explain exactly how they were funded. For want of the relevant documents, we are forced to conclude that the responsibility devolved upon the canons themselves, although we do not know who assumed which tasks. It is probable that sufficient sums had been saved to be drawn upon when the need arose. However, it is of interest to note that this had not always been the case, whether in the north or in the south, and that the bishop had sometimes had to play a fairly prominent role in fund-raising. Thus, at Coutances, it was Bishop Guillaume of Thiéville (1315–47) who embarked upon the construction of the precinct on the north flank of the cathedral. Likewise, at Lausanne, the prelate ruled in 1267 that half of the diocesan revenues should be used to finish the cloister. Formulae differed from one place to the next. Thus, at Rodez, Calmont of Olt bequeathed the vestry 10,000 Rodez *sous*, for the building of a cloister. The prelate played very much the same role at Lombez, where he twice embarked upon the construction of a cloister on two floors, as Arnaud of Barbazan (1317–57) did at Pamplona. However, for those cases where we have

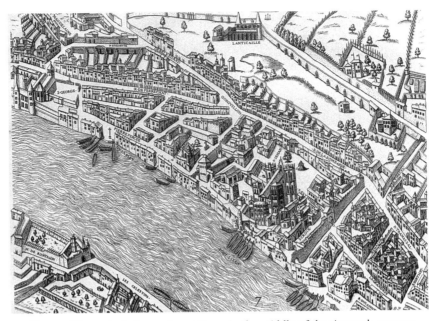

Fig. 141 The cathedral complex at Lyon in the middle of the sixteenth century.

some information, episcopal involvement concerned new structures of common concern rather than private houses. The same was true of various, carefully worded legacies. For example, a canon of Lausanne named the vestry in his will, stipulating that his legacy should be used for the building of the cloister. One should, however, bear in mind that in the fifteenth century, and especially in the latter half, it was invariably the chapter that took the decision to build, and therefore arranged the funding of the project.

THE POSITIONING OF CANONIAL PRECINCTS

When rebuilding programmes were launched in the Gothic period, the precinct was generally complementary to the palace. Where new constructions were concerned, this choice, which allowed each element to be independent of the other, generally went unchallenged. This is what the bishop of Lombez sought to achieve, when the abbey became a bishopric. There are, however, a few cases of palaces situated inside the canonial precinct. We have already mentioned the case of Narbonne, where the building programme entailed the juxtaposition of

318

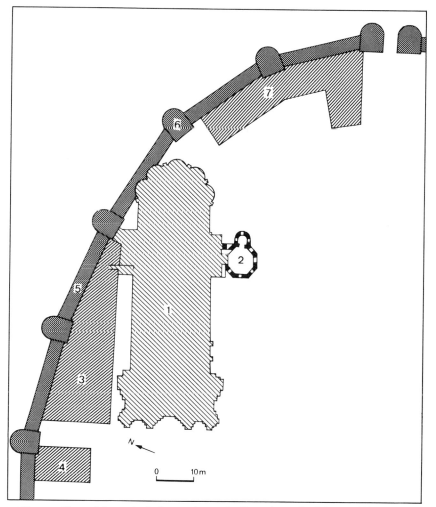

Fig. *142* Plan of the cathedral complex at Senlis at the end of the twelfth century (after Vermand). 1. The cathedral; 2. Saint-Gervais – Saint-Protais; 3. The chapter buildings; 4. The hôtel de Vermandois; 5. The ancient wall; 6. Saint-Michel; 7. The episcopal palace.

palace and cloister in a single ensemble, lying to the south of the cathedral. Work on the cloister had begun in 1349, on the initiative of Pierre Daniel, after the church of Saint-Théodard had been demolished, in 1343. Mention should also be made of Lyon and of Langres, which reflected the ancient traditions of the community.

Once a site had been chosen, one had to find free terrain, whether for

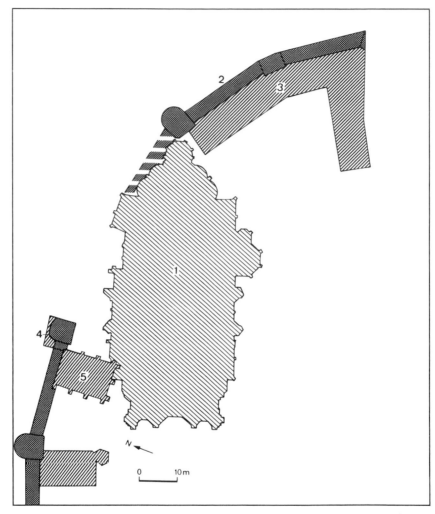

Fig. 143 Plan of the cathedral complex at Senlis in the twentieth century (after Vermand). 1. The cathedral; 2. The ancient wall; 3. The episcopal palace; 4. The library; 5. The chapter-house.

extending or for building. If the case of Senlis is anything to go by, this was an equally sensitive issue. In order to install a twelfth-century cathedral, an architect had to twist the plan of his edifice, so as to avoid, on the east, the ancient city walls, and on the north, the canonial precinct. His thirteenth-century successor showed fewer scruples when the decision was taken to add a transept to the cathedral, razing a part of the city walls and disrupting the precinct.

At Lombez, the elevation of the abbey to the status of a bishopric left one with no choice but to construct a palace and a precinct. Problems immediately arose, which Jacques Colonna (1328–61) and Antoine sought to smooth over by arranging a compromise with the canons, upon two different occasions, in 1334 and 1336. The chapter offered to surrender to the bishop the former abbey buildings together with the cloister, situated on the south flank of the cathedral, for the building of the palace. In exchange, the prelate agreed to build a new cloister on two floors on the square adjacent to the church, on the side of the new construction.

Such drastic steps were not always taken. Thus, the bishop, who naturally favoured a precinct that was conveniently placed, sought to find solutions to the problem. At Châlons, in 1255, Pierre of Hans made a gift of land, in order that the chapter might build a number of new houses upon it. The chapter in turn undertook to pay an annual sum of 100 *sous*.

Even though, at Amiens, the plan to move the precinct was soon abandoned, the very fact that it had been formulated at all serves to show what the bishops' wishes there had been. They had wanted to extend the canonial precinct and thereby to ensure the tranquillity of the canons. At that time, the precinct was located on the south of the cathedral, in a situation that precluded any extension, and it was also separated from the cathedral by one of the busiest thoroughfares in the town. The transfer to the north of the cathedral would have made it possible to resolve these two difficulties. Keeping it where it was, on the other hand, would merely have served to exacerbate the already acute tensions between the canons and the consuls.

ENCLOSURES: THE FORTIFIED PRECINCTS

The Carolingian legislators had been particularly concerned to ensure that the canons would enjoy as much peace and quiet as the monks in their monasteries. They had therefore instructed the prelates to build a wall around the precinct, which would guarantee such isolation and would allow communal life the requisite fervour. Whatever the use of the term *munitio* might lead one to suppose, it was in no sense a defensive system, but rather an enclosure. The limited number of doors confirms this intention. Cathedral and precinct were thus brought closer together, as much visually as materially. Although we cannot be certain of this point, it is probable that the majority of precincts had a symbolic enclosure. The increasingly dense texture of the town, from the

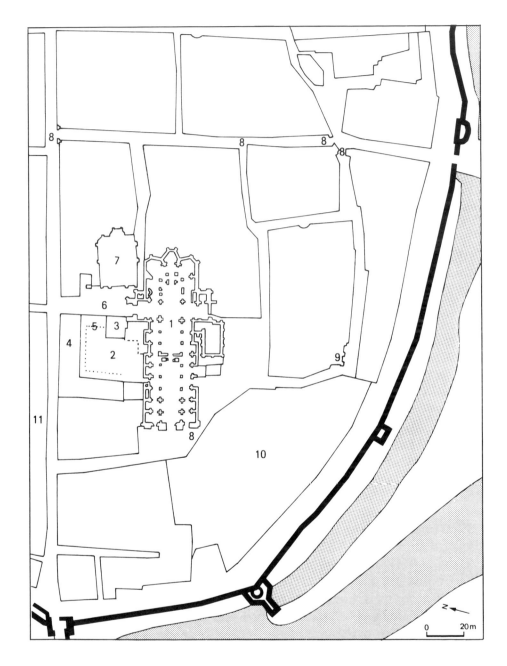

eleventh century onwards, rendered this enclosure indispensable, and it was around this period that the practice spread of building it in stone. The majority of canonial precincts of the late twelfth and early thirteenth centuries were probably hidden behind walls of a certain height, and pierced by an unspecified number of doors, the general effect being to create a separate quarter. There were four such doors at Laon, three at Paris and six at Châlons. At Béziers, prior to 1167, there had been only one such door; at that date, viscount Raymond Trencavel gave his authorisation for the piercing of a second. To render the isolation of the canonial quarter still more complete, all of these wooden doors were shut.

In a number of towns, even this degree of protection was soon to prove inadequate, for the wealth of the clergy was a source of bitter social tension. The resulting clashes, which sometimes ended in violence, caused the clerics to look to their own defences. We have already noted how, from the thirteenth century onwards, a number of palaces in the south had assumed a distinctly military guise, and how the north had followed suit in the fourteenth century, notably at Beauvais. Even prior to this date, the canons had struck a defiant attitude, turning the walls of the precinct into a genuinely fortified complex. Such cases remained few and far between in the first half of the thirteenth century, but became more commonplace subsequently, before becoming the rule by the end of the century.

In 1294, Robert of Harcourt, Bishop of Coutances, was granted permission to fortify his cathedral. He proceeded to build an enclosing wall which ringed cathedral, palace and canonial precinct. Admittedly, the circumstances were exceptional, and the measures taken unparalleled, yet this example gives us the measure of the new relations between townspeople and clerics.

Châlons is perhaps one of the earliest instances of the addition of such defences. Thus, in 1255, Pierre of Hans authorised the chapter to build walls around the precinct, their function presumably being defensive.

We have a fairly accurate idea of the circumstances under which the canons of Chartres found themselves having to adopt such a solution. Relations with the townspeople had deteriorated rapidly between the eleventh century and the early years of the thirteenth century. At first, there would seem to have been few

Fig. 144 Mass-plan of the cathedral complex at Châlons-sur-Marne (circa 1755). 1. The cathedral; 2. The cloister; 3. The chapter-house; 4. The refectory (?); 5. The library; 6. The parvis; 7. The collegiate church of the Trinity; 8. The precinct gates; 9. The prison; 10. The palace; 11. the hôtel-Dieu.

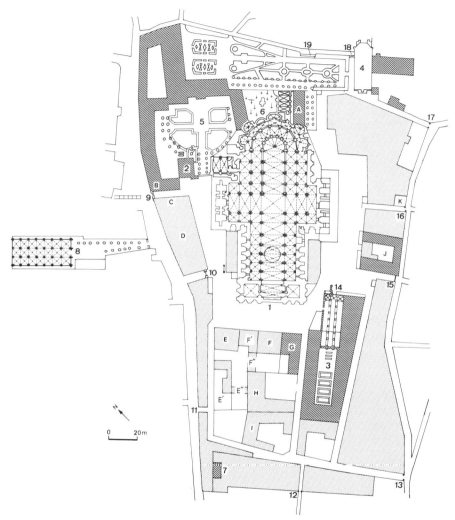

Fig. 145 Plan of the cathedral complex at Chartres (circa 1750). 1. The church of
Notre-Dame of Chartres; 2. The church of Saint-Nicolas-du-Cloître, formerly
Saint-Serge-et Saint-Bâche; 3. The former hôtel-Dieu of Notre-Dame; 4. The
chapel of Saint-Etienne-du-Cloître; 5. The Bishop's palace; 6. The cemetery and
chapel of Saint Jérôme; 7. Formerly the chapel of Saint-Même; 8. The Louans
storehouse; 9. The gate of the officiality; 10. Le Cadran gate; 11. Trois-Degrés gate;
12. The gate of the hôtel-Dieu; 13. Percheronne gate; 14. The former hôtel-Dieu;
15. Les Changes gate; 16. La Fruterie gate; 17. Saint-Jean gate; 18. The Vidame's
gate; 19. The ancient wall. A. The chapter library; B. The bishop's officiality (at
present a private dwelling); C. Notaries, secretaries of the chapter; D. Merchants'
hall; E. House dated 1600 (at present the Chamber of Commerce); E′. House dated
1626, now demolished; E″. A construction of 1954; F. 1286, canons' residence (at

discordances as regards either origin or way of life. However, at the end of the twelfth century, religious festivals were invariably marred by disputes or even brawls. Townspeople and clerics enjoyed such different standards of living that any contact between the two parties became tense. The canons sought to constitute, inside the city, their square meadow, and would therefore buy up houses situated near to the north of the cathedral. In 1251, they felt the need for a secure enclosure, and this led to still more tension. Saint Louis felt obliged to intervene in 1256, in order to quell the conflict: Jean of Châtillon, Count of Chartres, agreed that the precinct should be surrounded by a wall pierced with doors and posterns, of a reasonable height, topped with crenellations, but without any too obviously defensive elements such as towers and archers. The precinct, which had previously been a part of the everyday life of the town, was now completely isolated.

The case of Chartres was not unique in northern France. Thus, the canons of Langres created a defensive system for their precinct, in the beginning of the fourteenth century, with walls surmounted with crenellations and doors whose folding panels were reinforced with iron bars. This fortification was demolished in 1320, only to be rebuilt later.

The same was true of Lyon, where the canonial precinct, which contained a large part of the quarter of Saint Jean and of the cathedral complex, was shielded by a genuine surrounding wall pierced by six doors. However, this defence was to prove inadequate and on two separate occasions, in 1269 and 1310, the precinct was breached and looted by the townspeople.

We are better able to understand how the canonial precinct was defended if we consider the south, where a study has been made of the question, and where especially evocative traces survive. We have already drawn the reader's attention to Viviers, where the rocky spur at the top of the town constituted a natural defence. The defensive system was completed, in the Romanesque period, by a stone shield, part of which was formed by what was subsequently to become the cloister. The walls and towers were, however, less carefully constructed than the latter had been. In the course of the second half of the fourteenth century, steps were taken to mend these defences, by placing a watchpost at the summit together with a coping of merlons. At Béziers, the stylobate of the cloister

---

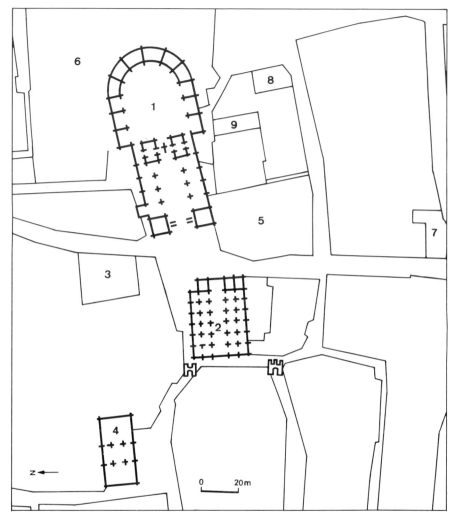

Fig. 146 Plan of the cathedral complex at Langres in 1784, with the canonial precinct
and its residences (after A. Bresson). 1. The cathedral; 2. Saint-Pierre; 3. The hôtel-
Dieu; 4. Saint-Didier; 5. The cloister; 6. The palace; 7. The chapter prison; 8. The
storehouses; 9. The choir school.

consisted of a wall reinforced with machicolation borne by arches stretched
between the buttresses. At Arles, the precinct was likewise fortified, but, in order
to strengthen their defences, the clerics had also recruited some horsemen.
Mention of such forces is also made at Viviers, in 1289, and we learn that they
lodged, as one would have supposed, within the precinct. They disappeared in

Fig. 147 Béziers, the cathedral, the canonial enceinte and the episcopal palace, after Martellange (1616).

the course of the fourteenth century and, in the middle of the fifteenth century, the defence of the canonial precinct was entrusted to the townspeople themselves. It is worth emphasising that here, as at Béziers, the strategic position of the canonial precinct meant that it was by definition an element in the city defences.

THE ORGANISATION OF THE PRECINCT

The construction of a perimeter wall inevitably led to a general restructuring of the canonial precinct. This accounts for the plan of a number of such precincts, for example, at Laon, where the individual houses were aligned along the Rue du Cloître and two other alleyways which gave on to the Rue Sainte-Geneviève. The houses, built in the twelfth and thirteenth centuries, numbered as many as forty by the end of the fifteenth century. In Paris, there were only thirty-seven such houses, and they were disposed in a far less orderly fashion. From around this period, these houses were built in stone, or this is what documents dated 1195–7 suggest for Noyon, where the precinct had an especially regular plan which was both imposed and respected. It was probably in the wake of the extension of the precinct at Noyon, in the twelfth century, beyond the enceinte,

Fig. 148 The canons' residences at Paris cathedral (after Raguenet).

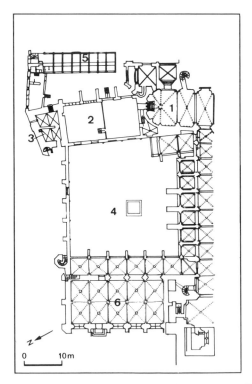

Fig. 149 Plan of the canonial buildings at Noyon (after P.-E. Devillers). 1. The north arm of the cathedral; 2. The chapter-house; 3. The prison; 4. The cloister; 5. The library; 6. The refectory and kitchens.

328

towards the north-east, that the decision was taken to build the houses in a concentric arrangement, with the gardens ending at the enceinte. The whole complex covered a surface area of 2 hectares 54 acres. The case of Noyon is, however, wholly exceptional.

Unencumbered land was in such short supply that the density of buildings became remarkably high. Indeed, numerous references to canons' residences built outside the precinct prove that there was in fact a shortage of land. There are two such sources for Laon, at the end of the fifteenth century, but this tendency had begun long before, in Langres, where there were already eight such houses outside the walls in 1214.

Cloisters

Canonial precincts of the Gothic period required communal buildings. If there were a genuine cloister, thought would have to be given to the organisation of such buildings, although, as we noted above, the decision to have a cloister was not related to the clerics' adoption of a secular or a regular rule. The lack of any such connection serves to account for the relatively high number of cloisters built during the Gothic period, both in the north and in the south or, in the case of the south and of Spain, for the concern with preservation. However, since the majority of such cloisters have disappeared without trace, save perhaps a rare mention in the archives, it is no easy matter to survey them. Here too, each diocese would tend to adopt a different formula, as regards both situation, positioning in relation to the choir or to the nave, number of galleries, terracing of cloisters or even the actual number of cloisters. In many cases the position chosen was dictated by that of an earlier building. The staging of the ritual and the ceremonial required in the religious life of the chapter may well have had a part to play in such decisions. A deeper analysis would perhaps enable us to grasp a reality which in general eludes us.

Once again, Noyon provides us with a particularly convincing example, as we have seen with regard to the organisation of the canons' residences. The rebuilding of the cathedral led to a complete reorganisation of the precinct, and as a consequence, to the construction of a number of new buildings. No sooner had the first stone of the cathedral been laid than a cloister was planned for Noyon, but its realisation occurred much later, very probably between 1240 and 1269. The cloister was originally supposed to have had only three galleries, rather than four – a point to which I shall return below – with the eastern gallery opening on to the ninth bay of the cathedral counting northwards, and

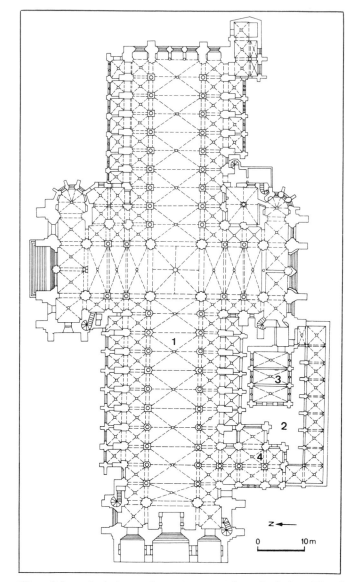

Fig. 150 Plan of the cathedral complex at Laon. 1. The cathedral; 2. The cloister; 3.
The chapter-house; 4. The chapel of the fonts.

with the west gallery opening on to the second bay; the north and east galleries
were eliminated in 1811. If the eastern gallery was slightly out of true, it was
because of the presence of the old wall, which still exists. This is not the only case
where there is no aisle running the length of the cathedral. This was true of the

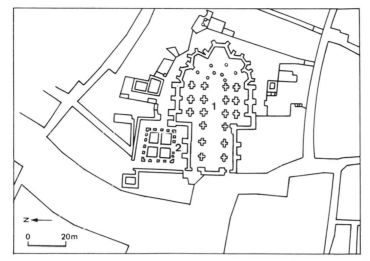

Fig. 151 Plan of the cathedral complex at Agen (after Lomet), 1784–9. 1. The
cathedral; 2. The cloister.

cloister at Lausanne, for example, begun around 1225, and of the cloister at Toul,
which was built at a later date. At Laon, the canons were satisfied, at the
beginning of the thirteenth century, with a single gallery with nine bays. It
turned back at the corner of the south arm of the transept so as to allow access,
via a complicated route, to the cathedral and to the chapter-house, which stood
in the middle of the cloister garden. To the west, the return was effected by a bay
opening out on to the so-called chapel 'of the fonts', whose ultimate purpose
remains obscure.

Nonetheless, it was more usual to have cloisters with four galleries, with
examples of this pattern being as commonplace in the north as in the south. The
most imposing were at Langres, Châlons-sur-Marne, Besançon, Reims, Agen,
Bayonne, Bordeaux and Lombez. In the case of the latter, the bishop undertook
to rebuild it on two storeys.

Irrespective of whether three or four galleries were involved, a number of
such cloisters were only realised at a fairly late date. Thus, at Rouen, work soon
stopped on the construction of the cloister, which was to have been within the
Albane courtyard. At Narbonne, the cloister was begun in 1369, but only
completed in 1432. The cloister at Bordeaux is perhaps of a slightly earlier date,
while the one at Toul is later still.

The existence of a cloister would necessarily lead to the building of a certain
number of other communal buildings, such as refectories and dormitories and,

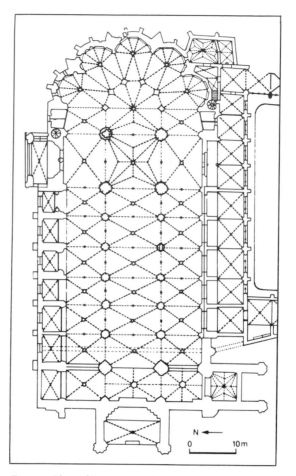

Fig. 152 Plan of Bayonne cathedral at the present time.

most important of all, the chapter-house. The significance of this building should need no further emphasis, for its purpose had hardly altered at all since the previous period, and, thanks to the increased number and greater prominence of the canons, it had if anything gained in importance. It was generally located near to the eastern gallery, on to which it usually opened, as was the case at Lyon, Noyon and Lausanne. If other sites were chosen, it was once again for topographic reasons, as, for example, at Reims, where the cloister was located on the west. We have already remarked upon the unusual location of the chapter-house at Laon, where there was absolutely no free ground available. At Châlons, it was located in the haunch of the western gallery and of the north flank of the

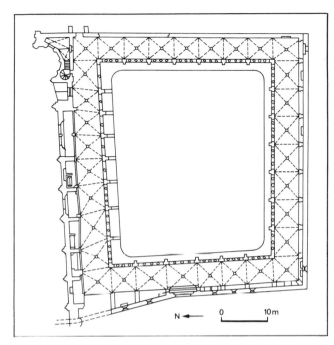

Fig. 153 Plan of the cloister of Bayonne cathedral (circa 1850).

cathedral, but access to the latter was exclusively by way of the gallery. At Toul, the chapter-house's situation was equally original, for it ran the length of three east-west bays, disposed along the south flank of the cathedral.

The majority of these constructions employed a longitudinal plan which matched the form of the gallery on to which they opened. Only the chapter-house at Pamplona, known as La Barbezine, which was square in plan, was an exception to this rule.

Chapter-houses

The chapter-house was so important that, in some bishoprics, it was built before there was even a cloister. The most illustrious examples are Senlis and Chartres, where the halls were for this very reason totally isolated. The former, realised to the north of the first bay of the nave, was undertaken by Pierre l'Orfèvre between 1390 and 1400, in order to replace those buildings which had been damaged when the arms of the transept were rebuilt. At Chartres, use was made of the basement of the chapel of Saint Piat, in the chevet of the edifice, which was built between 1323 and 1335. The hall featured three bays, and was flanked by

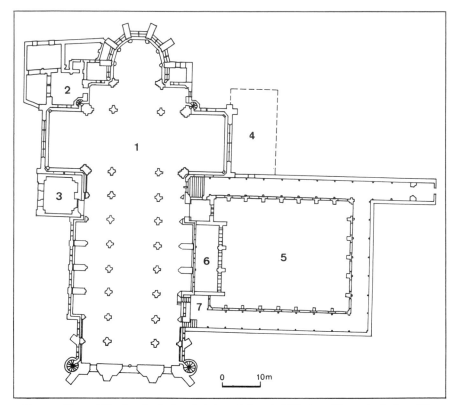

Fig. 154 Plan of Toul cathedral and cloister (after A. Villes). 1. The cathedral; 2. The great sacristy; 3. The bishops' chapel; 4. Saint-Jean-des-Fonts; 5. The cloister; 6. The old chapter; 7. The library.

two towers, one of which served as a prison, the other as an archive. The chapel had then been built above, and, in 1350, it was joined to the cathedral by a porch and a monumental staircase.

Refectories, dormitories, storerooms and libraries

We have already emphasised the degree to which the canons, from a very early stage, had turned against the communal life. This explains why it is that a refectory is so rarely to be found. Where such a thing did exist, the building either disappeared very early or else was quickly put to a new use. Here too, the case of Noyon is relevant. To the west of the western gallery of the cloister, there was a hall known today as the chapter-house; in fact, it is a refectory and kitchen, consisting of a double aisle with four bays, which opened on to the western gallery of the cloister and ran in a north-south direction. As was only to be expected, there was no access on the south side to the cathedral.

The same formula was employed at Pamplona, where the refectory was complemented by a kitchen. The refectory at Châlons dates from approximately the same period (1251–64), although the canons only assembled there to drink wine after their long and tiring processions through the town. The refectory at Reims has been turned into a place of worship, dedicated to Saint Michel.

References to dormitories are still rarer. At Reims, the dormitory was on the first floor of the western wing of the cloister, above the vestiary of the theology and law schools. The dormitory at Pamplona still exists today.

Inside the precinct were yet other buildings, some of which were service buildings, while others served a sacred purpose. Among the former, mention should be made of storerooms, which are often referred to in the texts (for example, Langres). The Louans storeroom, at Chartres, is one of the most famous, and by itself illustrates the wealth of the canons; sometimes it held as much as several thousand quintals of corn. The 'Vieux Chapitre' at Meaux may originally have served a similar purpose. The care taken over essentially utilitarian architecture is equally noteworthy in the case of Chèvremont granary at Metz.

Alongside these functional buildings, the fifteenth century saw a spectacular development in those which housed the libraries. With the invention of printing, the canons seem to have acquired a pronounced taste for books. Many bishoprics were therefore to undertake quite remarkable building programmes. Some canons, admittedly, were content merely to restructure the existing facilities, but they tended more often to embark upon especially burdensome and original projects, in order to house the works which they had procured, and to enable them to be read. Some of these libraries were truly spectacular. The library at Noyon, which had been planned as early as 1422 but only realised in 1504, was one of the most remarkable. Once the chapter had approved the design which had been submitted to it, the dean made a donation of 100 *livres*. Located on the east side, between the cathedral and the Corbeault gate, the library consisted of a gallery of nine wooden-partitioned bays, only the eastern facade of which was illuminated by bay-windows, and rested upon a double row of piers (measuring 23 metres by 57 metres). The preoccupation with conservation was evident in the suppression of the bay-windows on the west side and in the concern to raise the building above ground level.

At Troyes, the library was built in 1478–9 by Raguier, in an extension to the transept. At Rouen, Guillaume Pontifs erected the library on the edge of the

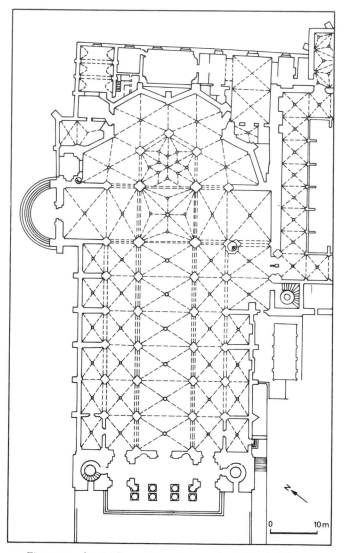

Figs. 155 and 156 Plans of Pamplona cathedral and cloister.

Cour des Libraires, access being by way of the monumental staircase inside the cathedral. The library at Bayeux, built in 1436 in order to house 192 volumes, was linked perpendicularly to the north gallery of the cloister. At Angers, it was located above the eastern gallery of the cloister, and the same was true of Châlons (1437). At Sens, the library was built of four bays, between 1517 and 1543.

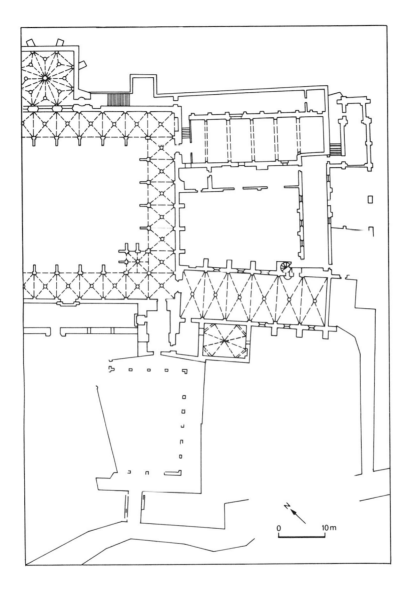

Buildings connected to the cathedral: treasury and sacristy

By contrast with the above buildings, which formed part of the canonial precinct, the treasury and sacristy appear to have had more tenuous links with the latter. This was by no means the case, however, for the treasury came under the authority of the chapter, while the sacristy represented an obligatory passage between precinct life and the community at prayer in the cathedral.

The treasury was not an invention of the Gothic period, but had its roots deep in the past. It housed cult objects, reliquaries, and the more or less precious items which constituted what was conventionally known as a treasure. It might also include objects which were of no venal value but to which some importance of another order was attached. Since the Romanesque period, the custom had arisen of placing the treasury in a confined, vaulted space, lit by very few openings. If the treasury grew in size during the Gothic period, it was largely because the cathedrals had by then acquired a greater number of pieces. It is no easy matter to retrace the history of such treasuries, and the reasons behind one or other arrangement usually elude us. At Rouen cathedral, the treasury was originally in a hall located on the floor which emerged on to the ambulatory on the south side, but it was subsequently moved to the chapter-house, above the cloister. There was only one access, which was from the inside of the cathedral, by means of the stairway installed in the north arm by Guillaume Pontifs. For obvious reasons, great care had to be taken to restrict the means of access to the treasury, although one had at the same time to guard against the threat of fire. A vaulted hall might thus be set aside for the purpose inside the cathedral, at first floor level. Such halls still exist in a fair number of edifices, at Bayeux, for example, and at Beauvais and Clermont. At Laon, it was the upper chapel of the south arm which served this purpose, and which was therefore guarded day and night by *coutres*. The chapel featured a chimney, and was heated, but this was not always the case. At Noyon, for example, the hall stood, prior to 1185, against the north arm of the transept.

What is conventionally known as the canons' sacristy was in fact the vestiary, the room in which they donned their choir vestments before proceeding to the choir; the vestments were therefore kept there. In addition, the canon would recite particular prayers while getting dressed. The siting of this hall was therefore connected to that of the canonial precinct and of the liturgical choir, and was invariably in the vicinity of the precinct and generally integrated into the cathedral (as at Chartres, Rouen, Laon, Tours and Meaux). It could be quite substantial in size as, for example, at Châlons, where it measured 14·6 by 7·8 metres.

The schools

The final point to be made concerns the schools, which, in the earlier period, were located within the precinct. They no longer played as significant a role as they had done before, for the advent of the universities had effectively marginalised them. At the same time, they had moved out of the precinct. The pioneers in this respect would seem to have been the schools in Paris, where the scholars were relegated, in 1128, to a space lying to the west of the palace, among the canons' residences, which were no longer part of the precinct. At Châlons, the scholars had been moved two years before.

9

The hôtel-Dieu

♣

The holy town, which had been profoundly disrupted during the Gothic period, when cathedral, episcopal palace and canonial precinct were all extended, was further shaken by changes affecting the hôtel-Dieu. This institution underwent alteration at three different levels, involving its administrative organisation, its architecture and its position. After these far-reaching changes, the hôtel-Dieu assumed a more or less fixed shape. This was in part because the Gothic holy town had acquired a stable form, with each of its constituent complexes at last assuming its definitive position, size on the ground and meaning. Subsequent modifications were minor by comparison with those which occurred at the beginning of the Gothic period.

THE WORLD OF THE HOSPITAL

The world of the hospital was influenced during this period by a number of different factors, all of which may be linked to demographic growth. Increased mobility had likewise prompted the founding or the expansion of charitable institutions along the main thoroughfares. In the towns, where demographic pressure was even greater, one had to respond to a much more intense demand, on the part of both handicapped persons and travellers. These changes effectively redrew the map of charitable institutions, and caused a proliferation in the religious orders responsible for the running of them.

With all due allowance for a wide margin of error, the increase in the number of lazar-houses in France has been estimated as follows: 33 in the twelfth century, 82 in the thirteenth century and 36 in the fourteenth century. A legacy of King Louis VIII states that in his time there existed around 2,000 institutions in which lepers lived as recluses.

Concern with the number and scale of the lazar-houses should not allow us to neglect the fact that as many charitable institutions of a different nature also existed. New social relations required new means, and the charitable movement which swept western Europe led to the founding of a large number of quite diverse institutions. Laymen now co-operated with clerics, and princes, lords and commoners combined to set up charitable foundations. At the same time, religious orders with a special concern with hospital work emerged; for example, the Antonine order, founded in the Dauphiné, cared for those afflicted by ergot poisoning, while the order of Saint-Esprit nursed pregnant women and the sick. The movement was so powerful that the figures advanced for the late thirteenth century reflect a universal awareness, with old, revived institutions being complemented by more recent foundations. Situations might differ markedly, with some institutions caring for a mere handful of sick persons while others were altogether more ambitious. The town of Lille is claimed to have had seven houses, while Arras, around 1300, had eight hospitals, eleven asylums and four lazar-houses. The figures for the south are even more striking. Thus, the county of Avignon had nine hospitals prior to 1300, and fourteen afterwards, not counting the lazar-houses.

With the proliferation of charitable houses, one had to address the particularly grave problems posed by their organisation. Not every institution offered the same level of service, and some were in fact plainly inadequate. Everyone was agreed as to the need for reform. Councils were held in 1212, in Paris, and in 1214, in Rouen, with the views expressed there achieving some sort of summation in the Fourth Lateran Council, held in 1215, where a number of decisions were taken as regards regulations. In the future, every new foundation was obliged to implement 'the rule and institution of approved religious orders'. The three vows and the wearing of a religious habit became compulsory, the number of carers had to be in a certain ratio to that of the sick, and financial management became more stringent. Statutes were subsequently drafted, at any rate for the larger institutions.

Those hôtels-Dieu which dated from Antiquity or from the Carolingian period could well have been swept away by this vast upheaval, and yet the majority of such institutions survived, although they were obliged to undergo far-reaching reforms. They had never enjoyed a monopoly of the welfare on offer in towns, but they were now confronted with severe competition. For all the violence of the shock, it had a levelling effect, sparing nothing and with administrative reorganisation and rebuilding being in effect interconnected.

ADMINISTRATIVE REORGANISATION

The Council of Paris of 1212 marked the turning-point, although its conclusions were reiterated at the Fourth Lateran Council. Thus, between 1217 and 1221, the chapter of Paris instructed Dean Etienne to draft the rule for the hôtel-Dieu. One should bear in mind that he was himself in charge of the institution, and therefore had access to all the information necessary for drafting a text which took the circumstances of the time into account.

This reform had two chief aspects, namely, the way of life of the clerics employed in the institutions, the principles invoked in this area being those formulated at the Council of Paris, and the care of the sick. A number of the decisions taken were in large part inspired by the statutes of the order of Saint John of Jerusalem. Many of the hôtels-Dieu that were dependent upon cathedral chapters consulted them in the drafting of their statutes. Some of them are fairly well known, thanks to illuminating monographs devoted to, for example, Paris, Laon and Bordeaux.

Thus, the hôtel-Dieu at Orléans, which was established in the twelfth century, was run by a religious community placed under the authority of the chapter. However, it enjoyed a degree of independence, which allowed it to develop further. In the course of the twelfth century, it managed to constitute itself as an independent authority, whose various acquisitions were ratified by the pope in 1171, 1186 etc. It had, for example, purchased some houses close to its existing buildings, which allowed it to expand. Etienne of Garlande, a well-known figure, had himself given the hôtel-Dieu a number of such houses. The chapter surrendered the schoolhouse, which was then used to house paupers, previously lodged in an excessively cramped space. In 1215, Philippe Auguste surrendered the Parisis Gate, which allowed the hôtel-Dieu to extend its territory beyond the ancient city walls. By the middle of the thirteenth century, the Orléans hôtel-Dieu was at its busiest, and could boast no fewer than ten friars and nine sisters, placed under the direction of a 'master'. The friars' chief responsibility was for the upkeep of the fabric and for the running of the hôtel-Dieu's own property. There were also clerics, a number of whom had entered the priesthood; their duties were to celebrate divine office and to administer the sacraments. The chapter wielded temporal and spiritual jurisdiction over the hôtel-Dieu, exercising its sovereign authority over both persons and property.

The development of the hôtel-Dieu at Laon is equally revealing. Up until the middle of the eleventh century, it was regarded as one of the departments of the chapter chaplaincy. However, the lexicon employed reflects a bid for independence. Thus, in the twelfth century, it was called *hospitale ecclesie Sancte Marie Laudunensis*, and in 1207, *Domus hospitalis Beate Marie Laudunensis*. In 1250, the bishop recognised the chapter's full and entire jurisdiction over the hôtel-Dieu, in both temporal and spiritual matters, but reserved his patronage in case of failure. The chapter would delegate a canon to run the hôtel-Dieu. The hospital community, known as a *fraternitas*, was composed of friars and sisters, as well as a very large number of lay servants.

In Paris, the chapter had obtained the right, in 1006, to have the hôtel-Dieu placed under its full and entire jurisdiction, and it possessed the high, median and low justice. The dean was *ex officio* a member of the standing committee. The *proviseurs*, who were delegated by the chapter, wielded executive authority.

I shall consider the growing independence of the hôtels-Dieu from the canonial chapter in greater detail below. Its undisputed success in the course of the thirteenth century, due in large part to the massive resources drained by the hospital institutions, necessarily lent itself to abuses. At the council assembled at Vienne in 1311, Clement V endeavoured to curb such abuses, by placing the management of these institutions in the hands of 'men who were honest, competent and of good reputation', who would agree to make an inventory of the property and who would give an annual report covering their period of office. The religious aspect of the institution also required reform, for it was necessary to restore priests to their former role. In the area with which we are concerned here, the thirteenth century saw some hôtels-Dieu becoming the canon's prebend. As a consequence, the prebends flourished, while resources were diverted away from the hôtel-Dieu, and therefore away from the sick. At Aix, displays of covetousness were sometimes so shameless that, between 1291 and 1303, scandals occurred. At the beginning of the fourteenth century, especially harsh criticism was levelled at the embezzlers, and real harm was done to the institutions. The Hundred Years' War and the plagues ravaging France made the difficulties still greater, and resources became so scarce that some hôtels-Dieu, even though richly endowed, were on the verge of bankruptcy. An abrupt fall in incomings was perceptible at Bordeaux, Coutances and many other places.

The measures taken by the Councils of the Lateran and of Vienne had been outstripped by events, all the more so given that a new social class – characterised by its seriousness, its domineering spirit, its sense of how to manage things and its efficiency – was in the ascendant. At the same time, the dramatic developments of the time had promoted the awareness that charity was the duty of one and all. This accounts for the tendency of the municipal authorities, from the end of the fourteenth century, to assume responsibility for such matters. Financial scandals had done much to facilitate such involvement in the affairs of the hôtels-Dieu, although it clashed with the de facto authority of the canons, who would not surrender their position easily. Yet this was not invariably the case. At Narbonne, for example, the consuls interfered more and more in the course of the fourteenth century. At Orléans, the problem of relations with the town had arisen at the end of the fourteenth century, and the idea of a communal administration had been mooted.

In Paris, the difficulties began at the end of the fifteenth century, during the reign of Charles VIII. The authority of the chapter-house was no longer recognised, and the ensuing problems were so grave that, in 1505, a far-reaching reform became necessary, which led fifteen years later to the drafting of new statutes. The administration of the hôtel-Dieu was entrusted to eight burghers.

The phenomenon was not restricted to France, but was Europe-wide even though few municipalities went so far as Köln, where an ordinance of 1510 decreed that no one save the members of the town council had authority over the hospitals of the town.

THE LOCATION OF THE HÔTELS-DIEU

Changes in urban topography were to have a significant impact upon the hôtels-Dieu, and upon their location in particular. Two other factors, of a quite different nature, should also be borne in mind. First of all, the canonial hôtel-Dieu had to expand, if it were to keep step with the demographic growth discussed above, and such expansion gave rise to difficulties of a topographic nature, which in turn prompted the search for original solutions. Secondly, one had to decide whether to locate the hospital *intra* or *extra muros*, a complex and already age-old debate over hygiene, which is not entirely resolved even today. One of three options had to be chosen, namely, to expand the original hôtel-Dieu, to move it further into the city or to shift it outside the town walls.

The first option was generally regarded as the most attractive, for a whole number of reasons, not least among them the greater convenience of the canons. We have already noted how the Carolingian legislators accorded great importance to the presence of the canons within the hôtel-Dieu. They had therefore drawn the conclusion that the building ought to be situated in the vicinity of the cathedral. Subsequently, the links between the two buildings had slackened to some degree, but too great a distance would have threatened the canons' charitable functions, and was not welcomed by those of a more conservative outlook. The usual haggling was therefore necessary, if free or developed land was to be acquired, such transactions being greatly facilitated by the purpose of the venture, which was to advance the cause of Christian charity. It was easy to make a convincing case and, by the same token, difficult to reject a claim if one's eternal salvation might thereby be jeopardised.

We have already observed that there had been no falling-off in the quantity of gifts and legacies. Indeed, the thirteenth century had been prosperous, and works of mercy had benefited. The fourteenth century had been stricken by economic crises, exacerbated by the Black Death, but the generosity of the faithful had not therefore diminished. Society's response to such traumas was to turn in upon itself, but it should also be borne in mind that every charitable act was meant to guarantee one's existence beyond the grave. One of the most remarkable consequences of the Black Death was the increase in the number of wills bequeathing property to hospitaller institutions. New hospitals were frequently founded, although obviously in lesser numbers than during the previous period, but gifts were also made to already existing institutions.

The building of the cathedral of Paris, embarked upon by Maurice of Sully, had had some fairly dramatic repercussions for the hôtel-Dieu. Among other things, it had been gravely damaged by the cutting of the Rue Neuve-Notre-Dame, which served to link up the parvis to the bridges further to the west. It had been necessary to demolish a number of houses belonging to the hôtel-Dieu, which stood in the proposed path of the new thoroughfare, or else to the north of it. The hôtel-Dieu was thus wedged between the Seine, to the south, and the street. Substantial financial compensation was paid for the damage caused. Thus, in 1208, the chapter again set aside an indemnity, to be paid out of the vestry budget.

Expansion on the original site

Study of comparative plans suggests that expansion of hôtels-Dieu where they stood was the usual practice, but we know of cases where they were moved into the city, although this procedure occasioned dramatic topographic problems, owing to the fact that land there was coveted and scarce. The most remarkable source, which has been the object of an exemplary study, concerns Laon, whose

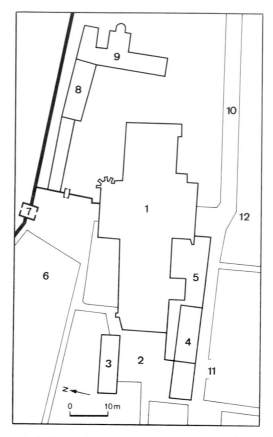

Fig. 157 The cathedral complex at Laon at the beginning of the thirteenth century (after Saint-Denis). 1. The cathedral; 2. The parvis square; 3. Saint-Martin; 4. The hôtel-Dieu; 5. The cloister; 6. The hôtel-Dieu after 1209; 7. The bishop's gate; 8. The episcopal palace; 9. The episcopal chapel; 10. Rue du cloître; 11. The precinct gate; 12. The canonial precinct.

hospital, although without a doubt of considerable age, is first mentioned as late as 1112. As one would expect at this period, links with the chapter were close: the hôtel-Dieu had been the responsibility of the chaplaincy, although it had subsequently, as we explained above, acquired a degree of independence. This ancient hospital was rebuilt in the years following 1167, and work came to an end in 1177. It was already in operation at this date, the community being definitively installed in 1193, in a new building overlooking the parvis. Already, by the beginning of the thirteenth century, the hospital was proving too small, and, being wedged between the canonial precinct to the east and the church of

Saint Remy to the west, no expansion was possible. A decision was therefore taken to build a new hôtel-Dieu further to the north, in the vicinity of the palace and of the cathedral, but it was further than it had been from the latter, being bounded on the south by the Rue de l'évêché and on the north by the city walls. The installation was realised in 1209, but work continued for a large part of the thirteenth century.

The canons pursued a lengthy and arduous policy of acquisition, their aim being to combine various plots of land around the original houses. The vital square of meadow was built up out of *post mortem* donations, legacies and purchases, and the documentary evidence suggests that the latter were at a particularly high price. In 1273, the hospital of Notre-Dame became the proprietor of the whole quarter. The chapter could then proceed with its highly ambitious plans for rebuilding, which would ultimately occupy 2,500 square metres of land in the heart of the city. The chapter funded the operation, although recourse was had to collections also. Once the removal had been effected, the former hôtel-Dieu was transformed, with the lower hall becoming a storeroom, and the upper floor an assembly hall. The case of Laon serves to show just how determined the canons were. The programme, as we shall see below, was one of the most ambitious of the whole period; its organisation was one of the most efficient, featuring a very large staff; and the reflections offered as regards its role the most advanced, with the fundamental distinction being posed, as it had not always been previously, between 'passants' and 'gisants'. Finally, the chapter had addressed the sensitive issue of its own link with the cathedral, for the removal had given rise to a degree of somewhat detrimental distancing. In order to make some reparation, in 1226 the chapter had the portal of Saint Nicolas cut, on the north side-aisle, thus permitting greater ease of access.

This determination to keep the hôtel-Dieu within the city reflected the canons' concern to hold on to such power as they already wielded, but also, and perhaps most crucially, to continue their charitable works. This would account for the huge financial sacrifices which were made, and which, though impossible to calculate with any accuracy, must have weighed heavily.

We should therefore investigate those hôtels-Dieu which remained inside the city, in close proximity to the cathedral, and which were rebuilt at the end of the twelfth century or at the beginning of the thirteenth century. They were fairly ambitious ventures, covering a particularly large area of ground. The scale upon which they had been conceived required, in this case too, the purchase of expensive houses or plots of land, which the canons showed no hesitation in

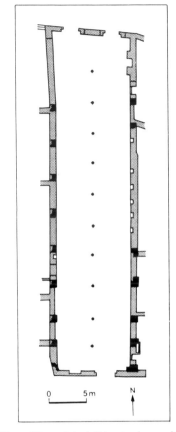

Fig. 158 Plan of Laon hôtel-Dieu in the twelfth century.

doing. However, there was not necessarily displacement, for there could also be expansion on the same spot: the chapters of Chartres, Langres, Paris, Reims, Sens, Soissons, Toul and many other dioceses were faced with identical problems.

Displacement extra muros

A number of displacements outside the town also occurred. The most famous example concerns the hôtel-Dieu at Amiens described above. Located to the west of the Gothic cathedral and, for that same reason obstructing its further development, the plan for its removal had been proposed, and agreed upon in principle, in 1220, when work on the cathedral site had begun. Admittedly, no written source survives, but the stated dimensions of the Gothic cathedral meant that the hôtel-Dieu was condemned as soon as the first stone was laid. The building was then named after Saint Jean, but the earliest explicit reference cannot be earlier than 1233–6. The hospital archives mention that the structure was too small to provide shelter for the multitude of poor people. Topographical requirements were no less urgent. It was crucial that Saint Firmin le Confesseur, whose remains were located in the cathedral transept, be moved; he would have to be placed to the north of the cathedral, where the hôtel-Dieu extended. In 1236, Bishop Geoffroi of Eu re-emphasised the urgency of the demolition, emphasising in addition that the building in fact posed a danger for the whole of the town. He then envisaged rebuilding it near to the Grand Pont, on a plot of land that a native of Amiens, Jean of Croï, had bought for the purpose. In 1238, Arnoul of La Pierre again remarked upon the urgent nature of such works. In 1241, the transfer was finally put into operation, and the new hôtel-Dieu was built on the fief of Heilly.

New foundations

A number of hôtels-Dieu were, admittedly, founded outside the town, either by the bishop, by the canons or by common agreement. The case of Coutances is well known. In 1209, Bishop Hugues of Mareville embarked upon an especially innovatory venture, calling upon chapter and burghers to collaborate in setting up a hôtel-Dieu outside the city. The administration of the venture was entrusted to the confraternity of the Saint Esprit. There were, however, comparable foundations within the city also, one of the most remarkable being at Bordeaux. This foundation, which has been the object of a very serious study, was remarkable as regards both its position, the date at which it occurred and the personality of the man responsible for launching it. The project owed its origin to a bequest made by one of the dignitaries of the chapter, the precentor Vitold of Carles. In his will, dated 24 December 1390, he set out to guarantee the future of the hôtel-Dieu by leaving it two houses, bought by him for this very purpose, which were near to the Saint-André Gate, together with a garden, various fields, rents and tolls. He had even made provision for the chapel and for the liturgical objects that were needed, and went so far as to append an original clause, in which he set aside funds for a child from his own native village, wishing to study, to be educated at the hospital. Vitold had stipulated that a layman should be in charge of the institution, and that two priests should be responsible for divine service. He wished the institution to be an asylum for the sick and a place of shelter. Even the name which he had chosen reflected his intentions, for he called it the Saint-André hospital, thereby placing its foundation under the tutelary name of the cathedral. The canons took grave offence at his desire to build a chapel in the 'Sauveté Saint-André' and, notwithstanding the pope's authorisation, they opposed the plan. To get round the problem, Vitold decided to place his foundation under the patronage of the mayor of Bordeaux.

THE ORGANISATION OF THE BUILDINGS

Reflection on the existing statutes, upheavals both anticipated and realised, and the widely felt need to face up to the new requirements could not help but have an impact upon the construction of buildings. It was in the course of the Gothic period that hospitals were organised in a more rigorous fashion, that buildings assumed a greater degree of order and that distinctions between persons were established. Admittedly, such rethinking was by no means limited to the canons, for it affected the laity also, throughout Europe. As far as France is concerned, the case of Laon is well known, and allows us to measure the difference between the twelfth-century hôtel-Dieu and its replacement in the thirteenth century, since both buildings have survived.

The twelfth-century hôtel-Dieu, insofar as it is possible to reconstruct it, was centred on the infirmary. To the north lay the reception courtyard, while to the east were the administrative annexes. We have very little information regarding the latter, and we cannot be certain that they were actually built of stone. Indeed, the predominant materials would seem to have been wood and daub. The same was not true of the infirmary, which, at this period, was necessarily made of stone, great care being taken with its construction. It was a huge space, oriented on an east-west axis, entrance to it being on the north side, by a staircase and an entrance-hall. The ground floor, which was partly submerged, was divided into three aisles vaulted with supported Gothic arches. The main floor was plastered, so as to give free expression to the uninterrupted volume. This floor, which is in a poor state of preservation, was blind to the north, but pierced with bay-windows on the south side; the infirmary was heated and could hold twenty double beds. From this period on, the distinction between 'passants' (in fact, travellers) and 'gisants' (the sick) became current. The main floor was reserved for the latter, who could thus enjoy a higher degree of comfort. Conversely, the ground floor must have been very rough and ready.

The thirteenth-century hospital became a genuine hospitaller complex, with

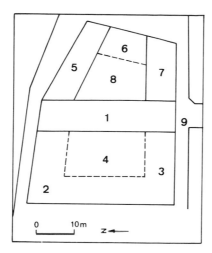

Fig. 159 Plan of the new hôtel-Dieu at Laon, at the end of the thirteenth century
(after Saint-Denis). 1. The sick-room; 2. The nunnery; 3. The monastery; 4. The
courtyard; 5. The passants' hall; 6. The guestroom; 7. The chapel; 8. The
courtyard; 9. Rue de l'évêché.

several buildings serving to guarantee the independence and autarchy of the
institution, and occupying a surface area of 2,500 square metres. The plan was a
very simple one, with the whole complex being centred upon the infirmary. To
the west stood the monastery, which was divided into two parts, one for the
friars and the other for the nuns, both parties being responsible for the physical
care of the sick. To the east lay lodgings, guest rooms and a chapel, which was
for the use of the whole community. Mention should also be made of the service
buildings, such as granaries, stables and various work-rooms. The great
infirmary was 5,000 cubic metres in volume, being 45·5 metres long (originally
50), 10·2 metres wide and 10 metres high. It was heated by a fireplace, and access
to it was by way of a door into the adjoining hall. To the south stood the chapel
for the sick, where Mass was celebrated daily. Physical and spiritual comfort was
thereby assured. One should further add that the existing distinction between
'travellers' and 'sick' was reinforced here, with the infirmary being reserved for
the use of the latter, and the former being welcomed in a second hall, which ran
alongside the ramparts. Beggars and pilgrims were given some food there, could
wash themselves, were clothed and, obviously, received shelter.

The majority of such institutions remained far more rudimentary, and could
not offer such a high degree of comfort. They undoubtedly had similar
aspirations, but, because most hôtels-Dieu were demolished in the seventeenth

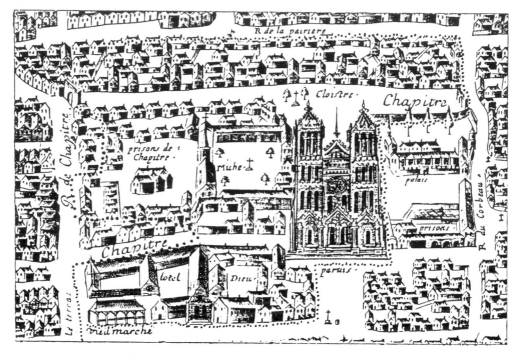

Fig. 160 Reims cathedral complex, by J. Colin (1665).

and eighteenth centuries (Paris), or in the nineteenth century (Chartres, Soissons, Bordeaux, Orléans), it is difficult to arrive at any firm conclusions. If, however, we scrutinise the surviving traces or the graphic documents, we can see what care was taken with the construction of the infirmary.

Such halls were made of stone, beautifully executed, generally above a submerged or half-submerged level, the arches of which rested upon rows of supports. At Reims, there survive two large submerged halls, from the early thirteenth century, one with two aisles, the other with three, built somewhat later. The actual hall might either have just one aisle, if the width permitted it, or would otherwise be divided up by rows of supports. The hall at Chartres was divided into three by two rows of columns, and extended across seven bays. It was usually covered by a panelled ceiling, so that the walls might be pierced at regular intervals, thus providing the indispensable light and ventilation.

When the hall was oriented on an east-west axis, which was generally the case (Paris, Chartres, Reims, Laon etc.), the chapel stood at the easternmost edge. Physical care could not by itself guarantee a return to health, for spiritual care was equally crucial, a point of view that anticipates, in this regard as in so many others, modern-day medicine, with its appreciation of psychosomatic factors. The easternmost bay was handled in a different fashion, adopted in many other medieval hospitaller institutions, being vaulted so as to house the altar. At Chartres, the three aisles of the final bay were covered in this manner. Even when the sick person was unable to rise from his bed, he was thereby able to attend the daily celebration of the mass.

The hôtel-Dieu at Orléans, demolished in 1846, is known to us through a series of surveys made by the architect Gabriel in 1728–9. Admittedly, the various buildings had been modified around 1560, but it is possible to imagine what their main lines were. The outstanding feature of the hôtel-Dieu was its location within the canonial precinct, although access to it was by way of two independent doors. As was the custom, the buildings were grouped around the great hall, oriented on an east-west axis and overlooking a courtyard in which convalescents could take the air. Next to the great hall stood the infirmary, which was occupied by those who were gravely ill. Those buildings designated for the use of the community extended towards the east, running along the city walls and coming close to the south arm. A distinction is evident, as at Laon, between the lodgings of friars and nuns. The former, reserved for the use of friars and chaplains – the monastery – stood next to the ramparts, and consisted of a dormitory and a refectory; the 'master' responsible for the running of the institution had an apartment to himself. The latter, which was separate from, but in close proximity to the monastery, consisted of individual rooms, a courtyard and a well. Both buildings overlooked a cloister, which was divided into two parts, one for the use of the nuns, the other for the use of the friars. To the south there stood a chapel, where friars, nuns and other staff worshipped. This chapel was adjacent to the great hall, and archways led from one to the other, a new arrangement which would soon become quite commonplace.

Paris featured a no less characteristic schema, dating for the most part from the thirteenth century. The hôtel-Dieu consisted of an already vast island, access to which was by way of two doors, namely, the door to the Palu market, which was the larger and was on the west, and the service door, which gave on to the parvis. It consisted of four rooms, which served to differentiate between the various categories of sick person: the Salle Saint-Thomas, which was for the use of the female convalescents, and was built between 1236 and 1240, thanks in part to the generosity of Blanche of Castilla; the infirmary (1225–50), which was for the care of the seriously ill; the Salle Neuve, which was for women; and, finally, the Salle Saint-Denis, which was for male convalescents. The Salle Neuve, which consisted of two aisles 12 metres wide, the infirmary and the Salle Saint-

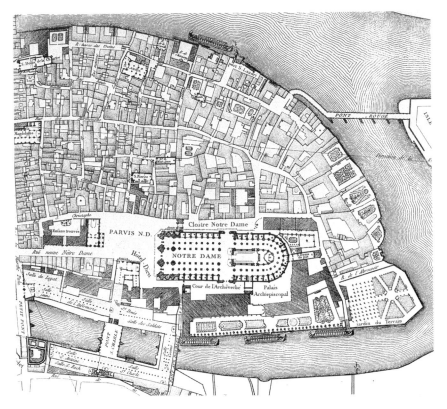

Fig. 161 Plan of the cathedral complex at Paris (after Abbé Delagrive, 1754).

Denis ran parallel to the Seine for 122 metres, each of them therefore benefiting from the southern light and from the vital supplies of water. The Salle Saint-Thomas was at right angles to the Seine.

The second complex of buildings was monastic in nature, for the use of monks and nuns, and it gave on to the parvis, to the east, and the Rue du Sablon.

A third complex was under construction in 1225, and completed in 1260, consisting of common rooms, outbuildings, refectory, dormitory, cloister, kitchen, bakehouse and stables.

The whole complex was an impressive affair, which included three different dormitories, one for the monks, one for the nuns, and a third for young girls. The existing buildings soon proved inadequate and, at the beginning of the fourteenth century, the chapter planned the extension of the clerics' infirmary and of their refectory, as well as the chapel. Pierre des Essarts set up a fund of 200 *livres* for the purpose, and a gift by Oudart of Mocreux made it possible to purchase the intervening houses, in 1383. The edifice could at last be enlarged, and was inaugurated, under the name of Saint Jean-Baptiste, in 1393. In 1399, a chapter-house was built. Yet more land was built on to the east, until, finally, the Petit Pont was reached. In 1463, a market square was purchased, and a new entrance marked by a portal created. In 1511, the closure of the Rue du Sablon isolated the hospital complex once and for all.

Conclusion

I have chosen to break off at the end of the Middle Ages since, in spite of the importance of the Classical period for the study of cathedrals, it occasioned no upheavals in the existing economy of the holy town. I would not wish to underestimate the repercussions, for the whole of Europe, of the Council of Trent, not least because of the admirable account that Emile Mâle once gave of them. Yet, though it is true that buildings were invaded by the presence of God, the architecture of the monuments remained all but untouched. Worship continued in buildings dating from the Middle Ages, with only their internal decoration being profoundly altered. Admittedly, a number of palaces became princely residences, and the tendency of hôtels-Dieu to come under municipal control continued, but the canonial precinct hardly evolved at all.

New constructions were few and far between. One of the most instructive for our purposes was undoubtedly the cathedral of Saint Louis at La Rochelle. Upon the capture of the town, after a famous siege (1 November 1628), Louis XIII had expressed a wish that it should be the seat of a bishopric. Twenty years later, the pope acquiesced, and the see of Maillezais was transferred to La Rochelle. The bishop immediately began to dream of building a cathedral, although the project only came to fruition a century later. In 1741, the king granted a subsidy of 100,000 *livres*, and Jacques V. Gabriel sketched out a preliminary plan. Work proceeded at a painfully slow pace, so much so that on 27 June 1784 the bishop was only able to bless the initial stages of the edifice, which had got no further than the second bay of the choir. The site was reopened in 1830, and work was finished in 1862. The clergy had encountered difficulties of every conceivable sort, affecting the decision-making process, the availability of land and funding.

It was no longer a question of building a palace, a canonial precinct or a hôtel-Dieu. The age of cathedrals had drawn to a close.

In fact, over a century was to pass before cathedral-building was to enjoy a new lease of life. In the wake of Vatican II, Roman Catholicism recovered some of the fervour which had formerly animated it, and which had found expression in so many different areas, including the domain of monumental architecture. In almost every part of the world, cathedrals are under construction or nearing completion. In New York, for example, the cathedral of Saint John the Divine, whose site was opened in the last century, is advancing at a great rate and will soon be finished. In black Africa, the president of the Ivory Coast has made a gift to the Vatican of the cathedral of Notre-Dame-de-la-Paix, a monument at Yamoussoukro which is nearing completion and which will vie with Saint Peter's at Rome. In Europe, the cathedral of Saint Sava in Beograd, begun in 1935, was consecrated on 25 June 1989. In France, the episcopate has consulted one of the greatest of contemporary architects, Mario Botta, over plans for Evry cathedral.

These projects are conceived on a scale to match those of the Middle Ages. Saint Sava, for example, covers 6,400 square metres on the ground. The architects are highly diverse, and the financing is often ingenious. In Yugoslavia, the cathedral has been funded by the gifts of the faithful and of expatriate Serbians. In Africa, Houphouët-Boigny's personal fortune has been used; in France, a national subscription has been launched. Malraux may perhaps have been right when he claimed that the twenty-first century would be 'a religious century, or it would not be at all'.

Selective bibliography

Since the bibliography regarding the subject of cathedrals is large, I have done no more here than mention the most fundamental articles and studies, which have the further advantage of referring to more detailed works.

GENERAL STUDIES

Chélini, J. *Histoire religieuse de l'Occident médiéval*, Paris, 1968.

Duby, G. *Le Temps des cathédrales. L'art et la société, 980–1620*, Paris, 1976, second edition.

Duby, G. (ed.) *Histoire de la France urbaine*, Paris, 1980, 2 volumes.

Favier, J. (ed.) *La France médiévale*, Paris, 1983.

Guillerme, A. *Les Temps de l'eau: la cité, l'eau et les techniques*, Paris, 1983.

Guyotjeannin, O. *Episcopus et comes. Affirmation et déclin de la seigneurie épiscopale au nord du royaume de France (Beauvais–Noyon, X^e-début XIIIe siècle)*, Geneva, Paris, 1987.

Le Goff, J. and Rémond, R. *Histoire de la France religieuse*, Paris, 1988, 2 volumes.

Lot, F. and Fawtier, R. *Histoire des institutions françaises au Moyen Age*, vol. III, *Institutions ecclésiastiques*, Paris, 1962.

Mortet, V. and Deschamps, P. *Recueil de textes relatifs à l'histoire de l'architecture en France*, Paris, 1929.

Mussat, A. 'Les cathédrales dans leurs cités', in *Revue de l'art*, 55, 1988, pp. 9–22.

Riché, P. *Les Ecoles et l'enseignement dans l'Occident chrétien, de la fin du Ve siècle au milieu du XIe siècle*, Paris, 1979.

Vicaire, M.-H. *Les Évêques, les clercs et le roi (1250–1300)*, in *Cahiers de Fanjeaux*, 7, Toulouse, 1972.

LATE ANTIQUITY AND THE EARLY MIDDLE AGES

Blanchet, A. *Les Enceintes romaines de la Gaule*, Paris, 1907.

Brühl, C.-R. *Palatium und Civitas. Studien zur Profantopographie spätantiker Civitates von 3. bis zum 13. Jahrundert*, vol. I, Vienna, 1975.

Durliat, J. 'Les attributions civiles des évêques mérovingiens: l'évêque de Didier, évêque de Cahors (630–635)', in *Annales du Midi*, vol. 91, 143, 1979, pp. 237–43.

Février, P.-A. *Le Développement urbain en Provence de l'époque romaine à la fin du XIVe siècle (Archéologie et histoire urbaine)*, Paris, 1964, ('Bibliothèque des écoles françaises d'Athènes et de Rome', t. 202).

Gauthier, N. and Picard, J.-C. *Topographie chrétienne de la Gaule, des origines au milieu du VIIIe siècle*, vol. I, *Trèves*, vol. II, *Corse*, vol. III, *Vienne et Arles*, vol. IV, *Lyon*, Paris, 1986; vol. V, *Tours*, Paris, 1987.

Heitz, C. *L'Architecture religieuse carolingienne. Les formes et leurs fonctions*, Paris, 1980.

Hubert, J. *Art et vie sociale de la fin du monde antique au Moyen Age*, Geneva, 1977.
Nouveau recueil d'études, d'archéologie et d'histoire. De la fin du monde antique au Moyen Age, Geneva, Paris, 1985.

Lesne, E. *Histoire de la propriété ecclésiastique du VIIIe siècle à la fin du XIe siècle*, Lille, 1922–40, 5 volumes.

Roblin, M. 'Cités ou citadelles. Les enceintes romaines du Bas-Empire d'après l'exemple de Senlis', in *Revue des études anciennes*, vol. 67, 3–6, pp. 361–91.

FINANCIAL PROBLEMS

Biget, J.-L. 'Recherches sur le financement des cathédrales du Midi au XIIIe siècle', in *Cahiers de Fanjeaux*, 9, Toulouse, 1976, pp. 127–64.

Chédeville, A. *Chartres et ses campagnes (XIIe–XIIIe siècle)*, Paris, 1973.

Fuchs, J. 'L'Oeuvre Notre-Dame de la cathédrale de Strasbourg à travers les archives', in *Bulletin de la Société des amis de la cathédrale de Strasbourg*, vol. 77, 1971, pp. 21–34.

Jusselin, M. 'La maîtrise de l'oeuvre à Notre-Dame de Chartres', in *Mémoires de la Société archéologique de Chartres*, 1915–22.

Legrand, M. *Le Chapitre cathédral de Langres, de la fin du XIIe siècle au concordat de 1516*, Paris, 1931.

Lopez, R. 'Économie et architecture médiévale. Cela aurait-il tué ceci?', in *Annales*, 1952, pp. 433–8.

Milet, H. 'La composition du chapitre cathédral de Laon: une analyse factorielle', in *Annales*, 1981, pp. 117–38.

Vroom, W. H. *De financiering van de kathedraalbouw in de middeleeuwen in het bijzonder van de dom van Utrecht*, Maarsen, 1981 (with a summary in English).

TECHNICAL PROBLEMS

Aubert, M. 'La construction au Moyen Age', in *Bulletin monumental*, 1961 and 1962.

Du Colombier, P. *Les Chantiers des cathédrales: ouvriers, architectes, sculpteurs*, Paris, 1973, second edition.

Gimpel J. *Les Bâtisseurs des cathédrales*, Paris, 1986, third edition.

THE HOLY TOWN

The canonial precinct

Esquieu, Y. 'Système défensif de quartiers canoniaux dans quelques cités épiscopales du Midi', in *Actes du 105ᵉ Congrès des Sociétés savantes*, Section d'archéologie et d'histoire de l'art, Paris, 1983, pp. 331–45.

'La cathédrale de Viviers et les bâtiments du cloître, xii–xiiiᵉ siècle', in *Bulletin monumental*, 1983.

The episcopal palaces

Carbonell-Lamothe, Y. 'Recherches sur la construction du Palais neuf des archevêques de Narbonne', in *Narbonne. Archéologie et histoire*, vol. ii, Montpellier, pp. 217–35.

Crépin-Leblond, T. 'Recherches sur les palais épiscopaux en France au Moyen Age (xiiᵉ–xiiiᵉ siècle), d'après divers exemples des provinces ecclésiastiques de Reims et de Sens', in *Positions de thèses...*, Ecole nationale des chartes, 1987, pp. 63–9.

Gardelles, J. 'Les palais dans l'Europe occidentale chrétienne, du xᵉ au xiiᵉ siècle', in *Cahiers de civilisation médiévale*, 1976, pp. 115–34.

Héliot, P. 'Nouvelles remarques sur les palais épiscopaux et princiers de l'époque romane en France', in *Francia*, vol. 4, 1976, pp. 193–212.

Jadart, H. *Le Palais archiépiscopal de Reims au point de vue de l'art et de l'histoire, du xiiᵉ au xxᵉ siècle*, Reims, 1908.

'Le palais archiépiscopal de Reims, notes et vues supplémentaires', in *Travaux de l'académie de Reims*, vol. 126, 1910.

Join-Lambert, O. 'Le palais épiscopal de Meaux', in *Bulletin monumental*, 1901, pp. 594–603.

Lejeune, J. *Liège et son palais. Douze siècles d'histoire*, Anvers, 1980.

Pradalier, H. 'Le palais de la Berbie', in *Congrès archéologique. Albigeois*, Paris, 1985, pp. 122–41.

'Les parties médiévales du palais épiscopal de Gérone', in *Les cahiers de Saint-Michel de Cuxa*, 18, 1987, pp. 207–48.

MONOGRAPHS

The hôtels-Dieu

Bouvier, P. 'Étude sur l'hôtel-Dieu d'Orléans au Moyen Age et au xvie siècle', in *Mémoires de la Société archéologique et historique de l'Orléanais*, vol. 3, 1914.

Candille, M. *Étude du Livre de vie active de l'hôtel-Dieu de Paris de Jehan Henry, xve siècle*, Paris, 1964.

Courteault, P. *Le Vieil Hôpital Saint-André de Bordeaux*, Bordeaux, 1944.

Coyecque, E. *L'Hôtel-Dieu de Paris au Moyen Age. Histoire et documents*, Paris, 1891, 2 volumes ('Société de Paris et de l'Ile de France').

Imbert, J. (ed.) *Histoire des hôpitaux en France*, Toulouse, 1982.

Le Cacheux, P. *Essai historique sur l'hôtel-Dieu de Coutances*, part I, *L'hôtel-Dieu*, Paris, 1895.

Legrand, H. *Statuts d'hôtels-Dieu et de léproseries. Recueil de textes xiie–xve siècle*, Paris, 1901.

Mollat, M. (ed.) *Assistance et charité*, in *Cahiers de Fanjeaux*, 13, Toulouse, 1978.

Saint-Denis, A. *L'Hôtel-Dieu de Laon (1150–1300)*, Nancy, 1983.

MONOGRAPHS

Aubert, M. (ed.) *La Cathédrale de Metz*, Paris, 1930.

Biget, J.-L. 'La cathédrale Sainte-Cécile d'Albi. L'architecture', in *Congrès archéologique. Albigeois*, Paris, 1985, pp. 20–62.

Branner, R. *La Cathédrale de Bourges et sa place dans l'architecture gothique*, Paris, Bourges, 1962.

Durliat, M. 'La cathédrale du Puy', in *Congrès archéologique. Velay*, Paris, 1976, pp. 55–163.

Erlande-Brandenburg, A. 'La façade de la cathédrale d'Amiens', Seventh International Conference of the Société française d'archéologie, 1974, in *Bulletin monumental*, 1977, pp. 254–96.

Chartres, Paris, 1987.

Favier, J. *L'Univers de Chartres*, Paris, 1988.

Gardelles, J. *La Cathédrale Saint-André de Bordeaux. Sa place dans l'évolution de l'architecture*, Bordeaux, 1963.

Kurmann, P. *La Cathédrale Saint-Etienne de Meaux. Etude architecturale*, Paris, Geneva, 1971.

Mortet, V. *Etude historique et archéologique sur la cathédrale et le palais épiscopal de Paris, du vi^e au xiie siècle*, Paris, 1888.

Ravaux, J.-P. 'Les campagnes de construction de la cathédrale de Reims au xiiie siècle', in *Bulletin monumental*, 1979, pp. 7–66.

Seymour, C. *La Cathédrale Notre-Dame de Noyon au xiie siècle*, Paris, Geneva, 1975.

Vermand, D. *La Cathédrale Notre-Dame de Senlis au XIIᵉ siècle*, Senlis, 1987.

Villes, A. *La Cathédrale de Toul. Histoire et architecture*, Metz, 1983.

La Cathédrale de Lausanne, Société d'histoire de l'art en Suisse, Berne, 1975.

It is worth consulting the series *Petites monographies des grands édifices de la France*, which contains over thirty studies of specific cathedrals. More recently, the sub-department of archaeology within the Ministry of Culture has embarked upon the publication of the *Guides archéologiques de France*.

The publications of the Société française d'archéologie provide access to original studies: the *Bulletin monumental* reviews publications concerned with the Middle Ages every three months; the *Congrès archéologique*, devoted each year to a specific region in France, brings out monographs on particular monuments. Its three alphabetic tables provide an overview of the whole of this information, which is especially abundant for the Middle Ages.

THE REDISCOVERY OF THE MIDDLE AGES

Boisserée, S. *Histoire et description de la cathédrale de Cologne*, Paris, 1823.

Frankl, P. *The gothic: Literary sources and interpretations through eight centuries*, Princeton, 1960.

Hubert, J. 'Archéologie médiévale', in *L'Histoire et ses méthodes*, Paris, 1961, pp. 275–328.

Leniaud, J.-M. *Jean-Baptiste Lassus (1807–1857) ou le temps retrouvé des cathédrales*, Geneva, Paris, 1980.

Mallion, J. *Victor Hugo et l'art médiéval*, Paris, 1962.

Viollet-Le-Duc: the architect's most important texts have been republished in a collection edited by B. Foucart, *L'Eclecticisme raisonné. Choix de textes et préface de B.F.*, Paris, 1984, with a bibliography by Viollet-le-Duc.

Yvon, P. *Le gothique et la renaissance gothique en Angleterre (1750–1850)*, Caen, Paris, 1931.

Actes du colloque international Viollet-le-Duc, Paris, 1980.

EXHIBITIONS

Auzas, P.-M. *Eugène Viollet-le-Duc, 1814–1879*, Paris, 1979.

Le 'gothique' retrouvé avant Viollet-le-Duc, Paris, 1980.

Viollet-le-Duc, Paris, Réunion des Musées nationaux, 1980.

Premiers temps chrétiens en Gaule méridionale. Antiquité tardive et haut Moyen Age, IIIᵉ–VIIIᵉ siècle, Lyon, 1986.

Index

Page numbers in italic indicate a reference to an illustration.